THE INSTITUTE OF ECONOMICS

OF

THE BROOKINGS INSTITUTION

The Carnegie Corporation of New York in establishing the Institute of Economics declared:

"The Carnegie Corporation, in committing to the Trustees the administration of the endowment, over which the Corporation will have no control whatsoever, has in mind a single purpose—namely, that the Institute shall be conducted with the sole object of ascertaining the facts about current economic problems and of interpreting these facts for the people of the United States in the most simple and understandable form. The Institute shall be administered by its Trustees without regard to the special interests of any group in the body politic, whether political, social, or economic."

PUBLICATION No. 46

THE BROOKINGS INSTITUTION

The Brookings Institution—Devoted to Public Service through Research and Training in the Humanistic Sciences—was incorporated on December 8, 1927. Broadly stated, the Institution has two primary purposes: The first is to aid constructively in the development of sound national policies; and the second is to offer training of a super-graduate character to students of the social sciences. The Institution will maintain a series of co-operating institutes, equipped to carry out comprehensive and inter-related research projects.

The responsibility for the final determination of the Institution's policies and its program of work and for the administration of its endowment is vested in a self-perpetuating Board of Trustees. The Trustees have, however, defined their position with reference to the investigations conducted by the Institution in a by-law provision reading as follows: "The primary function of the Trustees is not to express their views upon the scientific investigations conducted by any division of the Institution, but only to make it possible for such scientific work to be done under the most favorable auspices." Major responsibility for "formulating general policies and co-ordinating the activities of the various divisions of the Institution" is vested in the President. The by-laws provide also that "there shall be an Advisory Council selected by the President from among the scientific staff of the Institution and representing the different divisions of the Institution."

WAR DEBTS AND WORLD PROSPERITY

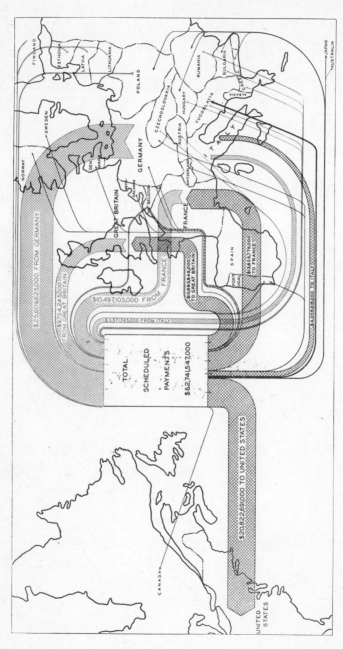

THE FLOW OF WEALTH INVOLVED IN WAR DEBT PAYMENTS
(Situation as of July 1, 1931)

WAR DEBTS AND WORLD PROSPERITY

BY

HAROLD G. MOULTON

AND

LEO PASVOLSKY

PUBLISHED FOR

THE BROOKINGS INSTITUTION

BY

THE CENTURY CO., NEW YORK

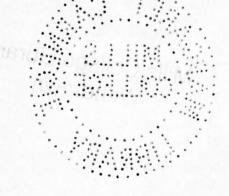

Printed in the United States of America by
George Banta Publishing Company
Menasha, Wisconsin

Each investigation conducted under the auspices of The Brookings Institution is in a very real sense an institutional product. Before a suggested project is undertaken it is given thorough consideration, not only by the Director and the staff members of the Institute in whose field it lies, but also by the Advisory Council of The Brookings Institution. As soon as the project is approved, the investigation is placed under the supervision of a special Committee consisting of the Director of the Institute and two or more selected staff members.

It is the function of this Committee to advise and counsel with the author in planning the analysis and to give such aid as may be possible in rendering the study worthy of publication. The Committee may refuse to recommend its publication by the Institution, if the study turns out to be defective in literary form or if the analysis in general is not of a scholarly character. If, however, the work is admittedly of a scholarly character and yet members of the Committee, after full discussion, can not agree with the author on certain phases of the analysis, the study will be published in a form satisfactory to the author, and the disagreeing Committee member or members may, if they deem the matter of sufficient importance, contribute criticisms for publication as dissenting footnotes or as appendices.

After the book is approved by the Institute for publication a digest of it is placed before the Advisory Council of The Brookings Institution. The Advisory Council does not undertake to revise or edit the manuscript, but each member is afforded an opportunity to criticize the analysis and, if so disposed, to prepare a dissenting opinion.

DIRECTOR'S PREFACE

At the close of the war it was rather generally assumed in this country that Europe's economic and financial problems, both external and internal, were of only remote concern to us. The American public in general saw no reason why we should not proceed to convert war prosperity into peace prosperity and project forward for an indefinite time a condition of great national economic well-being regardless of how Europe or the rest of the world might fare. In Europe, likewise, there was little appreciation of the economic inter-dependence of the world and the essential unity of international economic and financial processes.

With the passage of time, but especially during the three years since the present severe depression fell upon us, there has been a gradually clearing perception of the fact that the economic life of the world is strongly conditioned by international financial relationships. In particular, it has become more and more widely realized that the war debt problem has hung like a pall over the world's economic recovery and that its solution is today a factor of vital importance in the process of restoring world prosperity.

Over a period of ten years the Institute of Economics has devoted a substantial part of its energies toward searching and non-partisan investigation of the issues involved in the problem of reparations and other inter-governmental debt obligations resulting from the war. Beginning in 1923 with *Germany's Capacity to Pay*, we have sought to examine the principles upon which war debt settlements must rest and the relation which current efforts to deal with the international debt problem bear to private finance and business. In addition to special volumes dealing with the problem in particular countries —namely, Germany, France, Italy, Russia, Austria, Hungary, and Bulgaria—we have at various stages in the development of the problem published more general studies of the issues as a whole. Such volumes include *The Reparation Plan*, which appeared in 1924 after the announcement of the Dawes plan, and *World War Debt Settlements*, which appeared in 1926 following the completion of the World War Foreign Debt Commission.

The present volume is in a sense a synthesis of all our previous work in this field. Now that the Lausanne conference has enunciated a policy in the treatment of the war debts fundamentally at variance with that which was entertained wholeheartedly at the beginning of debt negotiations, and which was but grudgingly modified in numerous previous conferences, it seems opportune to review the several phases through which the problem has passed, and to re-state in the light of fuller knowledge the principles upon which sound adjustments must eventually be based. Furthermore the time has now arrived when a prolonged period of world-wide economic depression emphasizes the difficulties of fundamentally unsound or shortsighted debt policies, and calls for a clear statement of the relationship between the existing volume of inter-governmental debts and the future progress or retrogression of the world.

It is hoped that the analysis contained in this book will help to clarify the intricate and confused issues involved. Such understanding is of special importance at the present time when the war debts have again been brought to the forefront of public attention in every important country of the world and when far-reaching negotiations for a final solution of this tragic problem are in progress.

The members of the staff who served on the committee co-operating with the authors in the preparation of this volume were Cleona Lewis, Felix Morley, and Lewis L. Lorwin.

Edwin G. Nourse
Director

Institute of Economics
September 1932

CONTENTS

CHAPTER X

CHAPTER XI

APPENDIX C

PART I
INTRODUCTORY

CHAPTER I

SCOPE AND COMPLEXITY OF THE DEBT PROBLEM

For 14 years, almost from the moment when guns were stilled on the various battle-fronts of Europe, the reparation and inter-Allied debt question has commanded the attention of the world, unloosing passions and giving rise to bitter animosities and acrid controversies. With the coming of the economic depression which has overwhelmed the world with unprecedented difficulties, the war debt problem has emerged more than ever as a dominating factor in the whole international scene. Far-reaching action with respect to it has been brought about by the Hoover moratorium of June 1931 and by the decisions of the Lausanne conference of July 1932, and these two events have placed the problem on a new plane of discussion and controversy. As a result, it has become imperative to subject the whole question to thorough reconsideration in the light of changing conditions and of the experience yielded by a decade of attempts at fulfillment of the war debt obligations.

The war debt problem, for the purposes of this study, comprises the origin and liquidation of all inter-governmental obligations resulting from the world conflict—reparations, war loans, relief and reconstruction credits. This problem has evoked an immense amount of oral and printed discussion. A chronology of the reparation problem alone, dealing with the more important events in the official negotiations during only the first post-war decade, contains more than 600 items, some of

3

them referring to conferences that lasted days and weeks. As many as 30 specially convened conferences have devoted to the reparation question either their entire attention, or at least the major portion of it. These were meetings of premiers, ministers of finance, and other high government officials, as well as of bankers and economic experts. The Supreme War Council, the Reparation Commission, and the numerous committees and commissions set up by the latter, struggled for years with various aspects of the problem. To all this must be added the negotiations of the United States government with its European debtors, and of the creditor nations of Europe with their war borrowers. Each step in these endless parleys gave rise to extensive portfolios of notes, memoranda, reports, and other documents, while each decision requiring parliamentary ratification served to augment still further the constantly growing mass of documentary material. As a result, even a close student of the question finds himself today in a veritable maze. And this central maze of official negotiation and ratification is overgrown and surrounded on all sides by an even more extensive and tangled underbrush of unofficial discussion.

The emotional welter in which the debt problem has had its being has unfortunately tended to obscure the basic realities of the situation. The creation and the repayment of large international debts affect profoundly the economic life alike of the debtor and the creditor nations. They are, therefore, both in their immediate and in their far-reaching impact, economic problems of first magnitude. It is from this point of view that the war debt question is considered in the discussion which follows— in which we are primarily concerned with answering two fundamental questions:

(1) Would a complete obliteration of all reparation and inter-Allied war debt obligations promote, or retard, world prosperity?

(2) Would collection of these inter-governmental debts be economically beneficial to the creditor countries?

No fewer than 28 countries are involved in the war debt relations. Every European belligerent in the World War, with the sole exception of Turkey; every new state in Europe carved out of the territories of the former belligerents; every European neutral, with the exception of Spain; and, in addition, the United States and Japan—each of these nations stands today either as creditor or debtor on the war debt account, and some of them as both creditor and debtor. Five of these countries are debtors only; ten of them are creditors only; while 13 are both debtors and creditors. Ten of them are net debtors, and 18 are net creditors.[1]

Germany has eleven creditors. The United States receives payments from 16 debtors. Great Britain collects debt instalments from 17 countries, and France from ten. Even such smaller nations as Hungary, Bulgaria, Rumania, and Czechoslovakia have as many as nine or ten creditors each.

These debts, with very few exceptions,[2] have been

---

[1] The roster would be increased to 31 countries if we were to include all of the self-governing dominions of the British commonwealth of nations which share in the German reparation payments and are debtors to the British government on the war account. However, the share of the British Empire in the reparation instalments is received entirely by Great Britain and allocated by her to the dominions, and since we do not deal in this study with the debt relations between the British government and those of the dominions, these latter are brought into our story only in so far as they stand in a creditor position outside the intra-imperial debt arrangements.

[2] The only important exception is Russia, whose war debts, as well as other foreign obligations, stand repudiated.

funded. As the resulting contractual obligations evidencing the debts stood at the time of the announcement of the Hoover moratorium, the scheduled annual payments involved the international transfer of an enormous volume of wealth. During the moratorium year from July 1, 1931 to June 30, 1932 the total of such movements would have been the equivalent of over three-quarters of a billion dollars. If we think of this sum as one pool, Germany would have paid into it more than one-half of the total, or 385 million dollars; Great Britain would have paid 160 millions; France, 116 millions; Italy, 37 millions; and Belgium, 15 millions. Out of the pool, the United States would have received 262 million dollars; France, 196 millions; Great Britain, 188 millions; Italy, 48 millions; and Belgium, 30 millions. Of the other countries involved in the war debt situation, Austria, Hungary, Finland, Latvia, Esthonia, and Lithuania would have paid into the pool without receiving anything from it; Australia, Canada, the Netherlands, Switzerland, Sweden, Denmark, Norway, Luxemburg, and Japan would have received varying sums from the pool without paying anything into it; Greece, Yugoslavia, and Portugal would have made payments into the pool, but have received from it more than they had paid in; and Poland, Rumania, Czechoslovakia, and Bulgaria would have paid into the pool more than they would have received from it.[3]

Six of the countries involved in the debt situation—Germany, the United States, France, Great Britain, Italy, and Belgium—are of outstanding importance. Their relative weight in the movement of inter-govern-

[3] See Appendix D, Table II following p. 487.

ment debt payments, as they stood prior to the Lausanne conference, is indicated by the figures quoted above and even more strikingly by the table on this page, in which is shown the gross and net creditor or debtor

BALANCE SHEET OF INTER-GOVERNMENTAL WAR DEBTS AS OF JULY 1, 1931
Aggregate Amounts of Principal and Interest Scheduled, under the Existing
Debt Agreements, to Be Received or Paid by Each of the Countries
Indicated, after July 1, 1931
(In thousands of dollars[a])

Country	Total Receipts	Total Payments	Net Receipts (+) Net Payments (−)
Australia	782	—	+782
Austria	—	116,118	−116,118
Belgium	1,454,248	849,002	+605,246
Bulgaria	553	78,619	−78,066
Canada	13,207	—	+13,207
Czechoslovakia	1,090	424,836	−423,746
Denmark	478	—	+478
Esthonia	—	45,481	−45,481
Finland	—	19,050	−19,050
France	13,855,776	10,497,105	+3,358,671
Germany	210	25,609,625	−25,609,415
Great Britain	10,685,848	9,754,245	+931,603
Greece	216,079	164,539	+51,540
Hungary	4,246	35,041	−30,795
Italy	4,056,616	3,571,745	+484,871
Japan	109,548	—	+109,548
Latvia	—	24,652	−24,652
Lithuania	—	14,701	−14,701
Luxemburg	4,034	—	+4,034
Netherlands	18,273	—	+18,273
Norway	6,199	—	+6,199
Poland	4,353	666,096	−661,743
Portugal	159,546	109,557	+49,989
Rumania	447,184	422,562	+24,622
Sweden	1,914	—	+1,914
Switzerland	4,622	—	+4,622
United States	20,822,691	—	+20,822,691
Yugoslavia	874,050	338,573	+535,477
Total	52,741,547	52,741,547	

[a] All conversions at par of exchange. For details see Appendix D, Table I following p. 487.

Total Scheduled Receipts and Payments of Principal Countries as of July 1, 1931

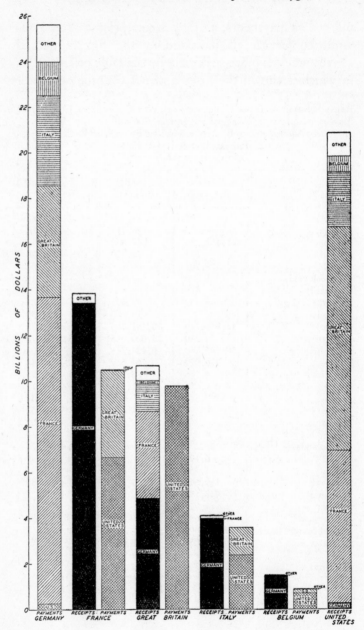

position of each of the countries concerned with the war debts, as of July 1, 1931.[4] The table shows Germany as the primary debtor and the United States as the primary creditor. These interrelations are represented graphically by the frontispiece map and the diagram on page 8.

The aggregate of Germany's obligations still outstanding at the time when all inter-governmental debt payments were suspended by the Hoover moratorium was almost equal to all the other payments to be made by all the other debtors to their creditors. The aggregate amounts scheduled to be received by the United States constituted 40 per cent of the total receipts of all the creditors. France, Great Britain, Italy, Belgium, and the United States, the principal creditors of Germany, were scheduled to receive together 94 per cent of the payments to be made by that country. Great Britain, France, Italy, Belgium, and Germany, the principal debtors to the United States, were scheduled to furnish together 95 per cent of our receipts from our war debtors. Germany, France, Italy, and Belgium, the principal debtors to Great Britain, were scheduled to furnish together 93 per cent of that country's total receipts. France, Italy, and Belgium were to receive from Germany more than the amounts owed their two creditors, the United States and Great Britain. Great Britain was to receive from her four principal debtors more than she was to pay to the United States.

The discharging of all these vast obligations requires a more complicated process than payments by all the debtors into a single pool, out of which all the creditors

---

[4] For a more detailed balance sheet of the inter-governmental debts and an explanation of the methods used in compiling it, see Appendix D, pp. 486-87.

receive payment. It is true that, because some of the important debtors are at the same time large creditors, a substantial part of the payments in effect becomes a mere series of bookkeeping transfers. But, in the end, each net debtor must discharge at least a portion of his obligations to each one of his creditors, and each net creditor must receive at least some portion of the debt payment owing to him. All this inevitably gives rise to a large number of international financial transactions. And while the bulk of these transactions, from the point of view of the amounts involved, concerns only the six countries we have just enumerated, the receipts and payments of the other debtor and creditor countries, although small in relation to the total, are nevertheless of great importance to each of them individually.

The whole process is extremely complex. It touches intimately the fiscal, currency, trade, and general economic conditions of all the countries concerned, and, as we shall see, its ramifications extend to the world as a whole. This complexity will become apparent if we examine the process by which international debt payments are made.

Such an examination is made in the next chapter, which serves to introduce the basic economic principles involved in the debt problem. It is followed, in Part II, by the story of the origin of the war debts and of the numerous agreements negotiated for the purpose of liquidating them. Part III is devoted to a discussion of the origin of the reparation obligations and of the long and tortuous negotiations that brought about the "final and definitive settlement" of 1929-30. In Part IV we discuss the attempts at fulfillment with respect to the various war debts and the breakdown of the payment programs. We show there the amounts paid and the manner in which these payments have been effected; the conditions which led to the breakdown, represented by the Hoover moratorium of 1931; the circumstances and negotiations attending the consequent deferment of the debt payments; and the results of the Lausanne conference of 1932. Finally, in Part V, we take up the basic economic implications of the war debt problem.

In order not to obstruct the flow of discussion and analysis by the introduction of detailed statistical data, we have sought, as far as possible, to avoid the use of tables in the text, relegating all such data to the statistical appendices given at the end of the book. There the reader will find the details of the war and post-war inter-governmental borrowing and lending and of the amounts paid to date on the numerous debt accounts; the complete schedules of payments for all war and reparation debt settlements; and the position of all inter-governmental debts as of July 1, 1931.

CHAPTER II

THE ECONOMICS OF INTERNATIONAL
DEBT PAYMENTS

At the time of the Armistice there was little popular understanding of the fundamental economic considerations involved in the payment of international debts. Although few subjects have ever been so widely discussed as have the war debts in recent years, there is even now so much obscurity as to make it desirable to re-state here, in very brief terms, the basic elements in the problem.

The primary source of popular confusion on the subject lies in the expression of the debts in terms of money. If the Treaty of Versailles had stipulated that the German government should each year for a certain number of years send to the Allied governments certain specific commodities, the nature of the problem would have been clear to anyone. It would have been necessary for the German government to raise, by means of taxes, the money required with which to buy the commodities in question; and then these commodities would have been sent directly by the German government to the Allied governments for such use or disposition as might in each case seem expedient. But instead of this direct process the debt settlements called for the payment of certain sums of money each year, and it was therefore popularly assumed that the debtor government need simply raise the required sums from its people and transfer the money abroad.

The transfer of money out of a country, however, has very limited possibilities. In the first place, the total gold supply of any country is so small that if used in the payment of international debts, such as those existing at the end of the World War, it would be very quickly exhausted. For example, the German gold supply in 1921 was sufficient to meet the reparations obligations for only about six months. Not only would the gold supply of any country be thus quickly dissipated, but if any considerable portion of it were shipped abroad the economic effects would be such as seriously to prejudice the making of any further payments. This lesson was brought home to the world in 1923 in connection with Germany, and as we shall see in Chapter XIV it was again brought home to us in connection with the international financial breakdown of 1931.

The paper currency of a country can be used only to a very limited extent in making payments abroad. This is because the value of the currency—unless the supply is very rigidly limited—depends upon its convertibility into gold. If paper currency were sent abroad in any considerable quantities it would lose its value unless it could be sent back for conversion into gold—and if this occurs it is gold, rather than paper, that becomes the real means of payment. Germany and various other European countries did for a time after the war sell paper currency abroad, but as soon as it became generally apparent that it would probably never be redeemable in gold at anything like its face value, it depreciated so rapidly that it could no longer be sold to foreigners at any price.

The only remaining possibility is to pay in the money of other countries, or in what is known as foreign exchange. In the case of debts owed to France, for example, the French government would accept either its own currency, or bills of exchange entitling it to dollars or any other currency convertible into gold. Such bills could then be utilized by the governments receiving them for making their own foreign debt payments or for meeting any other foreign obligations. They would thus be, to all intents and purposes, the equivalent of gold.

If payments have to be made by any debtor country in foreign currency, it is obvious that that country must be able somehow to *earn* the foreign currency required, for by hypothesis it is not to come as a *gift*. This foreign currency can be earned only by the sale of goods or the rendering of services to foreigners—services including such things as the carrying of the goods of foreigners, the entertainment of tourists, and the insurance of foreign goods. No other means are available, although, as we shall see, the funds required may for a time be borrowed. By goods or services alone, and chiefly the former, can international debts be paid.[1]

But it is not sufficient that the debtor country should export, say, two billion marks' worth of gold annually in order to be able to pay debts abroad to the extent of two billion marks. This is because some portion of a country's exports must always be utilized to pay for imports. In the complex economic world of today every nation has extensive trade and service relation with nearly every other nation, and a substantial volume of imports is an absolute necessity if the production of economic goods within the country is to be maintained.

Thus we arrive at the proposition that the total volume of exports cannot be used for the purpose of earn-

[1] The same thing is, of course, ultimately true in the case of domestic debts as well.

ing foreign money with which to meet foreign debts, but that only *the proceeds from the excess of exports over imports are available*. That is to say, the payment for the indispensably necessary imports must be regarded as a first charge against the proceeds of a nation's exports; and only what is left can, year in and year out, be utilized in liquidating international indebtedness.

It should be noted also that, in the main, the goods exported must be the result of current production. Temporary payments may be made by utilizing existing accumulations of movable property such as railway rolling stock, ships, livestock, and supplies; indeed, as we shall see in later chapters, a considerable volume of reparation payments was made by this process in the early post-war years. But the amount of available movable property is relatively limited, and, as in the case of the gold supply, its utilization in making debt payments is likely to lessen the volume of payments that can be made in the future, because of the effects upon the productive capacity of the country. As a long-run story, it is only through the processes of annual production and trade that payments can be made.

We have seen that if a country is to make payments abroad it must earn, by means of exports, or services, the foreign money required. But this foreign exchange derived from the sale of goods abroad is, in the first instance, owned by private citizens and not by the government. It is, therefore, necessary for the government to raise taxes, in domestic currency, with which to buy the necessary foreign exchange. That is to say, it must raise money from its citizens generally in order to be able to buy from some of its citizens the foreign bills which have come into their possession as a result of sales of goods abroad. Thus there are two stages in the process—one is the budget problem and the other is the foreign exchange problem, often referred to as the *transfer* problem. A surplus is necessary in the budget, over and above ordinary expenditures, in order that the government may have revenue with which to buy foreign bills of exchange. And a surplus, as we have seen, is also necessary in foreign trade if the requisite foreign exchange is to be available for purchase by the government. The ability of a debtor country to develop a budgetary surplus, as well as an excess of income over outgo in its international trade and financial relations, constitutes its capacity for meeting its inter-governmental obligations—its capacity to pay.

The procurement of a balanced international position presents more complications than the development of a budget surplus. The ability of a country to earn foreign exchange is dependent in no small degree upon the policies of other countries. Whereas the obtaining of a budget surplus depends in the main upon internal conditions and policies, the acquisition of foreign exchange is contingent upon foreign conditions and policies as well. This statement requires a word of explanation.

Just as a debtor country, in order to make a foreign debt payment, must sell to foreigners more goods and services than it buys from foreigners, so a creditor nation, in order to receive a completed debt payment, must be prepared to buy from foreigners more goods and services than it sells to them. It must accept in its international trade and service operations an excess of imports over exports. The degree to which such a creditor country accepts an import surplus measures its willingness to receive debt payments. For example, if the

United States is to receive payments from a foreign debtor the American people must import more goods than they export, for only thus will the necessary dollars be available in the foreign exchange market for purchase by the debtor government.

It should be made clear, however, that these trade and service operations may be to some degree *indirect* in character. That is to say, if Great Britain, for example, is the debtor, she might earn dollars by roundabout transactions. Americans might purchase goods in Brazil or Japan and pay dollars therefor. Then the Brazilians or the Japanese might purchase goods from the British, paying for them with the dollars obtained from American purchasers. But no matter through how many hands these dollars may pass, their acquisition by Great Britain indicates two things: first, that somebody in the United States has bought something outside his country; and, second, that somebody in Great Britain has sold something outside his country. These roundabout operations may facilitate the necessary trade processes, but they do not alter the fundamental nature of the problem. It still remains necesary for the citizens of the debtor country to sell more abroad than they buy abroad and for the citizens of the creditor country to receive more from abroad than they sell abroad. Only under these conditions can the debtor government procure the foreign money with which to pay the creditor government.

Emphasis has been placed upon the necessity of an *excess of exports* for the debtor country and an *import surplus* for the creditor country because it is commonly assumed that all that is necessary is for certain specific commodities to be shipped from debtor to creditor country. In fact, so-called payments in kind—coal, building materials, and so on—have been made on account of reparations. The shipment of specified commodities does not, however, change the fundamentals of the problem. If the value of the indispensable imports of the debtor country does not exceed the value of that country's *ordinary* exports, then the additional specific exports for debt payments can be made. But if the *total* exports merely equal the necessary imports, then utilization of a portion of those exports as payments in kind on debt account will lessen the capacity to pay in the following year. The resulting inability to pay for necessary imports will serve to restrict production and thus curtail future exports. The situation is analogous to that of a corporation which does not have a net income. It might pay certain obligations by using up some of its capital; but if it did, the chances of meeting current obligations in subsequent years would be reduced. A nation, like a corporation, can in the long run make payments abroad only out of *net income*, and this means out of an excess of exports over imports.

As opposed to payments out of current income it has often been contended that payments may be made out of capital—through the utilization of securities. In considering the use of securities it is necessary to distinguish between foreign securities owned by citizens of a debtor country and that country's own domestic securities. If the citizens of France, for example, own bonds of American railroads or of enterprises in other countries, the government of France might buy these bonds from their owners and turn them over to a creditor country in the liquidation of obligations. Or, for that matter, these bonds might be sold for cash in international markets and the proceeds utilized in meeting debt payments. In fact, France utilized this method to a very considerable extent in meeting the indemnity payments to Germany following the Franco-Prussian War of 1871.

When payments are made through the delivery of foreign securities, it is clear that the debtor country does not need to expand its current exports in order to make the payments. The sacrifice of capital assets, however, does mean that that country will henceforth be entitled to less interest from abroad, and hence its means of purchasing imports will have been reduced. The possibilities of effecting payments by the transfer of foreign securities are, in any event, usually limited in extent. Few countries possess large amounts of foreign securities, and only a portion of these are ordinarily of such character as to be readily accepted in the settlement of international obligations.

The utilization of a country's domestic securities or other property has often been suggested as a means of paying inter-governmental obligations. A moment's reflection will suggest that the international debts in question are themselves evidenced by domestic securities—in the form of government bonds. In any given case the creditor nation might possibly prefer to receive in lieu of the obligation of the debtor government the obligations of the railroads, public utilities, or other corporations in the debtor country. Indeed, this was done temporarily under the Dawes plan. But such a shifting of the form of the obligation in no sense changes the nature of the problem of payment; it is still necessary for the debtor country to procure an export surplus of goods and services and for the creditor countries to receive the

An alternative suggestion is the sale of domestic securities in foreign markets and the utilization of the proceeds in meeting inter-governmental debt obligations. payments in the form of imports of goods and services. This would again merely involve a shifting of creditors, for the bonds sold abroad would be new obligations replacing those that were liquidated.

Nor is the problem in any way changed by the so-called "commercialization" of inter-governmental debts. The hope was long entertained that the Allied governments might sell German reparation bonds in world markets for cash. While such a transaction might well be advantageous to the creditor governments it would merely result, from the debtor's point of view, in a substitution of private commercial and financial creditors for the public creditors, without in any way changing the nature of the problem of making payments. The same principles hold if direct ownership of physical properties in the debtor countries, such as land or buildings, is turned over to the creditor countries or if such properties are sold to foreign citizens and the proceeds utilized in meeting inter-governmental debts. All that can be accomplished by any of these processes is the liquidation of one form of indebtedness and the creation of another.

There only remains for consideration the possibility of liquidating inter-governmental debts through *new borrowing operations* as distinguished from the sale of existing securities. When a European government has to meet a debt payment to the United States Treasury, it may borrow the necessary funds in other countries, or from private American sources. In this manner the original debt obligations would be liquidated; but obviously a new debt would be created in their place, leaving the total indebtedness unchanged. Foreign loans may also be procured as a means of meeting interest instalments on international debts; but new, and increasing, obligations are again created in place of those which are being liquidated. In other words, one can borrow from Peter to pay Paul, but he cannot get out of debt by the process.

We shall have occasion in Part V to return to a discussion of the trade and loan aspects of the international debt problem. It will be sufficient to bear in mind at this place that the transfers of funds from treasury to treasury are but the pecuniary manifestations of a process which affects in fundamental ways the general economic relations of the countries concerned.

PART II

THE STORY OF THE DEBT SETTLEMENTS

CHAPTER III

ORIGIN AND CHARACTER OF THE WAR DEBTS

The inter-governmental indebtedness which is the subject of this analysis may be conveniently divided into three classes: (1) the war debts proper, resulting from the imperative need of the Allied countries for foreign loans; (2) the relief loans, occasioned by post-war borrowings for reconstruction and the relief of suffering populations; and (3) the reparation obligations, imposed upon the defeated Central Powers. In this chapter we are concerned only with the first two categories of this indebtedness. We shall set forth as succinctly as possible the origin, character, and extent of inter-governmental borrowings, covering not only loans from the United States to Europe but all inter-governmental loans arising from the exigencies of the war.

Under the conditions which existed at the outbreak of the war, three of the five powers which were then in alliance against Germany were in immediate need of foreign loans. Belgium and Serbia were quickly and almost completely overrun by the enemy. Deprived of their territory and consequently of all sources of income, the governments and the armies of these nations, which continued to function on foreign soil, could be financed only by means of foreign loans.

Similarly, Russia found herself in almost immediate need of foreign borrowings. This was because Russia had large payments to make abroad, particularly in France and England, as a result of a huge accumulation of foreign indebtedness and a deficit in her international

64059

trade and financial operations. As a matter of fact, pre-war Russia habitually borrowed abroad the sums needed for meeting interest charges on her foreign debt. This problem was greatly complicated after August 1914 by virtue of the fact that as much as 45 per cent of Russia's exports went to the countries of Central Europe, with which she was then at war, while over 90 per cent of her foreign debt was held in countries with which she was allied.[1] In these circumstances foreign loans with which to pay for indispensable war imports and to make regular payments on account of pre-war indebtedness were of paramount importance.

Italy, and such smaller belligerents as Portugal, Rumania, and Greece, after they entered the war on various dates subsequent to August 1914,[2] found themselves in much the same position as Russia, except that the burden of payments on account of pre-war debts was relatively much lighter. Their credit requirements were primarily for the purpose of paying for supplies, and so pressing were these needs that Italy, for example, made the acquisition of foreign credits a condition precedent to her declaration of war on the side of the Allied Powers.

None of these countries possessed sufficient gold reserves to meet more than a negligible proportion of its war requirements. Russia and Italy did, however, use for foreign payments a certain amount of gold in a manner which we shall presently describe.

The financial position of Great Britain and France at the outbreak of the war was essentially different from

---

[1] About 80 per cent was owed to France and 14 per cent to Great Britain.

[2] Italy became a belligerent in May 1915, Portugal in March 1916, and Rumania and Greece in August 1916.

that of the other Allies. This was due chiefly to the fact that they had large accumulations of foreign investments. Thus they did not have any interest charges to meet abroad and, on the other hand, they had liquid assets which could be more or less readily mobilized.

Great Britain, in fact, sold a substantial volume of foreign investments and utilized other foreign securities as a basis for loans. While she found it necessary to borrow large amounts as a means of financing purchases abroad, particularly in the United States, as we shall presently see she loaned much more during the first three years of the war than she borrowed.

The financial power of France was reduced from the very beginning of the war by two important factors. In the first place, the industrial sections of the country were occupied by the German armies, as a result of which France had to depend largely upon imported supplies. In the second place, the bulk of French investments was in the countries of Central and Eastern Europe and in the Near East, and such securities could not be utilized in paying for purchases in neutral countries. Accordingly it was necessary for France to borrow in order to pay for the large imports required. At the same time she was called upon to extend substantial loans to her Continental Allies.

I. PRE-ARMISTICE LOANS

The Allied borrowing during the war falls into two distinct periods, separated by the entry of the United States into the conflict. Prior to April 6, 1917 the primary responsibility for supplying the international financial requirements of the Allies devolved upon Great Britain. After that date, the United States assumed the role of banker for the Allied Powers, including Great Britain.

1. Prior to April 6, 1917. Early in the war the three principal Allied countries—Great Britain, France, and Russia—worked out a system of collaboration for meeting foreign payments.[3] The agreement dealt with transactions among members of the Allied group and payments to neutral nations.

The general principle governing payments by one Allied nation to another was that the government entitled to receive payments would facilitate the payment by providing the necessary exchange. For example, the French government would provide French exchange when the other Allies had payments to make in France, while the British government and the Russian government would similarly provide pounds sterling and rubles. Under the operation of this system of inter-Allied financial collaboration, each of the principal Allied Powers extended credits to the others, some of which, however, regularly cancelled each other. For example, the ruble credits provided by Russia for Great Britain and France were cancelled by some of the pound sterling and franc credits granted to Russia by these two powers. In the same way, the franc credits provided for Great Britain by France were cancelled by some of the

[3] The bases of the inter-Allied financial collaboration were laid down at the conference held in Paris in February 1915, attended by the British, French, and Russian Ministers of Finance. At this conference, the three Ministers undertook to recommend to their governments the following measures: (1) Co-operation in the making of advances to countries fighting on their side; (2) the issue of a joint loan; (3) the establishment of close relations among the three banks of issue; and (4) co-ordination of their purchases from neutral countries. These measures, with the exception of the second, were eventually carried out. The Paris conference was the first of a long series of meetings attended by the Ministers of Finance of the Allied governments.

pound sterling credits extended to France by Great Britain.

In the case of payments to neutral nations, Great Britain assumed the primary responsibility. In fact, during the first three years of the war, Great Britain undertook to provide a considerable part of the foreign exchange needed by all the Allied Powers in meeting payments in the neutral countries. Whereas the loans extended by France to her Continental Allies were exclusively for payments due in France, those extended by Great Britain were for payments due both in Great Britain and in other countries.

Practically all of these loans between the Allied nations were inter-governmental in character—that is, neither the borrower nor the lender was a private agency. The only important exceptions are found in a loan made directly by the Bank of England to the Bank of France, and in the sale of French Treasury bills and other securities directly to the British public, usually through the instrumentality, or at least with the assistance, of the Bank of England.

By the time the United States entered the conflict, all of the Allied Powers were debtors to Great Britain. In addition, France, a debtor to Great Britain, was also a creditor to Russia, Belgium, Serbia, and Greece.

During the first two years of the war both France and Russia borrowed substantial sums in neutral nations. Thus France borrowed in the United States, through various banking groups, the sum of 524 million dollars, of which 80 millions were repaid during the same period. In addition, France shared equally with Great Britain in the 500 million dollar Anglo-French loan which was floated in the United States in 1915. Russia also borrowed 136 million dollars in the United States. Moreover, both France and Russia borrowed considerable sums in Japan, in South American countries, and in the neutral countries of Europe.

These loans, however, were not sufficient in amount to provide the volume of exchange that was required to meet payments in neutral countries. The remainder, in accordance with the inter-Allied financial agreement mentioned above, was supplied by Great Britain. Some of the loans contracted in Great Britain by France specifically provided that a portion of the funds thus obtained (sometimes as much as two-thirds) should be made available for payments in the United States. There were similar arrangements in connection with British loans to Russia and Italy.

In her capacity as banker for her Allies, Great Britain was confronted with a very difficult task. In order to secure the necessary foreign exchange for her own payments and those of her Allies in the United States and other neutral countries, and at the same time maintain her currency at some approximation to parity, she had three possible courses of action: (a) to ship gold; (b) to sell foreign securities owned by her citizens; and (c) to borrow abroad. In fact, she resorted to all three methods of procuring the foreign exchange required.

Great Britain was not abundantly supplied with gold at the outbreak of the war. The stock at the Bank of England amounted to only 150 million dollars, but this was increased considerably during the course of the war by the withdrawal of gold from circulation and by new output from South African and Australian mines. Even so, the gold supply was meager indeed and very much smaller than that of France or Russia. The gold stock of the Bank of France amounted at the outbreak of the war to 840 million dollars, and that of the Bank of Russia to more than 750 million dollars.[4]

With a view to making a more effective utilization of the combined gold resources of these countries, arrangements were made under which substantial portions of the gold stock of France and Russia were transferred to Great Britain. Some of the British loans to France, Russia, and later to Italy, were accompanied by simultaneous shipments of gold from these countries to Great Britain. The major portion of these shipments represented loans to Great Britain which were made repayable after the war as a part of the subsequent debt adjustment. Some of the gold was, however, sold outright to Great Britain. The total shipments of gold under this arrangement, in millions of dollars, were as follows:[5]

Shipping Country	On Loan	For Sale	Total
France	$374	$170	$544
Russia	292	39	331
Italy	108	....	108
Total	$774	$209	$983

From the point of view of bookkeeping entries, the loans of gold to Great Britain represented British borrowing. Practically, of course, they served merely to offset portions of the loans extended by Great Britain to her three Allies. The reason why most of the gold shipped to Great Britain (or for her credit to Canada and other countries) was officially in the form of loans

[4] F. François-Marsal, *Les Dettes interalliées*, 1927, p. 10.
[5] The data for France are from François-Marsal, *Les Dettes interalliées*, p. 10; for Russia, from *La Dette publique de la Russie*, 1922, pp. 39 and 49-50; for Italy, from B. Stringher, *Momorie reguardanti la circolazione e il mercato monetario*, 1925, p. 20.

was that the shipping countries were extremely reluctant to part with their gold outright, fearing the unfavorable effects upon their financial position of a sharp contraction of their gold reserves. Under the system adopted, the British government handed them, in exchange for gold, non-interest-bearing Treasury bills, which they included in the metallic reserves of their banks of issue as "gold held abroad."[6] Eventually most of this gold found its way to the United States in meeting payments that had to be effected there by Great Britain.

Great Britain obtained a very large volume of foreign exchange through the mobilization of foreign securities. The British government began to mobilize the securities held by her citizens abroad about the middle of the year 1915. Under a system devised by Reginald McKenna, then chancellor of the exchequer, the Treasury instructed the Bank of England in July of that year to purchase for its account American dollar securities in London and transmit them to New York for sale. In December of that year, a special American Dollar Securities Committee was set up by the Chancellor of the Exchequer and thenceforth all operations in connection with the mobilization of foreign securities were concentrated in the hands of the committee.

[6] The authorship of this solution of the difficulty is attributed by Arthur Raffalovich, official representative of the Russian Ministry of Finance in France during the war, to John Maynard Keynes, who was at that time an official in the British Treasury. In the case of Russia, a special device was adopted for helping her to conceal her true monetary position: an arrangement was made under which, in exchange for Russian Treasury bills to the value of 2 billion rubles (200 million pounds sterling) handed over to the British Treasury, a non-negotiable book credit of the same amount was opened at the Bank of England in favor of the State Bank of Russia, which the latter also included in the item "gold held abroad." See *La Dette publique de la Russie*, p. 49.

The committee was authorized to purchase securities or to receive them on deposit as a loan. Its operations were gradually extended to include Canadian securities, those of some of the neutral countries, and sterling bonds and stocks. For the securities purchased outright, the Treasury paid in pounds sterling at the current quotation; for those deposited with it, it undertook to pay the owners the regular interest or dividends plus a specified bonus.

At the beginning, the offer of securities to the Treasury was made voluntary, but as the requirements of the Treasury increased faster than the voluntary offers, measures began to be taken to stimulate the latter. In May 1916 an additional income tax of 10 per cent was introduced on securities listed by the Treasury, the owners of which failed to present them for sale or deposit. In January 1917 the Treasury was given the power to compel the owners of securities desired by it to sell or lend them on demand.

Altogether, during the war—mostly during the period prior to April 1917—the volume of American bonds and shares obtained by the Treasury by purchase aggregated 866 million dollars and by loan 355 millions. In addition the Treasury acquired Canadian securities to the value of 34 million dollars by purchase, and 131 million dollars by loan, as well as small amounts of Dutch and Scandinavian securities.[7] The foreign securities purchased were as a rule sold in the

[7] A. W. Kirkaldy, *British Finance During and After the War*, 1921, pp. 188-97. The values given here in dollars were obtained by converting the amounts originally reported by the American Dollar Securities Committee in pounds sterling at the pre-war par of exchange. These amounts in pounds sterling were as follows: American securities obtained by purchase, 178 millions, and on deposit, 73 millions; Canadian securities obtained by purchase, 7 millions, and on deposit, 27 millions.

countries where they originated and thus directly provided American and other neutral exchange.[8]

The third means of procuring foreign exchange, namely, by borrowing, was also extensively utilized. As security for foreign loans, particularly in the United States, Great Britain usually hypothecated bonds and stocks. She utilized first the foreign bonds and shares discussed above which had been deposited as loans with the Treasury. She also pledged bonds and stocks of British railroad and other corporations which had been mobilized by the Treasury, chiefly in the form of loans to the government. The volume of sterling bonds and stocks thus mobilized amounted to 336 million pounds, or the equivalent at pre-war parity of exchange of 1,635 million dollars. During the period of the war prior to April 1917, Great Britain's total borrowings in the United States, including the British half of the Anglo-French loan, amounted to 1,065 million dollars, while her loans from other neutral countries aggregated 329 millions.

[8] France also utilized for the purpose of meeting her foreign payments a certain amount of foreign securities held by private French investors and mobilized by the French government mainly through the process of borrowing them from private holders, although a small amount was obtained by means of outright purchase. The securities of the following nations were thus borrowed: the United States, Canada, Argentina, Denmark, Norway, Sweden, Switzerland, the Netherlands, Brazil, Uruguay, and Egypt. In addition, a certain amount of Suez Canal shares and of bonds issued by the Province of Quebec were also obtained. In order to make the operation attractive to the holders of the securities, the French government undertook to pay them not only the regular interest or dividends, but also a bonus equal to one-fourth of the gross annual revenue. On the other hand, the government retained the right to purchase the securities lent to it, and subsequently did so acquire the greater part of such securities. The total value of the securities borrowed by the French government was about 2 billion francs. See G. Jèze and H. Truchy, *The War Finance of France*, 1927, pp. 301-03.

The results of Allied borrowing operations during the first period of the war may be briefly summarized as follows. The total inter-governmental loans amounted to 4,328.9 million dollars at par of exchange. Of this amount Great Britain loaned 3,814.4 millions, while France loaned 514.4 millions. During the same period, however, the French government borrowed 555 million dollars from the British government. All of the other Allies—Russia, Italy, Belgium, Serbia, Rumania, Portugal, Greece, the Belgian Congo, and the British dominions and colonies—were net borrowers.[9]

In addition to borrowing from each other, all of the important Allied governments borrowed from private interests abroad. France, for example, sold 500 million dollars of Treasury bills to British investors and negotiated loans in the United States amounting to 694 millions. Great Britain borrowed 1,065 million dollars in the American market, and Russia 136 millions. It is estimated that the combined borrowings of the Allies in other neutral markets aggregated 996 million dollars.[10]

2. *From April 6, 1917 to November 11, 1918.* By the beginning of 1917 the financial resources of the Allied countries had become strained almost to the breaking point. Not only had the exigencies of the war required a continuous augmentation of the physical volume of purchases in the United States, but the prices of war supplies had been rapidly mounting. By December 1916 the Bureau of Labor Statistics wholesale price index had risen to 146 (average for 1913 = 100), and by April 1917 to 172. As a result of these two conditions, the value of the purchases in the United States by the four

[9] For the detailed figures, see Appendix A, p. 425.
[10] See François-Marsal, *Les Dettes interalliées*, pp. 12-15.

principal Allies—Great Britain, France, Russia, and Italy—exceeded their purchases during the last pre-war year by approximately 700 million dollars during the first year of the war; by over 2 billions during the second year; and by more than 3 billions during the third year. Great Britain, upon whom fell the principal burden of procuring this ever increasing volume of dollars, found the task more and more difficult. We have seen that shortly before the United States entered the war, the British Treasury was compelled to seek and obtain the power to commandeer foreign, especially American, securities held by private investors in Great Britain. The difficulties of floating loans in the United States were also increasing.

After the United States entered the war in April 1917, the problem of financing Allied purchases was given immediate consideration. Notwithstanding the extraordinary financial requirements of America's own mobilization program, the United States Treasury undertook to provide the Allied governments with the funds they needed for the purpose of meeting their payments in the United States.

This method was considered preferable to merely facilitating access to the American capital market and letting the Allied nations supply their requirements out of loans offered to American banks and private investors. There were three principal reasons for this: First, foreign borrowers would thus be prevented from competing with the American Treasury as a borrower in the American market; second, it was not at all certain that the Allied governments would be able to obtain by direct borrowing sufficient funds to meet their requirements, and in any event the cost of such borrowing to them would have been very high; and, third, by becoming the banker for the Allied Powers, the Treasury could much more easily co-ordinate European purchases with those effected by the American government, thus bringing about a more efficient utilization of available supplies and keeping prices from rising as much as they might have risen under conditions of competition between American and foreign buyers acting independently of each other.[11]

In making loans to the Allied countries, the Treasury acted under the authority of the Liberty Loan Acts of April 24, 1917, September 24, 1917, April 4, 1918, and July 9, 1918.[12] In accordance with the provisions of these four acts, the Secretary of the Treasury was empowered, with the approval of the President, to purchase obligations of foreign governments at war with the enemies of the United States for a total amount not exceeding 10 billion dollars. The obligations were to be purchased at par and were to be made repayable on substantially the same terms as those on which the Liberty bonds were offered to the American public.

The total volume of credits established in favor of foreign governments by the time of the Armistice was approximately 8 billion dollars. Only a little over 7 billions, however, was actually advanced in cash prior to November 11, 1918. The remainder of the already established credits was utilized after the cessation of hos-

---

[11] In doing this, the American Treasury profited by the earlier experience of Great Britain, where the Treasury for similar reasons had taken over the financing of the Allies.

[12] For the text of these acts see *Annual Report of the Secretary of the Treasury on the State of the Finances for the Fiscal Year Ended June 30, 1917*, pp. 83-86 and 91-99; and similar report for the year ended June 30, 1918, pp. 159-63 and 174.

tilities, in addition to the new post-Armistice advances. These loans were extended to seven countries.[13] The manner in which the funds were spent is described in the last section of this chapter.

In the meantime, Great Britain and France also continued to make loans to their Allies in even greater amounts than had been the case during the first period of the war. The net amount of Great Britain's loans to her Allies increased, during the period from April 1917 to November 11, 1918 by the equivalent of about 3,200 million dollars; while the net amount of the loans made by France increased by the equivalent of approximately 1,700 millions. Great Britain's loans from the United States exceeded her loans to her Allies by nearly 500 million dollars, while the borrowings of France from the United States and Great Britain exceeded her loans to Continental Allies by about 1,500 millions.[14]

No precise data are available as to the status of Allied government debts to banks and private investors in other countries at the time of the Armistice. During the second period of the war, some repayments had been made and some new debts contracted. On the whole, there is reason to believe that the Allied government debts on this account were at the end of the second period of the war at least as large as they had been at the beginning.

II. POST-ARMISTICE LOANS

Inter-governmental borrowing continued for some time after the Armistice. A substantial part of the funds was used for the liquidation of war accounts, a portion

---

[13] A detailed statement of the loans is given in Appendix A, pp. 427-31.

[14] The details of the inter-Allied loans during the second period of the war are given in Appendix A, p. 426.

for the payment of interest on the war-time loans, and the remainder for reconstruction and relief purposes.

The bulk of the post-Armistice loans was provided by the United States. American government loans, in fact, continued to be made to a number of countries until the latter part of 1920. About three-fourths of the aggregate post-war advances were made under the authority of the war-time Liberty Loan Acts.[15] The remaining loans were made under special legislation. An act of July 9, 1918 empowered the War and Navy Departments to sell to foreign governments on credit any or all surplus war materials; an act of February 25, 1919 empowered the American Relief Administration to sell supplies on credit; and an act of March 13, 1920 conferred similar powers upon the United States Grain Corporation. The total volume of loans extended under these various acts following the Armistice was as follows (the three last items are commonly regarded as going for relief and reconstruction purposes):

Loans under the Liberty Loan Acts	$2,369,196,000
American Relief Administration credits	84,094,000
Surplus war supplies credits	574,977,000
United States Grain Corporation credits	56,859,000
Total	$3,085,126,000

[15] These acts provided that the authority of the Treasury to make loans for purposes specified in the acts ("of more effectually providing for the national security and prosecuting the war by establishing credits in the United States for foreign governments") "shall cease upon the termination of the war between the United States and the Imperial German government." However, Section 13 of the Second Liberty Loan Act stated that "for the purposes of this act the date of the termination of the war between the United States and the Imperial German government shall be fixed by proclamation of the President of the United States." Since the United States technically remained at war with Germany for more than two and one-half years after the Armistice (the presidential proclamation officially terminating the war between the two countries was not issued until July 2, 1921), the Treasury felt entirely justified in making post-war advances to the Allied nations.

The figure for the loans extended under the Liberty Loan Acts includes interest through April and May 1919. Late in 1919 the United States Treasury agreed to a postponement of interest payments on the war debts. During the war, and indeed until the spring of 1919, the debtor governments regularly met interest on all loans, the payments being made from the proceeds of new loans. Since it was apparent that this method of meeting interest charges could not be continued indefinitely, after the war was over, the question arose as to whether the Allies were in a position to undertake at once the payment of interest out of their own resources. It was recognized by Mr. R. C. Leffingwell, assistant secretary of the treasury, who was in charge of the war debts in the early post-war years, that because of unsettled economic conditions and depreciating exchanges this would involve serious difficulties. Accordingly, on September 26, 1919, the Treasury announced its willingness to defer all interest payments on debts due to the government of the United States, at that time amounting to 475 million dollars a year, for a period of two or three years.[16]

[16] This action on the part of the Treasury aroused a great deal of criticism at the time, especially in Congress, and led Secretary of the Treasury Carter Glass to set forth in letters addressed to Senator Boise Penrose and Representative Joseph W. Fordney the considerations by which the Treasury had been guided in the matter. In his letter to Mr. Fordney, Mr. Glass described the condition of foreign exchanges and then said: "Under these circumstances an impenetrable barrier exists which makes it impracticable for these governments to pay in dollars the amount of interest due from them to the United States. This involves no question as to the solvency or financial responsibility of those governments, . . . but results from the condition of the foreign exchange market. . . . If the Treasury does not defer the collection of interest and thus adds to the present difficulties in the financial and economic rehabilitation of the world by demanding an immediate cash payment of interest before the industry and trade of Europe have an opportunity to revive, we should not only make it impossible for Europe to continue

The moratorium period actually lasted much longer than three years in the case of some of our debtors. In 1922, at the expiration of the three-year period, Great Britain alone resumed interest payments on her debt to the United States. Meanwhile the arrears of interest continued to be calculated by the United States Treasury and added on its books to the total indebtedness of the debtor countries. The interest thus accrued by November 15, 1922 amounted to $1,554,791,903. Including these interest instalments, the first four years following the Armistice showed an increase of foreign indebtedness to the American government of more than 4.5 billion dollars.[17]

The British and French loans to other countries following the Armistice were relatively small in amount. Because of the post-war disorganization of foreign exchanges, it is difficult to convert the sums thus advanced into dollars. An approximate calculation would place the British loans for reconstruction and relief purposes at 150 million dollars, and the French loans for similar purposes and for military supplies to some of the smaller Allies at 250 millions. While the nominal amount of foreign indebtedness to the British Treasury grew substantially after the Armistice, the bulk of the increase is accounted for by the accumulation of interest.

III. NATURE AND PURPOSE OF AMERICAN LOANS

In view of the confusion that has existed as to the nature and purposes of the war loans, it is desirable to

---

needed purchases here and decrease their ultimate capacity to pay their debt to us, but should hinder rather than help the reconstruction which the world should hasten." See *Annual Report of the Secretary of the Treasury*, 1920, pp. 58-61.

[17] See Appendix A, pp. 430-31, for a detailed statement of foreign loans by the United States as of Nov. 15, 1922.

set forth the precise character of the financial arrangements that were adopted. The governing principle was that America's loans should be extended to each Ally individually and only for the purpose of meeting payments due in the United States. This principle, which was announced at the very beginning as that which would guide the Treasury, was on the whole adhered to, although in practice some important exceptions had to be made. The way in which the plan worked out may be best revealed by showing first a table which classifies the purposes for which the American loans were utilized.

A number of these items require a word of explanation. The amount included under "interest" represented

WAR EXPENDITURES IN THE UNITED STATES REPORTED BY THE ALLIED GOVERNMENTS FOR THE PERIOD APRIL 6, 1917–NOVEMBER 1, 1920[a]
(In millions of dollars)

Particulars	Apr. 6, 1917 to Nov. 30, 1918	Dec. 1, 1918 to Nov. 1, 1920	Total
Munitions (including remounts).	2,351.4	347.8	2,699.2
Cereals and other foodstuffs....	2,247.7	804.4	3,052.1
Other supplies................	425.0	333.4	758.4
Transportation and shipping....	197.6	111.9	309.5
Interest......................	435.0	295.5	730.5
Maturities....................	471.8	176.4	648.2
Exchange and cotton purchases..	2,167.2	477.5	2,644.7
Miscellaneous.................	506.2	519.0	1,025.2
Reimbursements..............	1,464.4	408.5	1,872.9
Total.....................	10,266.3	3,474.4	13,740.7

[a] The figures, representing total expenditures in the United States during the period covered, were given to the U. S. Treasury by the Allied governments after the close of the war. See *Annual Report of the Secretary of the Treasury*, 1920, pp. 338–48. A detailed summary of these expenditures is given in Appendix A of this book, pp. 427-29. The war period is taken to Nov. 30, 1918, rather than the date of the Armistice because that is the nearest date to the Armistice given in the official reports.

the interest payments made to the American Treasury, as well as to banking groups and private investors from whom the Allies had borrowed during the period prior to April 1917. Under "maturities" were included the payments of short-term obligations contracted before the United States went into the war and falling due within the period in question.

The item "reimbursements" did not represent actual expenditures. The United States Treasury, as already noted, desired to keep the loan accounts with each Allied nation separate and distinct. At the same time, however, it was important that purchases by the foreign governments should not only be co-ordinated as among the various European governments but also with the purchasing activities of the United States government. This co-ordination was achieved in several ways. First, each borrowing government was required by the United States Treasury to state the purpose for which the particular credits were requested, and after funds had been advanced the Treasury required further statements "showing the actual application of the proceeds of the loan."[18] Second, all purchases made in the United States by the Allied governments were, in August 1917, placed under the supervision of a special purchasing committee, which was in March 1918 merged with the War Industries Board. Third, in the autumn of 1917 the Inter-Allied Council on War Purchases and Finance was set up in Europe for the purpose of "considering and co-ordinating the demands of the Allies upon the American Treasury."[19]

[18] *Annual Report of the Secretary of the Treasury,* 1920, p. 69.

[19] The same, pp. 69-70. The purchasing commission consisted of Bernard M. Baruch, Robert S. Brookings, and Robert S. Lovett. The Inter-Allied Council was headed by Oscar T. Crosby, former assistant secretary

In practice, while each of the Allied governments received advances from the American Treasury corresponding to its individual needs, it was found advantageous in some cases for some one government to purchase supplies in bulk both for itself and for some of the other Allies. In order to maintain under these circumstances the principle of keeping the individual borrowings of the Allied governments separate, a system of "reimbursement" was adopted. This meant that the purchasing government would receive from the American Treasury the funds necessary to pay for the particular purchase. After the supplies had been allocated among the various governments for whom they had been purchased, an account would be drawn up and submitted to the Treasury. Sufficient funds to enable these other governments to reimburse the purchasing government for their shares would then be advanced to them, and, as a result, the indebtedness of the purchasing government on the books of the Treasury would be correspondingly diminished and the indebtedness of each of the other governments increased.[20] A certain amount of reimbursement was also made on account of purchases

---

of the treasury, at that time special finance commissioner of the United States in Europe.

[20] Practically all such purchases for joint account were effected by Great Britain, and this fact, among others, has led to some misunderstanding of the nature of the transactions involved. For example, in the Balfour note, of which we shall speak later (see p. 111), it is stated that when appeal was made to the United States government by the Allies for financial assistance, "under the arrangements then arrived at, the United States insisted, in substance if not in form, that, though our Allies were to spend the money, it was only on our security that they were prepared to lend it." This statement has been challenged both in the United States and in Great Britain. See Albert Rathbone, "Making War Loans to the Allies," *Foreign Affairs*, April 1925, and the *Economist* (London), Mar. 10, 1923. The article by Mr. Rathbone, who was an assistant secretary of the treasury in charge of foreign loans

made outside the United States, and to this extent the principle that the proceeds of the loans made by the Treasury should be spent here was not completely carried out.

The item "exchange and cotton purchases" in the table on page 42 also needs explanation. The extensive British purchases of American cotton had been financed habitually by means of sterling bills. During the first period of the war, most of such bills offered in payment to the American exporters found their way into the New York market, where they were purchased for dollars by the financial agents of the British government as a part of the general scheme of pegging the British exchange. This system continued after the United States entered the war, in spite of the fact that dollars were available to make the payments directly, and in this manner large amounts of sterling bills continued to be offered in New York. The amount of these bills was augmented by similar bills on London resulting from non-governmental financial transactions in the United States, and also by paper of the same sort given by British buyers in some of the neutral markets. As the system of pegging continued and as the dollar funds required were furnished by the American Treasury, all these bills were purchased for the account of the British government, and in this manner the credits extended by the American Treasury were used indirectly for financing some of the Allied purchases outside the United States. To a smaller extent than in the case of Great Britain, the same thing was done in the cases of France

and later a financial adviser of the American Peace Delegation in Paris, is probably the most comprehensive presentation of the methods and policies pursued by the United States Treasury in making war loans to the Allied nations.

and Italy, which countries also used a part of the credits received by them for pegging their exchanges.[21]

Of the total expenditures made by the Allied governments in the United States, as shown in the table on page 42, the sum of 9,466.2 million dollars was obtained by the Allies in the form of loans from the United States Treasury. Since the "reimbursements" did not represent real expenditures, there remained only 2,401.6 million dollars to be supplied out of their own resources. In fact, more than 60 per cent of this sum—to be precise, 1,490.4 million dollars—was also supplied by the American Treasury through the purchase of Allied currencies, mostly francs and pounds sterling, which were required for American military operations in Europe. The system adopted was that each of the Allied countries should supply the American military and civil authorities in Europe with the amounts of its own currency that would be required, while the United States Treasury should place at the disposal of its govern-

---

[21] The American Treasury attempted several times to put a stop to this method of utilizing, for purchases in neutral markets, the credits extended to the Allies, pointing out that in this manner an undue pressure was being put on the financial resources of the Treasury, especially from the point of view of the foreign exchanges. The officials of the Treasury in Washington and the American president of the Inter-Allied Council on War Purchases and Finance sought repeatedly to induce the Allies to finance their purchases in the neutral markets by means of their own resources or direct borrowing in those markets. To a certain extent, these efforts were successful, as was witnessed by the British borrowing in Argentina and Spain. The Treasury did not feel, however, that it could put too great a pressure on the Allies in this respect, because it recognized up to a point the seriousness of the representations made by some of the Allied governments to the effect that without American support the Allied exchanges might easily have crumpled, with disastrous consequences for the conduct of the war. The net result, however, was an added strain on the dollar exchange rate with respect to some of the neutral countries, which served to depress it considerably more than would have been justified by the direct trade and financial relations between the United States and these countries.

ment an equivalent amount of dollars. As a result of these arrangements, it was necessary for the Allies to obtain from sources other than the United States Treasury only about 680 million dollars during the period preceding the Armistice, and 230 millions after November 1918, or less than 8 per cent of their actual expenditures under the categories listed above.

In summary, the war loans made by the United States government amounted to approximately 10 billion dollars; British government loans reached a total of approximately 8 billion dollars, but this was substantially offset by borrowings from the United States which amounted to a little over 4 billion dollars and by gold shipments to Great Britain made by her Allies. While the French government loaned approximately 2.5 billion dollars, its borrowings from Great Britain and the United States were almost 5 billion dollars. All of the other Allies and all of the newly created states of Europe were, at the time of the formal re-establishment of peace, net debtors on the inter-governmental account.

Such, in brief, is the story of the circumstances and conditions which accounted for the enormous credit operations among the Allied and Associated Powers which began in 1914 and did not end until 1920. Financial exigencies forced what amounted to a virtual pooling of resources, first among the European nations ranged against the Central Powers and eventually as between the Allied Powers of Europe and the United States. The loans were made chiefly, though not wholly, for the purpose of financing purchases in the creditor countries; and the proceeds were devoted almost exclusively to the waging of the war, that is, the procurement of indispensable foodstuffs, supplies, and munitions.

CHAPTER IV

EARLY POST-WAR DEBT NEGOTIATIONS

It was only natural that amid the excitement and stress of the war years little thought should have been given to the difficult issues that would inevitably arise at the conclusion of the conflict. The absolute, compelling requirement of the moment was to win the war; everything else was secondary. Lavish expenditures, which in calmer surroundings might have appeared excessive, were deemed indispensable in the psychological atmosphere of the time, and loans in vast amounts were needed if such expenditures were to be made possible. Therefore, let the loans be made quickly and abundantly—on such terms as might appear to be reasonable among friends engaged in a common cause— leaving to the future any readjustments that might be necessary.

As soon as hostilities ceased, however, problems of liquidation and readjustment quickly took the center of the stage. Almost immediately after the Armistice, informal negotiations with respect to the war debts began and at once brought to a focus an important difference in point of view as between the American and Allied governments with reference to the character of the war debts.

I. DIFFERENCES IN VIEWPOINT

The promptness with which the United States began to render financial aid to the Allies may be indicated by the fact that within a few days of our entrance into the war the British Ambassador to the United States was handed a Treasury check for 200 million dollars. The American point of view with reference to the significance of the loans was set forth in an official bulletin issued by the Treasury in the latter part of 1917. It was pointed out that in placing at the disposal of the Allies a portion of American wealth, the government of the United States was helping not only them, but also American soldiers and sailors, since by making the Allies more powerful and effective we were "lessening the work and danger and suffering of our own men in bringing the war to an earlier close." It was also pointed out that, since we were producing more goods than we could use, the economic welfare of the American people required the sale of our excess production to the Allies.[1]

A similar estimate of the role of foreign loans was expressed immediately after the cessation of hostilities by Secretary of the Treasury Carter Glass, who, in his annual report for the fiscal year 1919, said:

> It is difficult to exaggerate the great purposes served and the great results accomplished by these advances to foreign governments. In the most critical stages of the war they immeasurably assisted America's gallant associates in obtaining the munitions, supplies, and equipment that were so imperatively needed to meet the enemy's offensives or to carry the fighting into his territory. . . . In the beginning before the creation of our great army, the principal assistance of America was necessarily through foreign loans, and it was then that these advances proved so very potent in contributing to the final victory. . . . The service of these loans in assisting to hold the battle-fronts of Europe until the might of our heroic army could be felt effectively, made possible, beyond the shadow of a doubt, the ending of the war in the fall of 1918. Without this aid to the Allied governments, the war unquestionably would have been prolonged, if not lost, with the resultant additional cost in life and treasure.

[1] See H. E. Fisk, *The Inter-Ally Debts*, pp. 173-74.

The loans were officially regarded as commercial obligations rather than gifts. While the financing of the
Allies was considered as an imperative necessity and
beneficial to us as well as to our Allies, no doubt whatever was entertained officially as to the character of the
advances. In the Treasury statement of 1917 emphasis
was laid on the fact that the advances were not in the
nature of contributions but were straightforward loans
to solvent nations with perfectly good credit but no
ready money. The Committee on Ways and Means of
the House of Representatives, in reporting the First
Liberty Loan Act to its parent body, stated: "It will be
observed that the credit proposed to be extended to foreign governments will take care of itself and will not
constitute an indebtedness that will have to be met by
taxation in the future."

The only instance in which the question ever arose
as to the desirability of regarding a portion of the advances in the nature of a gift was in connection with
France. During the Congressional debate on the First
Liberty Loan Act, sentiment was expressed in favor of
making a large pecuniary gift to France in recognition
of the assistance rendered the United States during the
Revolutionary War. This plan was given up when on
April 11, 1917 the American Ambassador in Paris
cabled the Secretary of State as follows:

The [French] Premier personally expressed the hope to me
that no resolution would be introduced or debated in Congress
tending to make a gift to the government of France from the
United States, however much the sentiment of good-will
prompting it might be appreciated by the French people.[2]

---

[2] *Combined Annual Reports of the World War Foreign Debt Commission,* 1927, pp. 60-61.

The loans to France, therefore, like those to all the other Allies, were evidenced at first by short-term obligations, renewed at maturity, and later by demand obligations. Technical difficulties alone prevented, while the war was still in progress, the conversion of these obligations into definitive long-term bonds. Long before the Armistice, the text of such bonds was a subject of discussion between the Treasury and its debtors.

Thus whatever may be said of the care with which the United States Treasury supervised the Allied expenditures made with the proceeds of the loans—and on this point opinions differ decidedly—the Treasury officials were extremely careful in obtaining evidences of indebtedness for every dollar advanced and in making it clear to the borrowers that the loans were being made with a definite expectation that they would be repaid in full after the termination of hostilities—without reference to other problems of war liquidation.

Loans between European Allies, on the other hand, had been regarded as subject to post-war adjustment. While accepting the point of view of the American government as to the nature of the advances made by the United States Treasury, Allied governments had from the beginning regarded the loans among themselves as a phase of war co-operation and had assumed that these credits would be adjusted at the end of the conflict as a part of the general liquidation of the war. In the statement issued by the British-French-Russian financial conference held in Paris in February 1915, at which the bases of inter-Allied financial collaboration were laid down, it was announced that "the Finance Ministers of Great Britain, France, and Russia . . . are agreed in declaring that the three powers are resolved to unite

their financial resources, equally with their military resources, for the purpose of carrying the war to a successful conclusion." On the basis of this and later agreements Great Britain, and to a much smaller extent
France, proceeded, as we have seen, to make advances
to the various Allies.

For example, the British Treasury was extremely
business-like in scrutinizing the needs of its borrowers.
It was, however, extremely unbusiness-like in the formal arrangements as to the security covering these advances and the terms of repayment. In most cases it accepted Treasury bonds of the borrowing governments
for the amounts of the advances, treating interest
merely as book entries covered later on by new Treasury
bonds of the borrowing governments. In the case of
some states, as for example Serbia, no evidence of borrowing was demanded.[3]

The difference of attitude with respect to the war
loans between the United States, on the one side, and
Great Britain and France, on the other, is clearly illustrated by the following incident recounted by Mr.
Oscar T. Crosby as having taken place at the time when
he served as president of the Inter-Allied Council on
War Purchases and Finance:

In December, 1917, in Paris, a conference occurred at
which the British, French, and American Treasuries were
represented on the one side as lenders, and the government of
Greece was represented on the other side as a borrower. Mr.

---

[3] On December 22, 1919, Mr. Andrew McFadyen of the British delegation to the Reparation Commission wrote to Assistant Secretary of
the Treasury Albert Rathbone: "There is no question at present of
getting long-term obligations from Serbia; all that we are proposing is
that she should now, for the first time, deposit short-term obligations.
So far we have had no security at all for the advances made to her."
See *Loans to Foreign Governments*, 67 Cong. S. doc. 86, p. 388.

Venizelos properly asked that the nature of the various loans to his government should be clearly made known. He produced evidence that earlier advances by Great Britain and France to Greece were made with the understanding that repayment might depend on the political results of the war. It became my duty to point out that I had no authority to consider such a transaction at all; that only straight loans could be discussed for consideration by representatives of our government acting for the Secretary of the Treasury under the controlling statutes providing for loans to foreign governments.[4]

This difference remained in the background during the period of hostilities. As the war proceeded, however, and the inter-governmental obligations mounted rapidly, the Allied statesmen began to turn their attention seriously to the possibility of winning the American government over to their point of view as regards the liquidation of inter-Allied war debts, including the loans made by the United States Treasury. It was not until after the end of the war, however, that any direct efforts were made to accomplish this end.

II. PROPOSALS FOR JOINT CONSIDERATION OF DEBTS

Shortly after the Armistice the principal Allied governments made an attempt to obtain the consent of the American government to a joint consideration of the war debts. The suggestion came originally from the French government, and it was the French Minister of Finance, M. Klotz, who first broached it in conversation with Mr. Crosby. The plan had, however, strong British support, for within a few days the same question was raised with Mr. Crosby by the British Chancellor of the Exchequer. To both suggestions Mr. Cros-

---

[4] *New York Times*, Feb. 2, 1925.

by replied that he had no authority to discuss the matter.[5]

The question was brought up repeatedly during the preliminary stages of the Peace Conference, usually in the form of a proposal that the debt question should either form a part of the general peace negotiations or else be considered by the powers concerned in Paris concurrently with the peace negotiations. At the same time, the French representatives in Washington were instructed by their government to approach the United States Treasury directly on this matter. Accordingly, the French Deputy High Commissioner in the United States, M. Edouard de Billy, after discussing the subject orally with Assistant Secretaries of the Treasury Leffingwell and Rathbone, wrote an official letter to Secretary of the Treasury Glass, dated January 15, 1919, in which he said:

Although prepared to abide by your final decision, my government is desirous of submitting to your kind consideration the reasons for which it appears that the question of the reimbursement of the debts of the Allies can be satisfactorily settled only at a conference to be held in Paris during the peace negotiations.

The financial relations among the Allies, brought about by the war, are closely interwoven. The British and French governments have both borrowed from the United States; but France is also a debtor of England. The French and Italian governments have both borrowed from the United States; but Italy is also a debtor of France. Although a debtor of the United

---

[5] In *Combined Annual Reports of the World War Foreign Debt Commission*, p. 63, it is stated that "the question of a general joint adjustment of all debts arising out of the war . . . first appears to have been informally suggested by the British Chancellor of the Exchequer to Assistant Secretary of the Treasury Crosby, who was then in Europe." Mr. Crosby informs us that as a matter of fact the first actual suggestion along these lines came to him from the French Minister of Finance.

States and of Great Britain, France has loaned about 10,000,000,000 francs to its Allies.

It appears to my government that, if the future adjustment of such mutual accounts is to be made the object of separate and distinct agreements, privileged situations might arise to the prejudice of some of the governments concerned. If, on the contrary, all questions of debit and credit were considered at the same time, and as a whole, it would be easier, according to equity, to settle the respective situation of these governments.

On the other hand, it appears that the possibility of reimbursement by certain governments may be deeply affected by the conditions of the treaty of peace, especially by the indemnities to be received eventually from Germany and, in the case of some countries, as Serbia for instance, by the distribution of territory and the establishment of new boundary lines.

In short, the French government looks upon these questions as concerning all the Allies and demanding a general and simultaneous settlement, in which, at the same time, would be taken into consideration the respective positions of each of the interested governments toward the others, and the reaction which the peace conditions might have on the financial possibilities of these governments.

To this communication Secretary Glass replied on January 29 as follows:

I am entirely in accord with the view that the scheme should take into account the recoveries from the enemy which are likely to be effected by your government. I do not, however, feel that these considerations lead to the conclusion that discussion of the plans for repayment of debts due to the United States can advantageously be undertaken in Paris in conjunction with the Peace Conference. The conclusion I draw therefrom is rather that the United States should be willing to postpone discussions until the probable amount, time, and form of recoveries from the enemy can be estimated and the financial position of the receiving government considered in the light of this information.

I have heretofore stated to representatives of various of the

Allied governments that, if they desire, I am quite ready to discuss with them the questions relating to any plan for the repayment of their obligations held by the United States. This I am prepared to do as I do not think the arrangements between the United States and the governments to which it has made advances can well be uniform or should necessarily be entered into simultaneously. On the other hand, I have no wish to press the immediate consideration and discussion of these questions upon any government.

I recognize that in case a country has borrowed of more than one of the governments associated in the war, it would be difficult to reach an equitable arrangement unless the arrangements which could be made by the borrowing country with the other associated governments which had lent it important amounts were taken into account, but I can not see that any country is concerned in such arrangements other than the borrowing country and the particular countries which have made advances to it. I agree with you that where two or more of the Associated governments have made loans to the same government, none should seek any unfair priority or advantage over others in terms of repayment, and I am confident that all the Associated governments will be animated by this principle. I assume that consideration of the advances to Russia must for a time be postponed and the other cases, where both the United States and France made advances to the same government, are few in number, and only Great Britain, besides the United States, has made loans to France, and I do not anticipate that the Treasuries of the respective countries will have any difficulty in arriving at arrangements which will be equitable and free from discrimination.

After giving the views of your government as expressed in your letter careful consideration (the more so in view of the cordial expression of readiness to accept the conclusion of the United States Treasury upon the question), I feel that discussion of the scheme of repayment of debts due to the United States should take place in Washington as soon as possible after the financial terms of the peace settlement have been decided, or earlier in the case of any government which so desires. I should expect that whenever such discussions are initiated by any

country that country will join with me in the desire that any
other Associated governments which shall have made loans to
the country in question will be asked at the same time to discuss
with the borrowing country the scheme for the repayment of
the debt held by such other Associated government, and that
no final conclusion would be arrived at in respect to the obligations, acquired during the war, of any one of the Associated
governments without the previous knowledge of all the Associated governments which have during that period made loans
of an important amount to the government in question.

The position taken by the American government was
thus made completely and repeatedly clear to the Allied Powers, and the unwavering adherence to this position by American representatives rendered futile the
efforts of the Allies to obtain a consideration of the war
debts in connection with the Peace Conference. The
question was not even inscribed on the agenda of the
conference in spite of the vigorous efforts made by some
of the Allies, notably Italy, to have it included in the
Paris program.[6]

[6] Italy's insistence on this point in the drafting committee of the Peace
Conference and the support given the Italian representatives on this
question by the French delegates led to an interesting exchange of correspondence between the American Treasury and the French War Mission in Washington. On Mar. 8, 1919, Assistant Secretary of the
Treasury Rathbone wrote French Deputy High Commissioner de Billy
as follows: "You will appreciate that the Treasury cannot contemplate
continuance of advances to any Allied government which is lending its
support to any plan which would create uncertainty as to its due repayment of advances made to it by the United States Treasury." M. de
Billy immediately transmitted Mr. Rathbone's letter to Paris and ten
days later communicated to the Treasury the reply of the French Minister of Finance, M. Klotz, in which the latter stated that "with reference to the attitude of the French officials toward the principle involved
in this question, the French government never made any declaration
favoring either the Italian proposition or any other similar proposition
reproduced in the press or in the French chambers." For the full text of
this correspondence see *Combined Annual Reports of the World War
Foreign Debt Commission*, pp. 66-67.

III. FUNDING PROPOSALS BY THE UNITED STATES, 1919

In the latter half of 1919 the American Treasury made its first concrete proposal for the funding of the war debts. The terms suggested were contained in a memorandum, dated November 1, 1919, which was handed by Assistant Secretary of the Treasury Rathbone, then in Paris, to Mr. Basil P. Blackett, the British financial representative there. The basic features of the plan were as follows:

It was proposed to divide all of the Allied obligations held by the United States (with the exception of some relief loans requiring special treatment) into two series of bonds, one representing the advances made by the American Treasury under the First Liberty Loan Act, and the other those made under the Second, Third, and Fourth Liberty Loan Acts. The bonds of the first series were to mature on June 15, 1947; those of the second series on October 15, 1938. Interest on all bonds was to be at the rate of 5 per cent, payable semi-annually. It was provided, however, that for the first three years no payments at all were to be made on account of either principal or interest. Regular interest payments were to begin during the fourth year. The deferred interest was to have been spread, without compounding, over twelve years, from the fourth to the fifteenth inclusive. Amortization payments were to begin in the form of annual sinking-fund instalments in the tenth year. The total annual payments were to rise from 5.5 per cent of the principal sums involved in the fourth year to a maximum of 7.5 per cent in the twelfth year. These sinking-fund provisions would have extinguished 17.8 per cent of the bonds maturing in 1938 and 55.7 per cent of the bonds maturing in 1947, leaving the remainder in each case to be met, presumably in a lump sum, at maturity.

After discussing the American proposal with the Chancellor of the Exchequer, Mr. Blackett informed Mr. Rathbone on November 8 that the general lines of action proposed in the American memorandum were acceptable to the British Treasury as a basis for negotiation. The Chancellor made one specific reservation. He expressed himself as being in favor of leaving out entirely all sinking-fund provisions. In any event, he thought that the amortization payments on the 1947 series of bonds were too large.

The Chancellor also made a general reservation to the effect that his tentative approval of the conversion proposal was given

on the understanding that such conversion will not in any way prejudice the general question of inter-Allied indebtedness, to the ultimate settlement of which along broad lines he attaches great importance.

This general reservation elicited the following blunt reply from Mr. Rathbone:

I note that the Chancellor attaches great importance to the ultimate settlement along broad lines of the general question of inter-Allied indebtedness. Just what is meant by that expression I do not know, but I feel confident there is no such question now under discussion or consideration. The United States Treasury has in no wise changed the views it has expressed, or modified the position that it has taken in the past, and regards the several obligations of the various Allied governments held by the government of the United States as representing the debt of each to the United States.

On the question of the British objections to the sinking-fund provisions, Mr. Rathbone stated that "the

Secretary of the Treasury feels very strongly that such a provision should be included in the long-time obligations." He expressed himself, however, as being inclined to agree that the sinking fund tentatively suggested for the 1947 bonds "would operate to redeem before maturity too large a proportion of the principal of the debt," and asked for suggestions "as to a rearrangement of the sinking-fund payment."

Conversations regarding the American proposal continued intermittently for several months as a part of intricate negotiations between the American and British Treasuries regarding the winding up of war accounts. They were never brought to a successful issue, their only result being a suspension of interest payments along the lines discussed in the preceding chapter.[7]

IV. GREAT BRITAIN'S PROPOSAL FOR GENERAL CANCELLATION, 1920

Early in 1920 a formal attempt was made to obtain America's consent to a general cancellation of the war debts. The initiative came from Great Britain at the time when negotiations for the funding of the Allied obligations to the United States were still carried on more or less half-heartedly. The direct bid for cancellation was made first in a letter from Mr. Blackett to Mr. Rathbone dated February 4, 1920, and repeated five days later in a direct message from the British Chancellor of the Exchequer handed to Assistant Secretary of the Treasury Leffingwell by the British Chargé d'Affaires at Washington. Up to that time, the question of cancellation, while distinctly in the background,

---

[7] See pp. 40-41. For the principal correspondence involved in the negotiations see *Loans to Foreign Governments*, 67 Cong. S. doc. 86, pp. 60-74.

had never been put in the shape of a formal proposal.[8]

In his letter to Mr. Rathbone, Mr. Blackett stated that he had been instructed by the Chancellor of the Exchequer to express in the following terms the view of the British government on the question of the war debts:

It has been the view of the British government that the existence of a vast mass of inter-governmental indebtedness not only involves very grave political dangers, but also forms at the present time a most serious obstacle to the recuperation of the world and particularly of Continental Europe from the immense strain and suffering caused by the war. They have more than once suggested informally to the representatives of the United States Treasury that steps should be taken by the two governments in concert to find some large solution of this problem, and as you are aware the Chancellor of the Exchequer expressed himself ready to take any steps toward relieving the governments which are debtors to the British government of the burden of their debts which the United States Treasury might feel able to propose in regard to the obligations of the governments which it holds. These suggestions have not hitherto been placed on formal record, and it is for the purpose of formal record that they are mentioned here.[9]

---

[8] In a memorandum for President Wilson on Feb. 21, 1920, Mr. Norman H. Davis, then assistant secretary of the treasury, said: "As you are aware, efforts beginning with the peace negotiations were made to bring about a cancellation of our debts against the Allied governments, but the question was not presented in such a definite way as to require us to take any formal action. Much to the surprise of the Treasury, in connection with the negotiations which have been under way with the British Treasury regarding the funding of short-time obligations of the Allied governments into long-time obligations and the extension of the interest accruing thereon during the next two or three years, the question has been formally raised by the British Treasury, both in a communication to Mr. Rathbone and also in a message from the Chancellor of the Exchequer through the British Embassy in which, among other questions, the Chancellor in effect invites the American Treasury to a consideration of a general cancellation of all inter-governmental war debts." See the same, p. 77.

[9] The same, p. 72.

In his message to Mr. Leffingwell, the Chancellor of the Exchequer said:

Turning to more general considerations it is evident that a financial crisis in America would gravely endanger the incipient recovery of Continental Europe. It is impossible to foresee the consequences. With the Continent a prey to bankruptcy and possibly to anarchy and with the United States unable to provide credits of any sort owing to the internal crisis, the world's position would be indeed serious. If I may venture on what I fear is controversial ground, I may say that it is largely because of these dangers that we should welcome a general cancellation of inter-governmental war debts. The moral effect would even be a greater practical change and fresh hope and confidence would spring up everywhere. The existence of these international debts deters neutrals from giving assistance, checks private credits, and will, I fear, prove a disturbing effect in future international relations.[10]

It should be recalled that this suggestion of the British government was in line with British policy at the conclusion of the Napoleonic wars a century earlier. During the long period from 1793 to 1816, Great Britain furnished financial aid to Continental Allies to the extent of approximately 61.3 million pounds. Of this total she obtained repayment to the extent of only 2.6 millions, voluntarily relinquishing all claims to the remainder. In fact, at least 53 millions of the total were advanced not as loans but as subsidies in a common cause, with no expectation that repayment would be made. To all intents and purposes, England thus wiped the financial slate clean, and this notwithstanding the fact that she was beset with economic and financial difficulties of the gravest character at home. The view held

[10] 67 Cong. 1 sess., *Refunding of Obligations of Foreign Governments*, Hearings on S. 2135 before Committee on Finance, July 14, 1921, p. 50.

by the British statesmen then in power—that "no arrangement could be wise that carried ruin to one of the countries between which it was concluded"—prevailed.[11]

An official reply to the British government was made by Secretary of the Treasury Houston in a message to the Chancellor of the Exchequer dated March 1, 1920. Replying to the British thesis as to the need of debt cancellation for the purpose of stimulating the economic recovery of the world and especially of Europe, Secretary Houston argued that the cancellation proposal "does not touch matters out of which the present financial and economic difficulties of Europe chiefly grow." He said:

The relief from present ills, in so far as it can be obtained, is primarily within the control of the debtor governments and peoples themselves. Most of the debtor governments have not levied taxes sufficient to enable them to balance their budgets, nor have they taken any energetic and adequate measures to reduce their expenditures to meet their income. Too little progress has been made in disarmament. No appreciable progress has been made in deflating excessive issues of currency or in stabilizing the currencies at new levels, but in Continental Europe there has been a constant increase in note issues. Private initiative has not been restored. Unnecessary and unwise economic barriers still exist. Instead of setting trade and commerce free by appropriate steps there appear to be concerted efforts to obtain from the most needy discriminatory advantages and exclusive concessions. There is not yet apparent any disposition on the part of Europe to make a prompt and reasonable definite settlement of the reparation claims against Germany or to adopt policies which will set Germany and Austria free to make their necessary contribution to the economic rehabilitation of Europe.

Moreover, Secretary Houston pointed out that the cancellation proposal "does not involve mutual sacri-

[11] See Edwin F. Gay, "War Loans or Subsidies," *Foreign Affairs*, 1926, Vol. IV, pp. 394-95.

fices on the part of the nations concerned; it simply involves a contribution mainly from the United States." He called attention to the fact that the United States had "shown its desire to assist Europe" by extending to European governments immense credits after the Armistice and by postponing interest payments. As for private credits, the Secretary expressed his conviction that "the foreign obligations held by the government of the United States do not constitute a practical obstacle to obtaining credits here," and that "the European countries would not obtain a dollar of additional credit as a result of the cancellation of those obligations." In conclusion he said:

It is very clear to me, however, that a general cancellation of inter-governmental war debts irrespective of the positions of the separate debtor governments is of no present advantage or necessity. A general cancellation as suggested would, while retaining the domestic obligations intact, throw upon the people of this country the exclusive burden of meeting the interest and of ultimately extinguishing the principal of our loans to the Allied governments. This nation has neither sought nor received substantial benefits from the war. On the other hand, the Allies, although having suffered greatly in loss of lives and property have, under the terms of the treaty of peace and otherwise acquired very considerable accessions of territories, populations, economic and other advantages. It would, therefore, seem that if a full account were taken of these and of the whole situation there would be no desire nor reason to call upon the government of this country for further contributions.[12]

Soon after this, an important meeting took place at Lympne, England, between the Prime Ministers of Great Britain and France, at which it was decided to link together the debts of the Allies to each other and

[12] See *Combined Annual Reports of the World War Foreign Debt Commission,* 1926, pp. 68-70.

the German reparation payments. So far as is known, there was no formal discussion of the debts to the United States, but apparently a decision was reached that an attempt should be made to obtain America's consent to the extension of this arrangement to the debts owed by the Allies to the government of the United States. Accordingly, on May 21, 1920 the Chancellor of the Exchequer informed Mr. Rathbone that the British government had decided to suspend for the time being the negotiations with regard to the funding of the war debts, since the decisions of the Lympne conference raised "questions of great importance unsuited for departmental treatment between our two Treasuries." He stated that the Prime Minister intended to take up the matter directly with the President of the United States.

V. LLOYD GEORGE—WILSON CORRESPONDENCE

The exchange of views between Prime Minister Lloyd George and President Wilson put an end to the early post-war debt negotiations. The letter of Mr. Lloyd George to the President was dated August 5, while Mr. Wilson's reply was made on November 3.

The British Prime Minister wrote as follows:

I come now to the other question I wish to write to you about, and that is the knotty problem of inter-Allied indebtedness. Indeed, I promised Mr. Rathbone long ago that I would write to you about it, but I have had to put it off for one reason and another till now. The British and French governments have been discussing during the last four months, the question of giving fixity and definiteness to Germany's reparation obligations. The British government has stood steadily by the view that it was vital that Germany's liabilities should be fixed at a figure which it was within the reasonable capacity of Germany to pay, and that this figure should be fixed without delay because the reconstruction of Central Europe could not begin nor could the Allies themselves raise money on the strength of Germany's obligation to pay them reparation until her liabilities have been exactly defined. After great difficulties with his own people, M. Millerand found himself able to accept this view, but he pointed out that it was impossible for France to agree to accept anything less than it was entitled to under the treaty unless its debts to its Allies and Associates in the war were treated in the same way.

This declaration appeared to the British government eminently fair. But after careful consideration they came to the conclusion that it was impossible to remit any part of what was owed to them by France except as part and parcel of all-round settlement of inter-Allied indebtedness. I need not go into the reasons which lead to this conclusion which must be clear to you. But the principal reason was that British public opinion would never support a one-sided arrangement at its sole expense, and that if such a one-sided arrangement were made it could not fail to estrange and eventually embitter the relations between the American and the British people with calamitous results to the future of the world. You will remember that Great Britain borrowed from the United States about half as much as its total loans to the Allies, and that after America's entry into the war, it lent to the Allies almost exactly the same amount as it borrowed from the United States of America. Accordingly the British government has informed the French government that it will agree to any equitable arrangement for the reduction or cancellation of inter-Allied indebtedness, but that such an arrangement must be one that applies all round. As you know, the representatives of the Allies and of Germany are meeting at Geneva in a week or two to commence discussion on the subject of reparation.

I recognize that in the midst of a presidential election and with Congress not in session it is impossible for the United States to deal with this question in a practical manner, but the question is one of such importance to the future of Europe, and indeed to the relations between the Allied and Associated Powers that I should very much welcome any advice which you might feel yourself able to give me as to the best method of securing that the whole problem could be considered and settled by the United States government in concert with its associates at the earliest possible moment that the political situation in America makes it possible.

There is one other point which I should like to add. When the British government decided that it could not deal with the question of the debts owed to it by its Allies except as part and parcel of an all-round arrangement of inter-Allied debts, the Chancellor of the Exchequer told Mr. Rathbone that he could not proceed any further with the negotiations which they had been conducting together with regard to the postponement of the payment of interest on the funding of Great Britain's debt to America. I should like to make it plain that this is due to no reluctance on the part of Great Britain to fund its debt, but solely to the fact that it can not bind itself by any arrangement which would prejudice the working of any inter-Allied arrangement which may be reached in the future. If some method can be found for funding the British debt which does not prejudice the larger question, the British government would be glad to fall in with it.

President Wilson's reply was as follows:

I turn now to the problem of inter-Allied indebtedness which you raise. I must deal with this matter with great frankness, as I am sure you wish me to do. It is desirable that our position be clearly understood in order to avoid any further delay in a constructive settlement of reparations which may arise from the hope that the debts to this government can form a part of such settlement. It will be helpful if first of all I indicate our legal situation.

The Secretary of the Treasury is authorized by United States law to arrange for the conversion of the demand obligations of the British government into obligations having a fixed date of maturity, in accordance with the agreement of the British government to make such exchange on demand contained in its existing obligations. In connection with such exchange, the Secretary of the Treasury has authority to arrange for the postponement of interest payments. No power has been given by the Congress to any one to exchange, remit, or cancel any part of the indebtedness of the Allied governments to the United States represented by their respective demand obligations. It would require congressional authority to authorize any such dealing with the demand obligations and the Congress has the same authority to authorize any disposition of obligations of the British government held by the United States, whether represented by demand obligations or by obligations having a fixed date of maturity. It is highly improbable that either the Congress or popular opinion in this country will ever permit a cancellation of any part of the debt of the British government to the United States in order to induce the British government to remit, in whole or in part, the debt to Great Britain of France or any other of the Allied governments, or that it would consent to a cancellation or reduction in the debts of any of the Allied governments as an inducement towards a practical settlement of the reparation claims. As a matter of fact, such a settlement in our judgment would in itself increase the ultimate financial strength of the Allies.

You will recall that suggestions looking to the cancellation or exchange of the indebtedness of Great Britain to the United States were made to me when I was in Paris. Like suggestions were again made by the Chancellor of the Exchequer in the early part of the present year. The United States government by its duly authorized representatives has promptly and clearly stated its unwillingness to accept such suggestions each time they have been made and has pointed out in detail the considerations which cause its decision. The views of the United States government have not changed, and it is not prepared to consent to the remission of any part of the debt of Great Britain to the United States. Any arrangements the British government may make with regard to the debt owed to it by France or by the other Allied governments should be made in the light of the position now and heretofore taken by the United States, and the United States, in making any arrangements with other Allied governments regarding their indebtedness to the United States (and none are now contemplated beyond the funding of the indebtedness and the postponement of payment of interest) will do so with the understanding that any such arrangement would not affect the payment in due course of the debt owed the United States by Great Britain. It is felt that the funding of these demand obligations of the British government will do more to strengthen the friendly relations between America and Great Britain than would any other course of dealing with the same.

The United States government entirely agrees with the British government that the fixing of Germany's reparation obligation is a cardinal necessity for the renewal of the economic life of Europe and would prove to be most helpful in the interests of peace throughout the world; however, it fails to perceive the logic in a suggestion in effect either that the United States shall pay part of Germany's reparation obligation or that it shall make a gratuity to the Allied governments to induce them to fix such obligation at an amount within Germany's capacity to pay. This government has endeavored heretofore in a most friendly spirit to make it clear that it cannot consent to connect the reparation question with that of inter-governmental indebtedness.

The long delay which has occurred in the funding of the demand obligations is already embarrassing the Treasury, which will find itself compelled to begin to collect back and current interest if speedy progress is not made with the funding. Unless arrangements are completed for funding such loans, and in that connection for the deferring of interest, in the present state of opinion here there is likely to develop a dangerous misunderstanding. I believe it to be highly important that a British representative with proper authority proceed to Washington without delay to arrange to carry out the obligation of the British government to convert its demand obligations held by our Treasury into long-time obligations.

The United States government recognizes the importance, in the interests of peace and prosperity, of securing the restoration of financial and industrial stability throughout Europe. The war debts of the Allied governments, the treaty obligations of Germany under the reparation clauses of the Treaty of Versailles and the annexes thereto and of other enemy and ex-enemy countries under the treaties negotiated with them, the administration of countries under the mandates provided for by such treaties, and the existing arrangements between the governments of various countries have or may have an important bearing in making plans to accomplish such restoration.

These two letters summarize clearly the views on the war debt problem held by the responsible statesmen of Europe and the United States. The differences were so sharp and distinct and the American position was so clearly defined that there was nothing left for the debtor countries but to let the matter rest. And so the question remained in abeyance, with the United States going through an important change of administrations, while the European nations concentrated their attention on the reparation negotiations which we shall discuss in Chapter VII.

CHAPTER V

THE AMERICAN DEBT SETTLEMENTS

Two and one-half years elapsed between the first concrete proposal by the United States for the funding of the war debts and the inauguration of a definite program of settlement with the several debtor governments. These formal negotiations began in 1922 and, in the course of the next nine years, funding agreements were signed with 15 countries—the debts of Russia and Armenia alone remaining unadjusted. The manner in which these debt negotiations were conducted and the terms of the settlements which were finally reached and embodied in funding agreements are described in this chapter.

I. THE TREASURY'S REQUEST FOR PLENARY POWERS

While the Treasury continued its informal conversations with the debtor countries described in the preceding chapter, the debt question became something of a political issue during the presidential election campaign of 1920. In the course of the campaign, the Democratic administration was frequently accused of holding nothing but "scraps of paper" to represent the billions of dollars advanced by the Treasury to the Allies, and promises were made by the Republican Party that if successful in the election the new administration would proceed without delay to a regularization of debt payments. These election pledges President Harding and Secretary of the Treasury Mellon began to carry out soon after they took office.

In June 1921 the Treasury asked Congress for full

powers to deal with the funding of the war debts. When he came to the Treasury, Mr. Mellon instructed his legal advisers to prepare a report on the nature of the authority with respect to the debts already possessed by the Treasury under existing legislation. The investigation revealed a confused situation and convinced the Secretary that it would be extremely difficult to conduct satisfactory funding negotiations with the debtor governments. At the same time the need of inaugurating such negotiations was becoming pressing, because some of the obligations held by the Treasury were about to mature. With respect to these maturing obligations it was recognized that some of the debtor governments could not meet the necessary payments at the moment; but the Treasury possessed no authority whatever to grant postponement of obligations due. Accordingly in a letter dated June 21, 1921 the Secretary communicated the facts to the President and suggested that Congress be asked to grant the Treasury plenary powers for dealing with the problem. Secretary Mellon's description of the situation was as follows:

I am advised that, except as to the advances made out of the proceeds of Liberty Loan bonds, this department is without authority to consent to any extension of the time for payment of the principal or of the interest of these obligations or to proceed with the refunding thereof. As to the advances made out of the proceeds of Liberty Loan bonds, the existing authority contains such diverse provisions as to interest rates, the maturity and other terms of the refunding bonds that may be accepted by the department as makes it difficult to formulate a plan whereby the interests of this government may be as well protected and the bonds to be received be in as desirable form as would be the case if the entire debt of each country could be dealt with as a whole and free from such restrictions.

In some cases the debtor nations owe large amounts to other

countries as well as to the United States, and it may be advisable, and in some cases indeed necessary, to consider comprehensively the entire debt of such countries, their financial condition and resources, so as to work out a refunding plan reasonably within the ability of such country to carry out.

In the case of some of the debtor countries it is impossible for them to make payment of their obligations as they now mature. It is impossible for some of them to make payment of the maturing interest. To insist on payment might be disastrous to the peoples of such countries; and besides there may have to be given consideration to the bearing of the adverse foreign exchange rates existing at the time against these debtor countries and which may make it desirable to defer payment of interest.

Under the circumstances I have briefly referred to, it is I think clear that by reason of the lack of any authority as to a part of these foreign obligations and the restrictions upon the existing authority as to the others, it is impossible in any refunding, under the varying conditions that exist, to deal fairly with the debtor countries and at the same time protect the interests of this country. To do this it is essential that the department have full authority as to all such foreign indebtedness to determine the form and terms of the settlements and of the refunding obligations, the rate or rates of interest, the maturity dates, and the right to extend the time for the payment of interest on the indebtedness to be refunded. It is also of importance that the department should have adequate authority to adjust and settle claims against foreign governments, which are not in the form of bonds or obligations, as for example the claim for costs of our military forces of occupation.

Enclosed with the Secretary's letter was a draft of an act of Congress, prepared by his advisers, which it was thought would make it possible for the Treasury to proceed with an adequate regularization of the debt situation.[1] President Harding immediately transmitted

[1] This draft read as follows: "*Be it enacted by the Senate and House of Representatives of the United States of America in Congress assembled,* That the Secretary of the Treasury, with the approval of the President, is hereby authorized from time to time to refund or convert, and to

the Secretary's letter and the draft bill to the chairmen of the appropriate committees in both houses of Congress, and in his covering letter said:

All the circumstances suggest the grant of broad powers to the Secretary of the Treasury to handle this problem in such a manner as best to protect the interests of our government. I hope your committee and the Congress will find it consistent promptly to sanction such an act as that which is suggested by the inclosed draft. If the Congress will promptly sanction such a grant of authority the Secretary of the Treasury may proceed to the prompt exercise of the powers granted to him, and we reasonably may expect a satisfactory handling of the obligations due and the claims of our government which are awaiting settlement.

Congress flatly refused to accede to the Treasury's request for full powers. On the contrary, under the terms of the debt funding bill which was finally enacted into law, the whole debt question was taken out of the hands of the Treasury and placed in those of a newly created body, the World War Foreign Debt Commission. On every point on which the Treasury had asked for full powers of negotiation, the powers of the commission were strictly defined and circumscribed. The

---

extend the time of payment of the principal or the interest, or both, of any obligation of any foreign government now owing to the United States of America, or any obligation of any foreign government hereafter received by the United States of America (including obligations held by the United States Grain Corporation), arising out of the European war, into bonds or other obligations of such, or of any other, foreign government, and from time to time to receive bonds and obligations of any foreign government in substitution for those now or hereafter held by the United States of America, in such form and on such terms, conditions, date or dates of maturity, and rate or rates of interest, and with such security, if any, as shall be deemed for the best interests of the United States of America, and to adjust and settle any and all claims, not now represented by bonds or obligations, which the United States of America now has or hereafter may have against any foreign government and to accept securities therefor."

Treasury's participation in the funding negotiations was limited to the provision that the Secretary of the Treasury should serve as chairman of the commission and that the reports of the commission should be included in the annual reports of the Secretary of the Treasury.

The draft bill prepared at the Treasury and transmitted to Congress by President Harding was formally introduced in the Senate by Senator Boise Penrose, chairman of the Committee on Finance, and in the House by Representative Joseph W. Fordney, chairman of the Committee on Ways and Means. The bill was referred back to these committees and became the subject of extensive hearings, in the course of which Secretary Mellon gave detailed and exhaustive testimony.

Both the Senate and the House committees were unwilling to clothe the Treasury with the blanket authority which was requested. Secretary Mellon was repeatedly questioned as to the reasons which led his department to seek such authority. The following are typical questions and answers that occur in the reports of the hearings:[2]

Mr. Hawley: I notice in this bill it is left entirely to the Secretary of the Treasury or to the Treasury Department to determine how long any bond shall run, when payments shall be made, the rates of interest to be paid, and when extensions shall be granted. Do you think such wide power as that is necessary?

Secretary Mellon: Yes. You see, it would be utterly impossible now to make any schedule of payments, because it depends in each country upon the conditions there existing; and, besides, these countries not only owe us but they also owe some of the other countries of the Allied Powers. For instance you

---

[2] 67 Cong. 1 sess., *Refunding Foreign Obligations*, Hearings on H.R. 7359 before Committee on Ways and Means, Oct. 6, 1921, p. 8.

may take one of those countries that owes money to our government, they also owe, perhaps, money to the British government, and to the French government, etc. Now, to a certain extent in arranging for the payment of the indebtedness, we have to consider their indebtedness to these other countries because, for instance, it is conceivable that one of those governments might endeavor to enforce some terms of payment that would be to our disadvantage; that is, that would be requiring payment ahead of our payment or possibly requiring some kind of security which, if it were given, might leave that country without resources to give us security. So that we have to work, to a certain extent, or have an understanding to some extent, with the other creditor nations of those powers in order to work out some orderly plan by which they can some time meet these payments.

One point which interested both committees greatly and on which Secretary Mellon was closely interrogated was the Treasury's request for power to accept obligations of other governments in lieu of obligations of the debtor governments themselves. Replying on this point to Senator Reed, Mr. Mellon said:[3]

It was considered desirable to be prepared for any contingency. You can imagine where a country that may be weak in its resources and that country may have, say, German bonds or bonds of some other country. It may add to the security if those other bonds can be accepted, and they naturally will be accepted with the indorsement or guarantee of the country having the primary obligation.

And, again, before the House committee:[4]

Mr. Oldfield: This bill also provides for the trading or exchanging of the bonds of one country for the bonds of another

---

[3] 67 Cong. 1 sess., *Refunding of Obligations of Foreign Governments*, Hearings on S. 2135 before Committee on Finance, June 29, 1921, p. 14.

[4] 67 Cong. 1 sess., *Refunding Foreign Obligations*, Hearings on H.R. 7359 before Committee on Ways and Means, p. 9.

country; for instance, the British for the French or the French for the Austrian.

Secretary Mellon: In regard to that, there is not any particular place where we expect that to apply. It was simply thought desirable to have broad authority so that if some contingency arose that would require an exchange of that kind, we would be in position to act on it. For instance, say, in Austria, there may be, in joining with these other nations, some other security we could take in exchange that might be better than the position we are in now. We have not anything in contemplation and there is not any contingency of that kind that we anticipate at all, but here are complicated negotiations with a variety of governments, and almost any contingency is liable to arise, and therefore it is desirable, and likely essential, to have that authority.

Mr. Oldfield: You have made that just about as broad as it could be made, Mr. Secretary.

Secretary Mellon: Yes.

Mr. Frear: In other words, there is no limitation whatsoever upon your acts under this language, either as to the rate of interest or the time of maturity of the obligations, or anything of that kind, is there, Mr. Secretary?

Secretary Mellon: No.

After prolonged discussion, the Treasury draft bill was fundamentally changed. The debt funding bill which finally emerged from the House committee was passed by both houses of Congress and approved by President Harding on February 9, 1922. It placed authority for negotiating debt settlements in a World War Debt Funding Commission, to be appointed by the President "by and with the advice and consent of the Senate"—though it was expressly provided that the Secretary of the Treasury should serve as chairman.

II. PROVISIONS OF THE DEBT FUNDING ACT

The debt funding act authorized the newly created commission to proceed with the refunding, or conversion, of the obligations of foreign governments to the United States, arising out of the World War, "in such form and on such terms, conditions, date or dates of maturity, and rate or rates of interest, and with such security, if any, as shall be deemed for the best interests of the United States of America," subject, however, to the following reservations:

(1) *Provided,* That nothing contained in this act shall be construed to authorize or empower the commission to extend the time of maturity of any such bonds or other obligations due the United States of America by any foreign government beyond June 15, 1947, or to fix the rate of interest at less than 4.25 per centum per annum:

(2) *Provided,* That when the bond or other obligation of any such government has been refunded or converted as herein provided, the authority of the commission over such refunded or converted bond or other obligation shall cease:

(3) *Provided,* That this act shall not be construed to authorize the exchange of bonds or other obligations of any foreign government for those of any other foreign government, or cancellation of any part of such indebtedness except through payment thereof.

In other words, the commission was instructed to arrange for the repayment of the principal of the debts within a period of not more than 25 years. This maximum period was, however, to be enjoyed only by those debtors who would fund their debts during the year 1922. Delays in the funding negotiations would automatically shorten the period of repayment, since the date by which the whole of the war indebtedness was to have been repaid was specifically fixed. The commission was instructed to charge interest at any rate it saw fit, but the rate of 4.25 per cent was fixed as the irreducible minimum. The commission was explicitly forbidden to accept from each debtor any obligations but its own. Finally, the law provided that a settlement once made by the commission was to be final and could not be revised by it at a later date.[5]

In the course of the debt funding negotiations, most of the provisions of the act of February 9, 1922 were substantially modified. In fact, only the limitation imposed upon the commission with regard to an exchange of obligations of one government for those of another was fully carried out. Provisions with regard to the commission's tenure of office, its membership, and the terms on which it funded the debts with respect to the dates of maturity and the rates of interest were all changed by later legislation.

The commission was originally set up with a membership of five for a period of three years. By an amendment to the act, approved February 28, 1923, the membership was raised to eight, and it was also provided that of the seven members appointed by the President, not more than four should be from the same political party.[6] By an amendment of January 21, 1925 the date

[5] For the full text of the act see H. G. Moulton and Leo Pasvolsky, *World War Debt Settlements*, pp. 221-23.

[6] The original members of the commission appointed by President Harding on February 21, 1922 were, in addition to the Secretary of the Treasury, A. W. Mellon: the Secretary of State, Charles Evans Hughes; the Secretary of Commerce, Herbert C. Hoover; Senator Reed Smoot; and Representative Theodore E. Burton. The three members added to the commission in 1923 were Representative Charles R. Crisp; former Representative Richard Olney; and Edward N. Hurley, formerly chairman of the United States Shipping Board. The only change in the membership of the commission during its tenure of office occurred in 1925, when Mr. Frank B. Kellogg, who had succeeded Mr. Hughes as secretary of state, took the latter's place on the commission. It is interesting to note that former Assistant Secretary of the Treasury Leffingwell, in an article on "War Debts," published in the *Yale Review* for October 1922, advocated the supplementing of the original commission by the inclusion of a number of leading Democrats. He said: "It [the commission] should, perhaps, if it is to have enlarged powers and re-

of the termination of the commission's authority was extended to February 9, 1927.

Modifications of the terms of settlement prescribed in the original act, which will be discussed in the next section, rendered it necessary for each debt agreement to be submitted to Congress for ratification by a separate legislative act. While Congress thus reviewed each agreement minutely, its assent was in fact given to all the departures from the original statute as agreed upon by the commission and the representatives of the debtor governments. Thus the settlements were in reality made by the commission on terms which it regarded as appropriate, without reference to the limitations imposed by the debt funding act—which was precisely what the Treasury had asked for at the start. The only difference was that the Treasury had sought authority to make the agreements without referring them to Congress for ratification, while under the conditions created by the act such reference became necessary.

III. AGREEMENTS NEGOTIATED BY THE COMMISSION

The World War Foreign Debt Commission held its first meeting on April 18, 1922. At that meeting two resolutions were adopted. The first was that "Congress be requested to appropriate $20,000 for the expenses of the commission." The second provided that "the Secretary of State be requested to inform each of the governments whose obligations arising out of the World War are held by the United States . . . of the organiza-

---

sponsibilities, be increased in personnel so as to include, like the American delegation at the Washington Disarmament Conference, a minority of leading Democrats, so that its recommendations may not have a strictly partisan reception when they reach Congress."

tion of the World War Foreign Debt Commission pursuant to the act of Congress approved February 9, 1922, and that the commission desires to receive any proposals or representations which the said government may wish to make for the settlement or refunding of its obligations under the provisions of that act."[7] With the dispatching of appropriate instructions by the Department of State to its representatives accredited to the various debtor countries, the process of negotiating the debt settlements formally began.

The commission negotiated 13 debt funding agreements. At the time when that body began its work, 20 foreign governments were debtors to the government of the United States on various accounts growing out of the World War. In three of these countries, Russia, Greece, and Armenia, the de facto governments of the time were not recognized by the United States and, accordingly, no negotiations could be inaugurated. The debts of Cuba and Nicaragua were regarded as already in funded form, requiring no further negotiations. Provision had already been made for the liquidation of the debt owed by Liberia from the proceeds of a new loan authorized by Congress. Finally, all negotiations regarding the debt owed by Austria had been adjourned for 20 years by a joint resolution passed by Congress on April 6, 1922 and subsequent action in the matter taken by the Secretary of the Treasury.[8] Debt agreements with the remaining debtors, after long, and in

[7] *Minutes of the World War Foreign Debt Commission,* 1927, pp. 1-2.

[8] The funding of the debts owed by Greece and Austria after the expiration of the commission's authority will be discussed later. Diplomatic relations between the United States and Greece were re-established during the life of the commission. See pp. 89-90.

some cases repeated, negotiations, were signed on the following dates:[9]

Finland	May 1, 1923
Great Britain	June 19, 1923
Hungary	April 25, 1924
Lithuania	September 22, 1924
Poland	November 14, 1924
Belgium	August 18, 1925
Latvia	September 24, 1925
Czechoslovakia	October 13, 1925
Esthonia	October 28, 1925
Italy	November 14, 1925
Rumania	December 4, 1925
France	April 29, 1926
Yugoslavia	May 3, 1926

The terms of settlement differed in all cases from the provisions of the debt funding act. From the very beginning of its negotiations with the debtor governments, the commission realized that it would be difficult to obtain in the agreements to be negotiated complete compliance with the terms laid down in the act. It was contended by representatives of some of the debtor governments that full or even substantial compliance was quite impossible and not for a moment to be considered.

The first important debtor government whose representative appeared before the commission was France. In the summer of 1922, M. Jean Parmentier, an important official in the French Treasury, was sent to the United States. His mission was not to negotiate a debt settlement, but merely to inform the commission that

[9] For the details of the negotiations see the following two documents issued by the commission: *Combined Annual Reports of the World War Foreign Debt Commission* and *Minutes of the World War Foreign Debt Commission.*

while France recognized her debt, she could not possibly proceed to its funding on the terms prescribed by the act of Congress. She objected not only to the actual terms of repayment, but also to a settlement that would treat the French debt to the United States apart from the other war debts. In a letter of instructions signed by Premier Poincaré and Minister of Finance de Lasteyrie, and handed to M. Parmentier on his departure, the character of his mission was described as follows:

Whatever might be the considerations of justice which it would have a perfect right to present, the French government does not in any way deny the political debt which it contracted during the war with the United States government; it recognizes the juridical obligations to which it agreed on that occasion, but it considers that the federal law of February 9, 1922, which deals with the payment of inter-Allied debts, is presented in terms not acceptable to France. The French government considers that its political debt to the federal government cannot be regarded separately from all the inter-Allied debts; the payment of it must be bound up with the general payment of all the war debts. . . . Your mission to the United States has no other object than to inform the members of the World War Debt Commission and to make clear to them that, under the present circumstances, France is not in a position to make any agreement concerning the payment of her political debt. . . . You will act in such a way that the government of the United States can not at any moment conclude from what you say to the World War Foreign Debt Commission or even from your silence that France has tacitly accepted the principles of the federal law of February 9, 1922.[10]

A British debt funding commission, headed by Mr. Stanley Baldwin, then chancellor of the exchequer, appeared before the commission on January 8, 1923. Al-

[10] The text of this letter of instructions appeared in the Paris newspaper *L'Avenir*, June 10, 1926; and an English translation in *European Economic and Political Survey*, Sept. 30, 1926.

though its purpose, unlike that of the Parmentier mission, was to negotiate a debt settlement, it also announced from the outset that the terms laid down by the act of February 9, 1922 could not be considered by the British government. Thereupon a series of informal negotiations ensued in the course of which it was sought to arrive at an arrangement, differing from the original terms, which would be acceptable to the British government and which, at the same time, the commission would feel "justified in recommending to the President for presentation to Congress for its consideration."[11] On January 14 the commission outlined to the British representatives a proposal along the lines which were eventually followed in the settlement. The British representatives felt unable to accept the terms proposed and returned to London. But on February 1 the commission was informed by the British Ambassador in Washington that his government had decided to conclude a settlement on the terms handed to Mr. Baldwin. These terms were as follows:

Great Britain undertook to repay the whole amount of the loans made to her by the American Treasury and the unpaid accrued interest from April 15 and May 15, 1919 to December 15, 1922 in 62 annual instalments, with interest at the rate of 3 per cent per annum during the first ten years and 3.5 per cent during the remaining 52 years.

The great extension of time over which the payments were to be made was for the purpose of lessening the amount of the annual payments. The 3 per cent interest rate in the early years was a concession to temporary exigencies, while the 3.5 per cent rate for the rest of

[11] *Minutes of the World War Foreign Debt Commission*, 10th meeting.

the period was a recognition of the soundness of the British contention that over long periods of time that was a fair average rate on government loans.

The principal of the funded debt on which current interest was to be charged was made up in the following manner: to the amount actually advanced to Great Britain, exclusive of advances made for the purpose of covering purchases of silver under the Pittman Act,[12] was added accrued interest, calculated at the rate of 4.25 per cent; from this total two deductions were made, one representing payments on account of interest made by Great Britain on October 16 and November 15, 1922, and the other—incidental in character and small in amount—for the purpose of rounding out the new principal sum.

It was stipulated that all payments on account of principal and interest were to be made "in United States gold coin of the present standard of weight and fineness, or its equivalent in gold bullion, or, at the option of Great Britain, upon not less than 30 days' advance notice, in any bonds of the United States issued or to be issued after 6th April, 1917, to be taken at par and accrued interest to the date of payment." Finally, it was provided that, while the original bonds issued in connection with the funding agreement were to be made payable to the United States government, Great Britain would, "at any time or from time to time, at the request of the Secretary of the Treasury of the United States," issue to the United States in exchange for these original bonds, "definitive engraved bonds in form suitable for sale to the public, in such amounts and denominations as

[12] Passed in 1918 to enable Great Britain to furnish India with silver. These advances aggregated 61 million dollars, half of which was repaid in April-May 1923, and the other half in 1924.

the Secretary of the Treasury of the United States may request, in bearer form." The purpose of this provision was to enable the United States government to commercialize the debt by marketing the obligations to the general public, thus substituting private investors for the government as the creditors of Great Britain.

The 62-year period of repayment, substituted in the British settlement for the maximum 25-year period stipulated in the act of February 9, 1922, was incorporated into all the other debt agreements negotiated by the commission. In some agreements, however, the interest rates differed substantially from the British model.

The funded principal in each case was made up of the amounts actually advanced on all accounts, after, as well as during, the war, plus unpaid accrued interest, calculated at the rate of 4.25 per cent for the period ending December 15, 1922 and at the rate of 3 per cent thereafter, minus small cash payments for the purpose of rounding out the sum funded. However, no accrued interest was charged on the Belgian pre-Armistice debt, and interest at the rate of 4.25 per cent was added to Hungary's debt up to December 15, 1923 and on Lithuania's debt up to June 15, 1924.

Current interest at the rate of 3 per cent for the first ten years and 3.5 per cent for the remaining 52 years was fixed, not only for Great Britain, but for the following eight countries: Czechoslovakia, Esthonia, Finland, Hungary, Latvia, Lithuania, Poland, and Rumania. For all these countries the average interest rate for the whole 62-year period works out at 3.3 per cent. However, various postponement options and arrangements were made in the case of some of these countries during the initial periods of payment. These will be discussed below. Belgium received special treatment. Not only was no interest charged on the pre-Armistice debt,[13] but interest during the first ten years of the paying period was charged at a lower rate than 3 per cent, and the payments were graduated rather than uniform. For the whole period, the rate of interest provided for in the case of Belgium works out at 1.8 per cent.

France, Italy, and Yugoslavia obtained important concessions in the matter of interest. In the case of France, no interest is charged for the first five years. Then for ten years the rate is 1 per cent; for the next ten years 2 per cent; for the next eight years 2.5 per cent; for the next seven years 3 per cent; and for the remaining period 3.5 per cent. In the case of Yugoslavia there is no interest charge for the first twelve years; the rate is one-eighth of 1 per cent for the next three years; one-half of one per cent for the next 14 years; 1 per cent for the next three years; 2 per cent for the next three years; and 3.5 per cent for the remaining years. In the case of Italy no interest is charged for the first five years; the rate is one-eighth of 1 per cent for the next ten years; one-quarter of 1 per cent for the next ten years; one-half of 1 per cent for the next ten years; three-quarters of 1 per cent for the next ten years; 1 per cent for the next ten years; and 2 per cent for the remaining seven years. The average interest rate for France works out at 1.6 per cent; for Yugoslavia at 1 per cent; and for Italy at 0.4 per cent.[14]

In the course of the negotiations, some of the debtor

---

[13] This was in accordance with an agreement made in Paris at the time of the Peace Conference, in which President Wilson acquiesced.

[14] These concessions are further discussed in Section VII of this chapter.

countries sought to obtain the debt commission's consent to an inclusion in the agreement of a special "safeguard" provision with regard to the German reparation payments. Under the terms of such a provision, the debtor country would have the right to reduce its scheduled payments to the United States in the event that reparation payments did not come up to expectation. The French delegation, sent to Washington in 1925 under the leadership of M. Joseph Caillaux, was especially insistent upon such a "safeguard" clause. The refusal of the American commission to grant its consent to this was one of the principal reasons for the breakdown of the negotiations conducted by M. Caillaux. When the negotiations were resumed in the spring of 1926, the French withdrew their demand for such a clause.[15]

The gold clause with respect to the form of payment, as well as the option of making payment with Liberty bonds, was inserted in all the agreements in the same form as in the British model, except that the provision for payment in gold bullion appeared only in the agreement with Great Britain. Similarly, stipulations regarding substitution of marketable obligations payable to bearer for the original bonds were included in all the agreements substantially in the same form as in that with Great Britain.

IV. AGREEMENTS NEGOTIATED BY THE TREASURY

With the signing of the Yugoslav agreement on May 3, 1926, the work of the commission was practically completed. The 13 debt settlements made by it repre-

---

[15] For a discussion of a similar proposal made by M. Caillaux to the British Treasury, see pp. 118-19.

sented "more than 97 per cent of the total principal amount of obligations held when the commission was created."[16] Negotiations with Russia and Armenia were still impossible because of the absence in those countries of governments recognized by the United States. The Austrian debt still remained adjourned. As regards Greece, negotiations had been carried on between the commission and the Greek government but since the latter insisted that a new advance be granted it as a part of the settlement of the war debt, the whole matter remained in abeyance pending a decision by Congress as to such an advance.

In view of this situation the commission felt that there was no reason for extending its life beyond February 9, 1927, when it would have terminated automatically. It suggested in its report for the fiscal year 1925-26 that "if the occasion should subsequently arise to undertake negotiations covering debts not yet funded, the matter might be handled informally by the Secretary of the Treasury, with such former members of the debt commission as are in Washington, and reported direct to Congress." Since the termination of the commission's existence, this rule has been applied in the cases of Greece and Austria.

The debt agreement with Greece was signed on May 10, 1929. Its terms were along the lines of the later, rather than earlier, settlements negotiated by the commission. In other words, it was based on the Italian and Yugoslav, rather than the British, model. The average interest rate charged works out at 0.3 per cent. At the same time, a new loan of $12,167,000 was extended by

[16] *Combined Annual Reports of the World War Foreign Debt Commission*, p. 58.

the Treasury to Greece—payable in 40 semi-annual instalments with interest at the rate of 4 per cent.

The agreement with Austria was signed on May 8, 1930. It differed materially from the other debt agreements. It was in effect a part of Austria's general agreement with the nine countries which had granted her relief credits during the early post-war years, under which each of the creditors received identical terms.[17] As regards the payments to the United States, Austria was given the option of liquidating her indebtedness in one of two ways: either by means of 25 annual instalments, beginning with January 1, 1943, and aggregating total payments of $33,428,500; or by means of 40 annual instalments beginning January 1, 1929 and aggregating $24,614,885, the present value of both sets of payments being approximately the same. Austria chose the second option.[18]

V. PAYMENT AND POSTPONEMENT PROVISIONS

The table on page 91 shows the total amounts to be received by the American Treasury from each of its debtors under the terms of the funding agreements, and the approximate interest rates, averaged over the whole period of payments. Principal and interest are shown separately, because each of the agreements contains detailed schedules of payments showing the amounts due each year on account of principal and interest respec-

[17] The other creditor countries involved were Great Britain, France, Italy, the Netherlands, Denmark, Sweden, Norway, and Switzerland. For a discussion of the general settlement of the Austrian relief debt, see pp. 133-34.

[18] For the details of the debt negotiations and settlement with Greece and Austria, see *Annual Report of the Secretary of the Treasury*, 1929 and 1930. There the reader will also find a complete explanation of the reasons for extending a new loan to Greece.

TOTAL PRINCIPAL AND INTEREST TO BE PAID TO THE UNITED STATES BY 15 WAR DEBTORS

Country	Principal	Interest	Total	Average Interest Rate (Approximate) Over the Whole Period of Payments (Per cent)
Austria...........	$ 24,614,885.00	—	$ 24,614,885.00	—
Belgium..........	417,780,000.00	$ 310,050,500.00	727,830,500.00	1.8
Czechoslovakia....	115,000,000.00	197,811,433.88[a]	312,811,433.88	3.3
Esthonia.........	13,830,000.00	23,877,645.76[a]	37,707,645.76	3.3
Finland..........	9,000,000.00	12,695,055.00	21,695,055.00	3.3
France...........	4,025,000,000.00	2,822,674,104.17	6,847,674,104.17	1.6
Great Britain.....	4,600,000,000.00	6,505,965,000.00	11,105,965,000.00	3.3
Greece...........	32,467,000.00	5,623,760.00	38,090,760.00	0.3
Hungary.........	1,939,000.00	2,815,431.42[a]	4,754,431.42	3.3
Italy............	2,042,000,000.00	365,677,500.00	2,407,677,500.00	0.4
Latvia...........	5,775,000.00	10,015,523.13[a]	15,790,523.13	3.3
Lithuania........	6,030,000.00	9,039,541.57[a]	15,069,541.57	3.3
Poland...........	178,560,000.00	303,114,781.29[a]	481,674,781.29	3.3
Rumania.........	44,590,000.00	77,916,260.05[a]	122,506,260.05	3.3
Yugoslavia.......	62,850,000.00	32,327,635.00	95,177,635.00	1.0
Total...........	$11,579,435,885.00	$10,679,604,171.27	$22,259,040,056.27	2.1

[a] Includes deferred payments, later funded into principal.

tively. Each agreement also contains provisions for temporary postponements of payments. These payment and postponement provisions are summarized below for each individual country; the actual schedules are given in Appendix B.[19]

1. Great Britain. The schedule of British payments was arranged in such a way that the total annual instalments would be practically uniform during the first ten years, and again practically uniform at a somewhat larger figure (because of the increase in the interest rate) during the remaining 52 years. This was done by arranging the payments on account of the principal on a rising scale and those on account of interest on a falling scale. The annual instalments during the first ten years range from $159,940,000 to $161,400,000; those during the last 52 years range from $178,240,000 to $187,350,000. Payments on account of principal are due annually on December 15 of each year; those on account of interest are due semi-annually, on June 15 and December 15 of each year.

Great Britain has the option of postponing any payment on account of principal for a period not exceeding two years, with the proviso that when this option is being exercised "the payment falling due in the next succeeding year cannot be postponed to any date more than one year distant from the date when it becomes due, unless and until the payment previously postponed shall actually have been made, and the payment falling due in the second succeeding year cannot be postponed at all unless and until the payment of principal due two years previous thereto shall actually have been made." Advance notice of not less than 90 days is required for each

[19] See pp. 432-54.

postponement. No interest payment on the postponed amounts is provided for.

The agreement provided that during the first five years of the paying period, Great Britain had the right of paying up to one-half of any instalment on account of interest, not in dollars or in Liberty bonds, but in British bonds, payable in the same manner as regards dates of maturity and rates of interest as the original bonds. This provision constituted in effect an additional postponement privilege and required 90 days' advance notice. It differed from the postponement option as regards payments on account of principal in that its exercise would have resulted in additional annual payments during the remainder of the paying period. Great Britain has not availed herself of either of the postponement privileges.

2. *Finland, Hungary, Lithuania.* The schedules of payments of these three countries are arranged in the same way as that of Great Britain. The total annual payments of Finland during the first ten years range from $313,120 to $315,000; those during the remaining 52 years range from $355,600 to $357,920. The payments of Hungary range from $67,382 to $67,995 during the first ten years, and from $76,025 to $78,885 in the remainder of the period. The payments of Lithuania range from $210,000 to $210,960 during the first ten years, and from $238,040 to $239,880 during the remaining 52 years. Payments on account of interest are due on June 15 and December 15 of each year for all three countries; payments on account of principal are due on December 15 from Finland and Hungary, and on June 15 from Lithuania.

All provisions with regard to the method of payment

and the two postponement privileges in the agreements with these three countries are identical with those contained in the agreement with Great Britain. Finland has not availed herself of either of the postponement privileges. On the other hand, Hungary and Lithuania exercised during the first five years of their payment periods the option of paying a part of the interest due in their own government bonds, rather than in cash, with the result that their actual annual payments have been in subsequent years somewhat larger than those indicated in the original schedules of payments.

3. *Poland, Latvia, Esthonia.* The schedules of payments of these three countries are arranged substantially in the same manner as that of Great Britain. Poland's total annual payments range from $5,916,800 to $6,265,000 during the first ten years; from $6,938,500 to $7,319,000 during the next 47 years; and then rise gradually during the last five years, reaching the maximum of $9,315,000 in 1984. Latvia's payments range from $201,250 to $201,760 during the first ten years; from $228,005 to $231,995 during the next 49 years; and then rise gradually during the last three years, reaching the maximum of $735,980 in 1984. Esthonia's payments range from $483,510 to $483,920 during the first ten years, and from $547,390 to $548,550 during the remaining 52 years. The payment dates are the same as for Great Britain.

All provisions with regard to the method of payment and the postponement privileges in the agreements with these three countries are identical with those in the agreement with Great Britain, with the exception of the provision governing the postponement of interest during the first five years. Instead of having the option of paying not more than one-half of the interest installments in their own bonds rather than in dollars, these countries received the right of limiting their cash payments to certain specified amounts, constituting considerably less than one-half of the total. Poland received the right of paying in cash $10,000,000 during the five years, instead of an aggregate of scheduled payments during these years of $30,957,300; Latvia, $400,000 instead of $1,007,550; and Esthonia, $1,000,000 instead of $2,419,200. All three of these countries exercised their option with regard to these payments, with the result that their annual payments in subsequent years have been somewhat larger than the amounts indicated in the original schedules of payments.

4. *Czechoslovakia and Rumania.* The debts of these two countries were funded on the same terms as the British debt, and nominal schedules of payments were drawn up along the lines of the British schedule. These nominal schedules were, however, used merely as a basis for the actual payment schedules which were arranged as follows: In the case of Czechoslovakia the nominal payments due annually during the first 18 years range from $4,022,700 to $4,565,425. The actual payments during this period, however, amount to only $3,000,000 a year, the difference being each year deferred to the nineteenth year. Interest is then computed on these deferred amounts at the rate of 3 per cent a year for the first ten years and 3.5 per cent for the remaining eight years. In the nineteenth year the value of the deferred amounts with interest is added to the amount of principal then outstanding, and that whole sum with current interest at the rate of 3.5 per cent is then paid off in 44 annuities ranging from $5,879,225

to $5,884,725. In the case of Rumania, the period of deferment is 14 years, during which the actual annual payments rise from $200,000 to $2,200,000. The annual payments during the remaining 48 years range from $2,245,050 to $2,248,020. Interest payments are due on June 15 and December 15 of each year; payments on account of principal, on June 15.

Both Czechoslovakia and Rumania have the same postponement privilege as regards payments on account of principal as has Great Britain, except that this right is denied them during the period of deferred payments. As a result, Czechoslovakia cannot exercise the postponement option until after June 15, 1943, and Rumania until after June 15, 1939.

5. *Belgium.* The Belgian debt agreement contains two schedules of payments, one covering the pre-Armistice debt and the other the post-Armistice debt. The first schedule calls for annual payments which rise gradually from $1,000,000 in 1926 to $2,900,000 in 1932 and then continue at this latter figure up to the last year of the 62-year payment period, the last payment being $2,280,000. The second schedule calls for graduated payments during the first ten years, rising from $2,840,000 to $6,650,000, and practically uniform annual instalments during the remaining 52 years, ranging from $9,752,000 to $9,968,000. The payment dates are the same as for Czechoslovakia and Rumania.

The privilege of postponing payments on account of principal is denied Belgium during the first ten years of the payment period. This privilege can be enjoyed by Belgium only after June 15, 1935.

6. *Italy and Yugoslavia.* The schedule of Italian payments calls for annual instalments of $5,000,000 dur-

ing the first five years, and is arranged thereafter, through the remainder of the period on a graduated, steadily rising scale. Beginning with $14,621,250 in 1931, the annual instalments rise to $80,988,000 in 1987.

The schedule of Yugoslav payments is arranged in such a way that the annual instalments during the first five years amount to $200,000 each; those for the next 30 years rise gradually from $225,000 in 1931 to $1,841,040 in 1960; and those for the remaining 27 years are practically uniform, ranging from $2,489,475 to $2,490,605. The payment dates are the same as for Czechoslovakia and Rumania.

The right to exercise the postponement privilege with regard to payments on account of principal begins in the case of Italy after June 15, 1930, and in the case of Yugoslavia after June 15, 1937. For both countries, all postponed payments under this provision are subject to interest at the rate of 4.25 per cent a year.

7. *France.* The schedule of French payments is arranged in such a way that the annual instalments during the first 17 years rise from $30,000,000 in 1926 to $125,000,000 in 1942. They then continue at this latter figure up to the last year of the period of payments. The final instalment for the year 1987 is $117,674,104.17. The payment dates are the same as for Czechoslovakia and Rumania.

The postponement privileges enjoyed by France differ from those granted to the twelve debtors whose agreements have just been discussed. During the period from June 16, 1926 to June 16, 1932, France has the right to postpone for a maximum period of three years "so much of any payment on account of principal and/or interest falling due in any one year. . . . as shall be in excess of $20,000,000 in any one year." After June 16, 1932 France has the right to postpone payments only on account of principal, for a maximum period of three years. All postponed payments are subject to interest at the rate of 4.25 per cent a year.

8. *Greece.* The debt agreement with Greece contains two schedules of payments, one covering the funded war debt and the other the new loan extended to Greece in 1928. Both schedules are in the form of semi-annual instalments, rather than annual, as in the debt agreements described so far. The payment dates are also different: the semi-annual instalments on account of the war debt fall due on January 1 and July 1 of each year; those on account of the new loan on May 10 and November 10 of each year. The first schedule provides for two semi-annual instalments (July 1, 1928 and January 1, 1929) of $20,000 each; two of $25,000 each; two of $30,000 each; two of $110,000 each; two of $130,000 each; ten of $150,000 each; and 104 of $175,000 each. The second schedule calls for 40 semi-annual instalments, almost uniform in size, ranging from a minimum of $444,040 to a maximum of $445,460.

With respect to the war debt, Greece has the right to postpone payments on account of principal for a maximum period of two and one-half years. All postponed payments are subject to interest at the rate of 4.25 per cent a year. Payments on account of the new loan cannot be postponed.

9. *Austria.* Under the option chosen by Austria, the schedule of payments calls for the following annual instalments, due on January 1 of each year: five in-

stalments of $287,556 each, beginning January 1, 1929; ten instalments of $460,093 each; and 25 annual instalments of $743,047 each. Austria on her own initiative has no right of postponing any of these payments. But the trustees of the reconstruction loan of 1923 may, during the period prior to 1943, raise objection to the payment of any annuity, in which case Austria is relieved from the obligation to pay the annuity in question. However, whenever this happens the unpaid amount will be repayable in 25 equal annuities starting with January 1, 1944, with accrued interest at the rate of 5 per cent compounded annually up to December 31, 1943, and current interest thereafter also at the rate of 5 per cent.

VI. EXTENT OF REDUCTION

The original obligations of foreign governments held by the United States Treasury called for current interest at the rate of 5 per cent, and in the case of the obligations transferred to the Treasury from the United States Grain Corporation at a 6 per cent rate. Prior to the funding of the debts, accrued interest on all these obligations was entered on the books of the Treasury at their original rates. Thus at the time of each settlement there was outstanding against the negotiating country a total indebtedness consisting of the amount originally borrowed, plus this accrued interest. For convenience, we may call this outstanding indebtedness "the debt prior to funding."

As noted above, the accrued interest was recalculated at the time of the settlements on a 4.25 per cent basis (3 per cent for part of the time in the case of the later settlements). The actual funded principal was thus made somewhat smaller than the debt prior to funding. This obviously represented a certain amount of reduction, or cancellation, of the outstanding indebtedness as recorded on the books of the United States Treasury. It will also be recalled that the rates of current interest charged in the settlements were reduced to a maximum of 3.5 per cent, as compared with the 4.25 per cent rate fixed as the minimum in the act creating the World War Foreign Debt Commission.

To estimate the amount of the reduction that has consequently occurred it is necessary to compare the amount of the debt prior to funding with the present value of the actual settlements. The present value of each settlement is the sum which in 62 years, at a given rate of interest, would yield a total equal to the principal and interest payments called for by the actual agreement. The amount of the present value will, however, obviously vary, depending upon whether interest is computed at 5 or 4.25 per cent.

The table on page 101 shows the amount of reduction in the debt settlements negotiated by the United States government with its war debtors. Two sets of present values are given in the table, one based on an interest rate of 5 per cent, and the other on a rate of 4.25 per cent. The column of percentages accompanying each set of present values indicates for each country the extent of reduction represented for it by the terms of settlement.

On a 5 per cent basis, the extent of reduction works out at approximately 30 per cent for Great Britain and for six countries—Finland, Poland, Hungary, Latvia, Esthonia, and Lithuania—which negotiated settlements based substantially on the British model. For Czechoslovakia and Rumania, the curtailment is about 37 per cent; for Belgium and France about 60 per cent; for Greece about 72 per cent; for Austria about 74 per cent; for Yugoslavia about 76 per cent; and for Italy it is a

AMOUNT OF REDUCTION IN THE AMERICAN WAR DEBT SETTLEMENTS
(In millions of dollars)

Debtor Country	Debt Prior to Funding (With accrued interest at original rates)	Reduction on a 5 Per Cent Basis		Reduction on a 4.25 Per Cent Basis	
		Present Value of Funded Debt	Percentage of Reduction	Present Value of Funded Debt	Percentage of Reduction
Austria.......	34.6	9.0	74.1	10.2	70.5
Belgium......	483.4	191.8	60.3	225.0	53.5
Czechoslovakia	123.9	78.0	37.0	92.0	25.7
Esthonia.....	14.1	9.9	29.9	11.4	19.5
Finland......	9.2	6.5	29.8	7.4	19.3
France.......	4,230.8	1,681.4	60.3	1,996.5	52.8
Great Britain.	4,715.3	3,296.9	30.1	3,788.5	19.7
Greece[a]......	19.7	5.5	72.1	6.4	67.3
Hungary.....	2.0	1.4	30.0	1.6	19.6
Italy.........	2,150.2	426.3	80.2	528.2	75.4
Latvia.......	5.9	4.1	29.8	4.8	19.3
Lithuania....	6.2	4.3	30.5	5.0	20.1
Poland.......	182.3	127.6	30.0	146.8	19.5
Rumania.....	46.9	29.5	37.1	35.2	25.1
Yugoslavia...	66.2	15.9	75.9	20.0	69.7
Total.....	12,090.7	5,888.1	51.3	6,879.0	43.1

[a] Exclusive of new 4 per cent 20-year loan of $12,167,000.

fraction over 80 per cent. For all the debtors combined, the extent of cancellation works out at slightly over 51 per cent.

These percentages represent the maximum alleviation of the burden that can be figured on the basis of the settlements as negotiated. In the case of commercial obligations between private parties, the rate originally stipulated would, of course, be regarded as the one and only rate to be considered. But in the case of the war loans, it was taken for granted that 5 per cent was merely a provisional rate and subject to reconsideration at the time of funding operations. Congress, in the act creating the debt commission, fixed 4.25 per cent as

AMOUNT OF REDUCTION IN THE AMERICAN DEBT
SETTLEMENTS

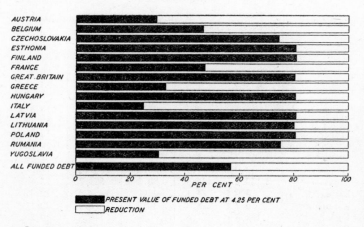

the minimum, though not necessarily the actual, rate at which the obligations should be refunded. This rate is perhaps a fairer basis on which to compute the extent of the curtailment that has occurred.

On a 4.25 per cent basis, the extent of reduction for all the debtors combined works out at 43 per cent. For the seven countries whose settlements are on the British model, the reduction is about 20 per cent; for Czechoslovakia and Rumania, it is approximately 25 per cent; for Belgium and France about 53 per cent; for Greece about 67 per cent; for Austria and Yugoslavia about 70 per cent; and for Italy a little over 75 per cent.

In considering the question of cancellation, it will be of interest to see how the present values of the payments scheduled in the settlements with the various debtors compare with the advances made to these countries before and after the Armistice. The following table gives such a comparison for the four principal debtors.[20]

PRE-ARMISTICE AND POST-ARMISTICE ADVANCES MADE BY THE AMERICAN TREASURY COMPARED WITH THE PRESENT VALUES OF THE DEBT SETTLEMENTS
(In millions of dollars)

Debtor Country	Cash Advances Made Prior to Nov. 30, 1918[a]	Cash Advances Made After Nov. 30, 1918[b]	Total Original Advances	Present Value of Scheduled Payments on a 4.25 Per Cent Basis
Great Britain....	3,796.0	278.8	4,074.8	3,788.5
France..........	2,010.0	1,330.5	3,340.5	1,996.5
Italy............	1,091.0	538.9	1,629.9	528.2
Belgium.........	185.5	191.5	377.0	225.0

[a] The amounts shown here represent actual cash advances, rather than credits established, during the period.

[b] Exclusive of accrued and unpaid interest.

It will be seen from the table that the present value of the payments scheduled in the settlement with Great Britain is equal to the advances made to that country after the Armistice and over 90 per cent of the pre-Armistice loans. In the case of France, the present value of the payments which that country has obligated itself to make equals all the post-Armistice advances and nearly one-third of the funds borrowed by it before the Armistice. The same is substantially true of Belgium, although in her case the present value of the payments

[20] The division of the advances as between pre-Armistice and post-Armistice periods is based on the detailed data contained in the *Annual Report of the Secretary of the Treasury*, 1920.

scheduled in the settlement equal, in addition to the post-Armistice loans, but 20 per cent of the pre-Armistice advances. Only in the case of Italy is the present value of the payments inscribed in the debt agreement

PRESENT VALUE OF PRINCIPAL AMERICAN DEBT
SETTLEMENTS COMPARED WITH ADVANCES

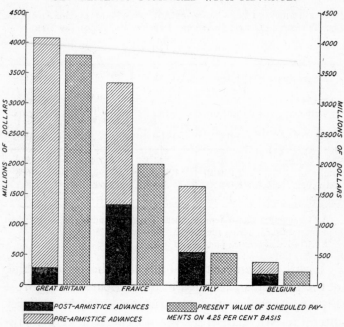

with that country less than even the post-Armistice loans. These comparisons are graphically represented on the accompanying chart.

VII. APPLICATION OF THE PRINCIPLE OF PAYING CAPACITY

The varying degrees of reduction granted by the United States government to its war debtors was a reflection of the extent to which the principle of paying capacity determined the formulation of debt policy. From this point of view, the position of the United States government underwent, with the passage of time, gradual, but far-reaching, modifications.

The terms of repayment contained in the first American funding proposal, which we described in the preceding chapter,[21] appear utterly fantastic when considered in the light of the actual funding agreements, especially those negotiated during the last two years of the debt funding commission's activities. It will be recalled that the proposal made in 1919 called for the liquidation of the debts within periods ranging from 20 to 30 years, and required annual instalments which rose to as high as 7.5 per cent of the original sums advanced. In none of the actual agreements negotiated do the maximum annual payments exceed 4.1 per cent of the funded principal.

At the time the first funding proposal was made, the principle of payments in accordance with capacity was not considered in any way. It was taken for granted that all of the European debtors could pay in full and on uniform terms as to the period of repayment and the rate of interest, if they really desired to do so. Even when the debt funding act was passed two and one-half years later, its underlying conception was exactly the same. The purely legal viewpoint still prevailed over economic factors involved in the principle of paying capacity.

However, the very first agreement negotiated under the act of February 9, 1922—that with Great Britain —represented a departure from this policy of literal

[21] See pp. 58-60.

fulfillment, caused by an emerging, though as yet very limited, appreciation of the problem of paying capacity. While the reduction of the standard rate of interest from 4.25 to 3.5 per cent was made by the commission on the ground that this was approximately the normal interest rate payable "by strong governments over a long period of years," the shading of this rate to 3 per cent during the first ten years was justified by the need of taking into account the exigencies of "readjustment and recuperation." Moreover, the provision permitting the payments to be spread over 62 years, rather than a maximum of 25 years, was a recognition that there were limits to the amounts that might be paid annually.

The fact that the commission prescribed for eight other debtors substantially the same terms as those laid down in the settlement with Great Britain, without any attempt to determine whether or not the relative paying capacity of each of these countries differed in any way from that of Great Britain, showed plainly that the principle of capacity to pay was only in a limited degree a guiding factor in the determination of policy. Even in the case of the Belgian settlement, which represented the first important departure from the British model, the concessions with reference to the pre-Armistice debt were in recognition of Belgium's sacrifices during the war and of the special commitments made at the time of the Peace Conference; and the only application of the principle of paying capacity was in connection with the provision for a graduated rate of interest on the post-war debt during the first ten years, this concession being granted because of the temporary trade and financial difficulties with which Belgium was confronted.

It was not until September 1925, when the French debt commission headed by M. Caillaux began its negotiations in Washington, that the principle of capacity to pay was given official recognition as a determining consideration in working out the settlement. In a statement issued by the American commission on October 1, 1925, this recognition was expressed in the following terms:

We believe it is fully recognized by the commissions that the only basis of negotiations fair to both peoples is the principle of the capacity of France to pay. The nub of the difficulty of the two commissions arises from a difference in judgment as to the future capacity of France to pay without, as we have stated, undermining her economic and social fabric; and this difficulty narrows itself to the future rather than to the present, for we are prepared to accept the views of the French commission as to the immediate difficulties of France.

Here we have for the first time a clear-cut recognition on the part of the American commission of the possibility that the debtor may have a limited paying capacity throughout the entire period of payments, as well as during the first few years of reconstruction and recuperation. In all of the earlier settlements the question was not considered as to whether a 3.5 per cent interest rate over the whole of the last 52 years of payment would be within the paying capacity of the debtor countries.

In the negotiations with the Italian debt commission in November 1925, the question of capacity to pay moved into the very foreground of the discussion, and the settlement which was concluded was worked out with much more regard to the economic factors in the situation both as regards the earlier and the later years than had been the case in any of the earlier settlements. In negotiations with France, in April 1926, which re-

resulted in the signing of an agreement, the principle that payment should be fixed in accordance with capacity to pay was taken for granted. The same was true of the negotiations with Yugoslavia and of the agreements concluded by the Treasury.

It may be noted in this connection that in estimating paying capacity the negotiators took into account the reparation receipts which the debtors were scheduled to receive, as well as other factors.

CHAPTER VI

INTRA-EUROPEAN DEBT SETTLEMENTS

The negotiation of debt funding agreements among the European war creditors and debtors was deferred for several years after the war. Most of the intra-European war debts, in fact, remained in abeyance much longer than the debts to the United States, while some of the settlements were deferred to as late a date as 1930. By the end of that year, however, practically all the war debt accounts, with the sole important exception of Russia's, had become the subject of definitive funding agreements.

In contrast with the American practice of not distinguishing between the war loans and the relief and reconstruction credits, the creditor nations of the former Allied group—Great Britain and France—followed the policy of treating these two sets of obligations separately. According to the phraseology insisted upon by the French, the war debts are considered as "political," and the relief and reconstruction obligations as "commercial," in character. And while the United States accorded the same treatment, as regards interest rates and periods of repayment, to both sets of obligations, Great Britain and France kept the negotiations regarding the "political" debts separate from those dealing with the "commercial" debts, the former, generally speaking, being regarded with much greater leniency than the latter. In this chapter the reader will find a discussion of the funding policies pursued by the European creditors on both the war and the relief debt accounts. A brief description is given of the numerous adjustments made with respect to intra-European debt relations.[1]

I. THE BRITISH DEBT SETTLEMENTS

Of the large advances to Allied governments made by the British government during the period of hostilities, almost 90 per cent went to France, Italy, and Russia. The first two of these principal borrowers, as well as the various smaller debtors, have negotiated funding agreements with Great Britain. An exception was made in the case of the war debt of Belgium, which, by an arrangement concluded at the Peace Conference between Great Britain, France, and the United States, was incorporated as a part of Germany's reparation obligation.[2] Great Britain's post-war loans, on various accounts, except the credits extended to the no longer existing government of Armenia, have also been regularly funded. The huge Russian debt is indefinitely in abeyance, although it is still carried in the official statements of the British national debt account as an unfunded obligation of more than 1 billion pounds sterling, inclusive of accrued interest.[3]

[1] No definitive official compilation of the agreements relating to the inter-governmental debts which had their origin in the World War is in existence. So far as the authors of this work can ascertain, all such agreements are mentioned in this book. It may be, however, that some very minor adjustments have escaped notice.

[2] This arrangement was carried out in the case of Great Britain and France, though not in the case of the United States.

[3] This item is a more or less nominal one, as may be seen from the fact that, starting with the budget for the fiscal year 1918-19, the British chancellors of the exchequer followed the practice of counting the debts due from the Allies at one-half of their face value, making allowance primarily for the probable default on the Russian debt and the possibility, contemplated even at that time, that some of the other debts would have to be scaled down. See F. W. Hirst and J. E. Allen, *British War Budgets*, 1926, pp. 204-05. In the Anglo-Soviet treaty re-

1. Great Britain's debt funding policy. The creation of the American debt funding commission was followed by a public formulation of a war debt policy on the part of Great Britain. Prior to that, the British government addressed no formal communications to its debtors. The amounts of the advances continued to be inscribed on the books of the British Treasury, and interest was regularly added. The British conversations with the American government described in Chapter IV were not accompanied by corresponding communications to Great Britain's own debtors. On August 1, 1922, however, Mr. Arthur J. Balfour, the British secretary of state for foreign affairs, addressed a note to the French Ambassador in London and similar notes to the diplomatic representatives in London of Italy, Yugoslavia, Rumania, Greece, and Portugal, which laid down the fundamental principles of British debt and reparation policy.

The Balfour note invited Great Britain's war debtors to inaugurate negotiations looking toward a funding of their obligations. It stated that the British government was doing this with "the greatest reluctance," since it had consistently advocated a general cancellation of all war debts. Such a course of action, however, had been rendered no longer possible by the steps taken by the United States in the direction of arranging for the collection of debts owing to that country. The note read as follows:

With the most perfect courtesy, and in the exercise of their undoubted rights, the American government have required

---

garding the settlement of debts between the two countries, the war debts were specifically "reserved for discussion at a later date." See H. G. Moulton and Leo Pasvolsky, *World War Debt Settlements*, p. 422.

this country to pay the interest accrued since 1919 on the Anglo-American debt, to convert it from an unfunded debt, and to repay it by a sinking fund in 25 years. Such a procedure is clearly in accordance with the original contract. His Majesty's government make no complaint of it; they recognize their obligations and are prepared to fulfill them. But evidently they cannot do so without profoundly modifying the course which, in different circumstances, they would have wished to pursue. They cannot treat the repayment of the Anglo-American loan as if it were an isolated incident in which only the United States of America and Great Britain had any concern. It is but one of a connected series of transactions, in which this country appears sometimes as debtor, sometimes as creditor, and, if our undoubted obligations as a debtor are to be enforced, our not less undoubted rights as a creditor cannot be left wholly in abeyance.

After stating at length the reasons why Great Britain was in favor of a general cancellation, Mr. Balfour went on to say that even if that proved to be impossible, the British government was so firmly convinced of the unwisdom, in the existing condition of the world, of insisting on a literal fulfillment of the debt obligations incurred as a result of the war, that it was prepared to go as far as it could in alleviating the burden. He pointed out that "Great Britain is owed more than it owes,"[4] but that, in spite of this fact, the British government will collect from its debtors only amounts sufficient to cover its own debt payments to the United

---

[4] According to the figures given in the Balfour note, the account stood as follows in 1922: Principal of British debt to the United States, 850 million pounds; principal of Russian debt to Great Britain, 650 million pounds; principal of debts owed to Great Britain by the other Allies, 1.3 billion pounds; British share of the German reparation payments on the basis of the London schedule of payments of 1921, 1,450 million pounds. Thus, exclusive of the reparation payments, Great Britain's loans to her Allies were more than double her borrowings from the United States; with the German reparation payments added in, the debts to Great Britain were four times her own debts.

States. This Balfour principle was stated in the note in the following terms:

The policy favoured by His Majesty's government is, as I have already observed, that of surrendering their share of German reparation, and writing off, through one great transaction, the whole body of inter-Allied indebtedness. But, if this be found impossible of accomplishment, we wish it to be understood that we do not in any event desire to make a profit out of any less satisfactory arrangement. In no circumstances do we propose to ask more from our debtors than is necessary to pay to our creditors. And, while we do not ask for more, all will admit that we can hardly be content with less.[5]

The policy thus enunciated became, generally speaking, the guiding principle in Great Britain's debt negotiations with her war debtors. Accordingly, each settlement was governed by two basic considerations: (1) the total annual receipts required by Great Britain to provide for her own debt payments to the United States, and (2) the relative financial strength of the individual debtors. This second consideration dictated more or less the character of the terms which the British Treasury was willing to grant, but always within the limitations of the first basic consideration.

As interpreted implicitly by the succeeding British governments, the principle established in the Balfour note was made applicable only to the war debts in a strict sense. The loans to the British dominions and colonies were excluded from the account, as well as the relief, reconstruction, and similar credits extended by the British Treasury after the war. Funding agreements regarding these debts were negotiated without reference to the Balfour principle. It was only in the settle-

---

[5] For the full text of the Balfour note, see Moulton and Pasvolsky, *World War Debt Settlements*, pp. 413-18.

ments on the war accounts with France, Italy, Portugal, Yugoslavia, and Greece that provisions were made to ensure the application of this principle. These provisions are stated explicitly, and in identical terms, in the agreements signed with the five countries. The character of these provisions is indicated by Article 5 of the Anglo-French debt funding agreement which reads as follows:

If at any time it appears that the aggregate payments effectively received by Great Britain under the Allied war debt funding agreements and on account of reparations or of liberation bonds exceed the aggregate payments effectively made by Great Britain to the government of the United States of America in respect of war debts, an account shall be drawn up by the British Treasury, interest at 5 per cent being allowed on both sides of the account; and if that account shows that receipts exceed payments, Great Britain will credit France against the payments next due by France under Article 1[6] of this agreement with such proportion of that excess as the payments effectively made by France under Article 4[7] of this agreement bear to the aggregate sums effectively received by Great Britain under all the Allied war debt funding agreements. Thereafter a similar account will be drawn up by the British Treasury each year and any further excess of receipts over payments shall each year give rise to the credit to France of a proportion of such excess calculated in the manner indicated above. On the other hand a deficit shall be made good by an increase in the payments next due by France up to a similar proportion of such deficit within the limit of the total amounts of the credits already allowed to France under this article.

For the purpose of this article, any capital sums, which may hereafter be realized by Great Britain in respect of reparations or liberation bonds, will be taken at their annual value, taking account of amortization.

---

[6] This article refers to the total payments to be made by France. See p. 117.

[7] This article refers to the postponement privileges granted France. See p. 118.

The agreement with Rumania, the first war debt settlement to be negotiated and signed,[8] does not contain any reference to the Balfour principle. Legally, therefore, the scheduled payments owed by that country are not subject to either decreases or increases resulting from the application of the principle.

2. *Arrangements with the war debtors.* Following the model of the American debt settlements, Great Britain's funding agreements with her debtors call for payments extending over a period of 62 years. The payment schedules make no distinction, however, between repayment of the principal sums due and current interest. Single annuities are provided, which, when met, will extinguish the entire indebtedness. Nevertheless, in all the British settlements, with the sole exception of that with Italy, the scheduled payments provide for the repayment of the debts outstanding at the time of each settlement (which include accrued interest) and for a certain amount of current interest.

The table on page 116 shows (1) the net amount of the debt outstanding at the time of settlement, after adjustment of all other war accounts between Great Britain and each debtor; (2) the aggregate scheduled payments; and (3) the aggregate amount of current interest payments. It should be noted, however, in connection with this table, that the ratio between the shares of the aggregate payments represented by principal and by interest is not a guide to the degree of leniency shown to each debtor. The relative size of instalments during the early and the later years of the period of payment

---

[8] Great Britain's war debt agreements were signed on the following dates: Rumania, Oct. 19, 1925; Italy, Jan. 12, 1926; France, July 12, 1926; Portugal, Dec. 31, 1926; Greece, Apr. 9, 1927; Yugoslavia, Aug. 9, 1927.

constitutes an extremely important factor in judging
the character of the terms granted. For example, as we
shall see later on, the amount of reduction represented
by the settlements with Yugoslavia and Greece is almost identical, although the aggregate amount of current interest is 22 per cent of the total scheduled payments in the case of the former and only 9 per cent in
that of the latter. The reason for this lies in the fact
that the payments to be made by Yugoslavia during the
early years are proportionately much smaller than those
which are to be made by Greece.

BRITISH DEBT SETTLEMENTS
(In thousands of pounds sterling)

Debtor Country	Amount of Debt at Time of Settlement	Total Scheduled Payments	Aggregate Amount of Current Interest
France..........	599.6[a]	801.5[a]	201.9
Italy............	588.6[a]	254.6[a]	—
Yugoslavia......	25.6	32.8	7.2
Greece..........	21.4	23.6	2.2
Portugal........	20.1	24.0	3.9
Rumania........	18.4	31.3	12.9
Total........	1,273.7	1,167.8	228.1

[a] Adjusted for return of gold shipped to Great Britain during the war in
the form of loans. See pp. 31-32.

The annuities scheduled in the agreements were
made payable in pounds sterling, without a gold clause,[9]
in equal semi-annual instalments. The due dates were
not made uniform. The instalments due from France
and Italy are payable on March 15 and September 15 of
each year; those from Yugoslavia and Greece, on June
1 and December 1; those from Portugal, on June 15

[9] In the case of the American settlements, it will be recalled, payment
was specified in gold dollars or their equivalent.

and December 15; and those from Rumania, on May 15 and November 15. After the Young plan went into effect, the system of monthly instalments was adopted for these debts.

Generally speaking, the British Treasury, in working out the terms of settlement, proceeded on the basis of establishing for each country a constant annuity and then arranging for deviations from this annuity in the form of smaller payments during initial periods varying in length from country to country. In the cases of France, Italy, and Portugal, the differences between the constant annuities and the actual payments during the initial periods were funded over the remaining periods; in the cases of the other three countries, these differences were simply written off in order to make it possible for these countries to meet their instalments on the relief debts due to Great Britain. The result of this was that each schedule of payments contains a period of graduated instalments, arising to a point where uniform annuities begin.

The agreement with France calls for aggregate payments over the 62-year period of 855 million pounds sterling (including a payment of 2 million pounds due in 1925 and still unpaid at the time the agreement was signed). Of this sum, however, 53.5 million pounds was not made subject to payment, but was left in abeyance in the form of a non-interest-bearing debt to be cancelled by a return to France of a similar amount of gold, representing the loans of that metal made to Great Britain by France during the war.[10] The procedure with regard to the return of this gold was left to future negotiations between the two governments.

[10] See pp. 31-32.

As regards the remainder of the debt, the agreement calls for annual payments rising from 4 million pounds sterling (plus the 2 millions due in 1925) during the first year to 10 millions during the fourth year. Starting with the fifth year, there are 27 annuities of 12.5 millions pounds each, followed by 31 annuities of 14 million pounds each. France has the right to postpone, for a period of not more than three years, a portion not exceeding one-half of each semi-annual payment. Any such postponement requires not less than 90 days' notice, and interest at the rate of 5 per cent is provided on any sums thus postponed.

In negotiating her debt agreement with Great Britain, France attempted to obtain from the latter a safeguard provision with respect to reparation payments. A similar attempt, it will be recalled, was made by the French negotiators with the United States. But while the Franco-American negotiations on this point did not result in any specific reservation, the Franco-British agreement was accompanied by the following exchange of letters between M. Joseph Caillaux, the French minister of finance, and Mr. Winston Churchill, the British chancellor of the exchequer. M. Caillaux wrote:

In assuming the responsibility of signing the agreement for the settlement of the French war debt to Great Britain and thereby accepting payment of the annuities fixed on the sole credit of France, I feel bound to explain that the payments of the amounts required to assure fulfillment of the debt settlements with the United States and Great Britain inevitably depend largely on the continued transfer of receipts from Germany under the Dawes plan. If, therefore, for reasons outside of the control of France, such receipts should cease completely, or to an extent greater than one-half, a new situation would be created, and the French government reserves the right in such an event of asking the British government to reconsider the question in the light of all the circumstances then prevailing. It is subject to this express reservation that I am ready to sign the agreement which we may draw up.

To this Mr. Churchill replied:

His Majesty's government must maintain that the position of the settlement which we have arrived at of the French war debt to this country depends, like that of the debt itself, on the sole credit of France. You will realize that in the hypothetical circumstances you mention Great Britain would already have suffered a diminution of receipts from the Dawes scheme, which we have taken into account in arriving at the various debt settlements, and this is one of the factors which would have to be borne in mind in the event of any reconsideration of the question being desired by the French government. Subject to this I do not object to the statement that you make.

In the event of any modification being made I should expect, in order to secure equal treatment among creditors, that the other creditors of France would take into consideration a corresponding modification of the debts due to them.

The practical value of this reservation cannot be considered as very great. In his reply Mr. Churchill made it clear that, in the event of a diminution of reparation receipts, Great Britain might find herself confronted with a deficit of the sort that was contemplated in Article 5 of the Franco-British agreement, in which case, far from relieving France of a part of her stipulated annuities, Great Britain might feel justified in asking for increased payments. Moreover, Mr. Churchill made a reopening of the question in the sense desired by France contingent upon the willingness of the "other creditors of France," that is, the United States, to agree to a similar procedure with respect to the debts owed to them by France.

The agreement with Italy calls for a payment of 2

million pounds sterling during the first year; 4 millions a year during the next two years; 4.25 millions a year during the next 4 years; 4.5 millions during the next 54 years; and 2.25 millions during the final year. It also provides for a return to Italy of gold, amounting to 22.2 million pounds, representing the loans of that metal made by Italy to Great Britain during the war. This gold is to be released to Italy in the following manner:

As to the sum of one million pounds sterling, in eight equal instalments on September 15 and March 15 of each of the four years commencing September 15, 1928; and as to the balance, in equal half-yearly instalments, commencing September 15, 1932, and terminating September 15, 1987; provided always that all the annuities due under Article 1 of this agreement have been integrally paid to date.

The return of gold was thus made to constitute small regular offsets to the scheduled payments during most of the 62-year period.

In accordance with the agreement, Italy has the right to "postpone such part of any of the half-yearly instalments falling due on or after September 15, 1928, as exceeds the sum of 1 million pounds to any subsequent March 15 or September 15, not more than two years distant from its due date." Any such postponement requires not less than 90 days' notice, and interest at the rate of 5 per cent per annum is stipulated for all postponed payments.

Detailed schedules of payments for France and Italy, as well as for Great Britain's four other war debtors—Portugal, Yugoslavia, Rumania, and Greece—are given in Appendix B.[11] In the agreements with these other

[11] See p. 456.

countries, no provisions are included allowing for postponements of payments, but a stipulation is made that "interest at the rate of 6 per cent per annum shall be charged on any instalment due and not paid at the due date."[12]

3. Arrangements with other debtors. In addition to her war loans, Great Britain extended post-war credits to a number of countries. These loans were for such purposes as relief, reconstruction, repatriation of prisoners of war, and the purchase of materials. The relief credits were extended by Great Britain jointly with a number of other countries, and the funding of these debts was also subsequently undertaken as a common enterprise. The funding agreements thus concluded will be described in a later section of this chapter.[13] With her other post-war debtors, Great Britain concluded individual agreements.

Great Britain's reconstruction loans to Belgium and the Belgian Congo were funded by agreements concluded on December 31, 1925. They provide for the repayment of the principal sums, with current interest at the rate of 5 per cent, in 30 annual instalments, extending from 1927 to 1956. During the first five years, the payments by Belgium amount to 450,000 pounds a year, and those by the Belgian Congo to 180,000 pounds. During the remaining 25 years, the Belgian payments amount to approximately 640,000 pounds a year, and those by the Belgian Congo to approximately

---

[12] For the details of Great Britain's debt negotiations with her principal war debtors, see Moulton and Pasvolsky, *World War Debt Settlements*, Chaps. III-V. For the official texts of the agreements, see British Parliamentary Papers, Cmds. 2580 (Italy); 2692 (France); 2791 (Portugal); 2848 (Greece); 2973 (Yugoslavia); and 2990 (Rumania).

[13] See pp. 130-35.

254,000 pounds. These payments are due in equal semi-annual instalments, payable on June 30 and December 31 of each year.

Repatriation and other credits were extended to Czechoslovakia, Poland, Rumania, Latvia, Esthonia, and Greece. Agreements with these countries call for annual payments, extending over varying periods, ranging from five to 30 years. No postponement provisions are included in any of these agreements, but in some cases a penalty at the rate of 6 per cent per annum is provided for instalments not met on the due dates. Finally, by means of special agreements, Great Britain funded the debts due to her from Poland and Lithuania, representing the British share of the costs of the Upper-Silesian plebiscite in the case of the former and of the Memel plebiscite in that of the latter.[14]

4. *Extent of reduction.* Great Britain's funding agreements with her war and post-war debtors represent, generally speaking, a large amount of reduction in the case of the former and practically no reduction in that of the latter. With the exception of Austria, as we shall presently see, the various relief, reconstruction, and other post-war debts were made subject to repayment in full with accrued interest to the dates of funding at the rate of 6 per cent, and current interest at the rate of 5 per cent. On the other hand, the amount of interest charged on the war debts is exceedingly low, and in the

[14] Detailed schedules of payments for all these agreements are given in Appendix B, pp. 457 and 467. For the text of the agreement with Belgium see Kingdom of Belgium, *Chambre des Répresentants, Situation du tresor publique*, Jan. 1, 1926; for that with Latvia, *League of Nations Treaty Series*, 1926, Vol. LVI, pp. 178-80; for that with Esthonia, *Esthonian Official Gazette*, 1925, No. 197/8; for the Upper Silesian agreement with Poland, *Dziennik Ustaw Rzeczypospolitej Polskiej*, 1932, No. 1.

case of some of the debtors even the original principal is not to be fully repaid.

We have already seen that the agreement with Italy calls for no current interest at all and for the repayment of only about one-half of the principal sum outstanding at the time of funding (original advances plus accrued interest). Substantial reductions from the amounts outstanding at the time of funding were made also in the cases of the four smaller war debtors—in these instances, however, to allow for adjustment of various war accounts. In the case of Portugal, the debt which was outstanding at the time the agreement was signed was reduced by 15 per cent "in consideration of the services and supplies rendered by Portugal to Great Britain during the war free of charge and in settlement of all outstanding claims in connection with the accounts relating to the war debt."

For similar reasons, the funded principal of the Yugoslav debt was made smaller than the debt actually outstanding by a little less than 15 per cent, and the Rumanian debt by almost 30 per cent. The debt of Greece was reduced slightly to allow for "claims in respect of damages caused by the British troops in Greece," and, in addition, the British government agreed "to remit all claims on Greece in respect of the military materials supplied under the agreement of February 10, 1918."

The rates of current interest charged on the net amounts funded are extremely low, ranging from no interest at all in the case of Italy to an average of approximately 1.5 per cent for France and Rumania. Since the original obligations called, generally speaking, for interest at the rate of 5 per cent, this meant, on the basis of present values, a very substantial reduction in the net amounts funded. The present value on a 5 per cent basis of the scheduled payments in the British settlements works out approximately as follows, in percentages of the net amounts funded: Rumania, 37.5 per cent; France, 37.2 per cent; Portugal, 35.5 per cent; Yugoslavia, 32.2 per cent; Greece, 32.1 per cent; and Italy, 13.3 per cent. On this basis, one can say that Great Britain cancelled a little less than two-thirds of the debts owed to her by Rumania, France, and Portugal; a little more than two-thirds of the debts owed by Yugoslavia and Greece; and almost seven-eighths of the debt owed by Italy.

II. THE FRENCH DEBT SETTLEMENTS

At the end of the war, Russia was by far the largest debtor of France, with Belgium and Italy following in order of importance. The Russian debt, although still inscribed in the official statements of the French national debt account as an unfunded obligation of almost 8 billion francs, is indefinitely in abeyance. The Belgian debt, as previously pointed out, was transferred by the Treaty of Versailles to Germany.[15] The French accounts with Italy, involving some loans from Italy as well as substantial credits, is still carried in the form of unfunded obligations on the books of the French Treasury. Three other small debts—of Portugal, Albania, and Georgia, contracted after the war but for reasons growing out of the conflict—also stand on the books of the French Treasury as unfunded obligations.

With three of her war-time borrowers—Rumania, Yugoslavia, and Greece—France has negotiated debt

---

[15] See p. 110.

funding agreements. In addition, France has made debt settlements with two countries whose obligations to her she also considers as war debts. These are Poland and Czechoslovakia, which did not become national entities until after the war, but were recognized as such by the Allied and Associated Powers during the period of hostilities. Military units, composed of the nationals of these two countries, fought in the Allied ranks, and loans to provide for the maintenance of these troops were extended by some of the Allies. Funds to provide for the repatriation of the troops and for similar purposes were also advanced after the Armistice to the two newly organized governments. So far as the French accounts are concerned, both the war and post-war advances were considered as unified transactions, and were eventually funded as war debts. Finally, France participated in the relief credits advanced to a number of countries through the International Relief Credits Committee, and her share was funded as a part of the joint agreements signed by the relief creditors and debtors.[16]

France was in no haste after the war to demand from her debtors a regularization of their war obligations. Her government did not at any time, as did the British government in 1922, announce formally any definite debt policy, although her responsible statesmen on numerous occasions made it known that France favored a complete cancellation of all war debt accounts as among the Allied and Associated Powers, while maintaining consistently a wholly different attitude on the question of the reparation obligations. It was not until January 1930 that France signed definitive funding agreements with her five war debtors, although with some of them

---

[16] These agreements are described in Section IV of this chapter.

she had carried on sporadic negotiations for some years previously.[17]

In her agreements with Rumania, Greece, and Yugoslavia, France made substantial reductions from the nominal figures of the debts as they stood on the books of the French Treasury at the time of settlement. This was done to allow for the counter-claims made against France by these three countries on various accounts growing out of the war. The net amounts arrived at for each country were made repayable in annual instalments, spread over a 61-year period in the case of Rumania, and a 37-year period in that of Greece and of Yugoslavia. For each of the countries, the schedules provided for graduated payments over initial periods, extending for 40 years in the case of Rumania and 20 years in that of the other two countries. The agreement with Poland provided for a division of the total debt into two parts. Part I was made repayable by means of 62 annual instalments, graduated over most of the period; Part II was made repayable by means of 40 annuities, graduated over the first 20 years. The agreement with Czechoslovakia made that country's debt repayable by means of 50 equal annuities.

The agreement with Rumania stipulated a 6 per cent per annum penalty on any instalments not met promptly on the due dates, and that with Yugoslavia a 5 per cent penalty. The agreements with Poland and Czechoslovakia granted to these countries postponement privileges covering any complete semi-annual instalment, for periods not exceeding two years, with interest on post-

---

[17] The final agreements between France and her war debtors were signed on the following dates: Rumania, Jan. 17, 1930; Greece and Yugoslavia, Jan. 20, 1930; Czechoslovakia, Jan. 21, 1930; and Poland, Jan. 24, 1930.

poned payments at the rate of 5 per cent per annum. The agreement with Greece contains no postponement provisions whatever.

In addition, the agreements with Rumania, Yugoslavia, Greece, and Poland contain a special clause, in accordance with which France agrees that, in the event she should obtain a modification in her favor of the terms of settlement embodied in her own debt agreements with the United States and Great Britain, she would modify accordingly the terms of her settlements with the four countries enumerated above. No such provision appears in the agreement with Czechoslovakia.

All annuities in the French debt settlements are made payable in equal half-yearly instalments,[18] although the due dates vary somewhat. The Rumanian and Yugoslav payments are due on March 1 and September 1 of each year; those of Greece and Czechoslovakia, on April 1 and October 1; and those of Poland, on April 15 and October 15. All annuities are payable in French francs, but whereas in the Yugoslav, Greek, Polish, and Czechoslovak settlements the franc is defined as having the gold content specified in the law of June 25, 1928, that is the equivalent at par of 3.92 cents, in the Rumanian agreement the franc is defined in terms of the pre-war unit, which was the equivalent of 19.29 cents. The adjustment of the debts to the changes in the gold value of the French monetary unit was one of the outstanding difficulties in the negotiations between France and her debtors. However, the deductions for counter-claims were so large and the current interest charged was made so low, that all the settle-

[18] There are some minor exceptions in the agreement with Rumania. As in the case of the war debts to Great Britain, the system of monthly instalments was adopted after the inauguration of the Young plan.

ments in reality represent the repayment of only small portions of the original advances. The adjustments are so numerous that it is extremely difficult to calculate the amount of reduction represented by the French debt settlements. It was, however, very substantial.[19]

In addition to her war debt settlements, in January 1930, France also concluded a special agreement with Poland for reimbursement of her share of the cost of the plebiscite in Upper Silesia. Annual payments under this agreement are due on April 15 of each year. In February 1930 a similar agreement was signed with Lithuania, relating to the French share of the costs of the Memel plebiscite. Finally, in February 1931 an agreement was signed with Latvia, providing for repayment to France of the costs of maintaining and transporting Latvian troops in 1918-20. This agreement calls for five annual instalments of 900,000 French francs each, payable on July 1 of each year from 1932 to 1936.[20]

III. THE ITALIAN DEBT SETTLEMENTS

As a result of the war Italy became a creditor of three countries, Rumania, Poland, and Czechoslovakia. Her advances to these countries, especially the last two, were

---

[19] For the detailed payment schedules contained in the French debt agreements, see Appendix B, pp. 458-59.

[20] For a general discussion of the French war loans, see French Ministry of Finance, *Inventaire de la situation financière de la France*, 1924, pp. 174-78; and H. G. Moulton and Cleona Lewis, *The French Debt Problem*, pp. 25-40. For the text of the agreements with Rumania, Yugoslavia, and Greece, see *Chambre des Députés, XIV Législature, Session de 1930, Annexe No. 3024 au Procès-verbal de la séance du 20 mars 1930*; of those with Poland and Czechoslovakia, *L'Europe Nouvelle*, June 28, 1930; for that with Poland regarding Upper Silesia, *Dziennik Ustaw Rzeczypospolitej Polskiej*, 1932, No. 1. The payment schedules in the agreements with Poland and Lithuania are given in Appendix B, p. 467.

made mainly after the cessation of hostilities, under circumstances similar to those under which France had extended credits to these same countries.

The debt funding agreement with Rumania was concluded in 1924, but was modified somewhat by later agreements. Under the terms of the original settlement, Rumania undertook to extinguish her obligations by means of 50 annuities, divided into five groups. Each group represented uniform annuities covering a decade, the payments for each successive decade being progressively larger. The annuities were made payable in Italian lire, in single instalments due on July 1 of each year.

However, by an agreement signed at The Hague on January 20, 1930, Italy agreed to cancel the last ten annuities provided for under the original settlement. This was done in view of the fact that the share of the German reparation payments assigned to Rumania under the agreements growing out of the Young plan appeared to be insufficient to cover that country's own payments on the war debt account. The surrender by Italy of the ten Rumanian annuities provided the basis for an acceptable adjustment.[21]

The agreement with Poland, signed in 1926, provided for the consolidation of the sums owed by Poland to Italy with accrued and current interest into a round sum, to be liquidated by means of eight semi-annual instalments. The payments were to begin on June 30, 1927 and to be completed on December 30, 1930.[22]

The agreement with Czechoslovakia, signed at the

[21] For the text of the Italo-Rumanian agreement, see *L'Europe Nouvelle*, Apr. 19, 1930. The full schedule of payments is given in Appendix B, p. 460.

[22] For the text of the agreement, see *Dziennik Ustaw Rzeczypospolitej Polskiej*, Jan. 11, 1930.

time of The Hague conference in January 1930, provided for the liquidation of that country's indebtedness to Italy by means of 37 annuities of 2.5 million gold marks each.

Finally, by means of agreements signed in January and February 1930, Italy regulated several special accounts with Poland, Lithuania, and Bulgaria. The account with Poland related to the Italian share of the costs of the Upper-Silesia plebiscite; that with Lithuania, to the costs of the Memel plebiscite; and that with Bulgaria, to the repatriation of the Bulgarian prisoners of war. The Bulgarian agreement calls for ten annual instalments of 61,000 gold lire each, payable on December 31 of each year from 1931 to 1940.[23]

IV. RELIEF AND MISCELLANEOUS DEBT ADJUSTMENTS

Relief credits were extended during the early postwar years to the following seven countries: Austria, Czechoslovakia, Esthonia, Hungary, Poland, Rumania, and Yugoslavia. Arrangements for making such credits available were made through the instrumentality of an International Relief Credits Committee, set up soon after the Armistice, and a number of countries participated in the granting of credits. In addition to the United States, Great Britain, and France, which furnished the bulk of the funds, five countries which remained neutral during the war—the Netherlands, Switzerland, Sweden, Norway, and Denmark—also became creditors on the relief account, while Italy supplied

---

[23] For the text of the agreement with Poland see *Dziennik Ustaw Rzeczypospolitej Polskiej*, 1932, No. 9, and for the schedules of Polish and Lithuanian payments, Appendix B, p. 467. For the text of the agreement with Bulgaria, see *Derjaven Vestnik*, Jan. 13, 1931.

a portion of the credits extended to Austria, and Australia made relief loans to Rumania and Yugoslavia.

The advances made by the United States for purposes of relief were, as we have already seen, assimilated with the other war and post-war loans extended by the United States Treasury, and all these obligations were funded together. The non-American relief creditors, on the other hand, handled the relief debts separately from the other obligations resulting from the war, and these debts became the subject of several collective agreements between each relief debtor and its various creditors.

In nearly all cases, the original evidence of indebtedness required under the scheme worked out by the International Relief Credits Committee was in the form of bonds maturing on January 1, 1925 and bearing interest at the rate of 6 per cent per annum. By the end of 1924, when the maturity date drew close, arrangements extending beyond that date had been concluded with respect to only two of the seven relief debtors.

In 1922, as a part of the League of Nations plan for the financial rehabilitation of Austria, the relief creditors of that country, including the United States, agreed to adjourn, for a period of 20 years, all consideration of the Austrian debts. In the same year, Hungary made an arrangement with Great Britain to extinguish her relief debt to that country by means of nine annual instalments, the last of which was to fall due in 1930.[24] Of the remaining five debtors, all, with the exception of Yugoslavia, negotiated funding agreements with their creditors in December 1924.

[24] The payments were duly met, and, as a consequence, Hungary is no longer on the list of relief debtors, except in so far as her debt agreement with the United States is concerned.

The Polish agreement, signed with the governments of Great Britain, France, the Netherlands, Switzerland, Sweden, Norway, and Denmark, provided for the repayment of the sums advanced to Poland with accrued interest to January 1, 1925 at the rate of 6 per cent, by means of 30 semi-annual instalments starting July 1, 1925 and ending January 1, 1940. Current interest during the period of repayment was stipulated at the rate of 5 per cent. The agreement covered all the relief bonds issued by Poland which matured on January 1, 1925. In addition to these bonds, a small amount of Polish relief bonds, maturing five years later, on January 1, 1930, was at the time held by Sweden. By means of a special provision in the agreement, Poland undertook to fund these bonds at their maturity on the same terms as those contained in the 1924 agreement, except that the period of repayment was to be ten years from January 1, 1930. This arrangement was duly concluded.

The Rumanian agreement was signed with the governments of Great Britain, Australia, France, Switzerland, and the three Scandinavian countries. The amount which was to be funded was made up of the sums originally advanced plus accrued interest at 6 per cent up to January 1, 1923. Rumania undertook to pay the accrued interest during the years 1923 and 1924 in cash, and to repay the funded principal, with current interest at the rate of 5 per cent, in 40 semi-annual instalments, starting July 1, 1925 and ending January 1, 1945.

The Czechoslovak agreement was signed with the governments of the same seven countries that were the creditors of Poland. It provided for the repayment by Czechoslovakia of the sums originally advanced to her, with accrued interest up to January 1, 1925 at the rate of 6 per cent, and current interest during the period of repayment at the rate of 5 per cent, in five annual installments, the last of which was to fall due on October 31, 1929. The period was made short because the amount of the debt was comparatively small.[25]

The Esthonian agreement was signed with the government of Great Britain alone, that country being Esthonia's only European relief creditor. It provided for the repayment of the Esthonian relief debt on the same terms as those contained in the agreement with Poland.

Yugoslavia did not negotiate a relief credit agreement until August 1927, when she finally signed one with her eight non-American creditors, namely, Great Britain, Australia, France, the Netherlands, Switzerland, and the three Scandinavian countries. The Yugoslav agreement provided for the repayment of the sums originally advanced to her with accrued interest at the rate of 6 per cent up to January 1, 1927. With the exception of her debt to Great Britain, Yugoslavia owed very small sums to the other creditors, and arranged to liquidate these obligations immediately by means of cash payments. The debt to Great Britain was made repayable in 30 semi-annual instalments, including current interest at the rate of 5 per cent, starting July 1, 1927 and ending January 1, 1942.

Austria decided in 1928 to negotiate a funding agreement, in spite of the fact that her debt stood adjourned under the terms of the 1922 arrangement. In accordance with this agreement, which was signed with the governments of the same seven countries that were the creditors of Poland, Austria undertook to extinguish her

---

[25] These instalments were duly met, and Czechoslovakia is no longer on the list of debtors to the European relief creditors, although still indebted on this account to the United States.

relief obligations by means of annuities, which aggregated less than the original sums advanced to her. She was granted this special concession in view of her difficult financial position. The agreement provided for two alternative schedules of payments. Schedule 1 called for 25 annuities extending from 1943 to 1967; Schedule 2, for 40 annuities, extending from 1929 to 1967. The annuities were so arranged as to have an identical present value. In her ratification of the agreement, Austria chose the second schedule, but with a proviso, accepted by the creditors, relating to possible postponements during the years 1929-42 inclusive. The period covered by these years represents the currency of the reconstruction loan floated under the auspices of the League of Nations, and under the terms of the proviso Austria was given the right, during this period, to suspend the payment of any annuity whenever the trustees for the League of Nations loan should demand such action. All annuities unpaid in this manner are to remain adjourned until January 1, 1943, but interest at the rate of 5 per cent is to accumulate on them. All such annuities, with the accrued interest, are to be paid in 25 annual instalments during the years 1943-67, with current interest at the rate of 5 per cent.

The Austrian relief debt to the United States was, it will be recalled, funded separately from the similar obligations to the other creditors, but on exactly the same terms. The relief debt to Italy was also funded separately, by means of an agreement signed on January 19, 1930, on terms similar to those granted by the other relief creditors.[26]

---

[26] In addition to this general settlement, a supplementary relief debt agreement was signed between Italy and Austria, providing for a total payment by the latter of 30 million gold francs. This agreement has not, as yet, been ratified.

All relief debt agreements provided for payments in the currencies in which the original loans were expressed, that is, generally speaking, in the currencies of the respective creditor countries. The detailed schedules of payments are given in Appendix B.[27]

A number of miscellaneous inter-governmental accounts growing out of the war had to be settled by means of negotiation. Two such accounts between Belgium and her neighbors, Luxemburg and the Netherlands, became the subjects of special agreements. Finally, an account between Greece and Canada was settled by negotiation.

The agreement between Belgium and Luxemburg related to the latter's share in the payments received by the former from Germany on the marks account. The two governments agreed that Luxemburg was to receive 3 per cent of each annuity on this account. The Belgian-Dutch settlement, signed in 1923, related to the debt owed by the government of Belgium to the Netherlands government for the expenses incurred by the latter in interning Belgian soldiers who had been forced to seek refuge on Dutch territory during the war. By the terms of the agreement, Belgium undertook to pay the amount agreed upon between the two governments, with current interest at the rate of 5 per cent in 30 equal semi-annual instalments of 2,233,032 Dutch florins each, beginning in 1923 and payable on June 30 and December 31 of each year.[28]

The Greek-Canadian account referred to a credit of

[27] See pp. 461-66. The texts of the relief agreements negotiated in 1924 are not available as published documents, but have been placed at our disposal in manuscript form. For the text of the Yugoslav agreement see *L'Europe Nouvelle*, Sept. 30, 1930, and for that of the Austrian agreement, the same, July 26, 1930.

[28] For the text of the agreement between Belgium and the Netherlands, see *Moniteur Belge*, May 1924, pp. 2586-87.

25 million Canadian dollars, extended to Greece during the war by the Canadian government to finance Greek purchases of wheat in the dominion. The actual advances under this arrangement amounted to slightly under 7.5 million dollars, and negotiations for the funding of this sum were begun in 1919. It was not, however, until December 27, 1923 that a definitive funding agreement was signed, providing for the repayment by Greece of 8 million dollars (original advances plus accrued interest) in 50 semi-annual instalments with current interest at the rate of 5 per cent per annum. The first instalment was made payable on June 30, 1924, and payments were to continue on June 30 and December 31 of each year until the end of 1948.[29]

[29] A complete schedule of payments is given in Appendix B, p. 468. For the text of the Greek-Canadian agreement see *Hellenic Government Official Gazette*, 1924, Vol. I, No. 198.

PART III

THE STORY OF THE REPARATION NEGOTIATIONS

CHAPTER VII

ORIGIN OF THE REPARATION OBLIGATIONS

While the war and relief debts had their origin in actual loans, the reparation obligations represented a bill for damages imposed by the treaties of peace upon the defeated countries. As regards Germany, Austria, and Hungary, the imposition of reparation liability rests on the acceptance by these three powers of full responsibility "for causing all the loss and damage to which the Allied and Associated governments and their nationals have been subjected as a consequence of the war imposed upon them by the aggression of Germany and her allies."[1] In the case of Bulgaria, the reparation liability is based on recognition by that country that "by joining the war of aggression which Germany and Austria-Hungary waged against the Allied and Associated Powers, she has caused to the latter losses and sacrifices of all kinds, for which she ought to make complete reparation."[2] These four countries are the only debtor nations on the reparation account.[3]

---

[1] Article 231 of the Treaty of Versailles (with Germany); Article 177 of the Treaty of St. Germain (with Austria); Article 161 of the Treaty of Trianon (with Hungary).

[2] Article 121 of the Treaty of Neuilly.

[3] The only country of the German group on which no reparation payments were imposed was Turkey. In Article 231 of the Treaty of Sèvres which was signed in 1920, Turkey recognized her liability for reparation in language similar to that contained in the Treaty of Neuilly. However, she was relieved of formal reparation payments because of the territorial losses she had sustained as a result of the war, although she did assume responsibility for a certain amount of indemnification of civilian nationals of the Allied Powers (Articles 235-36). The Treaty of Sèvres was never ratified by Turkey and was superseded in 1923 by the Treaty of Lausanne, which dealt also with the special

A set of similar payments was, however, imposed by the post-war treaty arrangements on the successor states of the Austro-Hungarian Monarchy, other than Austria and Hungary. These so-called "liberation" payments were considered in the nature of an indemnity to be paid by the national minorities of the former monarchy which had been freed as a result of the war, for the losses and damages sustained by the Allied Powers in effecting their liberation.

I. NATURE OF REPARATION CLAIMS

The nature of the damages for which reparation was to be made caused bitter controversy during the peace negotiations. Widely divergent views were expressed by the statesmen gathered in Paris as to what sort of claims could properly be made against Germany. At one extreme was the position taken by some members of the British Imperial delegation (notably Prime Minister Hughes of Australia) to the effect that Germany should be made responsible for the whole cost of the war and be compelled to reimburse the Allied and Associated Powers for every dollar they had expended in the prosecution of the war. At the other extreme was the argument presented especially by the American delegation which insisted that Germany and her allies

---

Greco-Turkish problems resulting from the occupation of Anatolia by Greece. This later treaty contains no mention of war guilt on the part of Turkey and no assumption of reparation liability by that country. Interestingly enough, however, the treaty contains an assumption by Greece of reparation liability with regard to Turkey. Article 59 reads as follows: "Greece recognizes her obligation to make reparation for the damage caused in Anatolia by the acts of the Greek army or administration which were contrary to the laws of war. On the other hand, Turkey, in consideration of the financial situation of Greece resulting from the prolongation of the war and from its consequences, finally renounces all claims for reparation against the Greek government."

could be held responsible only for repairing the damages actually done to the civilian populations of the invaded Allied countries.

The astronomical dimensions of the claims advanced in the early post-war days are evidenced by the following quotation from André Tardieu:

The figures revealed, that, if we were to insist upon the three claims—damage to property, damage to person, and war expenses—we would reach a total capital of 1,000 billion (one trillion) francs, the payment of which over a period of 50 years would represent, taking into account interest and sinking fund, more than 3,000 billion (three trillion) francs, a sum so great that it is unreal. If, faithful to this reasoning as logic demanded, we had demanded also on the ground of full and complete reparation and in accordance with full justice, payment of indirect damages, loss in operation, loss of profits, etc. . . . we should perhaps have reached some such fabulous total as 7, 8, or 10 trillions.[4]

The American argument was based on the proposition that the reparation claims should be governed by "the fourteen points contained in an address of President Wilson on January 8, 1918, which with certain qualifitions were accepted by the Allies, by the United States, and by Germany as the agreed basis of peace."[5] The fourteen points called for the evacuation and restoration of the occupied portions of the territories of France, Belgium, Rumania, Serbia, and Montenegro. The Allies accepted these provisions, although they qualified their acceptance by stating that "they understand that compensation will be made by Germany for all damage done to the civilian population of the Allies and their property by the aggression of Germany by land, by sea, and from the air."

[4] *The Truth about the Treaty*, p. 290.
[5] John Foster Dulles, in a speech before the Peace Conference Commission on Reparation on Feb. 13, 1919.

The reparation provisions finally written into the treaties of peace represented a compromise between the two points of view presented above. They made Germany and her allies responsible for the whole cost of the war, but stated that the Allied and Associated governments recognized that the resources of Germany, Austria, and Hungary, especially after taking into account their diminution as a result of the treaty arrangements, were not adequate to make complete reparation. Nevertheless, these three countries were made responsible for repairing the total damage under the following ten categories:

1. Damage to injured persons and to surviving dependents by personal injury to or death of civilians caused by acts of war, including bombardments or other attacks on land, on sea, or from the air, and all the direct consequences thereof, and of all operations of war by the two groups of belligerents wherever arising.

2. Damage caused by Germany or her allies to civilian victims of acts of cruelty, violence, or maltreatment (including injuries to life or health as a consequence of imprisonment, deportation, internment, or evacuation, of exposure at sea or of being forced to labor), wherever arising, and to the surviving dependents of such victims.

3. Damage caused by Germany or her allies in their own territory or in occupied or invaded territory to civilian victims of all acts injurious to health or capacity to work, or to honor, as well as to the surviving dependents of such victims.

4. Damage caused by any kind of maltreatment of prisoners of war.

5. As damage caused to the peoples of the Allied and Associated Powers, all pensions and compensation in the nature of pensions to naval and military victims of war (including members of the air force), whether mutilated, wounded, sick, or invalided, and to the dependents of such victims, the amount due to the Allied and Associated governments being calculated for each of them as being the capitalized cost of such pensions

and compensation, at the date of the coming into force of the present treaty on the basis of the scales in force in France at such date.

6. The cost of assistance by the governments of the Allied and Associated Powers to prisoners of war and to their families and dependents.

7. Allowances by the governments of the Allied and Associated Powers to the families and dependents of mobilized persons or persons serving with the forces, the amount due to them for each calendar year in which hostilities occurred being calculated for each government on the basis of the average scale for such payments in force in France during that year.

8. Damage caused to civilians by being forced by Germany or her allies to labor without just remuneration.

9. Damage in respect of all property wherever situated belonging to any of the Allied or Associated states or their nationals, with the exception of naval and military works or materials, which has been carried off, seized, injured, or destroyed by the acts of Germany or her allies on land, on sea, or from the air, or damage directly in consequence of hostilities or of any operations of war.

10. Damage in the form of levies, fines, and other similar exactions imposed by Germany or her allies upon the civilian population.[6]

The inclusion of pensions and separation allowances made a vast difference in the magnitude of the reparation account. It will be noted from the foregoing categories that Germany was made responsible not only for repairing the direct damage done to the civilian populations of the Allied countries, but also, in paragraphs 5, 6, and 7, for indemnifying the Allied governments for the outlays made, or to be made, by them on account

[6] Annex I to Part VIII of the Treaty of Versailles. The language of the corresponding provisions in the Treaties of St. Germain and of Trianon is exactly the same, except that in the former the word "Austria" and in the latter the word "Hungary" is substituted for the word "Germany" wherever that word occurs in the Versailles Treaty text.

of war pensions and separation allowances. As a result the reparation bill was more than doubled. The inclusion was insisted upon especially by Great Britain, because it provided the only method by which the British share in the reparation payments could have been raised to substantial proportions. It brought violent protests on the part of Germany and was strongly opposed by the United States, but in the end President Wilson yielded in the interest of other objectives of the peace negotiations.[7]

In addition to the damages enumerated above, Germany was also made responsible for assuming the whole of the foreign debt of Belgium contracted between the outbreak of the war and the date of the Armistice. On this question there was scarcely any controversy.

II. DETERMINATION OF TOTAL REPARATION LIABILITY

The total volume of German, Austrian, and Hungarian reparation payments was left undetermined in the treaties of peace. At the time of the Paris negotiations, it was felt that the evaluation of the claims for damages put forward by each individual country would be too long and too technical a process to be handled by the Peace Conference itself. It was, therefore, decided to set up, under the authority of the treaties, a Reparation Commission which was to act for the creditor governments (1) in drawing up a bill of claims against the reparation debtors and devising a schedule of pay-

[7] A brief survey of the circumstances attending the Paris discussion of this question is contained in World Peace Foundation, *Reparation*, Part I, Nov. 25, 1922. For a more extended treatment of the subject, see such works as B. M. Baruch, *The Making of the Reparation and Economic Sections of the Treaty*; H. W. V. Temperley, *A History of the Peace Conference of Paris*; and A. Tardieu, *The Truth about the Treaty*.

ments by means of which this bill would be paid; (2) in collecting from the debtors and distributing to the creditors the reparation payments made; and (3) in serving as the agency for changing, if necessary, as occasion might arise, the terms of payment—in any respect except the cancellation of any portion of the obligations once determined and agreed upon. Upon this commission, therefore, devolved the difficult task of determining the volume of reparation payments; and the treaties provided that this task was to be completed by May 1, 1921.

Pending the final determination of the reparation liability, certain interim payments were imposed upon the reparation debtors. First, the Central Powers were to make "restitution of such movable property and equipment as could be identified as having been removed from the invaded areas." Second, they were made responsible for certain payments in cash and in kind, the latter including the cession of mercantile ships and deliveries of coal and its derivatives, dyestuffs, and other chemical products, as well as of a large variety of goods and equipment necessary for the physical restoration of the invaded areas. The value of all such payments during the years 1919, 1920, and the first four months of 1921 was fixed for Germany at approximately 4,750 million dollars (20 billion gold marks); for Austria and Hungary the amounts were left to the discretion of the Reparation Commission.

The treaties provided that the total bill for damages drawn up by the Reparation Commission should include all the claims of all the creditors against all the debtors, with Germany, Austria, and Hungary assuming joint responsibility for the whole amount. After determining the total amount, the commission was to fix the amounts attributable to Austria, Hungary, and Bulgaria, subtract these, as well as the amount of Bulgaria's reparation payments fixed separately,[8] from the total, and make the remainder the direct liability of Germany. Against the amount of the debt thus assigned to each of the three principal reparation debtors was then to be credited the value of the interim payments made by it, less a deduction for the cost of the armies of occupation and certain other credits under various provisions of the treaties. The net indebtedness outstanding on May 1, 1921 was, according to the stipulations of the treaties, to be paid within 30 years from that date, although the Reparation Commission was given power to extend this period at its discretion.

In addition to the costs of the armies of occupation, certain other (supplementary) payments were imposed by the treaties of peace. These included the settlement of the pre-war debts and certain cessions of property and rights, such as military supplies delivered under the terms of the Armistice and claims of the Central Powers against each other. The handling of these accounts was also, generally speaking, placed in the hands of the Reparation Commission.[9]

The total reparation bill was finally fixed at 132 billion marks, or approximately 33 billion dollars. The procedure for the determination of this total as prescribed for the commission by the treaties of peace involved the presentation to the commission of claims by each of the creditor powers and a close scrutiny of such

[8] For the discussion of the Bulgarian aspect of the reparation problem, see pp. 148 and 246-48.

[9] For the details of all these payments and cessions, see the reparation, financial, and economic clauses of the treaties of peace.

claims by the commission, in the course of which the debtor governments would be given "a just opportunity to be heard."

The Reparation Commission set February 12, 1921 as the last date on which it would receive from the Allied Powers their official statements of claims for reparation payments. The volume of claims presented by that date amounted, at the prevailing rates of exchange, to about 53 billion dollars. All these creditors' estimates the commission submitted to the German government for acceptance or protest, and at the same time performed its own work of evaluation. Many of the claims were sharply disputed by the German representatives, and some of them were questioned by the commission itself. As the date by which the commission was bound by the treaty of peace to complete its task approached, the German government and the commission were still far from agreement. Accordingly on April 24 the German government officially declared that it could not acknowledge that "a just opportunity to be heard," in the sense of the Treaty of Versailles, had been accorded it. Nevertheless, three days later the commission announced its decision as to the total sum for which the Central Powers were to be held accountable, namely, 132 billion marks, to which was to be added the Belgian war debt, estimated at the time at approximately 4 billion marks.[10]

---

[10] Ten months before the Reparation Commission completed its evaluation "of the amount of damages for which reparation is due," the Allied Premiers, at a conference held at Boulogne, decided tentatively to demand from the reparation debtors an amount which (with current interest) would come to approximately 100 billion dollars. Nevertheless, the figure agreed upon by the commission was accepted by the creditor powers. See D. P. Myers, *The Reparation Settlement*, 1929, p. 5.

The commission's decision, together with a schedule of payments for the liquidation of the obligation to be assumed by Germany, also drawn up by the commission, was communicated to the German government on May 5, 1921 by the Supreme Council of the Allies, then sitting in London. In view of the persistent protests made by Germany, the communication was in the form of an ultimatum, refusal to accept which in the space of six days was to be followed by an occupation of the Ruhr Valley, as a form of economic sanction provided in the treaty of peace, and by the application to Germany of any military and naval sanctions which the Allies deemed necessary. In these circumstances, the German government accepted officially the terms which had been laid down. It still continued, however, unofficially to protest, as a matter of justice, against the size of the bill for damages and the nature of some of the items included in it, and to assert, as a matter of economics, its inability to meet the payments required.

The London settlement made Germany nominally responsible for the whole liability of 132 billion gold marks, but, as we shall see in the next chapter, the terms of payment called for monthly instalments sufficient to cover interest and amortization charges on only a portion of this debt. Against the remaining portion were to be credited the payments already made by Germany, as well as the payments already made and to be made by the other reparation debtors. Of the other debtors, Bulgaria's share alone was definitely fixed by that time, since the Treaty of Neuilly had provided that "Bulgaria agrees to pay and the Allied and Associated Powers agree to accept as being such reparation as Bulgaria is able to make, the sum of 2,250 million francs gold [approximately 450 million dollars.]" The share of reparation liability to be assigned to Austria and Hungary still remained undetermined. The figure of 132 billion gold marks specified in the London schedule, therefore, represented merely the theoretical maximum amount of reparation payments for which Germany, by virtue of the principle of joint responsibility on the part of all the reparation debtors, could be held liable. Germany's own actual liability was still left indefinite.

III. ORIGIN OF THE "LIBERATION" PAYMENTS

The liberation payments originated in a special agreement negotiated during the Peace Conference. This agreement, signed in Paris on September 10, 1919, contained the following provisions:

Article 1. Poland, Rumania, the Serb-Croat-Slovene State and the Czechoslovak State, as states to which territory of the former Austro-Hungarian Monarchy is transferred or states arising from the dismemberment of that monarchy, severally agree to pay, as a contribution toward the expenses of liberating the said territories, sums not exceeding in the aggregate the equivalent of 1.5 billion fr. gold, the gold franc being taken as of the weight and fineness of gold as enacted by law on January 1, 1914.

Article 2. The amount of the contribution referred to in Article 1 shall be divided between the said states on the basis of the ratio between the average for the three financial years 1911, 1912, and 1913 of the revenues of the territories acquired by them from the former Austro-Hungarian Monarchy, the revenues of the provinces of Bosnia and Herzegovina being excluded from this calculation.

The revenues forming the basis for this calculation shall be those adopted by the Reparation Commission, in accordance with Article 203, Part IX (financial clauses) of the treaty of peace with Austria, as best calculated to represent the financial capacity of the respective territories. Nevertheless, in no case shall the sum paid by the Czechoslovak State exceed the sum of 750 million francs. Should the contribution attributable to the Czechoslovak State exceed the sum of 750 million francs, the difference between that sum and the sum of 750 million francs shall be in diminution of the aggregate sum of 1.5 billion francs and shall not be attributable to the other states.

A similar agreement was signed with Italy, which had also benefited from the territorial dismemberment of the Austro-Hungarian Monarchy. By later agreements, notably one signed in Paris on March 11, 1922 by the Finance Ministers of the Allied Powers, a connection was created between these liberation payments and the reparation arrangements contained in the London schedule of payments. The details of these arrangements will be described in Chapter XI.

CHAPTER VIII

THE LONDON SCHEDULE OF PAYMENTS

The London settlement of 1921 was the first major agreement in the long and tortuous evolution of the German reparation problem. During the period preceding the acceptance by Germany of the Allied ultimatum of May 5 of that year and of the schedule of payments embodied in it, the principal question in connection with the reparation problem was the determination of the amount for which Germany should be held responsible, with little or no reference to Germany's ability to discharge the obligations which were thus to be imposed upon her. Claims, more or less fantastic in their magnitude, were being put forward by the creditor powers, and the center of the stage was held by the task of evaluating the correctness and justness of these claims.

With the evaluation completed and the total reparation liability definitely fixed, the emphasis shifted to the question of how Germany could be made to discharge these obligations. For the next two and one-half years, the reparation discussions were dominated by various attempts to enforce the terms of payment laid down in the London schedule. These attempts, as we shall presently see, broke down completely. Nevertheless, after the schedule went into effect the situation became at least much more definite than it had been before, when Germany was making large payments against a liability that had not been even remotely determined.

I. TERMS OF PAYMENT

Under the terms of the London settlement, the total amount of the reparation obligation was divided into three parts, each evidenced by a bond series. The first of these, Series A, had a face value of 12 billion gold marks; the second, Series B, of 38 billions; and the third, Series C, of 82 billions. The bonds of Series A were to be issued on July 1, 1921 and those of Series B on November 1, 1921, both series with coupons attached, calling for annual payments of 6 per cent, of which 5 per cent was to represent current interest and 1 per cent a sinking fund. The combined value of these bonds, namely 50 billion gold marks, thus became a definitely fixed obligation involving an annual payment of 3 billion gold marks. The bonds of Series C were to be delivered to the Reparation Commission on November 1, 1921, but without coupons attached and without any provision for annual payments. These bonds were to be held by the Reparation Commission until such time as the commission would determine the deductions to be made from the total amount of the reparation liability on account of payments and cessions already made and of the shares to be assigned to the other reparation debtors.[1]

The London schedule of payments did not, however, provide for a flat annual instalment of 3 billion gold marks, required to cover the interest and sinking-fund charges on the bonds of Series A and B. It called for the following annual payments:

(1) A sum of 2 billion gold marks; (2) (a) a sum equivalent to 25 per cent of the value of her [Germany's] exports

---

[1] The London schedule of payments did not state specifically that the deductions were to be credited to Series C, rather than to the other bond series. Arrangements covering this point were, however, definitely made by an agreement signed at Paris on Mar. 11, 1922 by the Finance Ministers of the Allied Powers. For the text of Article 11 of this agreement, covering the question under discussion here, see World Peace Foundation, *Reparation*, Part I, p. 19. All of the bonds were actually issued and were held by the Reparation Commission until the inauguration of the Young plan, when they were destroyed.

in each period of twelve months starting from May 1, 1921, as determined by the commission, or (b) alternatively an equivalent amount as fixed in accordance with any other index proposed by Germany and accepted by the commission; (3) a further sum equivalent to 1 per cent of the value of her exports as above defined or alternatively an equivalent amount fixed as provided in (b) above.[2]

The annual instalments under the London schedule were thus made variable, depending on the volume of Germany's export trade. It will be seen that if the value of the German exports was 4 billion marks, the total German payments would be just sufficient to cover the charges on the issued bonds.

The payments called for by the schedule were to be made partly in cash and partly in kind, and it was assumed at the beginning that the 2 billion mark instalments would be paid in cash, in four equal quarterly payments. It was provided that Germany should, within 25 days, turn over to the Reparation Commission in cash the sum of 1 billion gold marks, which was to represent the two first quarterly payments.

II. DEFAULT AND ITS CONSEQUENCES

The schedule remained formally in operation from the time it was accepted by Germany in May 1921 to the time when it was superseded on September 1, 1924 by the arrangements contained in the Dawes plan. While some payments were made during this entire period there was virtual default within 15 months. In fact, modifications had to be made from the very start.

The first change was in extending the period within which the first two quarterly cash payments might be made from 25 days to four months. After September 1,

[2] For the full text of the London schedule of payments, see H. G. Moulton and Leo Pasvolsky, *World War Debt Settlements*, pp. 160-68.

1921 there were numerous delays and postponements in the making of cash payments, and on March 21, 1922 the Reparation Commission officially reduced the cash payments for the year 1922 to 720 million marks. Even these instalments, however, could not be met, and on August 31, 1922 the commission agreed to a complete suspension of cash payments for a period of six months.

Payments in kind continued intermittently, though not in the amounts prescribed by the London schedule. These deliveries were made through the instrumentality of the Reparation Commission, except that Great Britain, in lieu of her share of such deliveries, imposed, by a reparation recovery act passed by her Parliament in 1921, a 26 per cent tax on all German exports to Great Britain.[3] Numerous attempts were made to work out methods of handling deliveries in kind. One important plan of this sort was embodied in the Wiesbaden agreement, signed on October 6, 1921 by the French and German Ministers of Reconstruction, under the terms of which Germany undertook to deliver to France, for a period of 14 years, various materials, mostly for building purposes. None of the methods devised, however, proved to be fully acceptable to all concerned or to be feasible in practice.[4]

The failure of the London schedule of payments program led to an important divergence of views between the two principal reparation creditors. This was mainly the result of the fact that the British government and the French government drew diametrically opposed conclusions from the circumstance that the payments prescribed

[3] For a discussion of this act, see pp. 274-76.

[4] For the details of these various attempts, see H. G. Moulton and C. E. McGuire, *Germany's Capacity to Pay*, Appendix H; and *Reparation*, Part II.

by the London schedule were not met. The interpretation which the former put on the situation and which became the basis of its policy, urged more and more strongly in the Reparation Commission and outside of it, was that a sufficient demonstration had been given of Germany's inability to comply with the London schedule of payments and to maintain at the same time financial and economic solvency, and that consequently a thoroughgoing revision of the schedule was imperatively needed. The French government, on the other hand, asserted its conviction that the sole reason for the failure of the London schedule program was lack of willingness on the part of Germany to carry out the obligations she had assumed.

This growing divergence of views between Great Britain and France, the latter supported more or less fully by the other two important reparation creditors, Belgium and Italy, came to a head at a conference of the Prime Ministers of the four countries held in Paris at the beginning of January 1923. At this conference the British Prime Minister proposed an entirely new plan, which involved a reduction of the total reparation liability assumed by Germany to approximately one-half of the figure fixed by the London schedule of payments, a complete suspension of all cash payments for four years, and a demand for very small payments during the four years following. However, before the British plan could even be fully discussed, the French government decided upon a new method of enforcing the London schedule.

This new method consisted of a strong military demonstration against Germany in an attempt to break down what the French held was her willful resistance to an honest fulfillment of her treaty obligations. A legal basis for such a show of force was not difficult to find. The Treaty of Versailles had reserved for the creditor powers the right of taking strong measures against Germany in the case of a "willful default" on her part. For some time prior to the January conference, Germany had been running behind the schedule in her deliveries of certain materials, notably timber and coal. The technical fact of default was, therefore, beyond any dispute, and it only remained for the Reparation Commission to declare the default a willful one, in which case the creditor powers would feel free to exercise their rights under the treaty.

The historic meeting of the Reparation Commission at which this question was decided took place on January 9, 1923. In spite of a strong argument presented by the German representatives in an attempt to prove that the default was a technical, rather than a willful one, and in spite of the fact that the British representative gave his support to the German position, the commission, by a vote of three to one, adopted a resolution declaring Germany in willful default—France, Belgium, and Italy voting for the resolution, and Great Britain voting against it. Two days later the French and Belgian troops marched into the Ruhr Valley, and the reparation problem entered upon a new phase of its evolution.[5]

[5] Before the vote on the resolution was taken by the Reparation Commission, the chairman asked the American unofficial observer, Mr. Roland W. Boyden, who was present at the meeting, whether or not he cared to make any remarks. Mr. Boyden responded with a strong plea against the action which was clearly in contemplation by the commission. His speech was received in dead silence, and upon its conclusion the chairman, without a word of comment, put the resolution before the commission to a formal vote. For the text of Mr. Boyden's speech and a graphic account of the commission's meeting by an eye witness see Guy Greer, *The Ruhr-Lorraine Industrial Problem*, Appendix B.

III. ABANDONMENT OF THE LONDON SCHEDULE

The occupation of the Ruhr led to an abandonment rather than enforcement of the London schedule of payments. From the time that the French and Belgian troops entered the great metallurgical center of Germany, all reparation payments were discontinued by the German government, and such payments were never resumed on the basis of the London schedule. During the whole period of occupation, which lasted from January 1923 to September 1924, the sole reparation receipts of the Allied Powers consisted of the reparation recovery tax levied by the British government on the German exports to Great Britain and of the revenues obtained in the Ruhr Valley by the occupation authorities.

Any direct payments by Germany during this period would scarcely have been possible in any event, because the occupation of the Ruhr, by completing the process of disorganization through which Germany had been passing since the end of the war, was largely responsible for the total economic collapse in that country. In a later chapter we shall describe the economic consequences of the various attempts to enforce the London schedule of payments. What is important to point out in this connection is that the failure to enforce that schedule, culminating with the occupation of the Ruhr, led to an abandonment of the program put forward by the London conference of May 1921, and to a fundamental change in the world attitude toward the reparation problem in general.

On the eve of the Ruhr occupation, an important pronouncement with regard to the reparation question was made in the United States. In a speech delivered before the annual meeting of the American Historical Association held at New Haven on December 29, 1922, Secretary of State Hughes suggested the appointment of a committee of experts for the purpose of studying the question of Germany's capacity to pay and of devising a financial plan under which such payments would be made. He argued that while on the one hand "we have no desire to see Germany relieved of her responsibility for the war or of her just obligations to make reparation for the injuries due to her aggression," on the other hand, "we do not wish to see a prostrate Germany," since "there can be no economic recuperation in Europe unless Germany recuperates." After reciting the repeated failures on the part of European statesmen to agree on a solution of the reparation problem, Secretary Hughes said:

There ought to be a way for statesmen to agree upon what Germany can pay, for no matter what claims may be made against her that is the limit of satisfaction. . . . If statesmen cannot agree, and exigencies of public opinion make their course difficult, then there should be called to their aid those who can point the way to a solution. Why should they not invite men of the highest authority in finance in their respective countries —men of such prestige, experience and honor that their agreement upon the amount to be paid, and upon a financial plan for working out the payments, would be accepted throughout the world as the most authoritative expression obtainable? Governments need not bind themselves in advance to accept the recommendations, but they can at least make possible such an inquiry with their approval and free the men who may represent their country in such a commission from any responsibility to foreign offices and from any duty to obey political instructions. In other words, they may invite an answer to this difficult and pressing question from men of such standing and in such circumstances of freedom as will insure a reply prompted only by knowledge and conscience. I have no doubt that distinguished Americans would be willing to serve in such a commission. If governments saw fit to reject the recommendation upon which such a body agreed, they would be free to do so, but they would have the advantage of impartial advice and of an enlightened public opinion. Peoples would be informed, the question would be rescued from assertion and counter-assertion, and the problem put upon its way to solution.

Secretary Hughes's suggestion was very well received in Great Britain and Germany, but met with little favor in France. It was not until the second half of 1923, when the disastrous consequences of attempting to collect reparation payments by force of arms became all too apparent, that the French government began to lend a receptive ear to proposals for a possible course of action along the lines suggested by the American Secretary of State. Such proposals came from a number of quarters: the idea was urged by the German and British governments, by influential American interests, and by groups in neutral countries, notably Holland. Finally, by the autumn of 1923, the French government decided to withhold its consent no longer, and the first steps were taken toward the carrying out of the idea.

Following an exchange of correspondence between Lord Curzon, the British foreign secretary, and Secretary Hughes, as to American participation in an attempt to reconsider the reparation problem along the lines suggested in the New Haven speech, an agreement was reached between Great Britain and France, under the terms of which the Reparation Commission was to proceed to the appointment of committees of experts for the purpose of inquiring into the whole reparation situation.[6] On November 30 the Reparation Commission announced the appointment of two such committees.

[6] For the text of the Hughes speech and of the Curzon-Hughes correspondence, see Moulton and Pasvolsky, *World War Debt Settlements*, pp. 168-81.

By this time financial and economic chaos existed in Germany. The currency system had become utterly demoralized; the government budget was hopelessly unbalanced; and the whole economic life of the country was almost at a standstill. There was a precipitous "flight from the mark." Private citizens in Germany sought to convert whatever liquid resources they possessed into stable foreign currencies, thus adding to the general economic disorganization of their country. Hence the first of the two committees of experts was instructed to find the means of restoring in Germany a stable currency and a sound budgetary system, while the second committee was assigned the task of determining the extent of German assets abroad and devising means for repatriating the funds that had left the country.

CHAPTER IX

AGREEMENTS BASED ON THE DAWES PLAN

With the decision of the creditor powers to seek the aid of technical experts, the reparation problem entered upon an entirely new phase. The issue was shifted from what Germany *should* pay or could be *forced* to pay, to how much Germany *could* pay and what should be done to *enable* her to make such payments. While merely provisional answers were obtained to these questions, the reports of the committees of experts served as the basis for a series of agreements signed in 1924 and 1925 under what came to be known as the "Dawes plan."

Five nations were represented on the committees of experts: France, Great Britain, Italy, Belgium, and the United States. The committees began their sessions on January 14, 1924 and completed their work on April 9 of that year, when they submitted their findings to the Reparation Commission. The chairman of the first committee was Charles G. Dawes of the United States, and, of the second committee, Reginald McKenna of Great Britain. The reforms suggested were shortly accepted by the creditor governments and the plan became operative on September 1, 1924.[1]

I. SIZE AND CHARACTER OF THE DAWES ANNUITIES

The Dawes plan substituted inclusive annuities for a large variety of payments. It also called for substantially smaller annual instalments than those required by the London schedule. It will be recalled that under the arrangements prevailing prior to the occupation of the

[1] For the full text of the two reports and an appraisal of the findings of the two committees see H. G. Moulton, *The Reparation Plan*, 1924.

Ruhr, Germany was held responsible for annual payments amounting to 2 billion marks and an amount equivalent to 26 per cent of her exports, as well as for additional sums required to cover the cost of the armies of occupation, of mixed claims awards, and so on. Under the Dawes plan all of these payments, with two unimportant exceptions, were consolidated into single annuities. Even the interest and amortization charges on an international loan of 200 million dollars extended to the German government under the Dawes plan were included in the annuity.

The Dawes Committee, after a careful study of the financial and economic position of Germany, came to the conclusion that, once currency and fiscal stability in that country was restored and the economic life of the nation properly reorganized, the German government should be able to meet a standard annuity of 2.5 billion marks. The plan provided, however, that this standard annuity was not to be demanded until the fifth year of the operation of the new reparation régime. The payments were to begin with the sum of 1 billion marks during the first year and then, as conditions improved, rise gradually during the next three years in the following progression:

	Gold Marks
First year	1,000,000,000
Second year	1,220,000,000
Third year	1,500,000,000[2]
Fourth year	1,750,000,000
Fifth year	2,500,000,000

Under the provisions of the Dawes plan specific revenues were assigned to the service of the reparation debt.

[2] The plan originally provided for 1.2 billion marks in this year. There were also certain supplemental payments, which were subsequently fixed at 300 million marks and added to the third annuity.

The funds required were to be derived from the following four sources: (1) interest and amortization charges on German railway bonds; (2) interest and amortization charges on German industrial debentures; (3) the transport tax; and (4) the budget proper, out of which the receipts from customs duties, the alcohol monopoly, and the taxes on tobacco, beer, and sugar were designated as the specific sources of the budgetary contribution.

Under the scheme worked out by the Dawes committee, the German railways were to be reorganized as a joint stock company, capitalized for 26 billion gold marks. Of this, 11 billions was to be represented by first mortgage bonds, 2 billions by preferred stock, and 13 billions by common stock. The first mortgage bonds, bearing 5 per cent interest and a 1 per cent sinking-fund charge per annum, were to be turned over to a trustee appointed by the Reparation Commission.

Of the preferred stock of 2 billions, one-fourth was to be the property of the German government, and three-fourths the property of the company. These shares were to be sold under such conditions that within two years the German government would be able to dispose of the whole 500 millions allotted to it. In the second year, 250 million gold marks derived by the government from the sale of these shares was to go for reparation purposes, the remaining 250 millions being a compensation to the German government for the loss of the transport tax. The common shares were to be owned by the German government and to be kept or sold as the government preferred.

In addition to the railroad bonds, Germany was also required to create 5 billion gold marks of first mortgage industrial bonds, which were to be turned over to a trus-

tee acting for the Reparation Commission and were to
bear interest at the rate of 5 per cent and a sinking-fund
charge of 1 per cent.[3]

COMPOSITION OF THE DAWES ANNUITIES

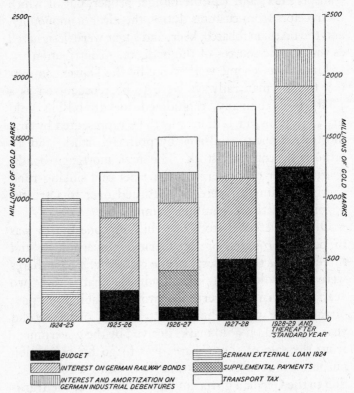

The amounts to be yielded by each of these sources

[3] The seizure of the first mortgage bonds of the railroads for reparation purposes was justified on the ground that the fall in the value of
the mark had practically wiped out the existing railway debt and that
it was only fair that the railroads should assume a mortgage debt for
the benefit of the Allies. Similarly, the justification of the imposition
of special contributions on the industries of Germany was that they had
greatly benefited as a result of currency depreciation.

of revenue during the first five years of the Dawes plan are shown in the chart on page 164.

It will be seen that during the first two years no contributions at all were required from the budget proper, and that four-fifths of the total annuity was to come from the proceeds of the international loan provided for under the plan. Not until the fifth year was the direct budget contribution to equal the amounts derived from the railroads and industries.[4]

II. SAFEGUARDS UNDER THE DAWES PLAN

The Dawes plan sought to ensure the maintenance of financial stability in Germany. The most important device for this purpose was the system of so-called "transfer protection" designed to safeguard the German exchange. The size of the annuities was also made dependent to some extent upon such broad indexes as the general economic development of Germany and the level of commodity prices.

The principle that the making of reparation payments involves two separate and distinct problems was recognized and incorporated as an integral part of the plan. The economics of this problem were discussed in Chapter II. It will be recalled that the making of reparation payments, just as the discharging of any inter-governmental debt obligation, requires first the collection in domestic currency of the amounts to be paid, and second the transfer of these sums abroad, through a process of conversion into forms of payment acceptable to the cred-

---

[4] It is interesting to note that in an offer made to the Allies on May 2 and June 7, 1923 the German government proposed that the funds required for the reparation payments should be derived from the hypothecation of the German railroads, industries, and taxes on luxuries, tobacco, beer, wine, and sugar. Germany offered, however, only 1.2 billion marks to be derived annually from these sources.

itors.[5] Under the Dawes plan, the first part of the process was made the direct responsibility of Germany, while the second part became a joint responsibility of Germany and her creditors.[6]

The Reparation Commission created a new organization, known as the Transfer Committee, to act as an intermediary between the commission, that is the creditors, and the German government. The Transfer Committee, which was to consist of six members, including an executive officer known as the Agent General for Reparation Payments,[7] was to receive, from the agencies responsible for the raising within the country of the funds needed to cover the prescribed annuities, their respective shares in the form of German marks.[8] These sums were to be deposited at the Reichsbank to the credit of the Agent General, and with the effecting of such deposit the direct responsibility of the German government was to end. The transfer of these sums abroad was to constitute the task of the Transfer Committee, the German government un-

[5] This principle was discussed at length in H. G. Moulton and C. E. McGuire, *Germany's Capacity to Pay*, published in June 1923.

[6] The device of transfer protection, the authorship of which belongs mainly to Sir Arthur Salter, director of the Economic and Financial Section of the League of Nations Secretariat, was first employed in connection with the Hungarian reparation payments and was embodied in the League Finance Committee's report on the Hungarian reconstruction scheme, presented to the League Council on Dec. 20, 1923. See p. 239.

[7] In addition to the Agent General, the committee was to consist of one national from each of the following countries: France, Great Britain, Italy, Belgium, and the United States. All members of the committee were to be appointed by the Reparation Commission.

[8] A foreign control officer was to be assigned to each of these agencies. Thus the Dawes plan provided for the appointment by the Reparation Commission of a commissioner for the German railways, a commissioner of controlled revenues, a trustee for the German railway bonds, a trustee for the German industrial debentures, and in addition a commissioner of the Reichsbank. These control officers were given the task of supervising the agencies to which they were assigned.

dertaking to facilitate the operation as much as possible.

The duty of the Transfer Committee consisted in providing out of the funds deposited to the credit of the Agent General the sums necessary for meeting such current expenditures in Germany as the maintenance of the armies of occupation, of international commissions, and of control officials administering the process of reparation payments, and in utilizing the remainder of each annuity for payments required by deliveries in kind and for the purchase of foreign bills of exchange to be turned over to the creditor powers. Such payments and purchases were to be effected, however, only "to the extent to which, in the judgment of the committee, the foreign exchange market will permit, without threatening the stability of the German currency." Should such a threat appear, the committee was authorized to suspend the transfer in whole or in part.

The suspension of payments was not, however, to be accompanied by a cessation of payments made within Germany. Such payments were to continue as before, and the committee was authorized to invest the accumulating funds within Germany. Only after the accumulation had reached a total of 5 billion marks was the committee authorized to suspend any of the internal payments, limiting such payments to sums that could be currently utilized for payments within Germany or for transfer abroad. The committee was given the power "to suspend accumulation before reaching 5 billion gold marks, if two-thirds of its members are of the opinion that such accumulation is a menace to the fiscal or economic situation in Germany or to the interest of the creditor countries." It was, however, also authorized to waive, by a similar majority, the limit of accumulation "in the event of concerted financial manœuvers either by the government or by any group [in Germany] for the purpose of preventing . . . transfers."

The protection accorded the German budget was less complete. The suspension of accumulation just referred to was an indirect safeguard. A limited amount of direct protection was also provided during the third and fourth years of the new reparation régime, when the budgetary contributions to the annuities could be diminished if the yield of the revenues assigned to the reparation debt fell below a specified figure.[9] Finally, the amounts might be reduced in the event of a pronounced fall in commodity prices.

It was stipulated in the plan that "the German government and the Reparation Commission each have the right in any future year, in case of a claim that the general purchasing power of gold as compared with 1928 had altered by not less than 10 per cent, to ask for a revision on the sole and single ground of such altered gold value," and that "after revision, the altered basis should stand for each succeeding year until a claim be made by either party that there has again been a change, since the year to which the alteration applied, of not less than 10 per cent." Under this provision, in the event of a fall in commodity prices the standard annuity which would normally be considered a minimum might be reduced. Similarly, this minimum might be increased in the event of a rise in prices. Disputes arising in connection with the application of the price index were to be submitted to arbitration by the League of Nations.

The standard annuity of 2.5 billion marks might also be increased by the application of an "index of prosper-

[9] This provision, however, worked both ways, since the budgetary contribution could also be increased if the yield of the assigned revenues rose above the specified figure.

ity."[10] This index was not to be applied during the first five years of the new reparation régime, and was to affect only the budgetary contribution during the next five years. Not until the eleventh year was the index to be applied to the entire annuity. Unlike the price index, the prosperity index was to be applicable only in one direction. If prosperity declined, Germany was nevertheless obliged to pay the full standard annuity—though she was to be given credit for the fact that prosperity had declined when an increase of prosperity subsequently occurred. Disputes arising in connection with the prosperity index were subject to arbitration by the Finance Section of the League of Nations.

The Dawes plan thus introduced more flexibility than was afforded under the London settlement. The new plan permitted reductions in payments, or even a complete suspension, while at the same time making possible an increase based upon a broad index of the nation's general economic condition. The London schedule, on the other hand, permitted variations in the annual payments in the light of changes in the volume of commodity exports alone.

III. POLITICAL ADJUSTMENTS

At the London conference in August 1924, at which the plan was officially accepted by the interested powers,

[10] This index was to be computed on the basis of the following statistics: (a) The total of German imports and exports taken together; (b) the total of budget receipts and expenditures taken together, including those of the States of Prussia, Saxony, and Bavaria (after deducting from both sides the amount of the peace treaty payments included in the year); (c) railroad traffic as measured by the statistics of the weight carried; (d) the total money value of the consumption of sugar, tobacco, beer, and alcohol, within Germany (measured by the prices actually paid by the consumer); (e) the total population of Germany (computed from the last available census data, vital statistics, and emigration records); (f) the consumption of coal (and lignite reduced to coal equivalent) per capita.

certain necessary political adjustments were also made. There were two important issues which had not been referred to the committees of experts but which were vital to the success of the plan. The first related to political guarantees and penalties for ensuring the execution of the plan, and the second to the still continuing occupation of the Ruhr by the Franco-Belgian troops.

Agreements were signed by the German government and the governments of the creditor powers providing for the setting up of arbitral machinery for the purpose of composing disputes. These related not only to important details in the inauguration of the new reparation régime, but also to the adjustment of disputes that might arise in connection with the application of the plan. In accordance with these agreements an arbitral tribunal was to be set up consisting of "three independent and impartial arbitrators," one of whom, acting as chairman, was to be a citizen of the United States.

The sanctions provided for under the Treaty of Versailles, whereby the Allied creditors might resort to punitive measures in the event of default, were retained in full. But, inasmuch as an international loan was to be floated, it was necessary to provide for the protection of the interests of foreign lenders in the event that sanctions should be in the future applied against Germany. Such creditors were accorded special protection and priority.

It was also agreed at the London conference that the fiscal and economic unity of Germany should be restored —which meant that the Ruhr should be evacuated, and that the administration of the occupied territory should revert to Germany.[11] While the Ruhr question, at the

[11] For the text of the final protocol of the London conference and of the various agreements signed there, see H. G. Moulton and Leo Pasvolsky, *World War Debt Settlements*, pp. 181-210.

insistence of the occupying powers, was formally excluded from the agenda of the London conference, direct negotiations on the subject were conducted during the conference between the German Chancellor and the Premiers of France and Belgium. These negotiations resulted in an announcement by the French and Belgian governments that they would begin the evacuation "on the morrow of the final signature" of the London agreements.

IV. DISTRIBUTION OF THE DAWES ANNUITIES

The Dawes Committee was not concerned with the distribution of reparation receipts among the creditor countries. The London conference of August 1924 decided that the problem was too technical and too involved for immediate adjustment, and accordingly it was agreed to call an official financial conference to deal with the problem. A special agreement covering the distribution of the annuities was finally signed at Paris on January 14, 1925.

Prior to the establishment of the new reparation régime definite arrangements existed only for the distribution of the major portion of the reparation payments proper. This arrangement was made at the Spa conference, held in July 1920, when the governments of France, Great Britain, Italy, Belgium, Japan, and Portugal—the only ones of the creditors represented—agreed as follows:

Sums received from Germany under the head of reparation shall be divided in the following proportions:

	Per Cent		Per Cent
France	52.00	Belgium	8.00
British Empire	22.00	Japan	0.75
Italy	10.00	Portugal	0.75

Six and one-half per cent shall be reserved for Greece, Rumania, and Serb-Croat-Slovene State, and for the other powers entitled to reparation which are not signatories of this agreement.[12]

The question of the distribution of the reserved 6.5 per cent was never definitely settled, some of the powers concerned, notably Rumania, refusing to accept the shares assigned to them by later agreements. Thus only the shares in the reparation payments proper assigned to the six signatories of the Spa protocol remained definitely fixed. The distribution of all the other payments made by Germany under the treaty of peace was made the subject of periodic determination by the representatives of the creditor powers.

The Dawes plan, by consolidating all payments to be made by Germany into inclusive annuities, raised two questions of distribution: the establishment of priorities as between the various kinds of payments, and the allocation of each group among the various creditors. Both of these questions were settled at the Paris conference, and the arrangements arrived at were embodied in an agreement signed there. In addition to allocating the Dawes annuities, the Paris agreement provided for the distribution of the amounts collected from Germany during the period of the Ruhr occupation.

Under the terms of the new agreement, the following priorities were established: (1) interest and sinking-fund charges on the 1924 external loan; (2) cost of the Reparation Commission and of the organization for the administration of the Dawes plan; (3) cost of the Inter-Allied Rhineland High Commission; (4) cost of the Military Commission of Control; (5) French and British ar-

---

[12] Article 1 of the Spa protocol. For the text of the protocol see Moulton and Pasvolsky, *World War Debt Settlements*, pp. 147-60.

rears on account of the cost of the armies of occupation prior to May 1, 1921; (6) cost of the United States army of occupation; and (7) cost of the Belgian, British, and French armies of occupation.

Next in the order of priority came the payments on the Belgian war debt, constituting 5 per cent of the amount remaining after the deduction of the charges enumerated above, and restitution payments, constituting 1 per cent (in later years somewhat more than 1 per cent) of the same amount. These were followed by payments to the United States on the mixed claims account, amounting either to 2.25 per cent of the amount remaining after the deduction of all the preceding priorities or to a round sum of 45 million marks, whichever happened to be the smaller. The net amount finally left over—for the standard annuity of 2.5 billion marks equal to approximately four-fifths of the total—was to be considered as reparation proper and made subject to distribution in accordance with the Spa percentages.

The Paris agreement, however, modified several of these percentages. The Belgian share was to continue as 8 per cent only during the first and a part of the second Dawes years; thereafter it was to be reduced to 4.5 per cent, this being the method of liquidating a previous priority arrangement. The 3.5 per cent thus released was to be divided between France and the British Empire in the ratio of 52/74 to the former and 22/74 to the latter. The Greek share was definitely fixed at 0.4 per cent, and the Rumanian share was increased from 1 to 1.1 per cent. As a result of these modifications, the Spa percentages as they were applied under the Dawes plan, starting with the end of the second Dawes year, were as follows:

	Per Cent		Per Cent
France	54.46	Rumania	1.10
British Empire[13]	23.04	Japan	0.75
Italy	10.00	Portugal	0.75
Yugoslavia	5.00	Greece	0.40
Belgium	4.50	Total	100.00

Thus the share going to France and Great Britain was slightly increased and that to Belgium was decreased. Allocations to Rumania, Yugoslavia, and Greece were for the first time definitely settled.

V. TEMPORARY CHARACTER OF THE DAWES PLAN

Following the announcement of the Dawes plan, it was widely assumed that the expert committees had found a permanent solution to the reparation problem. A careful reading of the report of the experts, however, indicates that the framers of the plan clearly recognized its provisional character. It was stated in the report that the plan "did not, as it properly could not, attempt a solution of the whole reparation problem." All that the ex-

---

[13] The share of the British Empire was allocated within the Empire in the following manner:

	Per Cent of the British Share	Per Cent of The Total
Great Britain	86.85	20.01024
Canada	4.35	1.00224
Australia	4.35	1.00224
New Zealand	1.75	0.40320
Ireland	1.20	0.27648
South Africa	0.60	0.13824
Newfoundland	0.10	0.02304
Crown colonies	0.80	0.18432
	100.00	23.04000

See World Peace Foundation, *Reparation*, Part VI, p. 305. For the text of the Paris agreement and a discussion of the negotiations connected with it, see the same publication, pp. 265-302.

perts claimed for the plan was that it constituted "a settlement extending in its application for a sufficient time to restore confidence," and was "so framed as to facilitate a final and comprehensive agreement as to all the problems of reparation and connected questions as soon as circumstances make this possible." While they set down definite figures as to Germany's ability to raise revenue in her own currency, they did not even "speculate on the amount which can annually be paid in foreign currency or on Germany's capacity to make a total payment."

The plan, moreover, did not extend to all phases of the problem. For example, the vital question as to the total amount of reparation liability was excluded both from the terms of reference of the committee of experts and from the agenda of the London conference. Legally, Germany was thus still bound by the provisions of the London schedule of 1921, and the Reparation Commission continued to hold the bonds issued to it in connection with the 1921 settlement. Yet even the standard Dawes annuity of 2.5 billion marks, after the deduction of the various payments for which priority had been established by the arrangements regarding the distribution of the sums collected, was less than the amount required to meet the 5 per cent interest charge on the bonds of Series A and B. Under these circumstances, with the accumulation of unpaid interest, the longer Germany met the standard annuity the larger would have been the total amount of her reparation debt. Difficulties in the transfer of the whole standard annuity would have served to make the total indebtedness grow still faster.

Another question connected with the general problem of the total indebtedness was the determination of the sums paid by Germany prior to the inauguration of the Dawes plan. The estimates drawn up by the German government and by the Reparation Commission differed widely from each other. But no provision was made either in the Dawes plan or in the agreements based thereon for a final reconciliation of these differences. Here again the question was left completely in abeyance.[14]

It was thus inevitable that the reparation problem would have to be considered anew at some future date. The only question was as to when sufficient experience would have been gained under the plan to test Germany's ultimate capacity to pay and when the political situation would be favorable for a reconsideration of unsettled issues. Several factors, as we shall see, combined to make the year 1928 seem a propitious time for inaugurating negotiations looking toward a "final" settlement. In order to understand the forces responsible for the evolution of the Young plan, which represented such a settlement, it will be necessary to review very briefly the trend of opinion during the period that the Dawes plan was in operation.

In his report for the year 1925-26,[15] the Agent General for Reparation Payments,[16] after quoting the Dawes

[14] For a discussion of these estimates see Chap. XII.

[15] Nov. 30, 1926, pp. 106-07.

[16] The office of agent general was held at the beginning by Mr. Owen D. Young, who, however, soon relinquished it to his successor, Mr. S. Parker Gilbert, the latter holding it until the end of the reparation régime instituted under the Dawes plan. Throughout his administration, Mr. Gilbert issued two reports a year: an interim report, published in May or June and covering the first nine months of each Dawes year (September 1 to August 31), and an annual report, published in November or December and covering the whole year. The only exception to this rule was the final report, which was not published until May 1930, and which covered the fifth Dawes year and the transitional period devoted to the institution of the Young plan.

Committee's description of its plan as an instrument facilitating "a final and comprehensive agreement," said:

Manifestly, the time for this has not yet come. The experience thus far available is still too limited, and it must grow and ripen before it will be possible to form the necessary judgments on the underlying questions involved.

In his next annual report,[17] reviewing the experience under the Dawes plan during the first three years of its operation, the Agent General said:

. . . We are still in the testing period, and further experience is needed before it is possible to form the necessary judgments. But confidence in a general sense is already restored. . . . And as time goes on, and practical experience accumulates, it becomes always clearer that neither the reparation problem, nor the other problems depending upon it, will be finally solved until Germany has been given a definite task to perform on her own responsibility, without foreign supervision and without transfer protection.

Less than a year later, in his fourth interim report,[18] the Agent General expressed his conclusions on this point in the following manner:

I believe . . . that it will be in the best interests of the creditor powers and of Germany alike to reach a final settlement by mutual agreement "as soon," to use the concluding words of the experts, "as circumstances make this possible."

This extremely rapid evolution of the view that the time was practically ripe for a final settlement of the reparation problem clearly could not have been due to any convincing demonstration as to Germany's capacity to pay. In this respect the situation was no different in June 1928 than it had been in December 1927. It is true that

---

[17] Dec. 10, 1927, p. 172.
[18] June 7, 1928, p. 108.

all through this period the instalments prescribed in the Dawes plan were duly met, but as we shall see in a later part of this discussion, the German payments were being made possible by foreign loans and there had been no experience as to what Germany could pay out of her own resources. The desire to proceed with a final settlement at this early date is attributable to a number of considerations which had very little to do with any demonstration of Germany's paying capacity.

The fact that no serious difficulties had been encountered in making the payments stipulated had led to a widespread view, shared by the reparation officials and even by some leading Germans as well, that the economic difficulties which had been anticipated, particularly in connection with the transfer problem, had been grossly exaggerated, and that there was little foundation for any pessimism as regards Germany's long-run paying capacity. Subsequent events have clearly demonstrated that it was this optimism which was without real foundation. It none the less had a potent effect upon the decisions as to policy which were in the making at that time.

The Agent General, the chief administrator of the Dawes plan, took the lead in urging at this juncture two far-reaching modifications of the existing system: (1) the fixing of the total reparation debt; and (2) the abolition of the controls on the part of the creditors over German economic activities—particularly over the foreign exchange as provided in the transfer safeguard provisions of the plan. It was the view of the Agent General and his advisers not only that the transfer system was unnecessary but that in practice it was tending to lull German borrowers and foreign lenders alike into a false sense of security which led to an over-rapid accumulation of for-

eign indebtedness, especially on the part of German governmental agencies, federal and local. As one of the
Agent General's advisers has put the contention:

> . . . the conditions under which the Dawes plan functioned
> were such as to remove two important checks which would
> otherwise have tended to correct a policy of over-spending and
> over-borrowing. . . . In the first place, Germany, being with-
> out knowledge of the total amount of her reparation debt, did
> not possess the normal incentive to conserve her finances against
> the ultimate extinguishment of that debt. In the second place,
> the factor of transfer protection tended to create a vague feel-
> ing of safety in the minds of both borrowers and lenders and
> so encouraged the too free use of credit.[19]

Whatever the merit of these contentions—and we are
not here interested in appraising their validity but
merely in setting forth the considerations which were in
the minds of those who were taking the lead in procuring
a final reparation settlement—the view that the time was
ripe for a new reparation settlement was also gaining
ground among some of the creditor nations, especially
France. One of the central ideas in the French attitude
toward the reparation problem had, for some time, been
the desire to "commercialize" the reparation obligations.
This meant a conversion of inter-governmental into
private debts by the issue of special German bonds which
were to be sold to private investors all over the world.
The proceeds of the bond issues would be used for
liquidating the obligations of the German government
to the governments of the reparation creditor countries,
private investors being substituted for the Allied governments as the creditors of the German government. Such

[19] Mr. Shepard Morgan in an address on "Conditions Precedent to
the Settlement," before the Academy of Political Science, Nov. 14,
1930.

a process appeared to have the advantage of removing the reparation problem from the sphere of political discussion; and in addition it would yield to the treasuries of creditor countries much larger immediate resources than would be provided by annual instalments.

Germany, on the other hand, opposed commercialization precisely on the ground that so long as the debt remained inter-governmental, or political, in character, there was always a possibility of adjustment through negotiation. Once commercialized, it would become an obligation much more difficult to adjust, since a default on a debt owed by the German government to private investors would constitute a much more serious blow to German credit than the inauguration of negotiations for the adjustment of an inter-governmental debt.

Technically, a commercialization program could have been carried out by force. The German government could have been compelled to issue the necessary bonds, and machinery could have been devised for offering these bonds in the markets of the world. But, apart from the economic factors involved, the experience of attempting to enforce the London schedule of payments had shown clearly the futility of any program not based on full consent by Germany. Unless such consent were forthcoming it is inconceivable that the reparation bonds would have been purchased by private investors anywhere. However, France had in her hands a weapon which she could use for bargaining purposes in obtaining Germany's agreement to a commercialization program. This was the issue presented by the occupation of the Rhineland, which finally proved to be the key to a reconsideration of the whole reparation question in the sense desired by France.

The Treaty of Versailles provided, in Articles 428-29, that, as a guarantee for the execution of the treaty, a portion of German territory situated to the west of the Rhine was to be occupied by the troops of the Allied and Associated Powers for a period of 15 years from the coming into force of the treaty. The occupied territory was divided into three zones, which were to be evacuated successively at five-year intervals, if the conditions of the treaty were "faithfully carried out by Germany." Article 430 stipulated further that "in case either during the occupation or after the expiration of the 15 years referred to above the Reparation Commission finds that Germany refuses to observe the whole or part of her obligations under the present treaty with regard to reparation, the whole or part of the areas specified in Article 429 will be reoccupied immediately by the Allied and Associated forces." On the other hand, Article 431 provided that "if before the expiration of the period of 15 years Germany complies with all the undertakings resulting from the present treaty, the occupying forces will be withdrawn immediately."

The treaty having gone into effect on January 10, 1920, the date for the evacuation of the first zone was January 10, 1925, and the zone was actually clear of foreign troops by February 26, 1926. The evacuation of the second zone was not due normally until January 10, 1930, and of the third zone, until January 10, 1935. But with the putting into operation of the Dawes plan and the completion of German disarmament as prescribed by the treaty, a feeling developed in Germany that the provisions of the Treaty of Versailles, for the execution of which the Rhineland occupation was to serve as a guarantee, had been faithfully carried out. The signing of the

Locarno treaties and the admission of Germany into the League of Nations were pointed out as proofs of this. The Germans felt more and more, therefore, that they had both a moral and a legal right to demand, on the basis of Article 431 of the treaty, an immediate evacuation of the still occupied Rhineland zones.

The French refused to concede to Germany the right she claimed, for to have done so might have precipitated difficulties with respect to interpretation of some of the provisions of the peace treaty. They were, however, willing to come to an agreement. On September 17, 1926, the Foreign Ministers of France and Germany, M. Briand and Dr. Stresemann, met at luncheon in the small French village of Thoiry, near Geneva, and discussed the matter. In the course of the discussion, M. Briand proposed that if Germany would give up her claim to an immediate evacuation of the Rhineland *as her right* and would agree to a commercialization of a substantial portion of the reparation debt, France would be inclined to favor complete evacuation at an early date.[20]

The Thoiry proposal was not acceptable to the Germans, because in their estimation it involved the payment of an economic price for something to which Germany considered herself already entitled. Moreover, the proposal could not in any event have been carried out, because a commercialization of any portion of the reparation liability was not feasible except as a part of a new

[20] Hjalmar Schacht, *The End of Reparations*, 1931, pp. 45-46. It is interesting to note that although no decisions were made at the Thoiry luncheon, the meeting itself took place under conditions of utmost cordiality. According to a story current at the time, when the luncheon was over and the bill was brought to the table, a friendly discussion arose as to who should pay. Finally, M. Briand took the bill, saying to his German colleague, "Let me do this; you still have reparation payments to make."

reparation settlement, involving the determination of the total reparation debt in an amount that would be acceptable to Germany. The French realized fully this phase of the problem, and when the Agent General began to stress the need of a definitive settlement, his proposals fell on receptive ears, so far as the French government was concerned.[21]

The attitude of Germany on the question of a definitive settlement was somewhat divided. On the one hand, some German leaders were in favor of such a settlement, first, because it would fix definite sums and a definite period during which payments would have to be made, and, second, because there was good reason for believing that it would bring immediate relief by establishing annual instalments which would be considerably smaller than the standard Dawes annuity. Moreover, a definitive settlement was bound to bring with it the withdrawal of foreign control, which was costly and was becoming increasingly irksome to the German people. Finally, in some German quarters it was felt that the negotiations for a new settlement should begin before the first "standard year" arrived lest the payment of 2.5 billion marks for even one year might render it more difficult to obtain the creditors' consent to smaller annual instalments in the future.

On the other hand, it was a foregone conclusion that a definitive settlement would involve the disappearance of

---

[21] One of the specific arguments urged by Mr. Gilbert in favor of a definitive settlement was that if Germany continued to accumulate an ever growing foreign debt the chances of floating reparation bonds would be greatly diminished. He developed this idea in a report to the Reparation Commission dated Feb. 24, 1928. Although this report has not been made public, it was referred to by M. Charles Dupont in his report to the French Senate on the Young plan. See Schacht, *The End of Reparations*, p. 43.

the transfer protection provisions of the Dawes plan, throwing upon Germany the whole responsibility for meeting the reparation payments. Some German leaders felt that, in spite of the immediate advantages offered by a definitive settlement, in the long run it was better to wait until there had been some real evidence as to Germany's capacity to pay. With all these differences of view, however, the weight of German opinion appeared to be in favor of a new settlement.

The inauguration of official negotiations leading to a new settlement was delayed by the failure of the French and the Germans to agree on the scope of the problems to be discussed. The French wanted the reparation problem and the Rhineland occupation question to be linked together, while the Germans insisted that these issues be treated separately and independently.

The situation called for a mediator, and Great Britain, the second largest creditor of Germany, seemed to be logically indicated for the role, especially since on several previous occasions the British government had played precisely such a part. Even at this date it is not clear what the attitude of the British government to the whole problem was at the time. But it seems certain that in 1928 the British government, occupied with difficult domestic problems, was extremely reluctant to see such important European issues as reparations and the Rhineland occupation come to a head. With Great Britain eschewing the initiative, the whole situation continued to drift, until it was finally brought to a head by the German internal political situation.

Through the summer of 1928 the question of the Rhineland evacuation was fast gathering momentum in Germany as an outstanding domestic issue, with the result that at the Ninth Assembly of the League of Nations, held in September of that year, the German Chancellor officially raised the question of Germany's right to demand the immediate evacuation of the Rhineland zones. The question received scant attention on the floor of the Assembly, but became the subject of serious discussion by the representatives of the interested powers, meeting privately at a Geneva hotel. Three such meetings took place, the whole situation was thoroughly surveyed, and on September 16 the following statement was issued for publication:

At the conclusion of the third conversation which has taken place today, the representatives of Germany, Belgium, France, Great Britain, Italy, and Japan are able to record with satisfaction the friendly conditions in which an exchange of views has taken place regarding the question under consideration. An agreement has been reached between them on the following points:

1. The opening of official negotiations relating to the request put forward by the German Chancellor regarding the early evacuation of the Rhineland.

2. The necessity for a complete and definite settlement of the reparation problem and for the constitution for this purpose of a committee of financial experts to be nominated by the six governments.

When the Geneva announcement was made, there was much indignation in Germany because, in the words of one vigorous commentator, "the same sheet of paper recorded the decision to discuss simultaneously the possibility of evacuation and the possibility of a final settlement of reparations." The Chancellor was openly denounced for having acceded to the French demand for the linking together of the two questions, or, as Dr. Schacht has since put it, because "the legal and moral problem of evacuation had become a question of money and debts." Chancellor Müller's defense was that the two questions would be discussed simultaneously, but independently, of each other. In any event, the way was open for new reparation negotiations and the stage was set for the next important step in the evolution of the reparation problem.

CHAPTER X

AGREEMENTS BASED ON THE YOUNG PLAN

The decision to create a new committee of experts, made at Geneva on September 16, 1928, marked the third major stage in the evolution of the reparation issue. The objective now was a "final and definitive settlement"—an agreement on a revised total liability and on annual payments that would be acceptable to both sides. A somewhat different technique was contemplated than that which had been previously employed. The new plan was not to be drawn up by the political representatives of the principal creditor powers alone, as had been the case with the London schedule of payments, or by experts who were nationals of the principal creditor countries alone, as in the case of the Dawes plan. German experts were also to be included. The final settlement, to a much greater degree than former plans, was therefore to represent the result of negotiation.

The Geneva conversations were followed by several months of further exchanges of views among the interested governments regarding the composition and the scope of activity of the new committee of experts. Agreement finally was reached on December 22, 1928, when it was officially announced that

... the German, Belgian, French, British, Italian, and Japanese governments, in pursuance of the decision reached at Geneva on September 16, 1928, whereby it was agreed to set up a committee of independent financial experts, hereby entrust to the committee the task of drawing up proposals for a complete and final settlement of the reparation problem; these proposals shall provide for a settlement of the obligations resulting from the existing treaties and agreements between Germany and the creditor powers.

The six governments also decided to invite American experts to take part in the work of the new committee, which was thus to consist of representatives of seven nations, rather than five, as had been the case with the 1924 committees. The two additions were Germany and Japan. Because of the interest which attaches to international negotiations of such far-reaching significance, we shall present a brief account of the deliberations of the Young Committee and of the first and second Hague conferences held in August 1929 and January 1930. In the final section of the chapter we shall summarize the essential features of the reparation arrangements.

I. WORK OF THE YOUNG COMMITTEE

The Young Committee—so called because its chairman was the principal American expert, Mr. Owen D. Young—sat in Paris from February 9 to June 7, 1929. It formulated a series of recommendations popularly known as the Young plan, which was intended to serve as the basis of a final adjustment.

The plan as formulated did not cover all aspects of the problem. Numerous detailed procedures were left for subsequent consideration, as also were certain political adjustments which could only be made by the governments directly concerned. The original Young plan therefore underwent considerable modification, elaboration, and supplementation before it was formally adopted as the "new reparation plan."

1. Fixing the total liability. Agreement on the total liability was the most complicated task of the committee of experts, and it was only achieved with great difficulty.

In fact, violent disagreement between Germany and her creditors on this point threatened on several occasions to disrupt entirely the work of the committee. The problem was one of determining the size and number of annuities for which Germany would be made responsible. The standard annuity prescribed by the Dawes plan, namely 2.5 billion marks a year, was taken as a point of departure, both sides agreeing readily that this amount was beyond Germany's paying capacity—at least for some time to come.

Early in the discussion the committee came to the conclusion that "the amounts were to a considerable extent contingent upon the machinery and the form of payment." Accordingly the committee laid aside, for the time being, the question of the size of the annuities and devoted its attention to such problems as the creation of a non-political agency for the collection, administration, and distribution of the annual instalments (to take the place of the Reparation Commission and the various other agencies created under the Dawes plan); the devising of general methods for the eventual commercialization of at least a part of the reparation debt; and agreement on the extent to which Germany would have the right to discharge a portion of her obligation by means of deliveries in kind. The character of the new agency, which took the form of the Bank for International Settlements, will be described in a later section of this chapter.

As the basis for the eventual commercialization which the French so much desired, it was agreed that the annuity, whatever its size, would have to be divided into two parts: the unconditional, which would represent an unequivocal obligation of the German government and could therefore be mobilized in the form of bond issues to be sold to private investors; and the conditional, in the discharging of which the German government would have a certain amount of protection, should the need for such temporary relief ever arise.

In the matter of deliveries in kind there were sharply diverging views. Germany was anxious to retain the right to make payments by the direct shipment of commodities, since such exports simplified the transfer problem. Some of the creditors, however, notably Great Britain, were anxious to eliminate this mode of payment, because of the adverse effect it was having on the competitive position of some of their industries. A compromise was finally effected, in accordance with which payment in kind would be permitted only for the first decade of the new reparation régime, the amounts gradually decreasing and disappearing altogether after the tenth year.

With agreement tentatively reached on these issues, the committee turned once more to the problem of annuities. At this juncture, the German experts made a definite proposal, in which they offered 37 annuities of 1,650 million marks each, divided into a number of categories.[1]

The German proposal contained two variants, representing the same total payments, but differing markedly in the character of the categories into which the annuities were to be divided. Under the terms of Variant 1, for the first ten years there were to be (1) a constant unconditional payment of 450 million reichsmarks a year; (2) a transfer-protected payment rising from 225 million marks during the first year to 500 millions during the tenth year; (3) a collection-and-transfer-protected in-

---

[1] For the full text of the German proposal see Hjalmar Schacht, *The End of Reparations*, pp. 63-71.

stalment of the same size; and (4) deliveries in kind diminishing from 750 million marks in the first year to 200 millions in the tenth year. During the last 27 years, the first category would remain the same, the second and third would be constant at 600 million marks a year each, and the fourth would disappear. Under the terms of Variant 2, there were to be no unconditional payments at all. Apart from deliveries in kind, the schedule for which was to be the same as in Variant 1, the annuities were to be divided equally between transfer-protected and collection-and-transfer-protected categories.

Neither of the German plans proved to be acceptable to the creditors. The total annuity was considered to be too small and the period of payment too short. Moreover, Variant 2 of the German proposal provided no basis whatever for a commercialization of any portion of the reparation debt, while the unconditional payments offered in Variant 1, which were capable of serving as a basis for commercialization, were regarded as inadequate.

Counter-proposals were made by the creditors, and after protracted argument a compromise involving the following general principles was finally reached. Annual payments were to be divided into two categories: unconditional—that is, payable without right of postponement of any kind—amounting to 660 million marks; and conditional, of varying magnitude—subject, under certain conditions, to postponement but not to remission. The provisions of the Dawes plan for adjustment in the light of indexes of prices and of prosperity were abandoned.

The payments were to be spread over a period of 59 years, and the total debt was thus the sum of the 59 annual instalments. The annuities during the early years represented a reduction of approximately 30 per cent as compared with the "standard" Dawes annuities of 2.5 billion marks, and at no time were the annuities to exceed that figure.

The committee recommended that Germany's previous obligations be entirely replaced by the obligations imposed by the Young plan, and that the payment in full of the proposed annuities should be accepted by the creditor powers as a final discharge of all the liabilities of Germany still remaining undischarged. In this manner the Young Committee proposed the final and official abrogation of the London schedule of payments. Three additional steps remained to be taken in order to make the amount of Germany's total financial liability really definite.

First, various unsettled accounts still existed between Germany and the Reparation Commission, referring particularly to the evaluation of the payments, deliveries, and cessions made by Germany during the period preceding the inauguration of the Dawes plan. The plan recommended that all such accounts be closed "at the earliest possible moment." The same recommendation applied to all other claims of the Allies against Germany and to German claims against the Allies, arising out of the Treaty of Versailles.

Second, extremely complicated accounts still existed between Germany and her former enemies with respect to German private property seized and liquidated by the latter. The plan recommended that

the governments make no further use, from the date of the acceptance of this report, of their right to seize, retain, and liquidate property, rights, and interests of German nationals or companies controlled by them in so far as not already liquid, liquidated, or finally disposed of, and that the outstanding questions concerning such property should be definitively cleared up within one year after the coming into force of this plan by arrangements between the governments concerned and Germany.

Third, the original provision of the treaties of peace regarding the joint liability for reparation of Germany, Austria, Hungary, and Bulgaria still remained officially in force. The Young plan recommended a formal dissolution of the joint responsibility and abolishment of "every obligation, present or future, in either direction which may result between these powers from this joint liability."[2]

2. *Linking annuities with Allied debt payments.* The annual payments by Germany were made subject to reduction in the event the creditors' own payments on account of the war debts should be reduced. This provision was contained in the so-called "concurrent memorandum," signed simultaneously with the Young plan by Germany and her principal creditors, and embodying agreement to the effect that any reduction obtained by Germany's creditors in their own payments on the war debt account should result in "a corresponding mitigation of the German annuities." It was agreed that during the first 37 years the current German payments would be reduced by eight-twelfths of the net relief obtained by the creditors; that one-twelfth would be deposited at the Bank for International Settlements for application to German payments after the 37th year; and that the remaining three-twelfths would be retained by the creditors. During the last 22 years, the whole of the relief would be applied to the reduction of the current payments by Germany.

[2] See pp. 145-46. The Young plan also recommended that definitive agreements for the liquidation of the non-German reparation obligations should be negotiated as soon as possible.

As a matter of fact, the size and the number of the Young annuities were to a large extent determined by the payments which the creditors had obligated themselves to make on the war debt account, rather than by any careful appraisal of Germany's capacity to pay. The annuities were so arranged that at no time during the first 37 years would the out-payments of the creditors, on account of their own war debts, exceed the conditional portions of the current German instalments. In this manner, the relief provisions suggested in the "concurrent memorandum" would not, during that period, affect the unconditional payments.[3]

3. *Changes in the distribution percentages.* The Young plan provided for a new distribution of the reparation payments among the creditors. The plan completed the work begun by the Dawes committee in consolidating into a single annuity all German payments arising out of the peace treaties by abolishing the priorities set up in the Paris agreement of 1925.[4] This required the establishment of a single set of distribution percentages, and in the process of working out these percentages, it was found necessary to rearrange the distribution scheme applicable theretofore.

The total annuities set up by the Young plan represented a compromise between the smallest amounts which each of the creditors was willing to accept and the largest aggregate amount which Germany would undertake to assume as a definite responsibility. Each of the principal creditors, with the exception of Great Britain,

[3] For the comparative figures of the German payments and the Allied out-payments, see Appendix B, p. 471. See also p. 296. For a detailed description of the methods used in establishing the Young annuities, see D. P. Myers, *The Reparation Settlement*, pp. 50-87.
[4] See pp. 172-73.

was determined to collect from Germany sufficient amounts to cover its own payments on account of the war debts and something besides to reimburse the cost of post-war reconstruction. Great Britain, in accordance with

ANNUITIES UNDER THE YOUNG PLAN

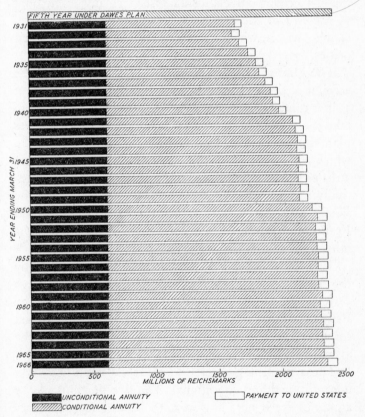

the Balfour principle, insisted on receiving from Germany as much as she needed, in addition to her receipts from her other war debtors, to meet her payments to the United States—although she was also anxious to obtain something in addition to reimburse her for the payments made to the United States before her receipts on reparation and war debt accounts became sufficient to cover her own current out-payments. Moreover, a certain percentage of the annuities had to be assigned to the United States to cover our claims against Germany on account of the cost of the armies of occupation and the mixed claims awards, which had formerly been treated as priorities.

The United States voluntarily reduced her claims on account of the costs of the armies of occupation by about 10 per cent, and the other creditors were also willing to take less than they would have received under the Dawes plan. But even with these reductions, the only way in which the claims of all the creditors could be acceptably satisfied within the limits of the global annuities tentatively agreed upon by everyone concerned was for the shares of some of them, notably Great Britain and France, to be reduced, and for the shares of some of the others, especially Italy and Belgium, to be increased.

The distribution percentages finally worked out by the Young Committee are shown in the table on page 197, in which the Spa percentages, as amended by the Paris agreement of 1925, are also shown in a parallel column. The Young plan percentages are based on the average receipts of each creditor over the whole period.

These percentages refer to the total annuities, both unconditional and conditional. The two portions of the annuities were not, however, to be distributed in accordance with these general allotments. The committee agreed that France was to receive 500 million marks a year out of the unconditional part of each annuity and the rest of her share out of the conditional part. Similarly, Italy was to be assigned 42 million marks of unconditional payments. The allotment of the remainder of the unconditional part was left to the future decision of the creditor governments.

The French experts accepted the reduction in the French share more or less readily because the committee was willing to give France a special advantage by as-

DISTRIBUTION OF REPARATION ANNUITIES UNDER THE YOUNG PLAN
(In percentages)

Country	Young Plan[a]	Amended Spa Scheme
France	52.3	54.46
British Empire	20.4	23.04
Italy	11.8	10.00
Belgium	5.6	4.50
Yugoslavia	3.9	5.00
Rumania	1.2	1.10
Portugal	0.6	0.75
Japan	0.6	0.75
Greece	0.4	0.40
Poland	—[b]	—
United States	3.2[c]	—
Total	100.0	100.0

[a] For the actual amounts to be received by each country annually, see Appendix B, pp. 472–73.
[b] Less than 0.1 per cent.
[c] Under the Dawes plan handled as a priority payment.

signing to her a very large share of the unconditional portion of the annuities. The British experts, on the other hand, were reluctant to make the concession required of them, since they were getting nothing in return, and finally agreed only in order not to disrupt the negotiations.

4. Modifications of safeguards. The Young plan proposed the abolition of all transfer safeguards provided by the Dawes plan, and of all foreign controls attendant upon transfer protection. In the language of the committee's report, it was intended, from the time that the new plan would go into effect, to "leave to Germany the obligation of facing her engagements on her own untrammelled responsibility." In practice, this meant that thenceforth Germany, and Germany alone, would be responsible for both stages of the paying process—the internal collections in marks, and the conversion of these marks into forms of payment acceptable to the creditors. With the assumption by Germany of full responsibility for the whole paying process, the foreign control agencies established under the Dawes plan ceased to be necessary.

Moreover, the Young plan envisaged a simplification in the scheme of internal collections from the point of view of the sources of revenue. In place of a complicated system of railway bonds, industrial debentures, transportation tax, and contributions from the general budget, secured by specially assigned revenues, it proposed that the sums necessary for the reparation payments should be drawn directly from the budget of the German Reich, without the pledging of any specific revenues, except in so far as such pledges continued to constitute a part of the contract with regard to the 1924 loan. The only feature of the Dawes plan machinery of internal collection which the Young plan proposed to maintain was the continuation during the first 37 years of a special contribution made by the German Railway Company fixed at 660 million marks annually, to be earmarked for reparation payments.

5. *The Bank for International Settlements.* The most distinctive feature of the Young plan was the proposal for the creation of a new financial institution to serve

as the intermediary between Germany and her creditors. This important function had, from the end of the Peace Conference, been performed by the Reparation Commission and its various control agencies in Germany. With the abolition of these agencies, the Reparation Commission itself, as set up by the treaties of peace, became no longer a suitable organization for the purpose in view. Moreover, it was frankly a political body, consisting of official representatives of the creditor governments, while the settlement foreshadowed by the Dawes plan and ostensibly carried out by the Young plan required the removal of the whole reparation problem, so far as possible, from the sphere of political relations to that of ordinary financial and commercial operations.

Hence the Young plan proposed the creation of an institution, to be known as the Bank for International Settlements, which would act as a trustee for the creditor powers in receiving from Germany the reparation instalments as they came due, in distributing the sums thus received among the creditor powers, and in managing such complicated technical operations as deliveries in kind and the eventual commercialization of the unconditional payments. It was recommended that, as soon as the bank began its operations, the Reparation Commission should cease to exist and its rights and duties should devolve on the bank.

The authors of the Young plan regarded the establishment of the bank as a necessary step in the removal of the reparation problem from the political to the economic field. In giving their reasons for setting up the bank they said:

A general plan for a complete and final settlement of the reparation problem, being primarily financial in character, involves the performance of certain banking functions at one or more points in the sequence between the initial payment of the annuities and the final distribution of the funds. A banking institution, designed to meet these requirements, justifies and makes logical the liquidation of all political controls and provides instead machinery essentially commercial and financial in character, which carries with it all the support and at the same time all the responsibilities that economic engagements imply.

The Young Committee also intended the bank to have very important general functions. They proposed that, in addition to its trustee functions with regard to the reparation payments, it should provide new financial facilities for the development of international trade and financial relations. In this manner, it would also serve as an instrument for general economic expansion, upon which the experts assembled in Paris predicated their faith in Germany's ability to meet increasing annual instalments. Accordingly, in defining the functions of the proposed institution, they said:

The bank will have (a) as its essential or obligatory functions those which are inherent in the receipt, management, and distribution of the annuities, and (b) as its auxiliary or permissive functions those which evolve more indirectly from the character of the annuities. . . . In the natural course of development it is to be expected that the bank will in time become an organization, not simply, or even predominantly, concerned with the handling of reparations, but also with furnishing the world of international commerce and finance important facilities hitherto lacking. Especially it is to be hoped that it will become an increasingly close and valuable link in the co-operation of central banking institutions generally—a co-operation essential to the continuing stability of the world's credit structure.

As a matter of fact, the authors of the Young plan proposed that the bank should be set up and controlled by the national central banks of the principal countries of the world. The scheme of organization suggested by them called for the creation of the bank as a corporation, with its shares allotted to the central banks of the seven countries whose nationals took part in the formulation of the plan and of any other countries which might be selected later on by the bank's board of directors. This board, which would serve as the highest administrative body of the institution, would consist of the governors of the participating central banks and their appointees.[5]

The Young plan did not propose a definitive scheme of organization for the bank, but rather a general outline. The experts who drew up the report recommended that an organization committee be created with full powers to devise a definite plan of organization. Only the bank's

[5] In view of the improbability that the Federal Reserve system of the United States or any of the Federal Reserve Banks would find it possible to participate in the Bank for International Settlements, the following alternative provisions were made for the selection of the bank's directors:

"If, in the process of organising the bank or in the performance of its functions after establishment, it is found that the central bank of any country or its governor is unable to act officially or unofficially in any or all of the capacities provided for in this outline, or refrains from so acting, alternative arrangements not inconsistent with the laws of that country shall be made. In particular, the governors of the central banks of the countries whose nationals are members of the present committee, or as many of them as are qualified to act, may invite to become members of the board of directors of the bank two nationals of any country the central bank of which is eligible under this outline to take part in forming the board of the bank but does not do so. The two nationals of that country upon acceptance of the invitation shall be qualified to act in the full capacity of directors of the bank as provided in this outline. Further, the directors of the bank shall be authorised to appoint, in lieu of any central bank not exercising any or all of the functions, authorities or privileges which this outline provides that central banks make or shall exercise, any bank or banking house of widely recognised standing and of the same nationality. Such bank or banking house, upon appointment and acceptance, shall be entitled to act in the place of the central bank in any or all capacities appropriate to central banks under this outline, provided only that such action is not inconsistent with the laws of the country in question."

duties with regard to the management of reparation payments were clearly defined in the plan. These will be discussed in detail in the last section of this chapter.

It is apparent from this analysis that the Young plan contemplated a really definitive settlement. The fixation of a total final liability and a definite schedule of payments, of which only a part was even postponable, together with the abolition of transfer protection and all foreign control devices, indicated a conviction that Germany could undoubtedly fulfill the obligations agreed upon. The committee expressed its belief that, when operating on the basis of restored financial freedom, Germany would have no difficulty in meeting the annuities inscribed in the plan. To quote from the final conclusions of the report:

> It has been our object to make proposals for financial obligations which, with the conditions and safeguards that accompany them, shall be within Germany's capacity to pay, and we believe that we have achieved this purpose.

The safeguards referred to are the provisions in the plan which afford facilities for temporary relief, under exceptional circumstances, in the form of postponement of the conditional annuities. These provisions, which we shall describe in detail in a later part of this chapter, are of a wholly different nature from the transfer protection and the other safeguards accorded Germany under the Dawes plan.

The members of the Dawes Committee, it will be recalled, emphatically refused to "speculate on the amount which can annually be paid [by Germany] in foreign currencies." Accordingly, they set up their system of complete transfer protection. The framers of the Young plan, on the other hand, did commit themselves definitely on this point and explained their position in the following terms:

Not the least part of the task was the determination of the figure which Germany could immediately undertake as a final and unconditional obligation. The point at which difficulties might begin to arise in making transfers into foreign currencies is not exactly definable in advance; but every care has been taken to be so far within this limit as to remove every possibility of the risk of error. We recognize that in fixing the figure payable by Germany in foreign currencies, without any right of postponement whatever, at 660 million reichsmarks, we have taken a conservative amount. But we are satisfied that it is wiser deliberately to under-estimate than to run the slightest risk of weakening German credit by proposing a figure which might not command instant acceptance by well-informed public opinion.

It is thus clear that the members of the Young Committee were still under the influence of the prevailing optimism of the boom era. The fact that the German representatives offered in their own proposal substantial unconditional annuities indicates that they were also still under the same spell.

II. DECISIONS OF THE FIRST HAGUE CONFERENCE

An official conference of fully accredited representatives of the governments concerned was necessary in order to give effect to the proposals of the Young Committee. Such a conference met at The Hague on August 6, 1929 and remained in session until August 31, when a number of preliminary agreements were signed.[6]

[6] The conference consisted of representatives of the following countries: Germany, France, Great Britain, Canada, Australia, South Africa, New Zealand, India, Italy, Japan, Poland, Portugal, Rumania, Yugoslavia, and Czechoslovakia. The United States was represented by an observer.

Between the time when the Young Committee had completed its work and the conference at The Hague, a change of government occurred in Great Britain. The Conservative Cabinet of Mr. Stanley Baldwin was superseded by the Labor Cabinet of Mr. Ramsay MacDonald. The new British Cabinet refused from the start to accept a number of features of the Young plan, especially those which referred to the British share of the new annuities and to the new program of deliveries in kind. This position was officially presented at The Hague conference by the principal British delegate, Mr. Philip Snowden, chancellor of the exchequer in the MacDonald Cabinet, and led to a bitter controversy there.

Mr. Snowden's most important criticism of the Young plan was concerned with the size of the share in the annuities assigned to Great Britain. He maintained that if the Spa percentages, rather than the new scheme of distribution worked out by the Young Committee, were to govern the allotment of the annuities, the British share would have been larger by an average of approximately 48 million marks a year. Under the Young Committee schedule, Great Britain's receipts from Germany and from her Continental Allies were barely sufficient to cover her current war debt payments to the United States, leaving no surplus that could be applied to the payments already made by Great Britain in excess of her own receipts. The additional 48 million marks a year which Great Britain would have received, had the Spa percentages been applied to the distribution of the new annuities, would have represented such a surplus. Accordingly, Mr. Snowden demanded a restoration of the Spa percentages as a basis for the distribution of the Young annuities.

This meant that, unless the total annuities were increased, the shares of some of the other creditors had to be diminished. Since it was generally considered undesirable to alter the total annuities, a compromise solution was sought which would leave them intact and at the same time satisfy the British demands. As a result of The Hague negotiations and later agreements, France and Belgium agreed to turn over to Great Britain 19.8 million marks a year of their reparation receipts.[7] Italy likewise agreed to pay 9 million marks a year. These payments were to continue for 37 years. Moreover, it was agreed that Great Britain should receive a lump sum of 100 million marks out of the payments made by Germany during the last five months of the fifth Dawes annuity, this sum representing, according to Mr. Snowden's calculation, an additional annuity of 7.2 million marks a year. Finally, the gain in interest resulting from a readjustment of the dates of monthly instalments payable by Germany was estimated by the British as the equivalent of another 4 million marks a year.[8] In this manner, 40 million marks a year were added to the British share, and the British government declared itself satisfied.

Mr. Snowden's second demand was in connection with the distribution of the unconditional part of the new annuities. The Young Committee had assigned no definite share to Great Britain, and it was quite apparent that if its proposal for allocating 500 million marks to France, 42 millions to Italy, and an average of 61.8

[7] By means of a later agreement, the responsibility for these payments was divided as follows: France, 16,650,000 marks; Belgium, 3,150,000 marks.

[8] The payment date was changed from the 30th to the 15th of each month.

millions to the interest and amortization payments on the 1924 loan were accepted, there would be very little left for Great Britain. Again after much discussion, a compromise was finally reached, this time putting the additional burden entirely on Germany. It was decided to fix the unconditional portion of the annuity at 612 million marks, exclusive of the loan payments, and to distribute this sum in the following manner:

	Millions of Marks
France	500.0
British Empire	55.0
Italy	42.0
Japan	6.6
Yugoslavia	6.0
Portugal	2.4
Total	612.0

Since the annual payments on the 1924 loan vary from year to year, this decision made the unconditional portion of the annuity somewhat variable. Over the first 37 years, however, it averaged 673.8 million marks a year, or 13.8 millions more than the figure arrived at by the Young Committee.[9] After some discussion, the German government decided to accept the additional burden represented by this adjustment.

Finally, on the question of deliveries in kind, the British were concerned particularly with the possible effects of German payments in this form upon the exports of coal from Great Britain, especially to Italy. Mr. Snowden demanded at first a complete re-examination of the whole question, but finally declared himself provisionally satisfied with the following arrangements: (1) France and Italy agreed to adjust their respective quotas

[9] See also p. 231.

in such a way that Italy's share would be made uniform for the whole ten-year period, instead of varying from 75 to 30 million marks a year, with the result that "the peak of the Italian purchases of coal in Germany on reparation account is therefore reduced"; (2) Italy agreed to purchase for her state railways one million tons of British coal a year for three years from November 15, 1929; and (3) Italy agreed "to abstain from importing reparation coal via sea over and above the maximum quantity of 1.5 million tons per year during the ten-year period."

After satisfying the British demands, The Hague conference drew up a set of regulations for the transitional period leading up to the full inauguration of the Young plan and reached agreement on the costs of the armies of occupation. On this latter question, the Young plan made no recommendations, except suggesting that, since the occupation was to come to an end, some sort of special arrangement should be made for handling the costs up to the completion of the evacuation. By a special agreement between the Belgian, French, British, and German governments, signed at The Hague, it was decided to set up a reserve fund of 60 million marks, out of which these costs would be met. Germany was to contribute 50 per cent of the fund; France, 35 per cent; Great Britain, 12 per cent; and Belgium, 3 per cent.[10]

These decisions of The Hague conference still left unsolved a large number of questions raised by the Young plan. Accordingly, the conference decided to set up a number of special committees to study these questions and report upon them to another conference which was

---

[10] Later on Germany agreed also to contribute an additional sum of 6 million marks to cover the costs of administering the Young plan prior to the establishment of the Bank for International Settlements.

to be convened at a later date. Seven committees were appointed to deal with the following subjects: (1) Organization of the Bank for International Settlements; (2) deliveries in kind; (3) ceded properties, liberation debts, and non-German reparation obligations;[11] (4) liquidation of past accounts; (5) adaptation of the system of controlled revenues to the new plan; (6) adaptation of the German law on the Reichsbank; and (7) adaptation of the German law concerning the German Railway Company.

The Hague conference also took up the question of the Rhineland evacuation. A political committee was set up by the conference, under the chairmanship of Mr. Arthur Henderson, the British foreign secretary, and the deliberations of this commission speedily resulted in complete agreement among the governments concerned. The terms of the agreement were embodied in official notes exchanged on August 30, 1929 by the Foreign Ministers of France, Great Britain, and Belgium on the one hand and Germany on the other.

In accordance with this agreement, the Allies undertook to begin the evacuation of the second zone on September 14, 1929 and to complete the withdrawal of their troops within a period of three months. The evacuation of the third zone, occupied exclusively by French troops, was to begin "immediately after the Young plan is ratified by the German and French parliaments and put into operation." It was to be completed "at the latest in a period of eight months terminating not later than the end of June, 1930."

---

[11] The Hague conference decided to proceed at once with an examination of these questions not only because of the recommendation of the Young Committee, but also because some of the additional payments guaranteed to Great Britain, especially by Italy, were to be derived from other than German reparation sources.

III. ADJUSTMENTS AT THE SECOND HAGUE CONFERENCE

The work of the seven committees set up by the first Hague conference was completed by the end of November, and on December 10 a committee of jurists was convened for the purpose of redrafting the reports of the committees into legal texts which could be embodied into formal agreements. These texts were then circulated to the governments concerned, and on January 3, 1930 a second conference met at The Hague. It remained in session until January 20, when signatures were finally affixed to a large number of documents which, subject to the necessary ratification, provided for the inauguration of a new reparation régime.[12]

1. Agreements between Germany and the Allies. The most important document executed at the second Hague conference was the general agreement between Germany and her creditors. It provided that "the experts' plan of June 7, 1929, together with this present agreement and the protocol of August 31, 1929 (all of which are hereinafter described as the "new plan"), is definitely accepted as a complete and final settlement, so far as Germany is concerned, of the financial questions resulting from the war."

The basic provisions of the Young plan were modified by The Hague agreement in only minor respects. In accordance with the plan, the agreement provided for the closing of all outstanding accounts between Germany and the Reparation Commission and for the liquidation of all pending financial claims and counter-claims "connected with the World War, the Armistice conventions,

---

[12] The second Hague conference consisted of representatives of the same 17 countries which were represented at the first conference, and in addition, since non-German reparation obligations were also to be discussed, by delegates from Austria, Hungary, and Bulgaria. Again, as at the first conference, an American observer was present.

the Treaty of Versailles, or any other agreements."[13] The agreement stipulated the abolition of the Reparation Commission, the creation of the Bank for International Settlements, and the constitution of the bank as a trustee for the creditor powers under the terms of a trust agreement, already drawn up and accepted by all the creditors. Comprehensive regulations were incorporated in The Hague agreement regarding deliveries in kind, the annual quotas of which were allocated somewhat differently than in the Young plan.[14]

The German government undertook to enact the necessary legislation for putting the new plan into effect. It also undertook to deliver to the Bank for International Settlements a debt certificate setting forth its payment obligations, as well as a similar certificate of the German Railway Company, the agreed text of both certificates being appended to the agreement. Finally, the German government confirmed "all the priorities, securities, and rights hitherto created for the benefit of the German External Loan of 1924." This priority of the payments on the 1924 loan was similarly confirmed by the creditor powers.

The creditor powers formally recognized "that their acceptance of the solemn undertaking of the German government replaces all controls, special securities, pledges, or charges" existing at the time of the conference. This was, however, a general provision to which there were several exceptions. The pledges given in connection with the 1924 loan remained in full force. The continuation for reparation purposes of contributions by

---

[13] Agreements to govern such liquidation had already been signed by Germany with most of the other powers concerned.

[14] Both programs of deliveries in kind are given in Appendix B. See pp. 474-75.

the railway company constituted another exception. Finally, a system of collateral guarantees was devised, in accordance with which Germany undertook to assign —without foreign control, however—for the service of the annuities and of any bonds that might be created on the basis of the annuities, the proceeds of the customs, and of the taxes on tobacco, beer, and spirits. The German government pledged itself not to create "any charge on the assigned revenues for any other loan or credit without the consent of the Bank for International Settlements."

Issues of interpretation were to be settled by arbitration. In line with procedure under the Dawes plan and the London agreement of 1924, The Hague agreement made the following provision:

Any dispute, whether between the governments signatory to the present agreement or between one or more of those governments and the Bank for International Settlements, as to the interpretation or application of the new plan shall . . . be submitted for final decision to an arbitration tribunal of five members appointed for five years, of whom one, who will be the chairman, shall be a citizen of the United States of America, two shall be nationals of states which were neutral during the late war; the two others shall be respectively a national of Germany and a national of one of the powers which are creditors of Germany.

Several exceptions were made to this arbitration procedure, the most important of which we shall indicate below in connection with the problem of sanctions. Comprehensive details regarding the operation of the tribunal, as well as relating to the other provisions of the agreement, were set forth in twelve voluminous annexes.[15]

[15] For a convenient collection of the documents signed at the two Hague conferences, see *International Conciliation*, September 1930.

In addition to the general agreement, a number of special instruments were negotiated and signed at The Hague. One of these gave formal effect to the concurrent memorandum signed in connection with the Young plan. Another represented an arrangement for the immediate commercialization of a sufficient portion of the unconditional annuity to provide for a 200 million dollar "mobilization" bond issue.[16] In connection with the latter arrangement, the German government undertook, for a specified period, not to float any foreign loans in order to give priority to the commercialization loan. Still another fixed the final details of the allotment of German payments among the various creditors.

2. *The American-German agreement.* The schedule of annual payments inscribed in the debt certificate handed by the German government to the Bank for International Settlements shows smaller amounts than those which appear in the Young plan. The reason for this lies in the subtraction from the Young plan figures of the share assigned to the United States, because between the first and the second Hague conferences the American government decided to dissociate its claims against Germany from those of the other creditors. Accordingly, a separate American-German agreement was negotiated, and was initialed on December 28, 1929. The final agreement was signed on June 23, 1930, after the terms of settlement worked out in December received Congressional approval on June 5, 1930.

The American-German agreement is in a form similar to the general type of debt funding settlements negotiated by the World War Foreign Debt Commission and the Treasury. The payments inscribed in it are identical

[16] See p. 268.

in amount with the share assigned to the United States by the Young Committee. Those on account of the armies of occupation run for 37 years, up to and including March 31, 1966, and range between 16.4 million and 35.3 million marks; those on account of mixed claims run through the fiscal year ending March 31, 1981 and are uniform throughout the period at 40.8 million marks a year. In counter-distinction to the Young plan, however, the instalments to the United States Treasury are to be made directly, rather than through the instrumentality of the Bank for International Settlements, and are due semi-annually, rather than monthly, on March 31 and September 30 of each year. Germany has the right to defer payments for a period not exceeding two and one-half years.[17] No pledge or security other than her duly executed bonds is required, and in this manner Germany is placed on exactly the same footing as all other debtors of the American Treasury. All payments must be made in United States gold coin at "the average of the middle rates prevailing on the Berlin Bourse during the half-monthly period preceding the date of payment."[18]

The second Hague conference took due cognizance of the American-German agreement and proceeded to adjust the paying schedules of the Young plan accordingly. However, the question arose as to the possibility that Germany might accord the American Treasury a preferred position in the case of a partial postponement of payments. The other creditors of Germany expressed

[17] For the postponement provision of The Hague agreement, see pp. 228-31.

[18] For the text of the agreement, see *Annual Report of the Secretary of the Treasury*, 1930, pp. 341-47. The complete schedule of payments is given in Appendix B, p. 470.

themselves as being anxious to forestall an eventuality in which Germany might decide to continue payments to the United States in full and at the same time exercise her option under The Hague agreements to postpone payment on a portion of her reparation annuity.

After some discussion, Germany undertook to give her creditors definite assurances on this score, which were embodied in an exchange of notes between the president of the conference and the principal German delegate. The German undertaking was stated in the following terms:

The German government will not exercise in relation to any one of the creditor powers the rights of postponement which it possesses under the agreements already signed or initialed without exercising at the same time any similar rights which it may possess in relation to all the other powers whose claims are included in the annuities, as set out in the experts' report on June 7, 1929. Moreover, in the future the German government will not, in connection with postponement, give any special advantage to any one of those powers.

3. The problem of sanctions. One of the questions which greatly disturbed the work of the second conference at The Hague was that of the guarantees provided by the Treaty of Versailles for ensuring the fulfillment by Germany of her reparation obligations. This problem of sanctions, as defined by Article 430 of the treaty,[19] had come up in the discussions of the committee of experts, and it was there agreed that the new plan would have to be predicated on at least a tacit understanding that the treaty sanction of a reoccupation of the Rhineland would not be applicable to a dispute between Germany and her creditors on any matter pertaining to the reparation obligations. Fulfillment of these obligations

[19] See p. 181.

by Germany was to be based on good faith, and any unavoidable disputes were to be the subject of arbitration.

During the interval between the first and the second Hague conferences, however, a situation developed in Germany which caused great concern in some of the creditor countries, especially France. The German Nationalists, who had shown a great deal of hostility to the Young plan from the outset, had finally crystallized their opposition into a demand for a popular plebiscite on the question of the reparation question in general. They succeeded in obtaining the legally requisite number of signatures (10 per cent of the total electorate, or over four million names) to a petition for a plebiscite, in the course of which the German voters were to be asked, by the sponsors of the movement, to repudiate the war guilt provisions of the Treaty of Versailles and to declare that "no further financial burdens or obligations based on the war guilt acknowledgment shall be assumed, inclusive of those arising from the recommendations of the Paris reparation experts and the subsequent agreements." The plebiscite was actually held on December 22, 1929. Although the number of votes cast in favor of the proposition put forward by the Nationalists was comparatively small (less than 5.5 millions as against the necessary majority of over 20 millions), the incident aroused strong apprehension in France.

Moreover, the action of the first Hague conference in introducing modifications in the original Young plan aroused opposition and bitter criticism in many German quarters. The most important feature of this opposition was the publication, on December 5, 1929, of a memorandum addressed to the German government by Dr. Hjalmar Schacht, president of the Reichsbank and principal German expert on the Young Committee. Dr. Schacht protested against what he regarded as new burdens imposed upon Germany by the decisions made at the first Hague conference, which, in his opinion, were likely to jeopardize the success of the plan as a whole.

As a result of these developments in Germany and of the French reaction thereto, the French delegates to the second Hague conference put forward a demand for a formal reaffirmation of the sanction provisions of the treaty of peace. In the face of strenuous opposition on the part of the Germans and lack of support from their fellow creditors, the French nevertheless succeeded in writing into the general agreement signed at The Hague a joint declaration giving effect to their demand.

This declaration began with a solemn pronouncement by the representatives of the Belgian, British, French, Italian, and Japanese governments to the effect that the object of the new plan "would not be attained without mutual good-will and confidence," and that "the creditor governments are convinced that, even if the execution of the new plan should give rise to differences of opinion or difficulties, the procedures provided for by the plan itself would be sufficient to resolve them." The declaration then continued as follows:

There remains, however, a hypothesis outside the scope of the agreements signed today. The creditor governments are forced to consider it without thereby wishing to cast doubt on the intentions of the German government. They regard it as indispensable to take account of the possibility that in the future a German government, in violation of the solemn obligation contained in The Hague agreement of January, 1930, might commit itself to actions revealing its determination to destroy the new plan.

It is the duty of the creditor governments to declare to the German government that if such a case arose, imperilling the foundations of their common work, a new situation would be created in regard to which the creditor governments must, from the outset, formulate all the reservations to which they are rightfully entitled.

However, even on this extreme hypothesis, the creditor governments, in the interests of general peace, are prepared, before taking any action, to appeal to an international jurisdiction of incontestable authority to establish and appreciate the facts. The creditor power or powers which might regard themselves as concerned, would therefore submit to the Permanent Court of International Justice the question whether the German government had committed acts revealing its determination to destroy the new plan.

Germany should forthwith declare that, in the event of an affirmative decision by the court, she acknowledges that it is legitimate that, in order to ensure the fulfillment of the obligations of the debtor power resulting from the new plan, the creditor power or powers should resume their full liberty of action.

The creditor governments are convinced that such a hypothetical situation will never in fact arise and they feel assured that the German government shares this conviction. But they consider that they are bound in loyalty and by their duty to their respective countries to make the above declaration in case this hypothetical situation should arise.

The representatives of Germany, on their side, made the following declaration:

As regards the . . . hypothesis formulated in this declaration, the German government regrets that such an eventuality, which for its part it regards as impossible, should be contemplated. Nevertheless, if one or more of the creditor powers refer to the Permanent Court of International Justice the question whether acts originating with the German government reveal its determination to destroy the new plan, the German government, in agreement with the creditor governments, accepts the proposal that the Permanent Court should decide the question, and declares that it acknowledges that it is legitimate, in the event of an affirmative decision by the court, that, in order to ensure the fulfillment of the financial obligations of the debtor power resulting from the new plan, the creditor power or powers should resume their full liberty of action.

The "full liberty of action" retained by the creditor governments in accordance with this declaration referred to their right, under the treaty of peace, to reoccupy the Rhineland in case of willful reparation default on the part of Germany. This act of The Hague conference, without adding anything tangible to the rights and privileges already enjoyed by the creditor powers, served to increase the growing unpopularity of the Young plan within Germany and to strengthen the rising opposition there to fulfillment of reparation obligations.

4. Convention regarding the International Bank. An important part of the task of the second Hague conference was to give final approval to the work of the organization committee for the Bank for International Settlements and to sign the various instruments necessary for the establishment of the new institution. These were a convention with the government of Switzerland, on the territory of which the bank was to be established; the bank's statutes, which became a part of the convention; and the trust agreement between the bank and the creditor powers, which became a part of the general agreement.

Since the Swiss city of Basle had been chosen as the seat of the Bank for International Settlements, the new institution had to be given the form of a Swiss corporation. However, because of the peculiar nature of the bank, its founders felt that it should enjoy a special legal status, the provisions for which were embodied in the convention signed at The Hague between the government of Switzerland and the governments of Germany, Belgium, Great Britain, France, Italy, and Japan.[20]

In accordance with the convention, the Swiss government undertook to grant the bank a constituent charter, the text of which was incorporated in the convention itself. Under this charter, the constitution, operations, and activities of the bank were defined by the statutes, annexed to the convention, which could be amended only in the manner set forth in its own relevant articles. The Swiss government agreed that the statutes and any amendments that might be made in them in this prescribed manner "shall be valid and operative notwithstanding any inconsistency therewith in the provisions of any present or future Swiss law." Moreover, the Swiss government granted the bank and its non-Swiss personnel a wide immunity from present and future taxation, and guaranteed that "the bank, its property, assets, and all deposits and other funds entrusted to it shall be

[20] These, with the exception of the United States, were the countries whose nationals sat on the Young Committee and whose central banks, in accordance with the Young plan, were to be the founders of the Bank for International Settlements. Although individual Americans played an outstanding part in the creation of the bank—Owen D. Young was president of the Paris committee of experts; W. W. Stewart, Shepard Morgan, and W. R. Burgess were the principal drafters of the suggested outline for the organization of the bank incorporated in the Young plan; and Jackson E. Reynolds was chairman of the organization committee which wrote the bank's statutes—the United States did not participate formally in the legal arrangements leading up to its founding. American participation after the bank was founded was arranged in accordance with the procedure laid down in the provision of the Young plan quoted in footnote 5 on p. 201. A group of banks, consisting of J. P. Morgan and Company of New York, the First National Bank of New York, and the First National Bank of Chicago, was selected to act, for the purposes of the Basle institution, as a substitute for an American bank. It may be noted that although Japan took full part in the legal steps leading up to the founding of the bank, her central bank also declined to participate in the new institution, and a substitute for it was created in the form of a group of 15 private banks.

immune in time of peace and in time of war from any measure such as expropriation, requisition, seizure, confiscation, prohibition or restriction of gold or currency export or import, and any other similar measures."

The convention was to remain in force for 15 years. During the period of its validity, "any dispute between the Swiss government and the bank as to the interpretation or application of the present charter shall be referred to the Arbitral Tribunal provided for by The Hague agreement of January 1930."

The bank's statutes, as drafted by the organization committee and approved by The Hague conference, were more general in their scope than the suggested outline incorporated in the Young plan. They defined the organization and activities of the bank without any specific reference to its functions as a trustee for the reparation creditors, merely empowering it to engage in operations inherent in the fulfillment of such functions. The detailed regulations for the handling of reparation payments were embodied by the organization committee in the trust agreement, which became the basic instrument governing the relations between the bank, the creditor powers, and Germany.

5. Supplementary agreements. Four supplementary agreements, growing out of the recommendations contained in the Young plan, were signed or implemented during the second Hague conference. These were the so-called "German marks agreement" between Germany and Belgium, which ended a long controversy between the two countries; a special arrangement between France and Yugoslavia; another between France and Italy; and one between Italy and Germany.

The controversy between Belgium and Germany went back to an important feature of the German occupation of the former during the war. In administering the country, the German military authorities caused a large amount of German mark notes to be put into monetary circulation. After the restoration of the Belgian government, following the cessation of hostilities, these mark notes were replaced by regular Belgian currency, and the Belgian government informed the German government that it considered itself as having a valid claim for the redemption of the retired mark notes. During the Peace Conference, the Belgian representatives attempted to have the claims on this account included in the formal reparation claims, but failed to obtain the agreement of the other Allies to such a procedure. The marks claim then became the subject of direct negotiations between Brussels and Berlin.

These negotiations were carried on sporadically, but unsuccessfully, for several years, and the account was still unadjusted at the time the Young Committee met. During the sessions of the committee, the Belgians once more raised the question of including their mark claims in the reparation bill against Germany, and again without success. It was recognized, however, by the whole committee, including the Germans, that the question should be settled. Accordingly, an agreement was made and embodied in Annex VI to the Young plan, to the effect that direct negotiations should once more be instituted between the two governments concerned and that a successful termination of these negotiations should become a preliminary condition to the institution of the plan itself.

Representatives of Belgium and Germany met soon after the signing of the Young report and, on July 13, 1929, signed a definitive agreement regarding the controversy. Germany agreed to pay Belgium 37 annuities, which were to be considered separate and distinct from the Young plan annuities, but were to coincide with the first period of the payment schedule inscribed in the plan. The annuities were made payable in equal monthly instalments, through the Bank for International Settlements. They were given the character of unconditional payments, though Germany reserved the right to make them by means of deliveries in kind.[21] During the course of the second Hague conference, on January 16, 1930, the Foreign Ministers of the two countries addressed identical notes to the president of the conference, informing him officially of the conclusion of the agreement and thus removing this particular condition to the final inauguration of the Young plan.

The special agreement between France and Yugoslavia, signed on January 20, 1930, was part of an extremely complicated series of arrangements, worked out by the first Hague conference and confirmed by the second, with regard to the payments made by Germany during the last five months of the Dawes plan (April 1 to August 31, 1929). According to the recommendations of the Young Committee (Article 83 of the plan), the payments by Germany during the five months were to be limited to the sums necessary for the service charges on the 1924 loan and such amounts as were needed by each of the creditors to cover, in addition to its share of the first Young annuity, its own out-payments on the war debt account during the fiscal year ending March 31, 1930. In view of the fact that the sums already received by Yugoslavia, together with the regular share allocated to her under the Young plan, exceeded her own requirements as defined in the plan, while the receipts of France

[21] For the text of the agreement, see *Federal Reserve Bulletin*, August 1929, p. 548. The schedule of payments is given in Appendix B, p. 476.

on the same basis were below her requirements, Yugoslavia agreed to pay to France 37 annuities that would
adjust the difference. Each annuity was made payable in
equal half-yearly instalments, due on March 1 and September 1. A penalty of 5.5 per cent was stipulated for all
instalments not met on the due dates.[22]

The French-Italian account was adjusted by an exchange of letters between the Ministers of Finance of
the two countries, in accordance with which France
agreed to make to Italy 37 annual payments of 3.5 million reichsmarks each, in partial compensation for the
latter's concessions made to Great Britain. These annuities were to be made up of the French share in the
Czechoslovak "liberation" payments,[23] which France undertook to cede to Italy, and additional instalments of
312,854 reichsmarks annually.[24]

The special agreement between Italy and Germany,
signed on January 20, 1930, related to the execution of
Articles 296-97 of the Treaty of Versailles (covering
clearing payments and property rights). Under its terms,
Italy agreed to pay Germany 1 million paper lire a year
for five years commencing in 1931.

IV. SUMMARY OF PAYMENT AND SAFEGUARD
PROVISIONS

The Young plan and the various agreements based
on it, which we have just described, laid down a com-

---

[22] The full schedule of payments under this agreement is given in
Appendix B, p. 469. For the details of the financial arrangements covering the transitional period, see Myers, *The Reparation Settlement*,
pp. 61-64, and for the text of the Franco-Yugoslav agreement, *Chambre
des Deputés, XIV Législature, Session de 1930, Annexe No. 3024 au
Procés-verbal de la séance du 20 mars 1930*, pp. 160-62.

[23] See p. 256.

[24] For the text of the letters, see *Annexe No. 3024* cited above, pp.
149-50.

plete schedule of reparation payments to be made by
Germany and a comprehensive and detailed procedure
for the handling of the prescribed annuities. The size and
character of the annuities and the salient features of the
machinery of payment are set forth below.

1. Size and character of annuities. The German schedule of payments was divided into two groups of annuities, the first group extending over 37 years, from
1929-30 to 1965-66, and the second group over 22 years,
from 1966-67 to 1987-88. The first of the 59 annuities
was made to cover only seven months, in order to provide for a transition from the so-called Dawes year to
the German fiscal year, which became the period of each
of the subsequent annuities.[25]

The first full annuity, payable between April 1, 1930
and March 31, 1931, was fixed at 1,641.6 million marks.
The amount was then to rise gradually, until the maximum annuity of 2,352.7 million marks would be reached
in 1965-66, the last year of the first period. Each of the
36 full annuities was divided into two parts: the unconditional, which was to remain uniform throughout the
whole period at 612 million marks, and the conditional,
which was to vary with the changes in the total annual
payment. The annuities during the second period were to
vary from 1,566.1 million marks to 1,703.3 millions in
the course of the 19 years from 1966-67 to 1984-85, and
drop to less than a billion marks during the final three
years. All these annuities were exclusive of the payments

[25] Under the régime established in accordance with the Dawes plan,
annual accounts covered periods from Sept. 1 to Aug. 31. The Young
plan was intended to go into effect at the expiration of the fifth Dawes
year, that is, on Sept. 1, 1928, but the annual accounting period was
made to coincide with the German fiscal year, which runs from Apr. 1
to Mar. 31. As a result, the first Young annuity was made to cover
only the period from Sept. 1, 1929 to Mar. 31, 1930.

to be made to the United States under the American-
German agreement, which were described on page
214.[26]

The interest and amortization charges on the 1924
loan, which had been included in the Dawes annuities,
were left out of the new schedule. They were made payable separately and were given the character of unconditional payments. Since the loan matures in 1949, these
payments are to continue only until that year. They
average 76.5 million marks annually over the 20-year
period 1929-49, and were to constitute, therefore, during
these years, a supplement of this average size to the unconditional portion of the reparation annuities.

2. *Normal mode of payment.* When the agreements
signed at The Hague went into effect, the German government handed over to the Bank for International
Settlements a certificate of indebtedness, to which there
were attached 58 coupons.[27] Each coupon was divided into two parts, A and B. Part A represented the unconditional, and Part B the conditional, portion of each annuity. Each coupon when properly endorsed by the Bank
for International Settlements and returned to the German government was to constitute full discharge of the
annuity represented by it.

[26] The full schedule of payments by Germany is given in Appendix
B, pp. 472-73. It should be noted that the annual instalments proposed
by the Young Committee, which included the payments to the United
States, were based, for the first 37 years, on a constant annuity of
1,988.8 million marks, the difference between this figure and the comparatively small payments during the early years being funded, with
interest, over the later years. Hence the graduated character of the actual schedule.

[27] The agreements did not officially go into effect until May 17,
1930, and the payments during the first Young annuity year (Sept. 1,
1929–Mar. 31, 1930) and the first two months of the second were
collected and distributed by the Agent General for Reparation Payments.

Each annuity was made payable in twelve equal monthly instalments, due on the 15th day of each month. Except when the postponement provisions, described below, had been invoked and were operative, the mode of payment was to be as follows: A portion of the monthly instalment, representing one-twelfth of the deliveries in kind quota for the year, was to be paid by the German government in marks to the account of the Bank for International Settlements at the Reichsbank. The remainder of the instalment, without any distinction as between the unconditional and the conditional annuities, was to be paid in currencies other than marks. Each such instalment was also to include one-twelfth of the charges on the 1924 loan for the current year. At least one month before each payment date, the bank was to inform the German government and the Reichsbank of its preferences with respect to the currencies in which it desired the payment to be made. This it was to do on the basis of instructions received from the creditor governments. If the German government found it impossible or undesirable to comply with these preferences, it had the right to make payment "entirely in the currencies of the creditor countries whose nationals were members of the committee of experts and as nearly as may be in proportion to the respective shares of these countries."

In other words, after deducting from any instalment the amount required for payments on account of deliveries in kind, the creditors might ask Germany to pay so much of the remainder in dollars, so much in pounds sterling, so much in francs, so much in yen, and so on. If Germany found it possible to make payment in this manner, well and good. If not, she had the right to pay approximately one-half in French francs; one-fifth in pounds sterling; one-tenth in Italian lire, etc. All payments in foreign currencies were to be credited in marks, the conversion being made on the basis of the average exchange rates prevailing on the Berlin Bourse during the last 15 days preceding the date of payment.

The contribution of the German Railway Company was also payable in twelve monthly instalments, but on the first day of each month. The amount represented by each instalment was to be paid by the company in marks into the account of the Bank for International Settlements at the Reichsbank. If the reparation instalment due on the 15th day of the preceding month had been duly received by the bank, the contribution by the railway company was to be placed at the disposal of the German government as soon as received. This contribution was, therefore, really in the nature of a collateral guarantee.

All payments made by Germany were to be received by the Bank for International Settlements into an annuity trust account. Out of each monthly instalment a sum equivalent to one-twelfth of the current annual charges on the 1924 loan was to be immediately deducted and transferred by the bank into a special account, out of which interest and amortization payments were to be made to the bondholders. The remainder, after a further deduction of the bank's commission, which amounted to one per mille on the actual payments received, was then to be allocated to the creditors and the funds held by the bank subject to their orders.

The bank was to pay no interest on the funds as long as they remained in the annuity trust account. The creditor governments were not, however, at liberty to transfer from the trust account all of the funds allocated to them.

They were under obligation, in accordance with the Young plan, to maintain a minimum deposit in the trust account aggregating for all of them the sum of 125 million marks.[28] Everything in excess of this minimum amount the creditors had the right to withdraw from the bank's custody, to transfer to an interest-bearing account at the bank, or to dispose of in any other manner they saw fit. The only exception to this rule was that whenever a portion of the unconditional annuity had been mobilized, an amount necessary to meet the annual charges on the bonds thus created was to be transferred by the bank to a special account, the deduction from each creditor's share being proportional to its participation in the mobilization.

3. *Safeguards.* The German government had the right, upon giving the bank 90 days' notice, to suspend, for a period of not over two years, the transfer of the whole or a part of the conditional portions of the current annuities. This constituted a safeguard in the event of temporary difficulties. During the period of suspension, however, the German government had to continue to

[28] This sum, in marks, was divided as follows:

France	68,037,500	Rumania	1,312,500
Great Britain	26,587,500	Portugal	862,500
Italy	13,887,500	Japan	862,500
Belgium	7,512,500	Greece	450,000
Yugoslavia	5,462,500	Poland	25,000
		Total	125,000,000

In addition, Germany was under an obligation to maintain in the annuity trust account a non-interest-bearing deposit equivalent to 50 per cent of the average deposit left in the account by the creditors, but not exceeding 100 million marks. The use of these funds by the bank was a part of its compensation for handling the reparation payments, although the maintenance of the deposits entitled the government to a share in the bank's net profits.

meet, in foreign currencies, the monthly instalments represented by the charges on the 1924 loan, the unconditional portion of the current annuity, and whatever part of the conditional portion it was still able to transfer. The remainder of the current annuity, during the first year, was to be paid in full in marks into the account of the bank at the Reichsbank. During the second year the payment in marks as well as the transfer of one-half of the conditional portion of the annuity could be suspended.

The maximum period of postponement was two years, with the proviso that if, during any annuity year, the German government availed itself of the power of postponement, "the transfers falling due during any second year cannot be postponed for more than one year from their respective due dates, unless and until the transfers due during the first year shall have been effected in full, in which case the transfers due during such second year may be postponed during two years from their respective due dates; and the transfers due during any third year cannot be postponed at all until the transfers due during the first year have been effected in full."

The funds paid by Germany in marks, after payments had been made on account of current deliveries in kind, could be utilized in one of three ways: (1) special programs of deliveries in kind could be arranged between Germany and individual creditors; (2) the funds could be invested in Germany by the Bank for International Settlements for the accounts of individual creditors; or (3) the funds could be left on deposit at the Reichsbank. On all such funds left with the Reichsbank, the German government was to pay, for the benefit of the creditors, interest "at the rate of 1 per cent per annum above the prevailing Reichsbank discount rate, or at 5.5 per cent, whichever is lower."

The amount of temporary relief which could be afforded Germany by the operation of these postponement provisions was very small. During the first year of the two-year period of suspension of transfers, the relief was wholly confined to the country's international balance of payments, and represented merely the removal of an obligation to find the necessary foreign currencies for the conversion of the amounts not absorbed by the deliveries in kind. The government budget was thus afforded no relief at all; on the contrary, it could, if interest had to be paid on funds remaining on deposit at the Reichsbank, be made to bear an even greater burden than if there had been no suspension of transfer. During the second year, with both the payments in marks and the transfers suspended in part, there was an appreciable amount of relief for both the balance of payments and the government budget.

Machinery had been provided for some permanent relief with respect to the conditional payments. The plan made provision for a special advisory committee, which had to be convened by the Bank for International Settlements whenever Germany declared her intention to suspend transfer or "at any other time when the German government declares to the creditor governments and to the bank that it has come to the conclusion in good faith that Germany's exchange and economic life may be seriously endangered by the transfer in part or in full of the postponable portion of the annuities." The purpose of the advisory committee was to consider the circumstances and conditions that led up to its convocation and "to indicate for consideration by the governments and the bank what are the measures that should be taken in regard to the application of the present plan."

This committee was to consist of seven members, one nominated by each of the following: the governors of the central banks of Germany, France, Great Britain, Italy, Belgium, and Japan, and by "a Federal Reserve Bank of the United States or some other agreed American financial institution." These seven members could, if they desired, co-opt four more members. It was specifically provided that the committee "shall play no part in connection with the unconditional annuity." There was no limitation, however, on the scope of its recommendations with regard to the conditional payments, and a part of its task, whenever convened, was to report its findings to the bank and to the governments concerned.

4. Guarantee Fund. The Young plan provided a rather complicated machinery for the distribution of reparation payments among the creditors in the event of a suspension of transfer. It stipulated that whatever amount Germany actually transferred during any year must be divided among the creditors strictly in accordance with their respective shares in the total annuity for that year. But it also stipulated that the distribution percentages relating to the unconditional portion of the annuity could not, under any circumstances, be disturbed. Conditions might easily arise under which it would be impossible to carry out both of these stipulations. It was in order to provide for such a contingency that the framers of the Young plan set up a device in the form of a special fund. The operation of this device may best be described by means of a concrete illustration.

Suppose that in any year Germany had suspended the transfer of the whole of the conditional portion of the current annuity. This would have meant that, apart from the sum required to meet the charges on the 1924 loan, she would actually pay into the Bank for International Settlements in foreign currencies only the unconditional portion of the annuity, or 612 million marks. Suppose further that the French share of the total annuity for that particular year was 52 per cent. Then, in accordance was the first stipulation, France would be entitled to 318 million marks, and all the other creditors to 294 millions. But in accordance with the second stipulation, France would receive her fixed share of the unconditional annuity, or 500 million marks. If, therefore, the second stipulation, which had priority over the first, was carried out, of the amount actually transferred by Germany there would have been left only 112 million marks for distribution among all the other creditors who, under the first stipulation, were entitled to 294 millions. Since the internal payments by Germany continued after the suspension of transfer, this amount was available in German marks. What was lacking was foreign currencies into which to convert the marks.

In order to make such foreign currencies available to bridge the gap, France, in consideration of the fact that she had been assigned a disproportionately large share of the unconditional annuity, agreed to create and maintain at the Bank for International Settlements a Guarantee Fund in foreign currencies equivalent to 500 million marks. In the eventuality described above, the bank would have drawn on the Guarantee Fund for the requisite supplies of foreign currencies—186 million marks under the conditions just outlined. The Fund would have been replenished as soon as the postponed transfers had been effected. In the meantime, the bank would have paid the French government interest on the unutilized portion of the Fund, while the amount in marks represented by the payments made out of the Fund would have been invested in Germany for the benefit of the French government.

Under the terms of the Young plan, France agreed to pay into the Fund 10 per cent of her share of the proceeds from the mobilization of any part of the unconditional annuity, and to make good the difference up to a maximum of 500 million marks on the demand of the bank. It was provided in the plan that the bank would not make this demand until after the suspension of transfer.

Whereas the Dawes plan was absolutely provisional in character, the Young plan, it is apparent, was conceived as a final settlement. The total obligation was definitely fixed as the sum of the scheduled annuities, adjustments in the light of price changes and conditions of prosperity were abolished, and all foreign controls were abandoned, the administration of payments being taken over by a newly created international banking agency. The only avenues left open for possible subsequent modification were (1) in connection with the "postponable" payments which might conceivably at some future date be reduced in the light of investigations by an advisory committee convened by the Bank for International Settlements, and (2) in connection with a general consideration of the whole war debt problem. Interestingly enough, as we shall see, the difficulties which arose within two years were of so grave and urgent a character that it proved impossible to utilize the safeguard machinery provided in the plan. Direct action of creditor governments became imperative in connection with both the unconditional and the postponable annuities. The "final" settlement proved to be merely provisional after all.

CHAPTER XI

OTHER REPARATION SETTLEMENTS

Reparation obligations were imposed by the treaties of peace on three of Germany's allies in the war—Austria, Hungary, and Bulgaria—while the countries which had received territorial concessions from the former Austro-Hungarian Monarchy were made liable for so-called liberation payments.[1] Although these debts were of negligible magnitude as compared with the obligations for which Germany was held responsible, the issues in connection with them were none the less of great importance to the countries concerned.

Prior to The Hague conferences of August 1929 and January 1930, only Bulgaria and Hungary were compelled to make regular payments on account of their treaty obligations. With the other countries, the question remained in abeyance until, upon the recommendation of the Young Committee, it was placed on the agenda of the first Hague conference. One of the seven committees set up by the conference was entrusted with the task of devising final and definitive solutions of all these issues, to the end that the whole complex of financial obligations resulting from the treaties of peace might be dealt with concurrently.

The committee on non-German reparations, which sat at Paris from September 16 to November 30, 1929, encountered almost insuperable difficulties in its attempts to grapple with the problems set before it. Its report, when finally presented, recorded agreement on very few of the matters under discussion. The difficult task of find-

[1] See pp. 149-50.

ing acceptable solutions devolved on the second Hague conference, and there consumed much time and effort. Eventually, however, all the problems were settled except those of Hungary, and even concerning them a sufficient degree of compromise was attained to open the way for a definitive arrangement negotiated at a later conference. Five of the 15 documents, signed at The Hague on January 20, 1930, related to the non-German settlements. In this chapter we shall survey briefly the history of each of these problems and set forth the terms of settlement governing the arrangements which are now officially in force.

I. AUSTRIA

The Reparation Commission never performed the task, assigned to it by the treaties of peace, of determining Austria's share in the total reparation liability assessed against the Central European powers. The commission presumably recorded the cessions and deliveries made by Austria in accordance with the Armistice convention and the Treaty of St. Germain, but, so far as is known, it never undertook a complete evaluation of the payments thus made. No regular schedule of annual reparation payments was ever imposed on Austria; and today she is entirely free of any reparation debt. By The Hague agreement all reparation claims against Austria were completely wiped out, and all undischarged accounts between Austria and the Allied Powers, growing out of the World War, were definitely and finally closed.

The only important official action taken with respect to Austria by the Reparation Commission during the twelve years of its existence was in connection with the League of Nations scheme of financial reconstruction in that country. The scheme called for the extension to Austria of an international loan, which was to be secured by the assignment of certain budgetary revenues. The Austrian government could not execute the assignment because, under the terms of the treaty of peace, the Reparation Commission held a general lien on all the resources of the Austrian state as security for reparation and other financial obligations growing out of the war. By a decision dated February 20, 1923 the Reparation Commission released, for a period of 20 years, the budgetary revenues necessary to secure the reconstruction loan. This release was intended to signify a general adjournment of any discussion of Austria's reparation liability for the same period, although the text of the commission's decision did not record this intention specifically.[2]

The Hague agreement stated that "the financial obligations of Austria arising under any provision of the Armistice of November 3, 1918, and the Treaty of St. Germain and any treaties and agreements supplementary thereto shall be finally discharged by the payments, deliveries, and cessions made by Austria up to the date of the coming into force of this agreement." It declared that from the date on which it became operative, all relations between Austria and the Reparation Commission should cease, all accounts between Austria and the commission should be considered as finally closed, and the general lien in favor of the financial obligations created by the treaty of peace should cease to exist.

The agreement excluded from its general liquidatory action certain special arrangements already signed and

[2] For the text of the commission's decision see The League of Nations, *The Financial Reconstruction of Austria*, 1926, pp. 151-52.

referring, in the main, to the settlement of administrative questions which arose out of the dismemberment of the former Austro-Hungarian Monarchy. With this exception, however, it provided that all other financial claims and counter-claims arising under the treaty of peace, the Armistice convention, or in any other manner as a consequence of the war, should be reciprocally waived. A similar provision applied to all war claims and counter-claims as among the former members of the Central European coalition of powers. Finally, the creditor powers undertook to surrender their right under the treaty of peace "to retain and liquidate the property, rights, and interests belonging at the date of the coming into force of the Treaty of St. Germain to nationals of the former Austrian Empire or companies controlled by them, in so far as such property, rights, and interests are not already liquid or liquidated or have not yet been definitely disposed of."[3]

II. HUNGARY

Hungary was not treated by her reparation creditors with the same leniency that had been accorded to Austria. As in the case of Austria, no determination was ever made of Hungary's share in the total reparation liability and there was no evaluation of the cessions and deliveries effected during the early post-war years. But a regular schedule of annual reparation payments was imposed on Hungary, first in a provisional form in 1924 and finally in a definitive form by agreements signed at The Hague on January 20, 1930 and at Paris on April 28, 1930. These agreements disposed also of an extremely vexa-

[3] For the text of The Hague agreement see *Agreements Concluded at The Hague Conference, January, 1930* (British Parliamentary Paper, Cmd. 3484), pp. 146-49.

tious controversy between Hungary and her three neighbors, Rumania, Czechoslovakia, and Yugoslavia, regarding property rights of Hungarian nationals in the territories detached from Hungary by the Treaty of Trianon
and incorporated in these three states.

1. Determination of total liability. The first official
action of the Reparation Commission with respect to
Hungary was, as in the case of Austria, taken in connection with the League of Nations financial reconstruction
scheme for that country. Here again the problem was one
of granting a release from the general lien on all the
resources of the Hungarian state for certain budgetary
revenues to be used as security for a reconstruction loan.
The commission granted this release in decisions dated
May 23, 1923, October 17, 1923, and February 21,
1924. But at the same time it also prescribed for Hungary a schedule of reparation payments, covering a period
of 20 years, from January 1, 1924 to December 31, 1943.

In accordance with this schedule, Hungary was to
pay during the period an aggregate sum of 200 million
gold crowns.[4] During the first three years no cash payments were required, but Hungary was to turn over to
her creditors deliveries in kind in amounts "corresponding to the value of 880 tons of coal per working day."
The actual deliveries were made in the form of coal shipments. During the remaining 17 years the schedule required annuities, rising in magnitude from 5 to 14 million crowns and payable on June 30 and December 31 of
each year. These payments were to be considered as made
in partial discharge of the total reparation liability, the
determination of which was adjourned to a later date.

[4] The crown, which was the currency unit of the Austro-Hungarian
Monarchy, was defined as having a gold content equivalent to 20.26
cents.

In view of the possibility that reparation instalments, added to the service charges on the reconstruction loan, might endanger the fiscal or currency stability of Hungary, safeguards were provided in the form of a transfer protection scheme. The reparation payments were to be paid by the Hungarian Treasury into the Hungarian National Bank in domestic currency. The task of converting these funds into foreign currencies devolved on the president of the bank, who, whenever he became convinced that the transfer operations involved in the process were likely to threaten the stability of the currency, had the right to suspend transfers and ask for the appointment of a special transfer committee.[5] Moreover, as a protection for the holders of the reconstruction bonds, it was provided that during the currency of the loan, the trustees representing the bondholders would have the right to ask the Council of the League of Nations to appoint a commissioner general for Hungary, whenever they could show that the budgetary equilibrium and the security of the loan were threatened. When such a commissioner general was in office, no reparation payments could be made if, in his opinion, they endangered the equilibrium of the budget or the security of the loan.[6]

The Hungarian reparation question remained in this form up to the convocation of the first Hague conference. In the meantime there developed between Hungary and three of her immediate neighbors a bitter controversy

---

[5] The same principle was later adopted by the Dawes Committee in setting up the system of transfer protection for German reparation payments. See p. 166.

[6] For the details of the reparation and reconstruction schemes for Hungary put into effect in 1924, see The League of Nations, *The Financial Reconstruction of Hungary*, 1926.

over the so-called "optant" question. Although there was no connection whatever between this question and that of reparation obligations, both involved financial accounts as between Hungary and the other three countries, and they were finally linked together in one comprehensive settlement.

The Treaty of Trianon had provided that the landed property of Hungarian nationals in those portions of the former Hungarian territory which had been detached from Hungary was not to be seized and liquidated with the state-owned property which was made subject to such seizure and liquidation as a part of the reparation program. However, Rumania, Czechoslovakia, and Yugoslavia, the three countries which had received territorial cessions from Hungary, all introduced far-reaching agrarian reforms, in the process of which Hungarian-owned landed properties were expropriated in common with other similar properties. The expropriation schemes provided for compensation, which in most cases was based on practically confiscatory prices. The Hungarian owners appealed to the government at Budapest on the ground that such a procedure amounted to the sort of liquidation specifically prohibited by the Treaty of Trianon and constituted, consequently, a violation of that treaty. The Hungarian government took up the cause of the expropriated property owners and raised the question formally before the Council of the League of Nations.

For several years this controversy plagued the League, which made several unsuccessful attempts to settle it. The whole matter finally came down to the question of how much compensation the dispossessed owners were entitled to receive, and it was in this form, stripped of its highly complicated political and legal aspects, that the problem came up before the committee on non-German reparations, when it was discovered that no separate and distinct solutions for the two problems appeared possible.

The committee made an attempt to settle the two questions at once by linking together the reparation obligations of the Hungarian government and the property claims of dispossessed Hungarian nationals. No agreement, however, was reached during the committee's sessions, and the problem was transferred to the second Hague conference. There, after much difficulty, at a dramatic all-night sitting of the conference on the very eve of its close, a compromise was reached on the principles which were to govern a final agreement. A formal document, embodying this compromise and providing for the convocation of a special conference to work out the necessary details of the settlement, was signed. The conference thus agreed upon met at Paris, and on April 28, 1930 its members signed a number of definitive agreements.

The Hague and Paris agreements confirmed the Reparation Commission's schedule of payments, established in 1924 and still in operation at the time. Hungary's reparation payments were to continue on the scale prescribed in the schedule until December 31, 1943. The agreements further provided that, starting with January 1, 1944, and up to and including the year 1966, Hungary was to pay a constant annuity of 13.5 million gold crowns. Subject to several minor exceptions, these payments were declared by the agreements to constitute a "complete and final settlement of the charges incumbent upon her [Hungary] by virtue of the Treaty of Trianon, of the Armistice of November 3, 1918, and of any agreements supplementary thereto."[7]

As in the case of Austria, the agreements with Hungary provided for the cessation of all relations between Hungary and the Reparation Commission; the final closing of all accounts between Hungary and the commission; the lifting of the general lien on the resources of the Hungarian state; the mutual waiving of all financial claims and counter-claims arising as a consequence of the war and the treaty of peace; and the surrender by the creditor powers of their right to any further liquidation of Hungarian property. All these provisions were to go into effect on the date on which the agreements became operative.

The Bank for International Settlements was substituted by the agreements for the Reparation Commission as the agency authorized to receive and distribute the payments made by Hungary. The scheduled annuities were made payable in equal semi-annual instalments, due on January 1 and July 1 of each year.

The agreements confirmed the transfer and other safeguard provisions which governed the operation of the 1924 schedule of payments. These provisions were, however, to remain in force only until the completion of that schedule. The payments prescribed for the years 1944-66 were made "an unconditional obligation, that is to say, without any right of suspension whatever," payable to the Bank for International Settlements "in gold or in currencies equivalent to gold."

2. *Provisions for the disposal of the payments.* By an arrangement signed at The Hague, the creditors of

[7] For the Hungarian schedule of reparation payments, see Appendix B, p. 477.

Hungary provided for the following distribution among themselves of the annuities payable up to 1944:

	Per Cent
Greece	76.73
Rumania	13.00
Yugoslavia	2.00
Czechoslovakia	1.00
Other creditors	7.27
Total	100.00

The share assigned to the "other creditors"—the British Empire, France, Italy, Belgium, Japan, and Portugal—was to be distributed in accordance with Article 2 of the Spa agreement of July 16, 1920. This provision, however, lost all significance when, by the Paris agreements of April 28, 1930, these creditors agreed to transfer their shares to the special "Funds" described below. No distribution provision for the annuities during the years 1944-66 was necessary, because the creditors had already agreed to turn them over in their entirety to the Funds.

Under The Hague and Paris agreements, the claims of the Hungarian nationals whose properties had been expropriated in Rumania, Czechoslovakia, and Yugoslavia, were to be liquidated out of two Funds which the powers concerned agreed to set up. Fund A, known as the Agrarian Fund, was to provide for satisfying the claims of individual property owners, while Fund B was to be similarly used to afford compensation for church property, local railway lines, and various other claims.

The maximum amount of compensation to be provided out of Fund A was fixed at a total of 219,500,000 gold crowns.[8] This Fund was to be constituted by means of annuities paid into it by Rumania, Yugoslavia, and Czechoslovakia; by the assignment to it of portions of the Hungarian reparation instalments; and by the payment into it of additional annuities by the British Empire, France, Italy, and Belgium.

Rumania undertook to pay 500,000 crowns a year into the Fund up to 1944, and 836,336 crowns a year during 1944-66. Yugoslavia's contribution was fixed at 1 million crowns a year up to 1944, and 1,672,672 crowns a year thereafter until 1966. These were to be maximums, subject to deductions resulting from later adjustments between the governments concerned and individual property owners. Czechoslovakia's payments were not definitely fixed, pending the completion of the agrarian reform in that country. These contributions were offset in part by the three countries' receipts on account of their respective shares in the Hungarian reparation annuities.

Out of the Hungarian reparation payments during the period prior to 1944, the share assigned to the "other creditors," or 7.27 per cent of the total, was reassigned by these creditors to Fund A. Out of the Hungarian annuities during the years 1944-66, the sum of 6.1 million gold crowns a year was earmarked for the Fund.

In addition, the British Empire, France, Italy, and Belgium agreed to pay into the Fund, during the years 1930-66 inclusive, annual amounts equivalent to their respective shares of the Bulgarian reparation annuities.[9] Moreover, the first three of these powers agreed to make

---

[8] This figure represented a compromise between the claims put forward by Hungary, which totalled 310 million crowns, and the estimates furnished by the other three countries.

[9] See pp. 252-53. The combined shares of these countries in the Bulgarian annuities work out at approximately 3.5 per cent of the total.

additional contributions, the maximum annual amounts
of which were specified in gold crowns as follows:

	1931-32	1933-43	1944-66
British Empire	—	827,528	579,269
France	400,000	1,680,000	1,340,000
Italy	400,000	1,630,112	1,260,027
Total	800,000	4,137,640	3,179,296

Finally, France and Italy agreed to pay into a "special
reserve" of Fund A combined annuities, not exceeding
326,000 crowns in 1933-43, and 545,291 crowns during
1944-66.

Fund B, which was fixed at 100 million crowns, was
to be constituted by means of the following annual instalments paid into it during the years 1931-44: Great
Britain, 600,000 crowns; France, 1.2 million crowns;
and Italy, 1.2 million crowns. During the years 1944-66,
the remainder of the Hungarian annuities for those years,
or 7.4 million crowns a year, was assigned to the Fund.

Elaborate regulations for the administration of the
Funds were laid down in the agreements. These involved
the establishment of arbitral tribunals for adjudicating
individual claims.

The payments into the Funds by the powers not directly concerned in the controversy were so arranged that
the combined contributions would be equivalent to their
respective shares in the payments prescribed for Czechoslovakia on account of her "liberation" liability. As we
have already seen, however, by a special agreement
France ceded to Italy her share in the Czechoslovak annuities.[10] These powers thus, in effect, surrendered their
claims to Hungarian, Bulgarian, and Czechoslovak pay-

[10] See p. 223.

ments in order to facilitate the solution of the difficult political problem confronting them at the time, or, as they stated in the preamble to one of the agreements signed at Paris, in order "to show their readiness for conciliation and their desire for peace."[11]

III. BULGARIA

Bulgaria was the only one of the reparation debtors whose liability was fixed by the treaty of peace. But although the Treaty of Neuilly made formal and detailed provisions for the discharging of this liability by Bulgaria, no actual reparation payments were made until 1923, that is, until three years after the payments were originally scheduled to begin. During these years, however, Bulgaria carried out, in whole or in part, many of the other financial liabilities assessed against her by the treaty. The inauguration of regular annual payments on the reparation account was preceded by an important revision of the original terms, and these terms underwent a further and far-reaching modification in the agreement which was signed at The Hague.

1. Arrangements prior to 1930. The Treaty of Neuilly fixed Bulgaria's total reparation liability at 2,250 million gold francs.[12] It stipulated that this amount should be discharged by means of 75 semi-annual instalments, beginning on July 1, 1920. The first two instalments were to represent only interest at 2 per cent per annum from January 1, 1920 on the whole amount assessed against Bulgaria. Thereafter, the treaty provided,

---

[11] For the text of the agreements signed with Hungary, see *Agreements Concluded at The Hague*, pp. 156-67 and 170-72; and *International Agreements Regarding the Financial Obligations of Hungary Resulting from the Treaty of Trianon* (British Parliamentary Paper, Cmd. 3577).

[12] The "gold franc" was defined as the equivalent of 19.29 cents.

"each half-yearly payment shall include, besides the payment of interest at 5 per cent per annum, the provision of a sinking fund sufficient to extinguish the total amount due by Bulgaria in 37 years from January 1, 1921."

The administration of the Bulgarian reparation program was placed by the treaty in the hands of an Inter-Allied Commission, to be stationed at Sofia, as a local organ of the Reparation Commission, and to be made up of the representatives of Great Britain, France, and Italy. The treaty provided that "the Inter-Allied Commission shall from time to time consider the resources and capacity of Bulgaria and, after giving her representatives a just opportunity to be heard, shall have discretion to recommend to the Reparation Commission either a reduction or a postponement of any particular payment due or a reduction of the total capital sum to be paid by Bulgaria." The treaty further provided that "the Reparation Commission shall have power by a majority of votes to make any reduction or postponement up to the extent recommended by the Inter-Allied Commission."

Bulgaria did not begin payments on the prescribed date. The Inter-Allied Commission itself was not constituted for some time after the treaty went into effect and did not actually arrive in Sofia until February 1921, after the first two semi-annual payments stipulated in the treaty had fallen due and had not been met. The commission regularized the situation created by this delinquency by granting Bulgaria a retroactive moratorium, and then proceeded to a study of the economic and financial condition of the country with a view to determining the manner in which the future reparation payments should be discharged. The study and the necessary negotiations with the Bulgarian government lasted two years, and during this period the commission granted extensions of the original moratorium, as they became necessary.

The result of the negotiations was a protocol, signed on March 21, 1923, by the members of the commission and the Bulgarian Prime Minister. Under the terms of this protocol, the total amount of the debt as fixed by the Treaty of Neuilly was retained, but provision was made for the current liquidation of only about one-quarter of that amount. The total reparation debt was divided into two parts, known as Tranche A and Tranche B. Only Tranche A, representing a capital sum of 550 million francs, was funded. All consideration of Tranche B, representing the remaining 1,700 million francs, was adjourned for 30 years, without interest. Eventually, it was against this Tranche B that all the payments, deliveries, and cessions already made by Bulgaria and all credit claims accruing to Bulgaria under the treaty of peace were to be charged.[13]

The funded part of the reparation debt was to be discharged in 60 years, by means of semi-annual instalments, graduated in size during the first twelve years and then remaining constant during the rest of the period. The first payment was to be on the basis of an annuity of 5 million francs. The amount was then to rise gradually until the maximum or standard annuity of 43,395,336 francs would be reached in 1935. These annuities represented principal and current interest at the rate of 5 per cent per annum.

By a special protocol, signed a year later, Bulgaria agreed to pay a total of 25 million gold francs in liquida-

---

[13] It will be noted that the plan thus applied to Bulgaria was similar to that on which the London settlement of 1921 concerning the German reparation question was based. See p. 152.

tion of her obligation to defray the costs of the Allied armies of occupation. The protocol provided for the extinguishment of this debt by means of 20 semi-annual instalments, representing the principal sum and interest at the rate of 5 per cent per annum. Finally, by means of special conventions, Bulgaria liquidated the war accounts held against her by Yugoslavia and Rumania because of requisitions on their territory by Bulgarian occupation authorities during the period of hostilities.

In connection with her international loan, floated in 1926 under the auspices of the League of Nations, Bulgaria received an important safeguard, so far as her reparation payments were concerned, in the form of transfer protection. In its decision dated July 23, 1926, in which it granted a release from the general lien held by it on all the resources of the Bulgarian state for certain revenues required as security for the loan, the Reparation Commission declared:

The Bulgarian government will have the right at any time during the existence of the said loan to make to the Inter-Allied Commission a request that, in the interest of the stability of the Bulgarian exchange, purchases of foreign currencies necessary for the payment of reparations under the protocol signed at Sofia on March 21, 1923, be suspended either in whole or in part.

In the schedule attached to the decision, provisions were made for the creation of a Transfer Committee to take over the operation of transfers immediately upon the receipt of such a request from the Bulgarian government.

2. *The Hague agreement.* The Bulgarian reparation problem was one of the questions assigned by the first Hague conference to its committee on non-German reparations. The committee, after a protracted discussion

in its Bulgarian sub-committee, failed to reach any agreement, and the whole question was referred to the second Hague conference. There the negotiations were successfully concluded, and a formal agreement was signed, superseding all previous reparations arrangements.

Under the terms of The Hague agreement, Tranche B of the original reparation debt was entirely cancelled. Moreover, Great Britain, France, and Italy waived their claim to the still outstanding payments in respect of the occupation costs. As for Tranche A, the following 37 annuities were substituted for the still undischarged payments inscribed in the 1923 protocol:

Period	Number of Annuities	Annual Payments (In gold francs)
April 1, 1930	1	5,000,000
April 1, 1930-March 31, 1940 . . .	10	10,000,000
April 1, 1940-March 31, 1950 . . .	10	11,500,000
April 1, 1950-March 31, 1966 . . .	16	12,515,238

The new annuities represented a substantial reduction in Bulgaria's reparation payments, as may be seen from the following table.

REDUCTION IN BULGARIAN ANNUAL TREATY PAYMENTS
(In million of gold francs)

Fiscal Year Ending March 31	Payments under the 1923 Arrangements			Payments under The Hague Settlement	Reduction
	Repara-tion	Occupa-tion	Total		
1931	10.0	4.0	14.0	10.0	4.0
1932	10.0	4.0	14.0	10.0	4.0
1933	20.0	1.0	21.0	10.0	11.0
1934	32.9	1.0	33.9	10.0	23.9
1935 - 40	43.4	—	43.4	10.0	33.4
1941 - 50	43.4	—	43.4	11.5	31.9
1951 - 66	43.4	—	43.4	12.5	30.9
1967 - 83	43.4	—	43.4	—	43.4

The Hague agreement provided for the liquidation of the Inter-Allied Commission and the cessation of relations between Bulgaria and the Reparation Commission; the final closing of all outstanding accounts between Bulgaria and the commissions; the lifting of the general lien on the resources of the Bulgarian state; the mutual waiving of all financial claims and counter-claims arising as a consequence of the war, with the exception of those

BULGARIAN REPARATION PAYMENTS BEFORE AND AFTER
THE HAGUE SETTLEMENT

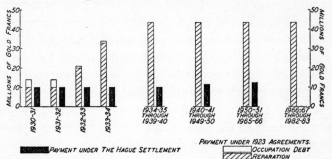

which had already been made the subject of special agreements;[14] and the surrender by the creditor powers of their right to any further liquidation of Bulgarian property. It was stipulated, however, that the revenues assigned as special security for reparation payments should continue to be so assigned.

[14] Three specific exceptions should be mentioned here. (1) Bulgaria agreed to pay Rumania 110 million Rumanian lei in liquidation of non-reparation war accounts between the two countries. This sum was made payable in two equal instalments, one of which was met in March 1931, and the other fell due in March 1932. (2) Under the terms of Article 141 of the Treaty of Neuilly, Yugoslavia still stood indebted to Bulgaria, as her share of the payments on the portion of the Bulgarian pre-war debt attributable to the territories ceded by Bulgaria to Yugoslavia, to the extent of an equivalent of $482,414, payable on July 1, 1931. (3) Greece stood similarly indebted to Bulgaria to the extent of an equivalent of $70,527, also payable on July 1, 1931.

The agreement confirmed the transfer safeguard provisions introduced in connection with the 1926 loan. Since the life of the loan extends until 1967, this provision was thus made to cover the whole period of reparation payments. In the application of these provisions, the role originally assigned to the Reparation Commission was transferred to the Bank for International Settlements, which in all other respects as well was substituted for the commission as the trustee for the creditor powers. The annuities were made normally payable to the bank in equal half-yearly instalments, on September 30 and March 31 of each fiscal year, in foreign currencies.

In addition to confirming the transfer safeguard provisions, The Hague agreement, by means of a declaration of the creditor powers annexed to it, extended to Bulgaria a privilege similar to that conferred upon Germany by the concurrent memorandum of the Young Committee and the subsequent formal agreement relating to it. This declaration read as follows:

> The creditor governments have taken note of the Bulgarian government's request to benefit by a remission of a portion of its debt in the event of the creditor governments themselves obtaining remission of the inter-Allied debts. They state their readiness collectively, if necessary, to consider favorably the possibility of allowing Bulgaria to have the benefit of advantages proportional to those which the special memorandum of the experts of the principal creditor powers and Germany concerning outpayments, appended to the experts' report of June 7, 1929, grants to Germany, without, however, any power having its share in Bulgarian annuities reduced by more than 50 per cent as a result of this possible reconsideration.

Finally, by an arrangement signed at The Hague, the creditor powers agreed on the following distribution among themselves of the Bulgarian reparation annuities:

	Per Cent
Greece	76.7
Rumania	13.0
Yugoslavia	5.0
France	2.4
Great Britain	1.0
Czechoslovakia	1.0
Others (Italy, Belgium, Japan, and Portugal)	0.9
Total	100.0

Greece was given, in addition, the whole of the first annuity. The British, French, Italian, and Belgian shares, it will be recalled, were assigned by a later agreement to the Agrarian Fund of Hungary.[15]

3. Bulgaro-Greek convention. A financial account between Bulgaria and Greece, growing indirectly out of the treaty of peace, caused a bitter controversy. It related to the compensation involved in the exchange of populations between the two countries after the war, and was finally settled, through the intervention of the League of Nations, by means of a special convention. The Treaty of Neuilly provided that Bulgarians living in Greece should be made to emigrate to Bulgaria, while Greeks living in Bulgaria should be likewise removed to Greece. In accordance with a convention signed between the two countries shortly afterward, the property left behind by these emigrants was to be taken over by the respective governments, which were to provide the necessary compensation. In this manner, the Bulgarian government became the debtor of the individual Greeks who had emigrated from Bulgaria, and the Greek government became the debtor of the individual Bulgarians

---

[15] For the details of the Bulgarian reparation problem and the texts of the principal agreements, see Leo Pasvolsky, *Bulgaria's Economic Position,* 1930, Chap. IV and Appendixes I-VI.

who had emigrated from Greece. The convention provided for the setting up of a mixed commission, which was to work out the basis of compensation and arrange for the payments to get into the hands of the rightful parties.

In spite of the fact that the mixed commission was duly set up, the question remained in abeyance for several years, until finally the League of Nations was requested to intervene. A new convention was prepared by the technical services of the League Secretariat, and on December 9, 1927 it was signed by the Finance Ministers of the two countries, M. Molloff for Bulgaria and M. Caphandaris for Greece. The convention provided that each government was to issue to its repatriated citizens its own bonds corresponding to the amount of compensation assessed by the mixed commission; that a balance was to be struck semi-annually by the commission between the payments effected by each of the governments on account of the bonds issued by it; and that only the difference was to be actually paid by one country to the other. Since more repatriated citizens were received by Bulgaria than by Greece, the Greek liability exceeded the Bulgarian. On August 19, 1931 the mixed commission fixed the sum of $7,615,000 as the net balance in favor of Bulgaria under the Molloff-Caphandaris convention. This amount was made payable in 60 semi-annual instalments, with interest at 6 per cent on unpaid balances outstanding at each payment date.

IV. CZECHOSLOVAKIA

The liberation obligations of the five countries which had received territorial cessions from the former Austro-Hungarian Monarchy—Italy, Rumania, Yugoslavia,

Poland, and Czechoslovakia—remained almost completely in abeyance from the time they were created by the Paris convention of September 10, 1919 until they came under the discussion of the first Hague conference in August 1929. The only action taken with respect to them in the meanwhile was at the conference of the Ministers of Finance of the Allied Powers held in March 1922, when the first three of the countries involved were given the privilege of extinguishing their liberation obligations by agreeing to surrender appropriate portions of their respective shares in the Series C bonds created by the London schedule of payments of May 5, 1921. Poland, as a reparation creditor of Germany, was similarly assumed to have the right of surrendering her claims on the Series C bonds in exchange for her "liberation" obligations. The liabilities of Italy, Rumania, Yugoslavia, and Poland arising from the 1919 Paris convention were automatically extinguished by the cancellation, at The Hague conference, of the bonds created under the London schedule. Czechoslovakia alone—not being a reparation creditor—remained obligated on the so-called "liberation" account.

By the terms of the 1919 convention, Czechoslovakia's liability in this respect was left for future determination on the basis of an extremely complicated procedure, but with a stipulation that it should not, under any circumstances, exceed a maximum of 750 million gold francs.[16] This determination was never actually made, but a plan for the liquidation of the liability on terms acceptable to both the creditors and the debtor was worked out by the committee on non-German reparations set up by the first Hague conference, and was embodied in a formal agree-

[16] See pp. 149-50.

ment signed at the second Hague conference on January 20, 1930.

Under the terms of this agreement, Czechoslovakia undertook to pay 37 annuities of 10 million gold marks each "in complete and final settlement of her debt arising out of the agreement of September 10, 1919." It was provided that the first annuity was to be paid in its entirety on March 15, 1930, and the subsequent ones in half-yearly instalments on July 1 and January 1 of each annuity year, taken to extend from July 1 to June 30. The final instalment was thus made payable on January 1, 1966. The agreement stipulated that "the instalments shall be paid by the Czechoslovak government to the Bank for International Settlements for the account of the creditor governments, in pounds sterling, at the average rate of exchange for the three days preceding the date of payment." The payments were made unconditional.

By an arrangement signed on the same day as the agreement, the creditor powers accepted the following distribution of each Czechoslovak annuity:

Country	Gold Marks	Country	Gold Marks
France	3,187,854	Belgium	418,816
Italy	3,146,632	Japan	51,920
Great Britain	1,384,519	Portugal	51,920
Greece	1,758,339	Total	10,000,000

Rumania and Yugoslavia agreed to refrain from participation in the distribution of the Czechoslovak payments.[17] The French share, as we have already seen, was reassigned to Italy, while Italy's own share, as well as that of Great Britain, was, in effect, earmarked for the Hungarian Funds.

[17] For the text of the agreement with Czechoslovakia, see *Agreements Concluded at The Hague Conference*, pp. 168-70.

PART IV

THE BREAKDOWN OF THE PAYMENT PROGRAMS

CHAPTER XII

ATTEMPTS AT REPARATION FULFILLMENT

In the two preceding divisions of our analysis, we have sketched the history of the war debt and reparation negotiations and the character of the settlements that had been effected prior to 1931. It is clear from this recital that with the passage of time policies with reference to both debts and reparations have undergone a steady evolution, particularly so in the case of the reparation negotiations. During the early post-war years it was assumed that the only reparation problem was the determination of the amount that Germany should be compelled to pay and the devising of means for enforcing such payments. Following the breakdown of Germany in 1923, the reparation policy shifted to a consideration of how much Germany could pay and what machinery could be devised to facilitate the making of such payments. Finally, reparation instalments under the Young plan were adjusted to the payment schedules arranged for in the principal war debt agreements. In the negotiation of these agreements there was a marked tendency in the direction of increasing recognition of the basic implications of the problem and of the close economic interrelation of all the obligations arising out of the war.

From this survey we turn to a consideration of the results of the policies that have been pursued. Discussion will be confined to an analysis of the process by which, and the extent to which, actual payments have been made in liquidation of the existing indebtedness—reserving for the final division of the study our consideration of the debt problem in terms of its profound and world-wide implications. The fulfillment process in relation to both the reparation payments and the war debts proper will be considered in the two chapters which follow, and an analysis of the breakdown of the payment programs which took place in the summer of 1931 will then be made. Finally, a discussion of the situation that has arisen as a result of the Lausanne conference of June-July 1932 will be presented.

I. AMOUNTS PAID BY GERMANY

Germany has been making payments on reparation and various other accounts growing out of the war ever since the end of hostilities. In fact, cessions of property, the value of which was to be credited later, were prescribed even by the Armistice convention. Since then, payments have been made, in one form or another, and in varying amounts. There is, however, no precise and generally accepted figure of the total volume of payments made by Germany. Such a figure exists only for the period covered by the operation of the Dawes and the Young plans (from September 1, 1924 to July 1, 1931) when payments were made either in cash or in current direct deliveries of goods and services, the value of which was never a matter of controversy. Even with regard to these payments, as we shall presently see, there is some question as to whether or not certain items ought to be included. Early post-war reparation payments by Germany were largely in the form of cession of German-owned properties located in other countries or in those portions of the German territory which had been detached by treaties of peace, and of deliveries to the Allies of such equipment and commodities as the merchant marine, inland water craft, railroad materials, marine cables, coal, coke, dyestuffs, chemicals, and livestock. Estimates of the value of all these cessions and deliveries vary widely.

1. Payments prior to September 1, 1924. Two official estimates of the early post-war payments have been made, one by the German government and one by the Reparation Commission. The German government claims that exclusive of the instalments paid under the Dawes and the Young plans, the payments made by Germany on the reparation account aggregated 42,059 million gold marks and on all other accounts arising out of the treaty of peace, 14,518 millions, or a total of 56,577 millions. The Reparation Commission, on the other hand, acting for the creditor governments, admits payments amounting, for all accounts, to a total of only 10,426 million marks.

This vast difference in estimates results primarily from three causes. In the first place, some of the items included by Germany were not admitted by the Reparation Commission. In the second place, the commission's accounts were incomplete. And, in the third place, the commission's methods of valuation, with respect to the items admitted for credit, differed widely from those employed by the German government.[1]

In the reparation account proper the following were the principal claims for credit put forward by the German government, but disallowed by the commission: 1,338 million marks as the value of the naval vessels

---

[1] This question is now only of historic interest, since, under the provisions of The Hague agreements, based on recommendations of the Young Plan, all outstanding unsettled accounts between Germany and the commission were declared closed. However, controversy over the difference between the two official estimates still flares up occasionally.

surrendered to the Allies; 1,200 million marks for the labor of German prisoners of war; and 617 million marks for "clearing" payments in the process of liquidating pre-war commercial debts. In the non-reparation accounts, the Germans claimed a credit of 8,500 million marks as the cost of military disarmament, including scuttled men-of-war, and a credit of 3,500 million marks as the cost of industrial disarmament. Neither of these huge claims was allowed by the commission.

Following are some of the principal items, given in millions of marks, in which the discrepancies between the two estimates were particularly pronounced:

Item	Credit Claimed by Germany	Credit Allowed by the Reparation Commission
Ceded and confiscated German property, public and private	19,845	2,312
Surrendered and confiscated ships	4,486	711
German non-military stores left at the various fronts	5,041	140
Railway materials	1,803	1,103
Deliveries of coal, coke, and by-products	2,374	927

The discrepancy in the two estimates relating to the value of the German property, private and governmental, seized and liquidated abroad, is in part attributable to the incompleteness of the commission's accounts, and in part to differences in methods of valuation. The commission admittedly had not and, indeed, could not have completed its task in this respect during the period of its existence, because the process of liquidation itself had not as yet been wound up. The Hague agreements, it will be recalled, and the series of supplementary agreements signed by Germany with each of the Allies in connection with The Hague conference, terminated the still unfinished process of liquidation and rendered no longer necessary the task of evaluation.

The fundamental disagreement on evaluation between the commission and the German government is strikingly illustrated by the difference between the two estimates of such items as the merchant marine and railroad equipment delivered by Germany. In general, the commission adhered to the principle that the value of each piece of property should be determined by the price at which it could be liquidated at a forced sale, while the German government maintained that each piece of property should be considered as a part of a going concern, with a value much in excess of what could be realized at auction.[2] It should be noted that while the treasuries of the Allied governments received in the main only the prices brought at auction, their citizens who purchased the properties may well have gained much greater use values. On the other hand, Germany's sacrifice, in terms of the going values which her people actually gave up, were undoubtedly greater than the amounts credited to her government.

Several independent unofficial estimates have been made of the total payments made by Germany during the early post-war years. The two most comprehensive ones are those of the Institute of Economics and of John Maynard Keynes. Both of these, although they differed in the values assigned to individual items, agreed

[2] For a detailed comparative statement of the two official estimates, see Appendix C, p. 479.

in placing the total at approximately 26 billion marks for the period prior to 1923. In each case, however, it was pointed out that the estimates were provisional in character and were based upon the economic value to Germany represented by the cessions, deliveries, and payments made by her, rather than upon the gain to the Allied treasuries resulting from these transfers of wealth.[3]

2. *Payments in 1924-31.* The amounts paid by Germany and received by her creditors under the Dawes and the Young plans are known with much greater precision. The annuities prescribed in the Dawes plan were punctually met by Germany during the five years of the plan's operation. Accordingly, Germany was credited on the books of the Agent General for Reparation Payments to the extent of 7,970 million marks. It should be noted, however, that under the Dawes plan interest and sinking-fund charges on the international loan of 1924 were included in the annuities. These disbursements, amounting in the five years to 439.8 million marks, were of course not reparation payments.

[3] For the Institute of Economics estimate, see H. G. Moulton and C. E. McGuire, *Germany's Capacity to Pay*, Chap. III and Appendixes D, E, and F, which contain also a comprehensive discussion of the valuation problem as relating to the official estimates by the German government and the Reparation Commission. It should be noted that the Institute of Economics estimate has often been incorrectly quoted as referring to *receipts by the creditors*, rather than to economic losses by Germany. The authors of *Germany's Capacity to Pay* placed a special emphasis on this very point when they said (p. 74): "We have arrived at the conclusion that the tangible values surrendered by Germany to the Reparation Commission, *as distinguished from the total credits to which Germany may or may not be entitled on the books of the Commission in reduction of her capital debt*, aggregate between 25 and 26 billion gold marks. This estimate is the best that can be made in view of the incomplete data thus far obtainable, and it may possibly be several billions too high or too low." For the Keynes estimate, see *The Nation and the Athenaeum*, Oct. 27, 1923.

In order to determine the amount actually received by the reparation creditors, it is necessary to make certain other minor adjustments. A sum, aggregating 75 million marks for the five-year period, had to be deducted to cover the cost of various commissions and bodies of control. Germany was allowed discounts on advance payments on industrial debentures and railway bonds amounting to 29.3 million marks. On the other hand, the Agent General's account showed a profit in favor of the creditors, resulting from interest on funds invested and net gains in exchange, amounting to 23 million marks.

The total account for the five years of the Dawes plan (closed as of May 17, 1930) was as follows, in millions of marks:[4]

Total amount paid by Germany under the Dawes plan	7,970.0	
Less service charges on the 1924 loan	439.8	
Net payments by Germany on reparation and other treaty accounts		7,530.2
Less cost of commissions, etc.		75.0
		7,455.2
Discount for advance payments		29.3
Portion of Dawes annuities available for distribution to individual creditors		7,425.9
Plus interest and gains in exchange		23.0
Total amount available for distribution to individual creditors		7,448.9

Between September 1, 1929 and June 30, 1931, that is, during the operation of the Young plan, Germany paid the first two annuities prescribed in the plan, and one-fourth of the third annuity, or a total of 2,871.9

[4] The manner in which this amount was distributed among the individual creditors is indicated on p. 267.

million marks. This sum included the payments made to the Allies, as well as those to the United States under the American-German agreement, but not the interest and sinking-fund charges on the 1924 loan, which were paid separately. In addition, Germany paid 30 million marks as her share of the cost of the Rhineland evacuation, and 6 million marks for the cost of the commissions administering the reparation payments prior to the establishment of the Bank for International Settlements. Finally, her payments to Belgium under the "marks agreement" amounted to 43.1 million marks during this period. The monthly instalments on the Young annuities were paid by Germany to the Agent General through the month of May 1930. Thereafter, the payments were made to the Bank for International Settlements.

Bringing together all the payments made by Germany on the reparation and other treaty accounts from September 1, 1924 to June 30, 1931, we find that the totals were as follows, in millions of marks:[5]

Under the Dawes plan	7,530.2
Under the Young plan and the American-German agreement	2,871.9
Under the marks agreement with Belgium	43.1
Special payments for evacuation and commissions	36.0
Total	10,481.2

[5] These figures differ from those given in the official German statement of payments made on these various accounts which we quote in Appendix C, p. 479. The differences are accounted for as follows: The German statement of payments made under the Dawes plan includes the charges on the 1924 loan and the interest and gains in exchange earned by the Agent General for the benefit of the creditors. Similarly, charges on the 1924 loan are included in the total of payments made under the Young plan. As a result of the inclusion of these items, which, as we have already seen, is not justifiable, the German figure is 11,096 million marks instead of 10,481.2 millions as given here.

The amounts received during the period by the individual creditors are shown in the table on this page. It will be noted that the totals differ somewhat from the figures given above. There are several reasons for this. The costs of various commissions and bodies of control under the Dawes plan and the special payments

RECEIPTS OF GERMANY'S CREDITORS, SEPTEMBER 1, 1924–JUNE 30, 1931
(In millions of marks)

Country	Under the Dawes Plan	Under the Young Plan	Proceeds of Mobilization Loan	Total
France..................	3,939.3	1,488.5	558.7	5,986.5
British Empire...........	1,654.5	505.6	211.7	2,371.8
Italy....................	555.1	242.7	55.4	853.2
Belgium.................	527.4	237.5[a]	—	764.9
Yugoslavia..............	275.2	170.7	7.9	453.8
Rumania................	67.2	13.0	—	80.2
Japan...................	45.1	29.1	8.7	83.0
Portugal................	44.9	22.3	3.2	70.4
Greece..................	23.7	5.3	—	29.0
Poland..................	1.4	1.2	—	2.5
The United States........	300.4	148.6[b]	—	449.0
Undistributed surplus.....	14.7	—	—	14.7
Total................	7,448.9	2,864.5	845.6	11,159.0

[a] Including payments under the marks agreement.
[b] Payments under the American-German agreement.

made under the Young plan are excluded. The same is true of the discounts for advance payments during the period of the Dawes plan. Two deductions are made from the Young annuities proper: one to cover the commission of one-tenth of 1 per cent stipulated in the trust agreement between the creditor powers and the Bank for International Settlements as a part of the bank's compensation for administering the payments;[6] and the other to represent the service charges on the mobiliza-

[6] See p. 228.

tion loan of 1930. Since, in order to show the total actual receipts of each of the governments that participated in the proceeds of the loan, such proceeds are included in their total respective shares, the corresponding service charges should properly be excluded.[7] Finally, "interest and gains in exchange" are added to the figures of the Dawes plan payments.

It should also be noted that the allocation shown in the table is only approximate. The distribution of the Dawes plan payments among individual creditors is taken from the closed accounts of the Agent General, but these accounts also show an undistributed balance of 14.7 million marks, presumably paid to the creditors later, for the final allocation of which no data are avail-

[7] This loan was issued on June 1, 1930 as the first attempt at commercializing or mobilizing the unconditional portion of the reparation annuities. In view of the fact that Germany was at the time in need of foreign credits, the arrangement provided for a German government bond issue, of which two thirds of the proceeds was to be distributed among the reparation creditors entitled to receipts out of the unconditional annuity in accordance with their respective shares, and one-third was to go to Germany for investment in the German Railway Company and the German Post Office and Telegraphs. The nominal amount of the issue was 350 million dollars, and the net proceeds 302 millions. Portions of the issue were placed in the United States, France, Great Britain, Holland, Sweden, Switzerland, Germany, Italy, and Belgium, the bonds of each portion being labelled in the currency of the country in which they were placed. The Bank for International Settlements handled the operation and now acts as trustee. The bonds bear interest at the rate of 5.5 per cent and are amortizable by means of a cumulative sinking fund, sufficient to extinguish the whole issue in 25 years. The annual interest and sinking-fund charges were, in the original contract, made payable as follows: the two-thirds representing the mobilization loan, by deduction of the requisite amounts from the monthly instalments on account of the unconditional annuity; the third representing the direct loan to Germany, by means of monthly payments to the bank by the German government. For the details of the loan see *First Annual Report of the Bank for International Settlements*, 1931, pp. 9-10 and Annex X; and *Standard Bond Descriptions*, Vol. V, No. 479, Sept. 19, 1931. For the changes in the original contract introduced by the Lausanne agreement, see p. 359 of this book.

able. The distribution of the Young plan payments is computed on the basis of the relevant provisions of the plan itself, since the Bank for International Settlements has not as yet published any detailed data showing the actual distribution. No account is taken of the various deposits left by the creditor governments at the Bank for International Settlements. No data are available regarding any receipts under the Young plan corresponding to the "interest and gains in exchange" item under the Dawes plan. However, the unavoidable inaccuracies resulting from all these factors are very small in comparison with the aggregate sums distributed, and the amounts shown in the table come very close to being the actual receipts of each of the creditor governments.[8]

In summary, since September 1, 1924 Germany's creditors have received, on reparation and other treaty accounts, an aggregate of 11,159 million marks.[9] Prior to that time they had received, according to the admittedly incomplete accounting of the Reparation Commission, approximately 10,426 million marks. Thus computed, the Allies have received 21,585 million marks. In view of the method of accounting which was employed during the period prior to the Dawes plan, the sacrifice to Germany was undoubtedly greatly in excess of the amounts for which she has received credit. For purposes of comparison it may be noted that Germany received from the French indemnity of 1871 approximately 4

[8] For all the details relating to the period of the Dawes plan and the first nine months of the Young plan, see *Report of the Agent General for Reparation Payments*, May 21, 1930. The only official statements regarding the subsequent period are contained in the first two annual reports of the Bank of International Settlements, issued in May 1931 and May 1932.

[9] See pp. 283-88 for a discussion of the relation of these payments to Germany's foreign borrowing.

billion marks, equivalent to a little over 5 billion marks on the basis of the price level of the years 1920-31. Of this amount about 10 per cent was paid in gold and silver, and nearly all of the remainder in foreign bills of exchange, of which about one half was obtained through the sacrifice of existing foreign investments and the other half by new foreign borrowings.[10]

II. HOW THE GERMAN PAYMENTS WERE MADE

It was pointed out in an introductory chapter that in order to pay foreign debts a nation must, in the long run, have both an excess of budgetary revenues over expenditures and a surplus from international trade and service operations. During the post-war period Germany has not, generally speaking, possessed either a budgetary or a foreign trade surplus. How then has she been able to make payments aggregating, as we have just seen, many billions of marks?

The fulfillment by Germany of her reparation and other financial obligations arising out of the treaty of peace falls into two distinct periods, one prior to the inauguration of the Dawes plan and one subsequent to it. Because the problems involved in each are quite different, these periods will be taken up separately.

1. Prior to the Dawes plan. The payments made by Germany before the inauguration of the Dawes plan on September 1, 1924, as we have already seen, primarily took the form of cessions of property located abroad and the surrender of movable equipment. Cash instalments and current deliveries of commodities were relatively unimportant. We may conveniently consider

---

[10] For an analysis of the process by which the French indemnity was paid, see Moulton and McGuire, *Germany's Capacity to Pay*, Chap. VII.

first how all these payments affected the German budget.

For the most part, the properties and equipment utilized were owned by private German citizens, and the government could procure them only through purchase. Payments for them were entered in the budget, and greatly swelled the expenditures of the state. In addition, there were disbursements on the various treaty accounts which had to come directly out of the budget.

The cost of treaty fulfillment, including the payments on the reparation account, absorbed, during the three fiscal years from 1919-20 to 1921-22, over 80 per cent of the total unborrowed revenues of the German Reich. During the fiscal year 1922-23 they actually exceeded such revenues. These outlays were superimposed on a constantly growing volume of general expenditures and an extremely ineffectual system of tax collections rendered more or less inevitable by the process of demobilization, the post-war disorganization of the country, the weakness of the newly established republican régime, and other similar factors. The result was enormous budgetary deficits, covered by means of new issues of paper currency, which merely added to the already existing difficulties and confusion.

The transfer problem was obscured for a brief period by the utilization of capital assets located abroad and at home. But, by the time the London schedule of payments was put into force in May 1921, the readily available capital assets were virtually exhausted. Accordingly, in addition to making current deliveries in kind financed by means of new issues of domestic currency, Germany in order to meet the quarterly cash instalments was forced to resort to expedients which quickly demoralized her financial and economic system. First, she parted with a considerable part of her already depleted reserves of gold and silver, which constituted the basis of her monetary system. Second, she sold large quantities of paper marks to foreign purchasers. Third, she utilized to some extent the proceeds from the sale of German securities and real estate to foreigners. Even so, as we have seen, the schedules had to be revised within a few months, and by the time of the occupation of the Ruhr in January 1923 virtually no means of making further payments remained. By completing the fiscal and currency disorganization of the country, the Ruhr occupation made this situation unmistakably apparent.[11]

2. *Under the Dawes and Young plans.* The payments by Germany under the Dawes and Young plans were made ostensibly out of current income. Before discussing the ultimate source of the income stream, however, it is desirable to describe the actual procedure of making payments.

a. Procedure. Of the 7,940.7 million marks actually paid by Germany to the Agent General for Reparation Payments during the five years of the Dawes plan, less than one-half, or a total of 3,530 millions, was supplied directly out of the budget of the German Reich. This amount included the special transport tax levied on the German railways for reparation purposes. Of the remainder, 3,610.7 million marks represented interest and amortization charges on the railway bonds and the industrial debentures; and 800 millions, the proceeds of the 1924 foreign loan.

In his final report, the Agent General stated that of

[11] For the details of the process by which Germany made reparation payments during the period prior to the inauguration of the Dawes plan, see Moulton and McGuire, *Germany's Capacity to Pay*, Chaps. III and V; James W. Angell, *The Recovery of Germany*, 1930, Chaps. I-II; and Hjalmar Schacht, *The Stabilization of the Mark*, 1927, Chaps. I-III.

the total amount distributed by him to the creditors,[12] 4,115.4 million marks was transferred by means of payments in marks, and 3,833.6 millions in foreign currencies. All payments, from whatever source, were in the first instance made in marks to the Agent General's account at the Reichsbank. The Agent General drew upon these deposits for such payments within Germany as those required for the current disbursements of the armies of occupation and for the maintenance of his own office and the various commissions and other bodies of control. He likewise drew upon the deposits for financing deliveries in kind and the transactions involved in the collections under the reparation recovery acts.

The deliveries in kind were handled substantially as follows: Orders for various commodities to be delivered were placed in Germany by public institutions and private interests in the creditor countries, and deliveries were made directly by the German firms to these foreign purchasers. Payment to the German firms, however, was made by the Agent General, while the purchasers turned over to their respective national treasuries, in their own currencies, the equivalents of the amounts involved. The German government was then credited, and the creditor governments were similarly debited, on the books of the Agent General, with completed payments of corresponding magnitudes. The Agent General and the Transfer Committee as a whole, acting in consultation with the governments of Germany and the creditor countries, exercised general supervision over the placing of orders.

For example, if a French railway company wanted

---

[12] The amount received from Germany, less the undistributed balance and the discounts on advance payment (a total of 44 million marks), plus interest and net gain in exchange (a total of 23 million marks).

to buy an amount of coal in Germany, worth, with the transportation charges, say 100,000 marks, the order would be placed and the delivery made after certain necessary formalities had been fulfilled. Then the Agent General would pay to the German exporter 100,000 marks, credit the German government with a completed payment of that amount, and debit the French share of the current annuity with a corresponding amount. The French railway company would pay to the French government the equivalent, in francs, of 100,000 marks, and the latter would thus come into possession of the funds represented by the operation. If the French purchaser happened to be a government department, the procedure would be exactly the same so far as Germany and the Agent General were concerned, but on the French side would merely represent a bookkeeping transaction on the books of the French Treasury.

Collections under the reparation recovery acts, while fundamentally akin to deliveries in kind, differed from them somewhat in procedure. Such acts were introduced in March 1921 by Great Britian, and in April of that year by France, but while the British act went into effect at once, the French did not become operative until September 1924. The British act, as applied at first, required all German exporters to Great Britian to hand over to the British Treasury 50 per cent of their proceeds, the German government undertaking to reimburse them with an equivalent amount in marks. The levy was imposed at the British frontier, in pounds sterling. After the London schedule of payments went into effect and called for payment by Germany of the equivalent of 26 per cent of her exports, the reparation recovery levy in Great Britian was reduced to 26 per cent. It continued at that level until February 1924 when, because of the financial disorganization of Germany, the German government found it no longer possible to reimburse the exporters, while a continued imposition of the full levy threatened to shut off trade between Germany and Great Britain. Accordingly, the levy was reduced to 5 per cent, but restored to 26 per cent in August 1924, just before the Dawes plan went into effect. The French act imposed a 26 per cent levy from the outset.

Prior to the inauguration of the Dawes plan, the British reparation recovery act was applied independently of the rest of the reparation collection machinery, which operated primarily through the Reparation Commission. After the plan went into effect, it became necessary to assimilate the British levy with the new machinery that was being set up, and to place it under the control of the Agent General. Accordingly, at the beginning of 1925, after prolonged negotiations between the British and German governments and the Agent General, a new method was worked out for administering the levy. Under this system, which continued in operation all through the existence of the Dawes plan, German exporters to Great Britain turned over the required portion of their proceeds in sterling to the Reichsbank, which in turn transferred these funds to the account of the Agent General at the Bank of England. The Agent General then reimbursed the German exporters through the Reichsbank and made payments to the British Treasury out of his account at the Bank of England. A similar procedure was followed with respect to France through the instrumentality of the Bank of France.[18]

[18] For a description of this complicated system, see *Report of the Agent General*, May 30, 1925, pp. 21-25.

From the point of view of the transfer problem, deliveries in kind and collections under the reparation recovery acts were essentially identical processes. In each case, the German exporters received marks for the goods shipped and the treasuries of the creditor countries received equivalent amounts in their own respective currencies. In each case, Germany as a country surrendered goods directly without receiving in return anything but a credit on her reparation liability. The only important difference was that for deliveries in kind there was an assured market and an agreed price, while the collections under the recovery acts represented proceeds of sales which had already taken place through the channels of ordinary trade.

With what remained of the marks paid into his account at the Reichsbank, the Agent General purchased foreign bills in the German money market, such bills originating in the general international trade and financial operations of the country. The respective shares of the creditors, after account had been taken of their receipts in the form of the payments described above, were completed by turning over to them the corresponding amounts of these foreign bills, which were in effect equivalent to gold and represented, internationally speaking, the only immediate cash payments.

The volume of such purchases of foreign bills effected by the Agent General during the existence of the Dawes plan was much smaller than the volume of payments in foreign currencies indicated in his final accounts. The reason for this lies in the fact that the Agent General reported the collections under the reparation recovery acts as payments in foreign currencies. As we have seen, however, since these collections were, from the point of view of the transfer problem, much more closely akin to deliveries in kind than to the purchase of foreign bills in the open market, the whole picture would probably be clearer if the amount of these collections was segregated from the payments in foreign currencies, as is done in the table on page 279.[14]

The table shows also in a similar manner the payments made under the Young plan. In connection with these payments, it should be borne in mind that the Young plan and The Hague agreements introduced a number of important changes. The Bank for International Settlements took the place of the Reparation Commission and its Agent General as the collecting agency. With the German government assuming full responsibility for both stages of the paying process—internal collection and transfer—the instalments became a direct charge on the budget and were made payable not in marks, as theretofore, but in the currencies indicated by the bank, in accordance with the provisions described on pages 226-27. Since the annuities dealt with here fell in the period during which deliveries in kind still continued, a portion corresponding to the fixed quotas of such deliveries was received by the bank in marks, the whole system being administered by the bank in substantially the same manner as had been done by the Agent General. Similiarly, the collections under the reparation recovery acts continued to be handled in the same manner as theretofore, except that, instead of imposing a levy of 26 per cent on the German exports

[14] It should be noted that the framers of the Dawes plan were emphatic in regarding collections under reparation recovery acts as merely a form of deliveries in kind, and The Hague conference, in drawing up the revised quotas of deliveries in kind included in the quotas the British and French reparation recovery levies.

to Great Britain and France respectively, the British government agreed to receive in this manner 23.05 per cent of each annual quota of deliveries in kind (including the reparation recovery levies), while the French government agreed to receive 4.95 per cent of each quota. The foreign bills required to cover the remainder of each annuity were procured by the German government and turned over to the bank for distribution among the creditors.

It will be seen from the table on page 279 that, under the Dawes plan, most of the payments made by Germany (76.9 per cent of the total payments on the reparation and other treaty accounts) were in a form which yielded the receiving countries their own currencies, either through the reparation recovery levies or through deliveries in kind. Less than one-quarter of the total was received in foreign currencies, that is, in such form as to represent for each creditor claims to gold outside its own frontiers and outside of Germany. Under the Young plan, payments in foreign currencies constituted 54 per cent of the total. For the whole period, such payments were approximately one-third of the aggregate amount.[15]

As regards individual creditors, the situation under the Dawes plan was as follows: About one-quarter of the amounts received by France and Italy was in foreign currencies and the remainder mainly in the form of

---

[15] It is assumed here, in the absence of any data as to the actual currencies in which the payments included in the category "cash transfers in foreign currencies" were made, that the receipts of each creditor included in this category were really in currencies other than either its own or marks. It may well be that as regards France, for example, some of these receipts were in French francs; as regards Great Britain, in pounds sterling, etc. In any event, however, these figures represent the *maximum* amounts that could have been received by the creditors in currencies other than their own or in marks.

deliveries in kind. Of Great Britain's receipts, less than 20 per cent were in foreign currencies, and most of the remainder in pounds sterling as a result of the application of the reparation recovery act. The other countries took the major portion of their receipts in the form of

CLASSIFICATION OF PAYMENTS MADE BY GERMANY UNDER THE DAWES AND YOUNG PLANS, BY TRANSFER CATEGORIES
(In millions of marks)

Category	Under the Dawes Plan	Under the Young Plan	Total
Cash tranfers in foreign currencies...	1,733.6[a]	1,611.0	3,344.6
Collections under reparation recovery acts........................	1,510.1	350.0	1,860.1
Deliveries in kind and other payments in marks................	4,257.2	990.0	5,247.2
Total......................	7,500.9[b]	2,951.0[c]	10,451.9

[a] The undistributed surplus of 14.7 million marks, mentioned on p. 267 is included in this figure.

[b] This figure is exclusive of (a) the service charges on the 1924 loan, which were paid in foreign currencies, and (b) discount for advance payments. See p. 265.

[c] This figure includes payments to the United States under the American-German agreement, to Belgium under the marks agreement, and the special payments for evacuation and commissions.

deliveries in kind. Under the Young plan, France and Portugal took slightly over one-half in the form of deliveries in kind, and Italy, Belgium, and Yugoslavia slightly less than one-half. Great Britain took more than one-half of her receipts in pounds sterling, resulting from the continued application of the reparation recovery act. Japan received over two-thirds of her collection in the form of foreign currencies, while Rumania and Greece took their entire shares in the form of deliveries in kind.[16]

[16] See Appendix C, pp. 480-81, for a detailed classification of the receipts of various creditors.

We may now turn to the underlying economic processes involved in these payments. Were the internal collections derived from current budget surpluses? Were the transfers made from an excess of current international income? Is there any truth in the assertion, commonly made, and almost as commonly disputed, that Germany has made no payments out of her own resources?

b. Budgetary deficits. The execution of the Dawes plan was predicated on the assumption that Germany must have a fully balanced budget. And, in fact, during the fiscal year 1924-25, when the Dawes plan went into effect, Germany had an excess of current revenues over current expenditures. The very next year, however, expenditures outstripped revenues, and ever since then the German budget has continuously shown deficits. The table on page 281 indicates the total current expenditures and non-borrowed revenues of the German federal government during the seven fiscal years from 1924-25 to 1930-31.

It should be noted in connection with this table that for the period of the Dawes plan only the direct budgetary contributions to the reparation annuities are included in the expenditures. Service charges on the railway bonds and on the industrial debentures, and the proceeds of the 1924 loan, which were handled outside the budget of the Reich, are excluded from both the revenue and the expenditure accounts of the budget. For the Young plan period, the entire annuities are included in the expenditures. The revenues and expenditures as given here are exclusive of the taxes collected by the federal government but transferred to the states and communes, and the surpluses or deficits consequently represent the net results of the current fiscal operations of the German Reich, exclusive of borrowing.

The table shows that during the seven-year period current expenditures exceeded current revenues by a little less than 4 billion marks. During the same period,

CURRENT REVENUES AND EXPENDITURES OF THE GERMAN GOVERNMENT
1924-1931[a]
(In millions of marks)

Fiscal Year Ending March 31	Revenues	Expenditures	Surplus (+) Deficit (−)
1925............	4,987	4,450	+537
1926............	4,738	4,848	−110
1927............	5,064	5,917	−853
1928............	5,945	6,300	−355
1929............	6,238	7,475	−1,237
1930............	6,223	7,153	−930
1931[b]...........	7,250	8,193	−943

[a] The figures for the years 1924–25 to 1928–29 are from *Report of the Agent General*, May 21, 1931, p. 102; for the year 1929–30, from *Statistisches Jahrbuch für das deutsche Reich*, 1931, pp. 438–39. The figure for the revenues during the year 1930–31 is from *U. S. Department of Commerce Yearbook*, 1931, Vol. II, p. 121, and for the expenditures during the same year, from *Report of the Special Advisory Committee*, convened by the Bank for International Settlements (British Parliamentary paper, Cmd. 3995), p. 8.

[b] Provisional figures.

the budgetary outlays for reparation payments aggregated, exclusive of the service charges on the 1924 loan, slightly over 5 billion marks.

The deficits incurred during the period were covered by means of internal and foreign borrowing. In the course of the seven years, the public debt of Germany (exclusive of the borrowings of the states, municipalities, and other local bodies) increased nominally by 6.6 billion marks. This figure, however, included the Dawes loan of 1924 and the whole of the Young loan of 1930. Since none of the former and only one-third of the latter could be applied to budgetary deficits, the German government's borrowings for budgetary purposes amounted, therefore, to approximately 4.8 billion marks, the difference between this figure and the aggregate current deficits being accounted for mainly by the cost of floating the loans. The entire new public debt was almost equally divided between foreign and domestic borrowing. A little more than two-thirds of it represented long-term borrowing, and the remainder floating indebtedness.[17]

A glance at the table will also show that the German fiscal situation grew distinctly worse during the year 1928-29. This conclusion is greatly strengthened by an examination of the position of the German Treasury, which reveals the fact that up to 1928-29 the German government had practically no floating indebtedness, long-term borrowing providing the necessary means with which to balance the budget. It was only starting with that year that short-term debts began to accumulate with great rapidity, making the position of the German Treasury progressively more precarious. It is worthy of note that this turn for the worse in the German fiscal situation coincided with the first "standard" annuity year under the Dawes plan, which brought with it a sharp increase in the amount of reparation payments, the whole increment of 750 million marks falling directly on the budget.

The German fiscal situation was rendered more difficult during this period by the financial operations of the German states and other local governments. Their budgets consistently showed large deficits, which were covered by means of borrowing. Of the total German

[17] *Statistisches Jahrbuch für das deutsche Reich*, 1931, p. 485.

public debt, federal and local, which aggregated, on March 31, 1931, the vast sum of 24.2 billion marks, 18.2 billions had been contracted during the seven-year fiscal period from 1924 to 1931, and of this amount, as we have already seen, the federal government was responsible for only 6.6 billions, or slightly over one-third. The local bodies borrowed during the period 11.6 billion marks, of which about 1.5 billions were obtained abroad, and the remainder at home.[18]

The question of whether or not it was possible for Germany to balance her budget during this period and keep her current expenditures, including the outlays for the reparation payments, within the limits of her current revenues, has been the subject of much controversy, to which we shall have occasion to refer in Chapter XIV, when we analyze the causes that led to the breakdown of 1931. In this connection it is only important for us to point out that, as matters actually stood, Germany did not, during the period under consideration, possess a balanced budget, and that consequently her non-borrowed revenues were insufficient to provide for the reparation payments as well as for her other governmental disbursements. As a result, far from decreasing its outstanding liabilities, as would have been the case had the reparation payments been met out of current revenues, the German government was going constantly deeper into debt to its own citizens, as well as to foreign lenders. This process of debt accumulation, on which interest had to be paid, rendered the attainment of budgetary equilibrium steadily more difficult.

c. International deficits. The Dawes plan recognized the necessity for adjusting transfers in the light of the

[18] The same, p. 485.

balance of international income. What was Germany's international income and outgo position during these years?

During the seven calendar years 1924 to 1930, Germany had a very substantial deficit in her current international accounts. That is to say, the total value of goods sold, and of services rendered to Germany by foreigners, exceeded the aggregate amount of goods sold and services rendered by Germany to foreigners to the extent of 3.3 billion marks. However, the deliveries in kind made by Germany on the reparation account and the goods and services representing the collections under the reparation recovery acts are included in the German sales. If we subtract the value of these items from the aggregate value of German exports of goods and services, we find that the funds actually procured by Germany as a result of her foreign sales, and of the international services rendered by her, in reality fell short of the payments which she had to make for the goods she bought and the services rendered to her, by approximately 9.8 billion marks.

In addition to the payments represented by the various deliveries mentioned above, Germany paid on reparation account, during the seven years in question, approximately 3 billion marks in foreign currencies. Moreover, her growing foreign indebtedness required annual interest payments, the net amount of which aggregated during the period over 3 billion marks, including the service charges on the 1924 loan. Finally, Germany during this period increased the stocks of gold and foreign currencies at her bank of issue by slightly over 2 billion marks, in this manner acquiring the monetary reserves required by her currency and credit system. All told, during the seven-year period, Germany's international income fell short of her international outgo by some 18 billion marks, or about 4.5 billion dollars. And of this vast sum considerably more than one-half was absorbed by the reparation payments.

The only means of covering these deficits on current accounts was through borrowing. The changes in Germany's international debt and investment position during these years may be summarized as follows: The increase of foreign debt amounted to about 25 billion marks. But during the same period, investments of German citizens in foreign countries increased by 6.8 billions—from approximately 2.9 billion marks at the end of 1923 to about 9.7 at the end of 1930. Thus to cover about 18 billions of deficit the net foreign debt was increased by a like amount. Whereas at the beginning of the period Germany was a net creditor, apart from reparation obligations, in the amount of about 3 billion marks, at the end of the period she was a net debtor to the extent of about 15 billion marks. That is to say, she had about 25 billions of foreign obligations, and nearly 10 billions of offsetting loans and investments.[19]

As much as 40 per cent of the German foreign debt outstanding at the end of 1930, or something more than 10 billion marks, was in the form of short-term indebtedness, maturing within periods under three years. A little over 9 billion marks was in the form of long-term securities sold abroad, and the remaining 6 billions represented direct foreign investment in German business enterprises or foreign purchases of German real estate.[20]

The bulk of the German foreign debt had been con-

[19] These figures are based on the data contained in the *Report of the Committee Appointed on the Recommendation of the London Conference, 1931* (the so-called Wiggin Report), Annexes I-III.

[20] The same, Annex IV. The volume of long-term German securities held abroad at the end of 1930 is given in *Statistisches Jahrbuch für das*

tracted by private, rather than governmental, agencies. Of the total debt outstanding at the end of 1930, the federal government stood responsible for 3.3 billion marks, and the states, municipalities, and other local public bodies for about 1.5 billions. Altogether, the public foreign debt constituted approximately one-fifth of the country's total foreign indebtedness, the remainder of the debt being owed by private business enterprises, banks, public utilities, churches, and other debtors.

No complete estimate is available as to the national origin of the funds borrowed by Germany. Generally speaking, the United States is undoubtedly Germany's principal creditor, so far as one can judge by two groups of indebtedness—long-term securities and short-term debts owed by the German banks—for the geographical distribution of which some material is available. About 55 per cent of the German long-term securities sold abroad was, at the end of 1930, held in the United States. Next in the order of importance as Germany's long-term creditors come Great Britain and Holland, with about 12 per cent each, followed by Sweden, Switzerland, France, and a number of smaller creditors. Approximately 37 per cent of the short-term foreign debts of the German banks was owed to the United States; 20 per cent to Great Britain; 14 per cent to Switzerland; 10 per cent to Holland; 7 per cent to France; and the remainder to a number of smaller creditors.[21]

---

deutsche Reich, 1931, p. 349, as 7.2 billion marks, or 2 billions less than the estimate of the Wiggin Committee. The difference is accounted for by the fact that the latter includes the Dawes loan and the whole of the Young loan, while the former excludes the Dawes loan and two-thirds of the Young loan.

[21] Wiggin Report, Annexes V-VI. For detailed analysis of German foreign loans in the United States, see Robert R. Kuczynski, *American*

Such was Germany's international financial position at the end of 1930. In the first half of 1931, the whole situation underwent a radical change. For the first time, the international movement of capital across German frontiers showed a net outflow, rather than an inflow. Instead of contracting new loans, Germany actually repaid some of her outstanding obligations. The accounts during the six-month period showed an excess of current international income over outgo, including reparation payments, of 1.2 billion marks, which was the amount of repayment of existing debts. The far-reaching significance of this change from the point of view of Germany's basic economic and financial condition will be discussed in Chapter XIV. It should be noted here, however, that the current income included as one of its items an export of gold and foreign bills from the monetary stocks of the Reichsbank, amounting to 1.4 billion marks, a sum sufficiently large to account for more than the whole excess of income over outgo.

d. Foreign loans and reparation payments. The relation of foreign borrowing to the reparation payments requires consideration both from the point of view of the transfer problem and the budget problem. It is sometimes contended that since the proceeds of the private loans, which made up the bulk of the German borrowings, were not available to the government, there is no connection between the foreign loans and reparation payments. It requires only a brief analysis to show that such is not the case.

In the first place, it was only as a result of foreign loans that Germany was able to achieve financial and

---

Loans to Germany, 1927; and *Bankers' Profits from German Loans,* 1932.

economic stability following the collapse of 1923. Her gold supply, her banking resources, her stocks of goods, were all depleted, and the void had to be filled. Foreign loans furnished the means by which stocks of goods were replenished and the foundation on which the monetary and credit system could once more be built up and the process of domestic capital formation could begin to operate. Under the boom conditions prevailing in the early years of the Dawes plan, the volume of business was very large and the earnings of business enterprises accordingly expanded very rapidly. It was this expansion which made it possible for the German government to make a fairly good showing in the budget and to borrow in the domestic market a portion of what could not be raised by taxation.

In the second place, so long as the loans continued, the German government, or rather under the Dawes plan the Agent General for Reparation Payments, found no difficulty in purchasing in the market the foreign bills required for cash payments on reparation account. The total supply of foreign bills available in the market for purchase, by importers or by anyone else having foreign payments to make, is determined by the volume of exports of goods and services plus the proceeds of foreign loans. With the loans steadily exceeding the amount of the deficit in the normal trading and financial operations, the supply of bills of exchange was always adequate.

III. PAYMENTS BY THE OTHER REPARATION DEBTORS

The payments made by the other reparation debtors were, naturally, extremely small in comparison with the sums which Germany had turned over to her creditors. Nevertheless, the process by which these payments were effected was substantially the same as that which operated in the case of Germany. This is equally true of Bulgaria and Hungary, the only two other reparation debtors that have made payments over a long period. Czechoslovakia, whose payments did not begin until 1930, may be left out of this account.

Bulgaria's total payments on the reparation and various other treaty accounts aggregated, during the period prior to July 1, 1931, approximately 30 million dollars. About half of this sum represented all sorts of cessions and deliveries made during the early post-war years. The remainder was paid mainly in foreign currencies.

These payments were made in spite of the fact that Bulgaria, like Germany, did not, generally speaking, possess either a budgetary surplus or an excess of income over outgo in her international trade and service operations during the period in question. As a matter of fact, the Bulgarian budget remained unbalanced up to the fiscal year 1929-30. The deficits during the first nine post-war years were covered by means of borrowing, mainly in the form of advances made to the Treasury by the bank of issue and of other types of floating indebtedness. A part of this domestic debt was paid off in 1928 and 1929 out of the proceeds of an international loan, extended to the Bulgarian government under the auspices of the League of Nations. The total deficit was approximately equal to the payments made on the treaty accounts.

In her international trade and service operations, Bulgaria consistently had an excess of current outgo over current income. These deficits were made up by means of long- and short-term loans.[22]

---

[22] For the details of the process of reparation fulfillment by Bulgaria, see Leo Pasvolsky, *Bulgaria's Economic Position*, Chaps. IV, VII, and VIII.

The exact volume of payments made by Hungary on reparation and other treaty accounts is not known, because the Reparation Commission did not perform the task of evaluating the cessions and deliveries she had made prior to 1924.[23] Hungary has since made payments prescribed by the reparation schedule of 1924, and these instalments aggregated about 8 million dollars during the period prior to July 1, 1931.

The Hungarian budget was balanced throughout most of the period since 1924, and the internal collection stage of the payment process therefore occasioned little difficulty. The transfer problem, on the other hand, was extremely difficult. Hungary, like Germany and Bulgaria, consistently had in her international trade and service operations an excess of current outgo over current income. Likewise she also made up the difference by means of long- and short-term foreign loans.[24] In both Bulgaria and Hungary, as in Germany, therefore, the process of reparation payments was accompanied by a more than proportional increase of foreign indebtedness.

[23] See pp. 237-38.

[24] For the details of the process of reparation fulfillment by Hungary, see Leo Pasvolsky, *Economic Nationalism of the Danubian States*, Chaps. XVI-XVII, and *The Financial Position of Hungary*, (report to the Council of the League of Nations on the work of the Financial Committee), Oct. 24, 1931.

CHAPTER XIII

ATTEMPTS AT ALLIED DEBT FULFILLMENT

The Allied debts to the United States Treasury, as indicated in the introductory chapter, constitute as much as 80 per cent of the funded non-reparation obligations resulting from the war. In analyzing the process of debt fulfillment as it relates to the war obligations of the Allies, we shall, therefore, center our attention on receipts of the American Treasury. In this chapter we shall indicate the amounts actually transferred to the United States since the cessation of hostilities as interest and amortization instalments; the relation of these payments to the reparation and other debt receipts of our principal debtors; and the significance of post-war lending by American citizens to the problem of war debt collections.

I. AMOUNTS RECEIVED BY THE UNITED STATES

The United States Treasury began collections on the war loans as early as the second half of 1917, and received some payments thereafter every year up to July 1, 1931, when the Hoover moratorium went into effect. The table on page 292 shows the aggregate receipts for each of the fiscal years from 1917-18 to 1930-31 from the 15 European debtors who have negotiated funding agreements with the United States government. Instalments representing repayment of principal are shown separately from payments on account of current interest.

The payments made during the year 1917-18 were exclusively on account of current interest. During the year 1918-19, while there was a small amount of amortization, interest payments still constituted practically the whole of the sums received. For the next three years, interest payments fell to very small amounts, but some payments on account of principal were received. The decrease in the interest payments was the result of the three-year moratorium, which, it will be recalled, was granted by the United States Treasury in the second half

ANNUAL PAYMENTS TO THE UNITED STATES ON THE WAR DEBTS
BY 15 EUROPEAN DEBTORS[a]
(In thousands of dollars)

Fiscal Year Ending June 30	Principal	Interest	Total
1918............	—	106,132.7	106,132.7
1919............	7,570.0	319,635.2	327,205.2
1920............	89,304.1	3,893.4	93,197.5
1921............	81,739.4	30,025.4	111,764.8
1922............	30,940.6	27,256.1	58,196.7
1923............	30,864.4	198,368.1	229,232.5
1924............	53,843.3	160,269.8	214,113.1
1925............	23,089.4	159,648.7	182,738.1
1926............	55,002.2	139,827.8	194,830.0
1927............	66,224.3	139,826.2	206,050.5
1928............	68,175.1	139,943.6	208,118.7
1929............	59,157.7	139,973.8	199,131.5
1930............	97,634.2	141,931.7	239,565.9
1931............	51,588.2	184,474.7	236,062.9
Total.........	715,132.9	1,891,207.2	2,606,340.1

[a] For detailed data see Appendix C, pp. 482–85.

of 1919. The receipts actually shown for these years were due to adjustments of various sorts, rather than to actual transfers of funds. The reader will also recall that the interest payments during the years 1917-18 and 1918-19 were made out of new loans extended by the Treasury.[1]

The years 1922-23 and 1923-24 again showed substantial receipts, which were primarily of British origin.

[1] See pp. 40-41.

PAYMENTS MADE TO THE UNITED STATES TREASURY ON THE WAR DEBT ACCOUNT PRIOR TO JULY 1, 1931[a]

(In thousands of dollars)

Debtor Country	Prior to Funding		Subsequent to Funding		Aggregate Payments		
	Principal	Interest	Principal	Interest	Principal	Interest	Total
Austria.........	—	—	862.7	—	862.7	—	862.7
Belgium........	2,057.6	18,543.6	17,100.0	14,490.0	19,157.6	33,033.6	52,191.2
Czechoslovakia..	—	304.2	18,000.0	—	18,000.0	304.2	18,304.2
Esthonia........	—	1.4	—	1,247.0	—	1,248.4	1,248.4
Finland.........	—	309.3	396.0	2,249.4	396.0	2,558.7	2,954.7
France.........	64,689.6	221,386.3	161,350.0	38,650.0	226,039.6	260,036.3	486,075.9
Great Britain...	202,181.6	357,896.7	202,000.0	1,149,720.0	404,181.6	1,507,616.7	1,911,798.3
Greece.........	2.9	1,159.2	981.0	948.9	983.9	2,108.1	3,092.0
Hungary........	—	.8	74.0	393.7	74.0	394.5	468.5
Italy...........	364.3	57,598.9	37,100.0	2,521.3	37,464.3	60,120.2	97,584.5
Latvia..........	—	130.8	—	503.3	—	634.1	634.1
Lithuania.......	—	1.5	234.8	892.3	234.8	893.8	1,128.6
Poland.........	—	2,048.2	1,287.3	19,310.8	1,287.3	21,359.0	22,646.3
Rumania........	1,798.6	263.3	2,700.0	—	4,498.6	263.3	4,761.9
Yugoslavia......	727.7	636.1	1,225.0	—	1,952.7	636.1	2,588.8
Total........	271,822.3	660,280.3	443,310.8	1,230,926.7	715,133.1	1,891,207.0	2,606,340.1

[a] For detailed data see Appendix C, pp. 482–85. Receipts from Germany are shown on page 295.

293

They represented payments by Great Britain in liquidation of a portion of the interest charges that had accrued during the moratorium period, in fulfillment of the debt funding agreement signed in 1923, and in repayment of the silver advances made to her under the Pittman Act of 1918. In 1922 France also began to make regular interest payments, amounting to slightly over 20 million dollars a year, on the war supplies sold to her by the War Department. After the negotiation of a funding agreement with France in 1926, these interest payments were consolidated with the instalments inscribed in the regular schedule of payments. The year 1930-31 showed for the first time normal scheduled payments by all 15 debtors.

In the table on page 293 are given the aggregate payments made to the United States Treasury by each of the 15 debtors on the war loan account during the 14 fiscal years ending June 30, 1931. The amounts paid by each country before and after its debt was funded are shown separately and, as in the table on page 292, a distinction is made between amortization and interest instalments.

Altogether, the Treasury has collected the sizeable sum of 2.6 billion dollars, of which 36 per cent was paid before the actual funding agreements were signed. In fact, every country, with the sole exception of Austria, had made some payments before it finally negotiated a formal settlement.

The relative size of the payments by the three most important debtors reflect not so much the differences in the size of the original loans made to these countries as the wide variations in the terms of repayment prescribed for them by the funding agreements. For example, Great Britain, which received 41 per cent of all the loans made by the United States Treasury to the 15 governments, has so far furnished 74 per cent of all the payments received by the Treasury from these debtors. The shares of all the other countries in the total payments to the United States have been smaller than their shares in the original loans.

The receipts of the United States Treasury from Germany aggregated, up to July 1, 1931, the sum of 155.2 million dollars. Of this amount, 103.5 million dollars represented reimbursement of the costs of the army of occupation, and 51.7 millions were on account of mixed claims awards.[2]

II. REPARATION RECEIPTS AND DEBT PAYMENTS

An examination of the tables on pages 267 and 293 will show that four countries—France, Great Britain, Italy, and Belgium—received, under the Dawes and the Young plans, 93 per cent of the payments made by Germany to all of her creditors, with the exception of the United States, and that these same four countries furnished 97 per cent of all the sums collected by the American Treasury under the funding agreements. These facts have inevitably given the appearance of a connection between the two sets of obligations. And indeed such a connection indubitably exists, although one must distinguish clearly between the legal and the economic aspects of the issue.

Legally, there is no relation whatever between the reparation payments and the other inter-governmental debts growing out of the war. No portion of any country's receipts on the reparation account is specifically

[2] *Annual Report of the Secretary of the Treasury,* 1931, pp. 84, 94. The receipts on account of the army of occupation include 37.5 million dollars representing cash requisitions made in Germany.

earmarked for the meeting of its current obligations on the war debt account. No debt funding agreement negotiated in connection with any of the war debts contains a provision making the discharge of the war obligations of the Allies to each other or to the United States contingent upon a continuation of their receipts from Germany. In the course of the debt funding negotiations, some of the debtor nations, notably France, sought strenuously to establish a legal connection of this sort between the two sets of obligations. Their efforts, however, were not successful.

The only significant instance in which a legal connection between reparation payments and war debts might be regarded as having been established is found in the so-called "concurrent memorandum" and The Hague agreement relating thereto, signed in connection with the Young plan by Germany and all of her principal creditors with the exception of the United States. It will be recalled that this agreement provided that in the event of a reduction in the war debt obligations of these countries, a part of the relief would be passed on to Germany in the form of a proportional reduction of the reparation annuities. This agreement is, however, not binding on the United States and in consequence has only a limited applicability.

But while there is no legal connection between the two sets of obligations, either inherently or as a result of accepted agreement, there is between them so important an economic relationship that the legal aspects of the problem have very little realistic significance. This relationship is so evident that it has long been recognized as a determining factor in public policy, and the Allied governments have assumed since the early post-war years that receipts from German reparations would furnish the means with which to liquidate their international war debts.

The economic connection between reparations and debts has also long been appreciated by responsible spokesmen of the American government. As early as December 1922, before any debt funding negotiations had been formally inaugurated, Mr. Charles Evans Hughes, at that time secretary of state, said in his New Haven address: "So far as the debtors to the United States are concerned, they have unsettled credit balances, and their condition and capacity to pay cannot be properly determined until the amount that can be realized on these credits for reparations has been determined." In 1926, in recommending to the 69th Congress the ratification of the debt funding agreement with France, the Committee on Ways and Means of the House of Representatives stated in its report that the settlement had been based on an estimate of France's capacity to pay, in the determination of which the principal considerations taken into account were an expected improvement of the general fiscal situation in that country and the fact that "the Dawes payments from Germany should, if all goes well, aggregate this year approximately 3.5 billion francs." The report concluded that "if the French government is permitted to derive the full benefit of all these favorable factors, the budget could be balanced and a surplus made available for the payments to the United States as contemplated in the settlement."

In practice, the tendency has been definitely toward an articulation of debt payments with reparation receipts. It will be recalled that the Young plan annuities were arranged in such a manner that each of Germany's principal creditors would receive sufficient sums to cover its own payments on the war debts. After the establishment of the Bank for International Settlements, the principal debtors of the United States followed the rule of accumulating in the form of deposits at the bank, mainly out of their own monthly receipts from Germany, sufficient amounts to enable them to meet their semi-annual instalments to the American Treasury. These operations are clearly indicated by the sharp drops, at the end of December 1930 and June 1931, in the amounts reported by the bank in its monthly statements as "deposits of central banks for the account of others," and by the steady increase of these deposits during the months immediately preceding the semi-annual due dates on the war debts to the United States.

We may now examine the actual relationship between the volume of reparation receipts and the volume of inter-Allied debt payments for the principal countries. The accompanying table shows the reparation receipts and debt payments of Great Britain, France, Italy, and Belgium for the period July 1, 1924 to June 30, 1931. Only these years are taken for purposes of comparison because no precise data are available for the payments made by Germany prior to the inauguration of the Dawes plan. All receipts and payments shown in the table are converted into dollars at par of exchange.

The table shows that for the seven-year period France received approximately three and one-half times as much from Germany as she paid to Great Britain and the United States. This is in part accounted for by the fact that France did not begin to make substantial payments on her war debts until 1926. Under the Young plan the amounts receivable by France continued to be greatly in excess of her own out-payments. The ratio of receipts to payments in the case of Belgium was approximately the same as that of France; and her position under the

Young plan also corresponded to that of France. Italy received about 50 per cent more than she paid; and under the Young plan she was scheduled to have a slight excess of receipts.

AGGREGATE RECEIPTS AND PAYMENTS OF PRINCIPAL COUNTRIES ON REPARA-
TION AND WAR DEBT ACCOUNTS, JULY 1, 1924 TO JUNE 30, 1931
(In millions of dollars)

| Country | Receipts from | | Payments to | | | Net Position |
	Germany	All Principal Debtors[a]	United States	Great Britain	Total	Excess receipts (+) Excess payments (−)
Great Britain	564.9	881.3	1,122.1	—	1,122.1	−240.8
France......	1,426.0	1,426.0	220.8	197.1	417.9	+1,008.1
Italy........	203.2	203.2	33.0	107.1	140.1	+63.1
Belgium.....	182.2	182.2	39.8	12.2	52.0	+130.2

[a] In the case of Great Britain these amounts include receipts from Germany as well as from her three principal war debtors, France, Italy, and Belgium; in the cases of the other three countries only receipts from Germany are shown here. The payments by other war debtors are of negligible importance.

Great Britain's situation is substantially different from that of the other three countries. Her receipts from Germany were sufficient during the seven-year period to cover only half of her payments to the United States, while her receipts from her three other important debtors, which in the last analysis also came from Germany, did not suffice by 240 million dollars to cover the remainder. If the receipts from Great Britain's smaller debtors be included, there is still a substantial deficiency which Great Britain had to cover from other resources. The British situation is attributable in part to the fact that she began making her payments to the United States prior to the negotiations of her own funding agreements. Under the Young plan schedules and funding agreements with Continental debtors, Great Britain would have received more than enough to cover her annual payments to the United States, thus making it possible in due course to make good the deficiency to date.

It is therefore clear that the Allies have thus far almost completely realized their hope of meeting their own debt obligations with funds received from Germany. While it does not necessarily follow from this fact that war debt payments should be considered as dependent solely upon reparation receipts, in practice these obligations have been from the outset inextricably interrelated parts of a single problem of world war liquidation, rather than separate and distinct issues.

Although the foregoing discussion appears to indicate that Germany has furnished the means of paying inter-Allied war debts, such is only nominally the case. As shown in the preceding chapter, while Germany paid some 11 billion marks on reparation account between 1924 and 1931, she borrowed abroad in one form or another some 18 billion marks, of which approximately 50 per cent came from the United States. The payments to the United States on the war debt accounts during this period were the equivalent of about 8 billion marks. Since the United States was making large loans to other European countries during this period, it will be seen that in the aggregate European indebtedness to the United States was steadily increasing rather than decreasing. American citizens were furnishing to the reparation and debtor countries of Europe sums much more than adequate to cover the payments made to the United States. The larger implications of these huge international operations from the point of view of the United States will be given consideration in Part V.

CHAPTER XIV

THE BREAKDOWN OF 1931

The analysis given in the last two chapters reveals the basic facts of the attempts at fulfillment, made since the war, with respect to the various inter-governmental obligations arising out of the conflict. We have seen that huge payments were made on the various war debt accounts—Germany being credited with the equivalent of over 5 billion dollars toward liquidation of her reparation liability, and Allied debtors with over 2.5 billion dollars in interest and amortization, on their debts to the American Treasury. We have examined the close economic connection between these two sets of payments, and the relation of the extensive international transfers of funds involved in the debt payments to the still greater movements across national frontiers of all kinds of new foreign loans and investments, made primarily by American citizens. It is clear from the foregoing discussion that the net results of the process of fulfillment have been: (1) a constant increase, rather than decrease, of international indebtedness; (2) a steady growth in the volume of annual foreign payments to be made by Germany and the other net debtor countries; and (3) a continuous disguising of the difficulties inherent in the situation by new international loans.

Although the breakdown of the payment programs which occurred in the summer of 1931 came with a dramatic suddenness, its inevitability had long been apparent to some observers. Moreover, it was anticipated that the first crack in the structure of payment programs, the long and laborious upbuilding of which we described in the first two divisions of this book, would occur in Germany, by far the largest of the debtors and the principal source from which the funds involved in the liquidation of the war debts were scheduled to come.

The necessity for some sort of major move with regard to the reparation payments and the war debts in general became the subject of earnest discussion in business and political circles both in America and Europe for some weeks prior to President Hoover's proposal for a debt holiday. Apart from its fundamental implications, such a move was coming to be more and more widely regarded as indispensable if the world was not to sink deeper into the morass of economic stagnation and retrogression into which it had been plunged by the profound economic depression that had overwhelmed it in the second half of 1929.

In the course of this discussion, the point was frequently brought out that the possible need for temporary relief from the war debt payments, far from having been ignored at the time when the various debt settlements were negotiated, was fully recognized by the negotiators, and that ample machinery had been provided for meeting emergencies by means of partial postponements of payments. All that was necessary, therefore, was for the relief machinery to be put into operation. Since the postponement of payments was optional with the debtors, it was within their power, if they so desired, to avail themselves of the possibility of relief agreed upon in advance. For such an action no initiative was required on the part of the United States, the largest creditor nation and the only important creditor not at the same time a debtor on the war debt account.

However, relief from the burden of the war debts came about through a dramatic gesture made by the

United States. Not only that, but the scheme put forward by the American President went far beyond the scope of the postponement machinery provided in the existing debt settlements. Why did it become necessary for America to take the lead? And why did President Hoover's proposal make such a clean sweep of the already existing machinery of relief, substituting for it a complete, rather than partial, adjournment of all war debt payments? An answer to these questions must be sought in an examination of the conditions which led up to the breakdown of the debt payment programs, and of the applicability of the postponement machinery to the emergency which confronted the world in June 1931.

I. CONDITIONS LEADING TO THE BREAKDOWN

All through the year 1930, in spite of the fact that the economic depression was manifesting itself more and more acutely, scheduled payments on the reparation and war debt accounts continued without interruption and apparently without difficulty. However, this absence of difficulty was, indeed, only apparent, especially in the case of Germany.

The crux of the German situation with respect to the reparation payments at this juncture was the state of the country's public finances, which, as we have already seen, was growing progressively worse during the period of the operation of the Dawes plan. The financial year 1928-29 showed a deficit of more than 1.25 billion marks, while the year 1929-30, in spite of the substantial alleviation brought about by the Young plan, still closed with a deficit of over 900 million marks.

The reasons for this continued lack of budgetary equilibrium were variously explained by the Germans and by some of their foreign critics. The former consistently maintained that the reparation payments represented the principal disorganizing influence in their fiscal situation. Although admitting that some aspects of their public finances had long been in need of thoroughgoing reform, they asserted that the domestic political situation made adjustments exceedingly difficult and that, in any event, no matter how far-reaching the budgetary reform might be, it could not be effective as long as the reparation payments continued.

Germany's foreign critics, on the other hand, believed that the Germans were inclined to exaggerate the difficulties in the way of a very necessary overhauling of their public finances. Perhaps the most authoritative of these critics, Mr. S. Parker Gilbert, former agent general for reparation payments, in the last annual report he issued in that capacity, characterized as follows the German fiscal situation:

During the financial year ended March 31, 1930, the German budget saw the culmination of the tendencies toward over-spending and over-borrowing which had been described in previous reports. . . . The public revenues, throughout the whole period of the Dawes plan, have shown beyond a doubt that the necessary material for budgetary equilibrium exists, and that under prudent administration the resources available to the budget would be ample to meet all legitimate requirements. What has been lacking, however, is any determined effort to control public expenditures, and the result has been a constantly mounting level of expenditure, exceeding even the greatly increased revenues and culminating in the serious financial troubles of the past year.

The financial troubles to which the former Agent General referred were largely the result of the fact that, starting with the fiscal year 1928-29, the German Treasury began to show substantial arrears. Up to that year the budgetary deficits were covered out of accumulated surpluses and new long-term loans. In 1928-29 and 1929-30 such additional resources decreased and became insufficient, and the floating indebtedness of the Treasury grew by leaps and bounds.

Whatever the cause of this deplorable state of the German public finances—and there is, probably, a great deal of truth in both points of view outlined above—Germany entered upon the financial year 1930-31 with a large accumulation of floating indebtedness and with the prospect of a new budgetary deficit. In the course of the year 1930, the German government introduced a number of emergency measures in an attempt at least to bring the current budget into equilibrium. These measures were, however, rendered only partly effectual by the unfavorable domestic political situation, and even more so by the growing difficulties of tax collections, resulting from the rapidly deteriorating business situation, and by the need of extending the scope of social relief imperatively demanded by the increase of unemployment. Whether or not it would have been possible to solve the German budgetary problem had the era of prosperity continued, it was a foregone conclusion that under conditions of depression stability could not be maintained.

On the other hand, the depression had a temporarily favorable effect upon Germany's international trade position. Instead of the prevailing import surplus, foreign trade showed a substantial excess of exports. In addition to this, there was also a small net income from international services. Thus, current trade and service operations in 1930 yielded Germany a net surplus of about 1.8 billion marks, which was available for debt payments.

While the export surplus was proclaimed by many unanalytical writers as conclusive evidence of Germany's steady progress and as an indication that the vexatious transfer problem had automatically taken care of itself, it was in fact little more than a depression phenomenon. The surplus was not achieved by a normal expansion of exports in relation to imports; in fact exports declined materially, while imports were sharply curtailed, as is shown by the following figures:[1]

Year	Exports	Imports	Balance
1925	9.3	12.4	— 3.1
1926	10.4	10.0	+ 0.4
1927	10.8	14.2	— 3.4
1928	12.3	14.0	— 1.7
1929	13.5	13.4	+ 0.1
1930	12.0	10.4	+ 1.6
1931	9.6	6.7	+ 2.9

When the depression came German factories got along for a time without the usual large purchases of raw material, while the demand of consumers for imported foodstuffs likewise decreased. At the same time, the prices of raw materials and foodstuffs, which comprise the bulk of German imports, fell much more rapidly than did the prices of finished products, which make up the bulk of German exports. A further explanation of the change in the trade balance should be sought in the fact that the German government during this period resorted to extraordinary measures for restricting non-essential imports and for forcing exports by dumping processes and by drastic reductions of wages, interest rates, and domestic prices.

[1] Figures for the years 1925-30 from *Statistisches Jahrbuch für das deutsche Reich;* for the year 1931 from *Wirtschaft und Statistik,* April 1932.

It happened that the net surplus of 1.8 billion marks derived from international trade and service operations in 1930 was almost exactly equal to the reparation payments required that year. There remained, however, interest and amortization charges on new public and private indebtedness, aggregating for the year about 800 million marks, and this had to be covered by means of new loans. Moreover, during this period the general fiscal and political uncertainty caused a flight of capital and substantial withdrawals of foreign short-term credits. Approximately 900 million marks were thus transferred abroad and this put an additional strain on Germany's balance of international payments. The outflow of funds on all international accounts exclusive of new borrowing thus still exceeded the inflow by 1.7 billion marks. Germany made up this deficit in her international accounts by decreasing her stocks of gold and foreign bills at the Reichsbank to the extent of 100 million marks and by means of new foreign borrowings, most of which were short-term in character.

The fiscal difficulties were intensified by an unexpected political development in the late months of 1930. The emergence of the National Socialist Party to a position approaching power, which took place in the parliamentary elections of September 1930, increased the political uncertainty, accentuated the flight of capital, and caused increased withdrawals from Germany of foreign short-term funds. While the German difficulties manifested themselves first in the budgetary problem, as soon as confidence in the stability of Germany began to be undermined the peculiar vulnerability of her international financial position was quickly revealed. The enormous volume of short-term foreign credits had to be continued, through renewals, and increased in amount by new credits, if stability was to be maintained and current international payments were to be met. A complete breakdown would occur the moment new foreign credits ceased to be granted and the payment of maturing ones was called for.[2]

The early months of 1931 witnessed a continuance of the budgetary and other difficulties which had become pronounced during the preceding year, as well as the emergence of a number of new problems. The withdrawal of foreign funds from Germany and the flight of German capital became more rapid. At the same time foreign loans practically ceased. Then in March a new and portentous factor was injected into the situation.

Suddenly and unexpectedly, Germany announced the conclusion of a customs union with Austria. Whatever may be said as to the merits of the case and as to the domestic political pressure that caused Germany to embark upon this enterprise, the action of the German government proved to be the first step toward catastrophe so far as the German financial situation was concerned. The announcement of the German-Austrian arrangement precipitated an international political crisis of first magnitude, since France and a number of other countries chose to regard it as a violation of existing treaties.[3]

The crisis had important economic repercussions for both Germany and Austria. It increased the uneasiness

[2] See pp. 352-53 for the conclusions on this aspect of the problem reached by the Special Advisory Committee set up in December 1931 by the Bank for International Settlements.

[3] After much heated discussion, the question as to the violation of treaties was finally submitted to the Permanent Court of International Justice, which decided, by a majority of one, that the arrangement did constitute a violation of existing agreements, especially those relating to Austria. The controversy, however, had been settled even before the court had rendered its verdict, by an announcement on the part of Germany and Austria of their decision to desist from putting the arrangement into effect.

already existing among Germany's short-term creditors and led, in consequence, to an accentuation of the withdrawals of foreign funds. This in turn made the flight of domestic capital more pronounced. It had similar consequences for Austria, whose international financial position was as vulnerable as that of Germany, for Austria, too, stood heavily indebted to the world on the short-term account.

It was Austria that showed the first visible signs of financial breakdown. Less than two months after the announcement of the German-Austrian customs union, the principal Austrian commercial bank, the Creditanstalt of Vienna, went into bankruptcy. This collapse was in large measure the result of general financial difficulties in Austria. About a year earlier, another important bank, the Boden-Credit-Anstalt, had failed and been taken over by the Creditanstalt. This merger weakened, rather than strengthened, the latter, and its operations during 1930 showed heavy losses, which were not disclosed, however, until early in May 1931. The belated disclosure of the difficulties under which the Creditanstalt was laboring had an extremely unfavorable effect on Austria's position as a short-term debtor, especially because the bank's own foreign liabilities were very heavy. Added to the international political crisis occasioned by the ill-fated customs union move, the situation of the Creditanstalt brought about a rapid increase in withdrawals of foreign funds and in flight of domestic capital. The crash of the Creditanstalt became inevitable.

In view of the outstanding importance of the Creditanstalt in the financial structure of Austria—it controlled approximately 70 per cent of the country's industries—and in order to prevent its collapse from disorganizing the whole economic life of the nation, the Austrian government and the Austrian National Bank found themselves compelled to pledge their own resources for the liquidation of the affairs of the bankrupt institution. The government even assumed a guarantee of the Creditanstalt's deposits. But all this, in turn, brought the public finances of the country and the situation of the bank of issue, already none too stable, to an extremely precarious position. In spite of international assistance extended by a group of central banks acting through the Bank for International Settlements, confidence in Austria was definitely shaken, and the withdrawal of foreign funds assumed threatening dimensions.

This blow to confidence was quickly transmitted to Germany. The gold and foreign exchange resources of the Reichsbank began to shrink at an alarming rate under the pressure of foreign withdrawals and a continued flight of capital. On June 2, after a thorough canvassing of the whole financial emergency confronting the country, the German Cabinet decided upon a series of new taxation measures, designed to strengthen public confidence. A decree embodying these measures was issued three days later. It was accompanied by a special manifesto addressed to the people, in which the German government said:

The expectation that the world economic crisis would ebb in 1931 and thereby relieve distress and unemployment in all industrial countries, and still more in the raw material and agricultural countries, has proved deceptive. Germany . . . cannot save herself from the common distress under which even nations victorious in the war are suffering severely. Our cares and difficulties are aggravated because in addition to the general crisis in which we live we have to carry the special burden of having to make payments as the vanquished in the World

War. These payments were undertaken on presuppositions which have not been realized and deprive our economic system, impoverished by the war and by inflation, of the capital it needs for its preservation and development. Deprivation of capital means the stoppage and restriction of plants, unemployment, diminution of private income, and last, but not least, diminution of the revenues of the state. In addition, our purchasing power in the world's markets is diminished by the amounts we have to pay in reparations for which we do not receive any returns. The tribute payments weaken us as purchasers and compel us to restrict our imports. They compel us to increase our exports, against which other countries are raising stronger and stronger barriers. The consequence is embittered intensification of the struggle for the world's markets.

The manifesto denied the accusations made against the German government, at home and abroad, that it had not "managed its affairs economically enough," and asserted that, on the contrary, it had done everything in its power to balance its budget. It then continued:

The putting forth of the last power and reserve of the nation entitles the German government, and makes it its duty toward the German people, to say to the world: The limits of the privations we have imposed on our people have been reached. The presuppositions upon which the new plan [Young plan] came into being have been shown by the course of world developments to have been wrong. The alleviations which the new plan was to bring to the German people, as was the intent of the participants, . . . have failed to be realized. The government is conscious of the fact that the direly menaced business and financial position of the Reich calls imperatively for alleviation of the unbearable reparation obligations. The economic recovery of the world also depends upon it.

The promulgation of this manifesto was made on the eve of a meeting between heads of the German and British governments at Chequers, England. This meeting—originally called to discuss other problems but delayed for various reasons—was interpreted by the world at large as centering upon the reparation problem. The tenor of the German manifesto was, no doubt, largely responsible for this. The Chequers meeting produced no positive results, and in the light of the conclusions which were widely drawn from this fact, it made the promulgation of the manifesto another fateful step on the part of the German government.

Far from allaying doubts and restoring confidence, the developments of the first week of June intensified the critical nature of the situation. The outflow of funds from Germany assumed the nature of a frenzied torrent. Between May 30 and June 6 the Reichsbank lost 38 million dollars of its reserves of gold and foreign exchange; but between June 7 and June 15 the loss was 130 millions. In a little more than two weeks the monetary reserves of the German central bank had shrunk from 613 million dollars to 445 millions, and the outflow still continued. Germany was plunging headlong into a new financial and economic collapse, as sinister in its dangers as that of 1923. The German currency was once more threatened with disorganization, as its basic reserves were sapped by the outflow of gold. With currency stability destroyed, the whole fabric of credit was bound to crash, carrying with it demoralization and chaos in every phase of the country's economic life. And the experience of the early post-war years had demonstrated clearly that financial and economic prostration in Germany was bound to bring with it immense difficulties for all the surrounding countries and produce serious repercussions in the United States, as well as elsewhere in the world.

Apart from the rapidly growing danger of German collapse, the course of the world-wide economic depression was making the discharging of the payments required by the vast body of international indebtedness more and more difficult. The depression was expressing itself everywhere in a precipitous fall of commodity prices, a severe contraction of the volume of international trade and service operations, and a shrinkage of international loans, approaching the point of complete cessation. With the reduction in the volume of international financial transactions, the burden of the debt payment transfers was becoming heavier and heavier, while the disappearance of loans rendered it no longer possible to disguise the situation by means of new borrowing and lending, as had been done for some years prior to the depression. As a result, even aside from the extraordinary factors which were operating in such countries as Austria and Germany, the normal course of international trade and financial relations was bringing about a continuous and increasingly alarming flow of gold from the debtor to the creditor countries. The former were thus exposed more and more to an imminent danger of currency disorganization, and to all of the economic and social difficulties consequent upon monetary instability, which were bound, sooner or later, to engulf the creditor countries as well in widespread economic disaster.

Such was the situation that confronted the world in the first half of June 1931. In the midst of this gathering storm, the routine of war debt payments went on without interruption. On June 15 the German government duly met the monthly payment required from it under the Young plan. On the same day the semi-annual instalments on the war debts due to the American Treasury were also met. The funds for these payments to the United States had been accumulated by the principal debtors out of the sums they had received from Germany during the preceding six months. If things had gone on as before, with Germany meeting the July instalment and the ones to follow, the debtors of the American Treasury would again have begun accumulating out of their receipts the funds required for their December payments. But as the situation developed, it appeared much more likely that by the time the July payment became due, Germany would have been plunged into financial and economic chaos, as a result of which no payments at all could be expected. Apart from the general consequences of a German collapse for trade and finance throughout the world, the whole structure of war debt liquidation would have been profoundly affected.

II. INADEQUACY OF EXISTING POSTPONEMENT PROVISIONS

With the continuation of regular reparation payments rapidly becoming an impossibility, and with the consequent prospect that the creditors of Germany would suddenly and without any preparation be thrown upon their own resources in meeting their war debt obligations, in June 1931, some form of action appeared imperative to relieve the economic situation from the disorganizing influence of the war debt, and especially reparation, payments. The greatest immediate danger threatened Germany, and upon her, therefore, it was logically incumbent to initiate a course of action leading to an alleviation of the debt burden.

Under existing agreements, the only way open to Germany was to invoke the safeguard machinery of the Young plan. Let us now visualize what would have happened in such a case. In order to do this, we shall take the period covered by the Hoover moratorium, the year from July 1, 1931 to June 30, 1932, and see what would have been the position of each of the principal countries involved, under the operation of the existing relief machinery.

The reader will recall from our discussion in Chapter X that the Young plan gave Germany the right in the first instance merely to postpone the transfer of the whole or a part of the conditional portion of any annuity. It was specifically provided that payments in marks be continued in full during the first year of the postponement period. Not until a year after the transfer postponement had gone into effect was Germany given the right to suspend some of the payments in marks as well. Since a 90-day notice was stipulated for any exercise of the postponement option, this would have meant, in June 1931, that Germany could obtain no relief for her budget for a period of 15 months, that is, let us say, until September 1932. Moreover, unless the payments in marks had been utilized for deliveries in kind or investment in Germany, the burden on the German budget would have been increased by the amount of interest on the unutilized balances required under the plan to be paid by the German government.

Even on the transfer side the amount of relief would have been very small. The twelve monthly payments during the year from July 1, 1931 to June 30, 1932 would have aggregated 1,698.3 million marks, with the conditional or postponable portion constituting 1,086.3 millions. Under the 90-day rule, if Germany had announced the suspension of transfers before June 15, the July and August instalments would not have been affected at all, leaving 906.3 million marks as the amount subject to postponement. The quota of deliveries in kind for the ten months during which the suspension of transfers would have been operative works out at 539.7 million marks. Assuming that this quota had been utilized in full, Germany would have been relieved merely of the obligation of procuring foreign currencies to the amount of 366.6 million marks (about 91 million dollars), or only about one-fifth of the aggregate payments due during the year.

Under these conditions the loss to the principal creditors would have been small, especially since approximately half of the cash transfers to most of them would have been made up out of the Guarantee Fund,[4] which would automatically have come into operation. Moreover, if they exercised the postponement options provided for in their agreements with their own war debt creditors, the position of all of them, with the exception of Great Britain, would have been but slightly affected.

It is true that France might have been under an obligation to create immediately a Guarantee Fund of 119.1 million dollars (500 million marks) at the Bank for International Settlements.[5] However she already had on deposit at the bank, as part of this Fund, the sum of 13.3 million dollars, representing 10 per cent of her

---

[4] See pp. 231-33.

[5] In its negotiations with the government of the United States, which we shall describe in the next chapter, the French government insisted that it was not under any obligation to pay into the bank, for the purpose of creating the Guarantee Fund, a lump sum representing the difference between 500 million marks and the amount already deposited by it out of the French share of the mobilization loan, but that it was obligated merely to provide the funds currently needed for deficiency transfers under the Young plan. The French interpretation was finally accepted by the other creditors, who, after a prolonged discussion, conceded that there was a certain amount of vagueness as to the mode of procedure in the language of paragraph 199 of the Young plan, which provided that "on the coming into force of this plan, France will give to the Bank for International Settlements an undertaking to deposit in a trust fund, on the demand of the bank, foreign currencies to a total value of 500 million reichsmarks."

share in the mobilization loan. This would have meant that her outlay for the Guarantee Fund would have been approximately 106 million dollars. On the other hand, she would have received her normal share of the German annuity in full (her receipts from the unconditional portion of the annuity and the quota of deliveries in kind and reparation recovery levy adding up to the amount of her share in the total annuity), and she would have had the right to postpone portions of her scheduled payments to the United States and Great Britain, aggregating slightly over 60 million dollars. Since she normally collected much more than she paid out, the only consequence for her would have been a diminution of her net receipts by about 45 million dollars, against which, however, she would have had an interest-bearing deposit at the Bank for International Settlements, represented by the Guarantee Fund.

Great Britain, on the other hand, on condition that all the postponement provisions of the existing reparation and war debt settlements had been invoked, would have found herself with a deficit in the debt account. Her receipts from Germany would have fallen short of her normal share, and this diminution, together with the loss of receipts resulting from the exercise of postponement options by her other debtors, would have wiped out the small surplus of receipts over payments normally accruing to her. The portion of her payments to the United States which she in turn would have been in a position to postpone would have been smaller than her combined losses of revenue, although the net deficit would not have been large.

The position of the American Treasury on the war debt account during the fiscal year ending June 30, 1932 is indicated in the table on page 318. The "postponable" part, except in the case of France, comprises the payments on account of principal which were made subject to postponement in the debt agreements.[6] The table shows that, if all the postponement provisions

SCHEDULED RECEIPTS OF THE AMERICAN TREASURY ON THE
WAR DEBT ACCOUNT, 1931–32
(In thousands of dollars)

Country	Postponable	Non-Postponable	Total
Austria.........	—	287.6	287.6
Belgium.........	—	7,950.0	7,950.0
Czechoslovakia...	—	3,000.0	3,000.0
Esthonia........	108.0	492.4	600.4
Finland.........	55.0	257.3	312.3
France..........	30,000.0	20,000.0	50,000.0
Great Britain....	28,000.0	131,520.0	159,520.0
Greece..........	660.0	449.1	1,109.1
Hungary........	12.3	57.1	69.4
Italy...........	12,200.0	2,506.1	14,706.1
Latvia..........	44.7	206.0	250.7
Lithuania.......	38.6	185.9	224.5
Poland..........	1,325.0	6,161.8	7,486.8
Rumania........	—	800.0	800.0
Yugoslavia......	—	250.0	250.0
Total........	72,443.6	174,123.3	246,566.9
Germany........	6,000.0	—	6,000.0
Grand total..	78,443.6	174,123.3	252,566.9

stipulated in our debt agreements had been invoked, the American Treasury would still have collected during the year almost 70 per cent of the total scheduled payments.

It is clear that if the postponement provisions contained in the debt settlements had been invoked in June 1931, their operation would have affected the general situation but slightly. The major portion of the sched-

[6] For the special provisions regarding France and the countries indicated in the table as not possessing any postponement privileges, see pp. 92-99.

uled debt payments would have had to be continued, and the strain of such payments on the international trade and financial relations, therefore, would have been relieved to only a negligible degree. Moreover, the extraordinary difficulties confronting Germany and some of the other countries of Central Europe—the run on their gold and foreign exchange resources resulting from loss of confidence—might easily have been enhanced if action were initiated by the debtor countries themselves, as would have been the case if relief had been sought by way of the machinery inherent in the existing debt agreements. Furthermore, relief was particularly urgent in the case of Germany, and it was with respect to Germany that the existing machinery would have been least adequate: it could not have been made operative immediately, and when finally put into effect it would have brought no alleviation for the German budget and but a slight lessening of the strain on the German balance of payments. Action outside the scope of the existing agreements was required.

Germany made a bid for a major move with respect to the reparation payments in the manifesto of June 5, and even this request, couched as it was in general terms, brought a sharp turn for the worse in the country's international financial position. A more definite appeal to her reparation creditors would have made Germany's position with respect to her short-term creditors worse than before, and would merely have intensified the very danger that action with regard to the reparation payments would have been designed to forestall.

As it turned out, Germany was not, in the end, saved from a situation almost approaching national bankruptcy. The course of events which brought this about will be described in the next chapter. But in the meantime the whole complex of factors relating to the debts was already in the sphere of international discussion and action, and this fact rendered possible a greater measure of control over unfolding developments than would have been the case had Germany been forced into a position of virtual default. As matters stood in the middle of June 1931, swift and decisive action that promised at least some hope of success could have been, in the very nature of things, initiated only by the largest of the ultimate creditors, the United States. Fortunately, the American government took the lead with reasonable promptitude and admirable decisiveness.

III. THE HOOVER PROPOSAL

The fact that Germany and, consequently, the whole world were on the brink of a major catastrophe began to be clearly realized in many well-informed quarters in the United States soon after it became apparent that Germany was being subjected to an irresistible run on her foreign exchange resources. American diplomatic representatives in Central Europe, and especially in Berlin, had for months been sending increasingly disquieting reports. Moreover, in the words of Secretary of the Treasury Mills, "as early as the 12th or 13th [of June], men like Mr. Owen Young, Mr. Parker Gilbert, who had spent four years in Germany and was thoroughly familiar with German economy, Governor Harrison of the Federal Reserve Bank of New York, who has an intimate knowledge, of course, of situations of this kind, had all reached the conclusion that something had to be done."[7] As this evidence was accumulating, the admin-

---

[7] 72 Cong. 1 sess., *Postponement of Inter-Governmental Debts*, Hearings on H. j. res. 147 before Committee on Finance, Dec. 16, 1931, p. 9.

istration was rapidly arriving at the conclusion that action was necessary.

The President, however, was confronted with a number of peculiar difficulties. The United States is not a reparation creditor, and moreover, it has been the consistent policy of the American government to regard the reparation payments and the war debts as totally separate and distinct obligations. Yet relief from the burden of the war debts had to begin with the reparation payments by Germany. It was clear that only by throwing everything into a melting pot and adjourning all inter-governmental payments resulting from the World War, including the payments due to the American Treasury, was it possible to bring about an adequate measure of relief in such a manner as to help the situation, rather than make it worse. But Congress, not the President, has power over the obligations of foreign governments to the United States. Without authority from Congress, the President and the Secretary of the Treasury are bound by law to collect the instalments scheduled in the funding agreements. Semi-annual payments from 13 foreign governments were coming due on June 15. Congress alone could authorize the adjournment of these payments, and Congress was not in session. Prior to June 16, therefore, no move involving payments to the United States could have been undertaken by the President. After the June 15 payments had been met, there was a possibility for the President to act, subject always to subsequent ratification by Congress.

The President decided to act on June 19 and embarked at once upon an almost unprecedented procedure—an attempt to obtain the consent to his action, in advance, from leading senators and representatives. Again in the language of Secretary Mills's dramatic testimony,

We sat here from June 6 to the evening of Friday, June 19, watching this run on this great nation [Germany], which was comparable to a run on a great bank, with the reserves gradually being depleted, until it was perfectly obvious by Friday and Saturday [June 19 and 20] that the end was at hand. And it was clear, after the President began, on Friday morning, to lay this situation before the members of both houses who could be reached, that each and every man before whom these facts were laid had said unqualifiedly, "There is only one thing for you to do, Mr. President"—and by noon on Saturday he definitely decided to issue that statement.[8]

Almost to the last day, action was contemplated in terms of a two-year moratorium. On the very eve of the momentous pronouncement of July 20, however, principally under the pressure of domestic political factors, the program was changed to a moratorium covering but one year. President Hoover's proposal with respect to action along these lines, as embodied in his statement to the American people, read as follows:

The American government proposes the postponement during one year of all payments on inter-governmental debts, reparations, and relief debts, both principal and interest, of course, not including obligations of governments held by private parties. Subject to confirmation by Congress, the American government will postpone all payments upon the debts of foreign governments to the American government payable during the fiscal year beginning July 1 next, conditional on a like postponement for one year of inter-governmental debts owing the important creditor powers.

The statement contained the names of 21 senators and 18 representatives, of both parties, with whom the President had conferred and who had expressed their approval of the action to be undertaken. Accordingly, he was able to announce that his contemplated action had been "as-

---

[8] The same.

sured cordial support of leading members of both parties in the Senate and the House."[9]

In explaining the objective which his proposal was intended to achieve, the President said:

The purpose of this action is to give the forthcoming year to the economic recovery of the world and to help free the recuperative forces already in motion in the United States from retarding influences abroad.

The world-wide depression has affected the countries of Europe more severely than our own. Some of these countries are feeling to a serious extent the drain of this depression on national economy. The fabric of inter-governmental debts, supportable in normal times, weighs heavily in the midst of this depression.

From a variety of causes arising out of the depression such as the fall in the price of foreign commodities and the lack of confidence in economic and political stability abroad there is an abnormal movement of gold into the United States which is lowering the credit stability of many foreign countries. These and the other difficulties abroad diminish buying power for our exports and in a measure are the cause of our continued unemployment and continued lower prices to our farmers.

Wise and timely action should contribute to relieve the pressure of these adverse forces in foreign countries and should assist in the re-establishment of confidence, thus forwarding po-

---

[9] The second paragraph of President Hoover's statement read as follows:

"This course of action has been approved by the following senators: Henry F. Ashurst, Hiram Bingham, William E. Borah, James F. Byrnes, Arthur Capper, Simeon D. Fess, Duncan U. Fletcher, Carter Glass, William J. Harris, Pat Harrison, Cordell Hull, William H. King, Dwight W. Morrow, George H. Moses, David A. Reed, Claude A. Swanson, Arthur Vandenberg, Robert F. Wagner, David I. Walsh, Thomas J. Walsh, James E. Watson; and by the following representatives: Isaac Bacharach, Joseph W. Byrns, Carl R. Chindbloom, Frank Crowther, James W. Collier, Charles R. Crisp, Thomas H. Cullen, George P. Darrow, Harry A. Estep, Willis C. Hawley, Carl E. Mapes, J. C. McLaughlin, Earl C. Michener, C. William Ramseyer, Bertrand H. Snell, John Q. Tilson, Allen T. Treadway, and Will R. Wood. It has been approved by Ambassador Charles G. Dawes and by Mr. Owen D. Young."

litical peace and economic stability in the world. . . . The essence of this proposition is to give time to permit debtor governments to recover their national prosperity. I am suggesting to the American people that they be wise creditors in their own interest and be good neighbors.

Further in the statement, the President took occasion to emphasize the view that the course of action he was proposing was "entirely consistent with the policy which we have hitherto pursued." He reiterated the policy of the American government with regard to the separateness of the war debts and the reparation payments and stated clearly that he did not "approve in any remote sense of the cancellation of the debts to us." He went on, however, to say:

But as the basis of the settlement of these debts was the capacity under normal conditions of the debtor to pay, we should be consistent with our own policies and principles if we take into account the abnormal situation now existing in the world. I am sure the American people have no desire to attempt to extract any sum beyond the capacity of any debtor to pay and it is our view that broad vision requires that our government should recognize the situation as it exists. This course of action . . . represents our willingness to make a contribution to the early restoration of world prosperity in which our own people have so deep an interest.

President Hoover's proposal was the official expression of a growing realization that the payment programs contained in the existing debt settlements were no longer capable of fulfillment under the conditions in which the world found itself in the summer of 1931. It marked a definite breakdown of these programs. It was a demonstration of the fact that the framers of the debt settlements had failed to foresee the sort of economic dislocation which had made the breakdown inevitable and to provide for this type of emergency. The machinery of relief from the debt payments which had been provided proved to be woefully inadequate and had to be swept aside in favor of much more far-reaching action.

That action was initiated by the President's proposal. It did not—as it probably could not—change the immediate course of the world crisis. Its beneficent effects were soon offset by factors of dislocation in other branches of the world economy, and even these effects themselves were in part neutralized by the character of the negotiations which attended the acceptance of the Hoover proposal and which we shall describe in the next chapter. But the debt holiday did remove, at least for the time being, one important element of strain in a world already over-burdened with great economic difficulties, and it served to direct the world's attention to the basic implications of the debt problem, which had been so badly obscured by the disguising factors that had characterized the process of debt fulfillment.

CHAPTER XV

MORATORIUM ARRANGEMENTS

President Hoover's proposal for a debt holiday was clearly conditional on two actions: its approval by the Congress of the United States, and its acceptance by the other important creditors. Congressional approval had already been virtually assured in the process of the President's consultations with members of Congress, and since no debt payments to the United States Treasury, save for some minor obligations, were due until December 15, 1931, the submission of the proposal could well be postponed until the next regular session of Congress. Acceptance by the other important creditors, on the other hand, was of immediate urgency. It was necessary that the proposal be put into force as soon as possible if it was to have the desired effect, especially since the next instalment on the German reparation payments was due on July 15, and other instalments were due monthly thereafter.

Announced under the pressure of what was considered at the time to be an emergency that brooked no delay, the President's proposal was made with scarcely any consultation with the other important creditors. Although all of these, with the exception of France, accepted the proposal immediately, the reservations insisted upon by that country for reasons of general policy necessitated a series of negotiations. The result was that full acceptance of the moratorium idea could not be announced for more than two weeks after the original proposal had been made by President Hoover, and even then many important problems concerned with the detailed arrangements for the adjournment of the debt payments still remained in abeyance.

I. FRANCO-AMERICAN AGREEMENT

In a note delivered at the Department of State on June 24 by the French Ambassador in Washington, the government of France accepted in principle the proposition that payments on inter-governmental debts should be adjourned in the interests of world economic recovery, but firmly refused to accede to the proposal that the whole existing machinery of debt payments be completely swept aside. In particular, the French government protested against the suspension of German instalments on account of the unconditional portion of the Young annuities. The French note argued that such action went "directly against a fundamental principle and express stipulations" and created a "great risk of shaking confidence in the value of signatures and contracts, and thus of proceeding contrary to the aim in view." The French government also made a number of other reservations and suggested an exchange of views between the two governments. Accordingly, negotiations were begun, the successful termination of which was not announced until July 6.

The position taken by France in the note of June 24 and subsequent declarations was substantially as follows:

1. All payments on inter-governmental debts should be adjourned for one year, but an exception should be made of the unconditional portion of the Young annuities.

2. Monthly instalments representing the unconditional annuities should be continued in full, but the funds, after proper deduction had been made to cover the service charges on the mobilization loan, should be placed by the creditors at the disposal of the Bank for Inter-

national Settlements and utilized as follows: (a) to provide for financing the contracts already approved with respect to deliveries in kind; (b) to provide credits aggregating approximately 25 million dollars for countries of Central Europe, other than Germany, which would experience difficulties as a result of the suspension of German reparation payments; and (c) to return the remainder to Germany in the form of loans to German industrial and financial concerns, but not to the German government. France was thus proposing that the unconditional annuity payments be continued without interruption, but that the funds should not be retained by any of the creditors, except in so far as the contracts for the deliveries in kind were concerned.

3. All payments by Germany, suspended during the Hoover year, and all loans made to Germany out of the unconditional instalments, should be made repayable within two years after the moratorium went into effect.

4. During the Hoover year, France should be freed from her obligation to create, at the Bank for International Settlements, the Guarantee Fund stipulated in the Young plan. In the event of a suspension of payments by Germany under the procedure laid down in the Young plan in 1932-33, the French share of the unconditional annuity reloaned to Germany during the year 1931-32 should be regarded as the source from which funds would be obtained for the purpose of creating the Guarantee Fund.

In the course of the Franco-American negotiations, the original French position was modified in a number of important respects. The American government conceded the French thesis that the continuity of unconditional payments by Germany should be maintained, but France agreed that complete relief be afforded to Germany by reloaning to her the whole of such payments, with the exception of the amounts required to cover service charges on the mobilization loan. Under the terms of the Franco-American agreement, it was arranged, subject to later approval by the other reparation creditors of Germany, that the contribution of the German railways, amounting to 660 million marks a year, should be continued. However, instead of serving merely as a collateral guarantee, the necessary portion of these payments, namely, 612 million marks, was to be credited as unconditional annuity instalments, the remainder to be applied to the service charges on the Dawes loan. The sums representing the difference between the amount assigned to the unconditional annuities and the sums required for the service charges on the mobilization loan were to be used by the bank to purchase, for the account of the creditor governments, specially created bonds of the German railways. The administration of the railways, however, was to retain the right of placing the proceeds of such bonds at the disposal of the German government in the form of direct or indirect loans.

On the question of the period during which the suspended instalments should become payable, the original American position was that all the payment schedules should be pushed up one year, the moratorium year being simply dropped out. This was modified into a proposal that the suspended payments be funded over a period of 25 years. A compromise was finally reached between this proposal and the French insistence on limiting the period of repayment to two years, in the form of a scheme for extending the funding period over ten years, starting with July 1, 1933. It was agreed that the same treatment be accorded the suspended payments and the railway bonds, the French thus giving up their demand for linking the loans to the German railways with the Guarantee Fund.

On the question of the Guarantee Fund, the French government recognized that any modifications in the provisions regarding it were not a matter of direct concern to the American government, and agreed to take it up with the other creditors of Germany and with the Bank for International Settlements. Similarly, France recognized that the problem of financial assistance to other governments adversely affected by the moratorium on the reparation payments and the question of deliveries in kind were not matters of direct concern to the American government. It was agreed, however, that central banks should be requested to organize the necessary financial assistance through the Bank for International Settlements, and that a committee of experts be named by the interested powers to study the question of deliveries in kind and other technical matters with a view to reconciling "the material necessities with the spirit of President Hoover's proposal."

Immediately after the Franco-American agreement was announced, the British government issued official invitations to the interested governments to appoint their representatives to a committee of technical experts, which was to convene in London on July 17. The committee was duly created, but before it could meet the German crisis took a sharp turn for the worse and necessitated the convocation of a diplomatic conference to deal with the new problems thus suddenly thrust forward.

II. THE SEVEN-POWER CONFERENCE AND THE COMMITTEE OF EXPERTS

In its note addressed to the American government on June 24, the government of France expressed its belief that "the mere general suspension of payments would not furnish an adequate remedy" for the dangers which threatened German economy and, more generally, European economy, since these dangers "have another origin and are especially due to important restrictions of credit and withdrawals of foreign funds." While recognizing that the proposed adjournment of inter-governmental payments would be a step in the direction of attenuating the consequences of the current crisis, the French government argued that "the solution of the German crisis does not appear to lie only in the diminution of the charges on the budget of the Reich, but in an extension of credit."

The existing situation pointed clearly to the correctness of this analysis. The immediate German crisis was largely a matter of credit confidence, and President Hoover's proposal was intended, in part, to strengthen precisely this factor in Germany's position. Yet the delay in making the moratorium effective, which France felt constrained to occasion by insisting upon her reservations, operated strongly in exactly the opposite direction from that in which, according to the French view itself, the way out of the crisis logically lay. Far from reassuring the short-term creditors of Germany, the uncertainty produced by the delay served to increase their apprehensions, with the result that an unceasing, though somewhat slackened, strain continued to be put on the gold and foreign exchange resources of the Reichsbank, the reserve ratio of which still hovered perilously near the statutory minimum. If the financial collapse of Germany was to be avoided, it was even more necessary after the Franco-American agreement had been reached than it had been when the Hoover proposal was announced that withdrawals of foreign funds from Germany should cease and, possibly, that new credits be placed at her disposal.

Three days after the Franco-American agreement, Dr. Hans Luther, the president of the Reichsbank, flew to London to confer with the British regarding new foreign credits for Germany. The next day, in company with the Governor of the Bank of England, he visited Paris and continued his negotiations there. On July 11, he returned to Berlin with nothing accomplished. Rumors to the effect that the French government had insisted on political conditions as a part of any new credit arrangement and that the German government had flatly refused to accept any such conditions accompanied Dr. Luther's return to Berlin. On the day of his arrival there, the withdrawals of gold and foreign exchange from the Reichsbank doubled by comparison with the preceding day.

In the meantime, the general financial position within Germany had deteriorated at a rapid pace. Runs had begun on some of the German banks, and on July 12, in a desperate effort to forestall disaster, the German government issued a statement announcing its decision to guarantee the liabilities of the leading commercial banks. This announcement came too late. On the next day, the Darmstädter und National Bank, one of the four great banking institutions of Germany, went into bankruptcy. The German government at once closed the Berlin Bourse and ordered all commercial and savings banks in the country shut down for two days. On July 15, the reserve ratio of the Reichsbank dropped below the statutory minimum, and the German financial situation definitely reached a point requiring extraordinary measures.[1]

---

[1] The widespread nature of the immediate repercussions of the German crisis may be seen from the fact that, on July 14, a bank holiday

On the same day, the British government invited the governments of the United States, France, Germany, Italy, Belgium, and Japan to send representatives to an official conference for the purpose of considering the situation. This seven-power conference met at London on July 21, and remained in session for three days. The United States was represented by Secretary of State Stimson and Secretary of the Treasury Mellon, both of whom were in Europe at the time. As never before the trans-oceanic telephone served as a means of communication in the conduct of international negotiations.

The principal problem confronting the London conference was the devising of emergency measures for preventing the German crisis from developing into an utter collapse. It was clear that the crux of the situation was still Germany's position with respect to foreign short-term credits. An official *communiqué* issued after the first session of the conference stated that the ministers assembled in London were considering "methods of financial co-operation whereby confidence in Germany's economic stability may be restored in the immediate future as a preliminary to an examination of further measures which may be necessary to effect a permanent restoration of Germany's financial situation." The conference had before it from the start a series of concrete proposals submitted by the government of the United States, and its final recommendations were based in the main upon these proposals.

The conference proceeded on the assumption that no

---

was declared in Hungary, bank failures were reported in Austria, Rumania, and Latvia, and banks in Danzig fixed maximum limits for withdrawals of deposits. The next day, the principal stock exchanges of the world showed heavy liquidations and sharp breaks in prices, and a heavy drain of gold began from England. For a dramatic diary of the crisis, see the *Economist* (London), July 18, 1931 ff.

direct action by governments appeared feasible in the circumstances. Private financial interests and, to a lesser degree, central banks, were primarily involved in the situation. Accordingly, the recommendations of the conference were addressed primarily to the financial institutions concerned, the governments undertaking merely to use their influence in bringing about a speedy and successful carrying out of the measures proposed.

The London conference recommended strongly that the short-term creditors of Germany cease withdrawals of their funds and arrange for concerted action looking toward maintaining the volume of such credits at the disposal of Germany at the then existing level. The conference further recommended that assurances be given to Germany that the credit of 100 million dollars advanced to the Reichsbank on June 25 by the principal central banks (including the Federal Reserve Bank of New York) and the Bank for International Settlements, and renewed for three months on July 16, would be renewed for another period of three months at its next maturity. Finally, the conference recommended that "the Bank for International Settlements should be invited to set up without delay a committee of representatives nominated by the governors of the central banks interested to inquire into the immediate further credit needs of Germany and to study the possibilities of converting a portion of the short-term credits into long-term credits."

The final official *communiqué* stated the conviction of the conference that the loss of confidence, which was playing so tragic a role in the German situation, was "not justified by the economic and budgetary position" of Germany. This blanket assurance, together with the specific measures proposed, was intended to restore confidence in Germany and put an end at last to the devastating run on liquid resources which had been rapidly sapping the economic life of the country.[2]

The carrying out of the recommendations put forward by the London conference required the setting up of two committees—one representing the central banks and one acting for private short-term creditors. These bodies were created in very short order. On the day following the close of the conference, the Bank for International Settlements, through its president, Mr. Gates W. McGarrah, informed Prime Minister MacDonald that it was "proceeding without any delay to an examination of the best and most expeditious methods of giving effect to those recommendations of the conference which fall within its power and sphere of action." The central banks' committee met at Basle, the seat of the Bank for International Settlements, on August 8. It became known as the Wiggin Committee, because its American member, Mr. Albert H. Wiggin, presided over its sessions. In the meantime, representatives of banking groups in various countries concerned with short-term credits to Germany began negotiations with their German debtors. On August 14 these negotiations were transferred to Basle at the invitation of the Wiggin Committee.

The Wiggin Committee's report, issued on August 18, contained a brief, but thorough, survey of the credit position of Germany. As regards the first part of its agenda

[2] One of the American proposals submitted to the London conference was that the German government should be asked to continue the enforcement of a complete control of foreign exchange in order to prevent flight of capital. The conference did not include this among its recommendations, mainly because the German representatives had already given positive assurances that their government was doing everything in its power along these lines.

—"the immediate further credit needs of Germany"—
the committee came to a definite conclusion "that it is
necessary in the general interest as well as in that of Germany (1) that the existing volume of Germany's foreign credits should be maintained, and (2) that part, at
all events, of the capital which has been withdrawn
should be replaced from foreign sources." Effect was
to be given to the first conclusion by means of an agreement already negotiated between the German short-
term debtors and their foreign creditors in the form of a
so-called "standstill arrangement," under the operation
of which all maturing credits were to be renewed up to
their full amount for a period of six months. With respect to the second conclusion the committee expressed
its conviction that "the internal economy of Germany
will continue under a condition of extreme strain until
the situation of the Reichsbank has been relieved and a
part at least of the circulating capital that has been suddenly withdrawn from the German economy has been
replaced." On this point, the committee made the following observation:

It is, however, obvious that if the additional capital required
by Germany were supplied in the form of short-term credits
she would be faced with still greater difficulty than at present
in meeting the obligations that will become due in six months'
time, when the period of prolongation of existing credits comes
to an end. . . . We are, therefore, of opinion that in order
to ensure the financial stability of Germany, any additional
credits provided should be in the form of a long-term loan and
that such parts of the existing short-term debt as may suitably
be treated in this way should be converted into long-term obligations.

This brought the committee to a consideration of the
second part of its agenda—"possibilities of converting
a portion of the short-term credits into long-term cred-

its." The committee expressed its conviction that the economic and financial position of Germany was basically sound, but that there were two fundamental difficulties which obstructed the extension to Germany of long-term loans. The first was the political risk, regarding which the committee said that "until the relations between Germany and the other European powers are firmly established on a basis of sympathetic co-operation and mutual confidence and an important source of internal political difficulty for Germany thereby removed, there can be no assurance of continued and peaceful economic progress." The second was the question of Germany's external obligations. In the opinion of the committee, "so long as these obligations, both private and public, are such as to involve either a continuous increase in a snowball fashion of the foreign debt of Germany or alternatively a disproportion between her imports and exports on such a scale as to threaten the economic prosperity of other countries, the investor is unlikely to regard the situation as stable or permanent." The committee, accordingly, recommended to the governments concerned that far-reaching action along these two lines was indispensable to a restoration of Germany's credit, and urged strongly that the necessary measures be taken without delay.[3]

Paralleling the efforts to provide the necessary breathing spell for Germany made by the seven-power conference and the Basle committees set up in accordance with its recommendations, the international committee of financial experts, convoked in accordance with the terms of the Franco-American agreement, duly met in

[3] The full text of the report may be found in 72 Cong. 1 sess., *Moratorium on Foreign Debts*, Hearings on H. j. res. 123 before Committee on Ways and Means, Dec. 15, 1931, Part I, pp. 27-43.

London on July 17 and remained in session until August 11. It consisted of representatives of the United States and of all the nations which had signed The Hague agreements of 1930, and had before it for consideration a large number of technical questions which needed to be settled before the Hoover proposal for a debt holiday could be given full effect.

The most important task confronting the committee of experts was to reach an agreement on the conditions which were to govern the adjournment of reparation payments by Germany. These conditions were finally embodied in an official protocol, signed by plenipotentiary representatives of the respective governments, and attached to the final report of the committee as Appendix I. On the whole, the basic terms laid down in the Franco-American agreement were adhered to, although some of them became the subject of heated discussion in the meetings of the committee, and underwent a certain amount of modification. Since the reparation problem has already entered upon a new phase, it is unnecessary to indicate here the ways in which the various interested countries sought to obtain concessions which only a few months later had already proved to be of no consequence.[4]

III. THE MORATORIUM BEFORE THE UNITED STATES CONGRESS

The postponement of payments due to the American Treasury during the fiscal year 1931-32 was formally

[4] The interested reader will find a description of the controversies and of the detailed decisions of the committee of experts in Leo Pasvolsky, "The Results of the London Conference of Experts," the *Annalist*, Aug. 21 and 28, 1931. For the text of the principal documents see *Report of International Committee of Experts* (British Parliamentary Paper, Cmd. 3947).

approved by the two houses of Congress by means of a joint resolution. As soon as Congress convened in December, a draft resolution prepared by the Administration was submitted to it and was introduced in the Senate by the chairman of the Committee on Finance on December 10, and in the House by the chairman of the Committee on Ways and Means on December 14. The draft resolution authorized the Secretary of the Treasury, with the approval of the President, to postpone the debt payments owed to the Treasury and to arrange with the debtors for the repayment of the deferred amounts in ten annual instalments, starting July 1, 1933, with interest at the rate of 4 per cent. It was provided in Section 3 that

no such agreement shall be made with the government of any country unless it appears to the satisfaction of the President that such government has made, or has given satisfactory assurances of willingness and readiness to make, with the government of each of the other countries indebted to such country in respect of war, relief, or reparation debts, an agreement in respect of such debt substantially similar to the agreement authorized by this joint resolution to be made with the government of such creditor country on behalf of the United States.

Finally, it was provided (Section 4) that agreements regarding the repayment of postponed instalments should not differ in technical respects from the original debt settlements. This was done in order to cover special stipulations relating to mode of payment and postponement clauses in the settlements with Greece and Austria.

Although the moratorium idea had been informally approved by a large number of the individual members of both the Senate and the House of Representatives at the time when the original proposal was made, either before or subsequently to the issuing of President Hoover's statement of June 20, 1931, the joint resolution became the subject of a long and, at times, acrimonious debate. Extensive hearings on the resolution were held by the Committee on Finance and by the Ways and Means Committee, in the course of which several witnesses were examined, among them being Secretary of State Stimson, Mr. Ogden L. Mills, at that time undersecretary of the Treasury, and others. In the course of the deliberations of the Ways and Means Committee, strong opposition to the whole moratorium idea developed among some of the members of the committee, based principally on conviction, expressed by a number of committee members, that the moratorium, if approved, would become merely a prelude to a partial reduction or even a complete cancellation of the debts. In order to meet these objections, the committee added another provision to the draft resolution, which became Section 5 of that document as finally adopted, the other four sections remaining as in the original draft. This provision read as follows:

Section 5. It is hereby expressly declared to be against the policy of Congress that any of the indebtedness of foreign countries to the United States should be in any manner canceled or reduced; and nothing in this joint resolution shall be construed as indicating a contrary policy, or as implying that favorable consideration will be given at any time to a change in the policy hereby declared.

In this new form, the joint resolution was submitted to the House of Representatives, with a majority report recommending its adoption, and a minority report urging a rejection of the moratorium proposal. The House, after an eight-hour debate, voted the adoption of the resolution in the form in which it had emerged from the committee.

The Finance Committee of the Senate, after holding hearings of its own, decided to submit to its parent body the text as finally worked out by the House committee, with the recommendation that it be approved. Such approval was finally given by the Senate, again after a long debate.

The joint resolution did not become law until December 23, when it was signed by President Hoover. In the meantime, debt instalments from twelve of the debtors had fallen due on December 15. However, by means of an informal arrangement, no demand for payment was made on these debtors and they were given assurances that they would not be considered in default by virtue of that fact.

In the joint resolution the Treasury was authorized to fund the postponed payments on the same terms as those worked out by the London committee of experts, except that the interest rate to be charged was changed from 3 to 4 per cent. In explaining this change to the Ways and Means Committee of the House of Representatives Secretary Mills stated that this was done "in recognition of the fact that money conditions have changed since August and that the United States long-term bonds are selling on about a 4 per cent basis."[5]

The debt of Germany covered by the resolution referred only to the payments on account of army costs, and not to the instalments required to cover the mixed claims awards. The United States government sought to

---

[5] 72 Cong. 1 sess., *Moratorium on Foreign Debts,* Hearings on H. j. res. 123 before Committee on Ways and Means, p. 12.

exempt these latter obligations from the operation of the moratorium on the grounds that they belonged to the category of government payments to private parties. Such treatment of the mixed claims instalments was considered especially desirable because it would have been for the benefit of Germany, since the amounts paid by the United States to German claimants on this account exceed our receipts from Germany. For the fiscal year 1931-32, the former amounted to 18 million dollars and the latter to 9 millions. Such an arrangement required, however, the waiving by the other creditors of Germany of their rights under the letters exchanged at The Hague conference in connection with the American-German agreement.[6] France alone among the creditors withheld her consent, and as a result it became necessary to arrange for a suspension of German payments on the mixed claims, as well as on the army costs, account. However, these payments were treated in a different manner than were the other war obligations. The governments of Germany and the United States agreed to postpone the instalments on the mixed claims account in accordance with the relevant provisions of the American-German agreement, rather than the terms agreed upon in London. This meant that these instalments were postponed for two and one-half years, to bear current interest in the interval at the rate of $3\frac{5}{8}$ per cent.[7]

The German payments on account of army costs, as well as the instalments due from all other European debtors, became subject to funding on the terms pre-

---

[6] See pp. 213-14.

[7] Notice of postponement of payment was given by the German Embassy in Washington on Sept. 11, 1931. Since an instalment was due on Sept. 30, the Secretary of the Treasury waived the 90 days' advance notice, as he was empowered to do under Article 8 of the American-German agreement.

scribed in the joint resolution. Accordingly, the United States government invited each of the debtor governments to proceed with the conclusion of an appropriate agreement to this effect. Shortly before the expiration of the moratorium year, such agreements had been concluded with all of the debtors with the exception of Yugoslavia, which, alone of all the countries concerned, had refused to agree to the moratorium.

CHAPTER XVI

THE LAUSANNE SETTLEMENT

The Hoover moratorium was to expire on June 30, 1932. All the payment schedules were, thereafter, to be resumed as though nothing had happened in the meantime. For a period of one year, the regular payment schedules were to be operative. Then, starting July 1, 1933, not only were the regular schedules to continue in full operation, but for a period of ten years, one-tenth of the postponed annual instalments, plus current interest, was also to be paid annually. This was the program envisaged in the protocol with respect to the German reparation payments, signed in London on August 11, and in the special agreements negotiated by all other creditors with their respective debtors.

Every factor in the world situation, however, which could fairly be taken as an indicator of unfolding developments, clearly pointed to the improbability of a resumption of payments by Germany at the expiration of the debt holiday period, and to consequent difficulties in an integral reapplication of the inter-governmental debt payment schedules in general. This improbability was greatly enhanced by the succession of events which occurred during the months of September and October 1931, and which served to intensify the economic and financial dislocation already existing.

In addition to the grave financial difficulties which spread over Central Europe in the wake of the German crisis, a number of other factors of utmost importance were suddenly thrust forward. Great Britain's enforced departure from the gold standard, which took place on

September 20, and which was followed by similar developments in a number of countries, plunged the world once more into a condition of monetary instability and foreign exchange restrictions comparable to those which existed in the early post-war years. This was reflected in the state of international trade and in the course of commodity prices, which in turn had far-reaching repercussions in every phase of economic life everywhere.[1]

In the face of these developments, the measures envisaged by the seven-power conference of July 1931 as "a basis for more permanent action to follow" necessarily acquired added importance and difficulty. Of primary significance among such measures was the question of a resumption of inter-governmental debt payments, and, first and foremost, of reparation payments by Germany. It required almost a year of intermittent negotiations before the powers concerned really came to grips with the whole problem at the Lausanne conference of June-July 1932, which marked the fourth stage in the evolution of the reparation problem.

I. THE HOOVER-LAVAL CONVERSATIONS

The question of a resumption of reparation payments was clearly of most immediate concern to the nations directly involved, and especially to Germany herself and to her principal reparation creditor, France. Negotiations were begun between France and Germany shortly before the seven-power conference, when Chancellor Brüning and Foreign Minister Curtius of Germany stopped at Paris, on their way to London, and conferred with the principal members of the French Cabinet. They were continued intermittently after the London confer-

---

[1] For further discussion, see Chap. XX.

ence. At the end of September, Premier Laval and Foreign Minister Briand of France paid a return visit to Berlin, and as a result of this visit, the conversations between the two countries began to crystallize into a scheme for the formation of a French-German Commission of Co-operation.

However, the statesmen who were at that time in control of the government of France felt that, before they could act definitely, it was necessary for them to reach an understanding with the United States. Hence, in the second half of October, Premier Laval visited Washington, and his conversations with President Hoover led to an important development in the status of the debt problem.

The primary purpose of Premier Laval's visit appears to have been to reach an understanding with the American government concerning the general lines of policy to be pursued with respect to the inter-governmental obligations, which then stood adjourned. Other important problems, such as disarmament, the future of the gold standard, and a general co-ordination of efforts in finding a way out of the current economic depression, were also discussed. But the debt question undoubtedly constituted the crux of the conversations.

So far as the reparation payments aspect of the debt problem was concerned, France was still determined to maintain, as far as possible, the framework of the arrangements comprised in the Young plan and the agreements based on it. During the Franco-American negotiations at the end of June and the beginning of July, she had succeeded in retaining a formal continuity of that part of the arrangement which was of special interest to her, namely, the unconditional annuities. Fully realizing

that in view of the existing circumstances the debt holiday would inevitably have to be prolonged beyond the
one-year period stipulated in the original proposal,
France was extremely eager that any future action should
be entirely within the framework of the existing agreements.

The only light which we have on the nature of the
understanding arrived at by the heads of the two governments is found in the joint statement issued by President Hoover and M. Laval on October 25, 1931. After
a preamble on "the traditional friendship between the
United States and France," the statement referred to
the debt problem in the following terms:

We canvassed the economic situation in the world, . . .
the effects of the depression on payments under inter-governmental debts, . . . and other financial and economic subjects.
An informal and cordial discussion has served to outline with
greater precision the nature of the problems. It has not been
the purpose of either of us to engage in commitments binding
our governments, but rather, through development of fact, to
enable each country to act more effectively in its own field.
. . . In so far as inter-governmental obligations are concerned, we recognize that prior to the expiration of the Hoover
year of postponement some agreement regarding them may be
necessary covering the period of business depression, as to the
terms and conditions of which the two governments make all
reservations. The initiative in this matter should be taken at an
early date by the European powers principally concerned within the framework of the agreements existing prior to July 1,
1931.

This pronouncement was sufficiently general and
vague to cover almost any contingency. No commitments
of a binding nature were entered into, and each of the
two governments reserved complete freedom of action.
And yet the statement contained two propositions of

great significance. The first was that the two principal creditors on the inter-governmental debt account were in agreement on the probable need of prolonging the adjournment of debt payments beyond the limits of the then current moratorium, although the question of how extensive a prolongation might be needed was covered by the indefinite phrase, "the period of business depression." The second was that the initiative this time must come from the debtors, that is, in the first instance, Germany. In other words, if there was to be any further modification in the reparation payment programs, the machinery necessary for devising such modifications was to be formally set into motion by Germany.

Although no promises on either side were recorded in the joint statement, France served notice to the world in sufficiently unmistakable terms that as far as the reparation aspect of the inter-governmental debt problem was concerned, she, as the principal creditor, was determined that thenceforth there should be no substantial deviations from the procedures laid down in the arrangements growing out of the Young plan. The United States readily accepted a position of neutrality in this matter, which formally, and in accordance with repeatedly announced policy, was not of direct concern to it. Armed with this pronouncement, which was greatly strengthened by the fact that it was made from Washington and over the signatures of the heads of the American and the French governments, Premier Laval returned to Paris, where a new series of Franco-German negotiations was immediately inaugurated.

II. WORK OF THE SPECIAL ADVISORY COMMITTEE

It was clear that the procedure which the French government meant to be invoked was that provided for in the safeguard arrangements of the Young plan and The Hague agreements. The German government had perforce to be content with this line of action on the formal side, but it insisted that while the letter of the existing agreements be carried out scrupulously, their spirit should be interpreted with a sufficient degree of liberality to take account of newly arisen circumstances. The Franco-German negotiations centered, accordingly, around the scope of the terms of reference on the basis of which the Special Advisory Committee, when convoked through the proper channels, should proceed with its task.

The German government, in its negotiations with the government of France during the first half of November, contended that a committee, with its scope of discussion limited to a consideration of the conditional annuities alone, as provided in the Young plan, would not in the least meet the needs of the situation. Its spokesmen insisted that if such a committee was to develop its full usefulness, it should be given power to examine the whole financial and economic position of Germany, with a view to appraising all the factors involved in the country's paying capacity; that an examination of this sort should extend to the whole reparation liability of Germany, the unconditional, as well as the conditional payments; and, finally, that the committee should be authorized to deal with the commercial, as well as the political, obligations of Germany and to establish, if need be, priority as between reparation payments and other foreign obligations, especially short-term debts, covered by the "standstill" agreement, which was due to expire in February 1932.

The French government, on the other hand, maintained that it was in no way concerned with the German foreign debts on the non-reparation account.[2] Based on solemn treaty obligation and on equally solemn subsequent undertakings assumed by Germany, the reparation payments, in the opinion of the French government, constituted a first lien on the resources of Germany and had undisputed priority over commercial loans, made to Germany mainly on the basis of speculative expectations of profit and consequently clearly on the risk of lenders. Neither was the French government willing to permit an extension of the committee's terms of reference, enabling it to make a pronouncement with respect to the unconditional annuities.

After more than two weeks spent in search of a formula to express an acceptable compromise between these two opposing views, agreement was finally reached. The German request for the creation of a Special Advisory Committee was to be made strictly in accordance with the procedure laid down in the Young plan, but this request was to be accompanied by a statement of the German government's views as to the basic needs of the situation and as to the task to be performed by the committee. France agreed to give tacit endorsement to this position by interposing no formal protest to the convocation of the committee under these circumstances. At the same time, it was agreed that the committee was not, under any circumstances, to make any pronouncement on the question of priority as between the reparation and the commercial obligations; that the short-term debts were to become the subject of new negotiations between the foreign creditors and their German debtors; and

[2] The French government was strongly supported in this view by the press and the financial circles of the country, principally because the French share in the German foreign debt on the non-reparation account is very small.

that, subsequently to the sessions of the committee and the conclusion of the commercial debt negotiations, an official conference of government representatives should be convoked to deal with the debt problem in its entirety.

Accordingly, on November 20, the German government addressed a formal request to the Bank for International Settlements for the setting up of a Special Advisory Committee. Upon the receipt of the German note, the bank immediately issued invitations to the governors of the seven central banks, who were to name members of the committee[3] to make the nominations. As soon as these had been made, the bank officially convoked the committee, which met at Basle on December 7.

The committee consisted of one member of each of the following nationalities: British, French, German, Italian, Belgian, Japanese, and American. At its first meeting, it decided to exercise its option of co-opting four additional members, and the members thus brought in were of Swiss, Swedish, Dutch, and Yugoslav nationality. On December 8, the full committee met at its first plenary session and entered upon its task, which was completed on December 23, when, after a series of stormy sessions, a unanimous report was signed.[4]

The committee's report dealt with the general condition of affairs in Germany; with the circumstances that had brought about the existing situation; and with the special measures taken by Germany to meet the emergency. Such factors as the foreign debt, the trade bal-

---

[3] For the provisions regarding the convocation of the committee, see pp. 230-31.

[4] The chairmanship of the committee devolved upon its Italian member, Professor Alberto Beneduce, who was chosen after the American member, Dr. W. W. Stewart, the first choice of the committee, had found it impossible to serve in that capacity.

ance, the balance of payments, the position of the Reichs-bank, the state of production and employment, and the government budget were subjected to a searching analysis, after which the committee announced the following conclusion:

It is evident from the facts outlined in the preceding chapters that Germany would be justified in declaring—in accordance with her rights under the Young plan—that in spite of the steps she has taken to maintain the stability of her currency, she will not be able, in the year beginning in July next, to transfer the conditional part of the annuity.

In stating this conclusion and in reporting its findings as to the general state of Germany, the committee discharged its formal duty as required in its official terms of reference. But it went beyond that and supplemented its conclusion with the following general statement:

The committee, however, would not feel that it had fully accomplished its task and justified the confidence placed in it if it did not draw the attention of the governments to the unprecedented gravity of the crisis, the magnitude of which undoubtedly exceeds the "relatively short depression" envisaged in the Young plan—to meet which the "measures of safeguard" contained therein were designed. The Young plan, with its rising series of annuities, contemplated a steady expansion of the world trade, not merely in volume but in value, in which the annuities payable by Germany would become a factor of diminishing importance. In fact the opposite has been the case. Since the Young plan came into effect, not only has the trade of the world shrunk in volume, but the very exceptional fall in gold prices that has occurred in the last two years has itself added greatly to the real burden, not only of German annuities, but of all payments fixed in gold.

In the circumstances, the German problem—which is largely responsible for the growing financial paralysis of the world —calls for concerted action which the governments alone can take. But the problem has assumed a world-wide range. We can recall no previous parallel in time of peace to the dislocation that is taking place and may well involve a profound change in the economic relations of nations to one another. Action is most urgently needed in a much wider field than that of Germany alone. . . .

When governments come to examine the whole group of questions allied to the present report, they will have to take account of many matters relevant to these complex problems— which can only be solved in conformity with economic realities. In this connection, certain considerations seem to us of great importance.

The first is that transfers from one country to another on a scale so large as to upset the balance of payments can only accentuate the present chaos. It should also be borne in mind that the release of a debtor country from a burden of payments which it is unable to bear may merely have the effect of transferring that burden to a creditor country which, in its character as a debtor, it, in turn, may be unable to bear. Again, the adjustment of all inter-governmental debts (reparations and other war debts) to the existing troubled situation of the world —and this adjustment should take place without delay if new disasters are to be avoided—is the only lasting step capable of re-establishing confidence which is the very condition of economic stability and real peace.

We appeal to the governments on whom the responsibility for action rests to permit of no delay in coming to decisions which will bring an amelioration of this grave crisis which weighs so heavily on all alike.[5]

Thus while it made no concrete proposals, the committee definitely stated its view that the Young plan was no longer applicable and that the whole complex of reparation arrangements based on it was in need of thoroughgoing revision. Moreover, the committee took the position that while Germany as a debtor undoubtedly stood in pressing need of permanent and substantial relief with respect to her foreign obligations, there ap-

[5] For the official text of the committee's report, see *Report of the Special Advisory Committee* (British Parliamentary Paper, Cmd. 3995).

peared to be no possibility of dealing with the German problem apart from the whole problem of inter-governmental debts and the effect upon them of such factors as fluctuations in the volume of international trade and alterations in the purchasing power of gold. Because of the importance of Germany in the general world situation, the committee urged that a reconsideration of the German reparation problem be made the occasion of a general canvass of, and agreement upon, measures relating to the wide range of financial and economic factors involved in the current depression.

In the meantime, the Foreign Creditors' Standstill Committee was meeting in Berlin to consider the fate of the "standstill" agreement negotiated for a six months' period in August 1931. It completed its labors on January 23, 1932, with the elaboration of a new agreement which comprised a prolongation, subject to a number of conditions, of the "standstill" arrangement for one year from the date of the expiration of the first agreement, that is, from February 29, 1932. The agreement covered a body of indebtedness amounting to approximately 5,360 million marks, representing short-term credits, already matured at the time or maturing prior to March 1, 1933.

III. PROVISIONS OF THE LAUSANNE AGREEMENT

The report of the Special Advisory Committee clearly called for the convocation of a conference of government representatives. The initiative was assumed by Great Britain, and in the invitation sent out by the British government to the powers concerned, it was proposed that the conference should meet on January 13, 1932 at Lausanne, Switzerland. The meeting did not occur, however, on that date, because the French government took the position that preliminary negotiations among the principal interested powers were necessary for the success of the whole enterprise. Accordingly, the British proposal was adjourned indefinitely. It was renewed, however, a month later, after preliminary agreement among the governments of Germany, France, Great Britain, Belgium, Italy, and Japan had been announced at Geneva on February 13. This second invitation took the form of a joint act of the six powers, and June 16 was fixed as the opening date of the parley. On that day the Lausanne conference duly assembled.

All the powers that had taken part in The Hague conference of 1930, with the sole exception of Austria, were represented at Lausanne.[6] While the German reparation problem naturally held the center of the stage, similar problems of the smaller reparation debtors were also discussed. However, the final act of the conference recorded full agreement only in so far as Germany was concerned, the other problems being left to future adjustment.

The conference remained in session until July 9, when an agreement between Germany and her creditors was signed. This accomplishment was, in the words of the document itself, "arduously attained," for in spite of its brief duration, the conference worked under conditions of great tension and was on numerous occasions threatened with disaster because of difficulties in recon-

[6] Austria was not present because The Hague conference had freed her completely from any obligation on the reparation account. In addition to the six inviting powers, the following 13 governments were represented: Poland, Portugal, Czechoslovakia, Rumania, Greece, Yugoslavia, Hungary, Bulgaria, Canada, Australia, New Zealand, India, and the Union of South Africa. Unlike the previous reparation parleys, the Lausanne conference was not attended by a specially designated American observer.

ciling the various opposing national viewpoints, especially between Germany and France.

The Lausanne agreement proclaims, subject to its subsequent ratification by the signatory powers, the termination of the Young plan and of The Hague agreements based on that document, in so far as they relate to reparation payments. For the obligations comprised in the so-called Young annuities, it substitutes a new set of obligations, on a vastly reduced scale and made subject, moreover, to a complete cancellation under certain conditions resulting mainly from the general economic state of the world.

Under the Lausanne agreement, Germany assumes the responsibility for delivering to the Bank for International Settlements, acting as trustee for the reparation creditors, German government bonds to the amount of 3 billion gold marks "of the present standard of weight and fineness" (approximately 715 million dollars), bearing interest at the rate of 5 per cent per annum and redeemable by means of a 1 per cent sinking fund. The bonds are to be held by the Bank for International Settlements, but not offered for sale by it until the expiration of a three-year period from the date of the signing of the agreement. Subsequently to that, the bonds may be negotiated by means of public issues "as and when possible and in such amounts as it [the bank] thinks fit," providing, however, that "no issue shall be made at a rate below 90 per cent." The bonds are to bear interest and amortization charges only from the date on which they are negotiated.

The agreement provides that if any bonds remain unsold at the expiration of a 15-year period from the date of signature, they shall be cancelled. However, it also stipulates that after the first five years the bank's board of directors may, by a two-thirds majority, change the minimum price at which the bonds may be offered for sale, if, in its opinion, "the credit of the German government is restored, but the quotation of its loans remains, none the less, below the minimum price of issue" fixed in the agreement. Moreover, the German government, which retains the right to redeem at par any bonds remaining unissued, is obligated, if it should issue or guarantee any foreign loan, maturing within periods in excess of twelve months, to make an offer "to apply up to the equivalent of one-third of the net cash proceeds of the loan raised to the purchase of bonds held by the Bank for International Settlements," the purchase price being such "that the net yield of the bonds so purchased would be the net yield of the loan so raised." This provision becomes applicable immediately after the agreement goes into effect. The creditors clearly retain the right to refuse the German offer, if the purchase price should appear to them unsatisfactory.

The determination of all details such as the currency and denomination of bond issues and the costs of operations is left to the bank, which is required to consult on all such matters with the president of the Reichsbank. However, the final decision rests solely with the bank's board of directors and requires merely a majority vote of the board.

No provision is made in the agreement for the allocation of the proceeds of any bond issues that may be effected by the bank, beyond a statement that all such funds shall be placed in a special account. The question of allocation is left to future agreement among the creditor governments.

The new bonds are substituted for all previously existing German obligations on the reparation account, including those covered by the London agreement of August 11, 1931 relating to the liquidation of the reparation instalments deferred under the terms of the Hoover moratorium, and the payments made by the German government and reloaned to the German railways during the Hoover year. However, the 1924 loan and the mobilization loan of 1930 are specifically excepted. They are to retain their full validity, and special arrangements are to be made between the German government and the Bank for International Settlements for the handling of the service charges on these loans. Finally, the agreement retains the arbitration tribunal set up at The Hague conference, and empowers it to adjudicate disputes relating to the interpretation or application of the new instrument.

It is stipulated in the agreement that the new instrument will go into effect upon its ratification by the following six powers: Belgium, France, Germany, Great Britain, Italy, and Japan. To cover the period preceding such ratification, the Lausanne conference adopted a number of transitional measures.

First, it was agreed that all payments by Germany should cease under the terms of the declaration made by the principal creditor powers on June 16, the opening day of the conference. In this declaration, the creditors agreed to suspend all war debt payments among themselves for the duration of the conference. By the Lausanne agreement, this arrangement was prolonged indefinitely and was made to cease being operative only upon the coming into force of the Lausanne agreement or, failing this, "on one of the governments of the following countries, Belgium, France, Germany, Great Britain, Italy, and Japan, notifying the governments concerned that it has decided not to ratify." Second, the German government and the Bank for International Settlements were authorized to enter into negotiations for the working out of arrangements relating to the service of the Dawes and the "mobilization" loans. And third, provision was made for the creation of a committee consisting of representatives of the German government and of the other governments concerned to deal with still uncompleted contracts relating to deliveries in kind.

The ratification provisions of the Lausanne agreement were supplemented and amplified in the so-called "Gentlemen's Agreement." This was a memorandum initialed by the principal creditors simultaneously with the signing of the document itself, but not incorporated in it and not made public until after its presumed existence had aroused a great deal of controversy and discussion. This memorandum read as follows:

The Lausanne agreement will not definitely go into force until after the ratifications foreseen in those accords.

Concerning the creditor governments in whose name this *procès verbal* is initialed, ratification will not be effected before a satisfactory settlement is obtained between them and their own creditors.

They will have every liberty to explain their position to their respective parliaments, but no precise reference to the present arrangement will appear in the text of the accord with Germany.

If it follows that a satisfactory settlement of their own debts is obtained, the governments of the above-named creditor countries will proceed to ratification, and the accord with Germany will take its full effect.

But in case the settlement in question cannot be obtained, the accord with Germany will not be ratified. A new situation will thus be created and the interested governments will have to agree on what they should do. In this eventuality the legal position of all the interested governments would become what it was before the Hoover moratorium.

Notification of this accord will be made to the German government.

Under the terms of the agreement itself and of the supplementary memorandum, the ratification of the new reparation settlement was, therefore, made contingent upon a modification of the existing debt arrangements between Germany's creditors and their own war creditors, that is, the United States and Great Britain. The question of the American debts was necessarily left in abeyance, since the United States was not represented at Lausanne.

As for the debts to Great Britain, a letter was addressed during the conference by the British Chancellor of the Exchequer to the government of France, in which he, in the name of his government, stated that "in the present circumstances, it [the British government] regrets not to be able to take any definite measure modifying the agreement on Franco-British war debts." He announced, however, his government's decision to extend to the debt owed by France to Great Britain similar arrangements to those made applicable to the German payments by the prolongation of the declaration of June 16, 1932. Finally, he stated that "in the eventuality of non-ratification of the Lausanne agreement, the legal position of all interested governments in relation to one another would again become that which existed under the terms of The Hague agreement of January 20, 1930, and the accord on war debts funding; in this case the British and French governments will have to examine the whole situation thus created." This policy is also being followed in the case of other debts to Great Britain.

No procedure to be followed in the event of non-ratification was laid down either in the Lausanne agreement or the supplementary memorandum. The official documents record agreement merely to the effect that the legal position of the creditor governments will revert to what it was prior to the Hoover moratorium. However, the proceedings of the Lausanne conference contain a far-reaching declaration of the creditor powers dealing with this important point. When the agreement was formally submitted to a vote of the conference, Chancellor von Papen, the head of the German delegation, put the following question to Prime Minister MacDonald, who was president of the conference:

In the event, which in my opinion is rather improbable, that the six governments fail to ratify the Lausanne agreement, what will be the resulting situation and the procedure to be followed? In my view, it will be indispensable that representatives of our governments should then meet as soon as possible in order to examine the situation thus created. I should be very grateful, Mr. President, if you would be good enough to assure me that such is also the view of the conference.

To this Prime Minister MacDonald replied:

I am very happy to make a declaration which will be incorporated in the proceedings, since it would have been difficult to state in the agreement itself the procedure that we envisage. I declare, in the name of the inviting powers, that in the event that we find it impossible, for any reason whatever, to carry out the provisions of the agreement, a new conference shall be assembled before any action is taken.[7]

The final act of the conference recorded three other decisions: first, to set up a committee to deal with non-German reparations and cognate questions "viewing them within the framework of the general settlement"; second, to create a committee for the purpose of studying the measures required for the restoration of the

[7] Translated from the French text of the proceedings, as given in *L'Europe Nouvelle*, July 16, 1932, p. 867.

countries of Central and Eastern Europe and of reporting its findings to the Organization Committee of the
European Union; and third, to request the League of
Nations to convoke a monetary and economic conference
and invite the government of the United States to participate in such a conference.

IV. SIGNIFICANCE OF THE LAUSANNE SETTLEMENT

While the Lausanne settlement did not literally put
an end to reparations, it wiped the slate nearly clean.
Prior to this agreement, the aggregate instalments still
due from Germany under the Young plan amounted
to an equivalent of approximately 25 billion dollars. The
new bonds will, if issued in their entirety, represent a
volume of interest and amortization payments aggregating the equivalent of less than 2 billion dollars. Moreover, counting the Hoover moratorium period, Germany will be entirely free from any reparation payments
for four years, instead of meeting annuities of more
than 400 million dollars each. And even starting with
the fifth year, that is after July 1, 1935, the size of
her annual payments will depend upon whether or not
the new bonds are negotiated through public sale and
the rapidity with which this process takes place. Under no circumstances can such payments exceed an annual total of 43 million dollars. By this settlement,
therefore, over nine-tenths of Germany's vast reparation liability was completely obliterated. The residue of
the Allied claims against Germany which still remain
valid is relatively so small and is moreover so hedged in
by the conditions governing the issue of the new bonds,
that for all practical purposes the reparation problem
may now be considered entirely removed as an element

of strain in the economic and financial affairs of the world.

It is true that the Lausanne agreement is subject to ratification by the creditor powers, who have agreed to delay putting it into force until they have effected "a satisfactory settlement" between themselves and their own creditors, that is, the United States and Great Britain. It does not appear likely, however, that Germany will give her consent to any revision of the Lausanne settlement on terms more favorable to the creditor powers, and consequently that the reparation question will ever be seriously reopened.

So far as Germany is concerned, therefore, the reparation question may, in all probability, be considered as definitely closed. In this manner, the Lausanne settlement represents an important aspect of the "permanent action" envisaged by the seven-power conference, although it does not, by any means, solve all of Germany's problems.

It has cleared away an important obstacle to conciliatory and mutually helpful relations between Germany and her neighbors. It has removed a primary source of social and political unrest within Germany. It has served to clarify the financial and economic situation in Germany and to open the way for a more hopeful approach to the solution of such difficult problems as the relation of German debtors to their foreign private creditors, the repatriation of German capital, and the general revival of German economic life.

This general economic revival of Germany, which is a factor of great importance in the world situation, does not, however, depend solely on German action or on the solution of the reparation problem alone. The Lausanne settlement removes only a part of the strain imposed upon international economic and financial relations by the war debt payments. A glance at the balance sheet of the war debts given in Appendix D will show that with the disappearance, as a result of the Lausanne settlement, of the major portion of reparation obligations, the payments required for the liquidation of the war debts would be cut in half. But were the Lausanne agreement to go into effect and the other war debt schedules to undergo no alteration, the position of most of the important countries concerned would be profoundly altered.

Receipts by the United States Treasury would represent almost four-fifths of the new aggregate movement of funds required in the process of debt payments. On the other hand, the position of eight countries—Great Britain, France, Italy, Belgium, Rumania, Yugoslavia, Greece and Portugal—would change from that of more or less substantial net creditors to that of much more substantial net debtors. The ability of these countries, the first seven of which are war debtors to the United States, to meet their debt payments would clearly be affected.

While the debt funding agreements negotiated by the World War Foreign Debt Commission and by the United States Treasury contain no provision for periodic reconsideration of payment schedules in the light of changing conditions of paying capacity, the United States is, by virtue of official utterances on the subject and as a matter of practical necessity, committed to the principle of regarding the repayment of the war debts as being governed by the debtors' ability to pay. In his message to Congress on December 10, 1931, President Hoover said:

As we approach the new year it is clear that a number of the governments indebted to us will be unable to meet further payments to us in full pending recovery in their economic life. It is useless to blind ourselves to an obvious fact. Therefore it will be necessary in some cases to make still further temporary adjustments. The Congress has shared with the executive in the past the consideration of questions arising from these debts. I am sure that it will commend itself to the Congress that the legislative branch of the government should continue to share this responsibility. In order that we should be in a position to deal with the situation, I recommend the re-creation of the World War Foreign Debt Commission, with authority to examine such problems as may arise in connection with these debts during the present economic emergency, and to report to the Congress its conclusions and recommendations.

The adjustments envisaged in President Hoover's message related to *temporary* alterations in the payment resources of the debtor countries resulting from the current depression. The Lausanne settlement, by depriving these countries of their reparation receipts, has introduced into the situation a new and *permanent* factor. The original debt funding agreements, to the extent to which the principle of paying capacity was taken into account in the course of their negotiation, were predicated on a position of our principal debtors in which substantial reparation receipts constituted a permanent part of their resources. The changed situation renders inevitable a reconsideration of the existing war debt agreements.

The profound significance of the Lausanne settlement lies in the fact that it represents the first clear-cut evidence that the world is beginning to appreciate the economic lessons taught by the application of the policy of debt collection pursued since the war. The nature and significance of these lessons will be discussed in the chapters immediately following. We shall then be in a position to consider the remaining issue which, as a result of the Lausanne agreement, has been forced into the foreground of discussion, namely, the future policy of the United States with reference to the war debts.

PART V

ECONOMIC IMPLICATIONS OF THE DEBT PROBLEM

CHAPTER XVII

FOURTEEN YEARS OF DEBT POLICY

Having completed the story of reparation and debt settlements and of the unsuccessful efforts at fulfillment, we turn to a consideration of the basic economic issues involved in the war debt problem. As was stated in the introductory chapter this analysis is primarily concerned with answering two fundamental questions: (1) Would a complete obliteration of all reparation and war debt obligations promote, or retard, world prosperity? (2) Would collection of these inter-governmental debts be economically beneficial to the creditor countries? Before attempting to answer these questions, which constitute the real issues of the war debt problem, it will be useful to recapitulate, in broad economic terms, the story of the last 14 years—for only thus can one extricate oneself from the maze of details inherent in the manifold problem of the relation of war debts to world prosperity and obtain the perspective necessary for an appreciation of the lessons which the post-war era has taught.

I. ECONOMIC CONSEQUENCES OF THE WAR

The economic burden imposed upon the world by the Great War manifested itself in diverse ways. Certain of the resultant costs could be observed with the eye, while others belonged to the realm of the unseen and the intangible. These invisible consequences have been of much more fundamental and far-reaching significance than the visible ones.

The actual warfare resulted in an enormous destruction of human life and of physical property in many parts of Europe. The battle-front was an irregular but almost continuous girdle encircling the Central Powers. Belgium and Northeastern France; Northeastern Italy and the Adriatic littoral of Austria-Hungary; Serbia, Montenegro, and Rumania; portions of the Ottoman Empire along the Dardanelles, the eastern coast of the Mediterranean and the southern boundary of Transcaucasia; Galicia, Russian Poland, a wide strip of territory in the western and southwestern portions of Russia and along the Baltic; and East Prussia—all of these regions were devastated by prolonged and furious fighting or by incessant movement of troops. Millions of people were killed or incapacitated, cities and villages were stripped, industrial plants dismantled, agricultural lands rendered unfit for cultivation, livestock slaughtered, forest areas denuded, railways, bridges, and roads destroyed, and thousands of square miles of territory once densely populated and productive were rendered temporarily uninhabitable.

In addition to the destruction of life and fixed property, there was an enormous loss of industrial working capital and supplies of semi-manufactured and finished products. Raw materials of many kinds were scarce, manufacturers' inventories were depleted, and the stocks of goods in distributive channels and in the hands of ultimate consumers were very greatly reduced. Such property losses, though not so painfully manifest to the eye as the horrors of the devastated areas, were nevertheless readily apparent to the average citizen, for they affected his every-day livelihood.

The invisible costs of the war manifested themselves in financial and economic maladjustments which vitally affected the functioning of the economic system. The changes which occurred relate to fiscal and currency organization, to agricultural and industrial production, to the status of private international investments, and to the emergence of huge inter-governmental indebtedness. The significance of these changes lay in their effects upon production and trade both in Europe and elsewhere. The financial exigencies of the war left to every European nation a direct heritage of unbalanced budgets, of monetary instability, and of foreign exchange disorganization. For years these financial dislocations impaired the functioning of the productive mechanism of the countries concerned and impeded the movement of international commerce.

Related to these problems were the profound international economic and financial changes which the war produced. While the industry and the agriculture of the European belligerents were being thoroughly disrupted, elsewhere the reverse was occurring. The European shortage of commodities, coupled with an intensified demand, served to stimulate new industries in nearly every non-belligerent country. This was true not only of the neutral nations of Europe, but of North and South America, Australia, and the Orient as well. Agricultural production, particularly in Canada and the United States, both of which countries had the advantage of lower transportation costs to Europe, was enormously expanded to meet the European war demands.

The resulting vast stream of commodities which flowed into the belligerent countries brought about far-reaching alterations in international financial relations. Exports from the nations at war were not available in sufficient volume to pay for the foreign purchases, and the deficits, as we saw in Chapter III, were made up by the sacrifice of previously accumulated foreign investments and in a much greater measure by the flotation of foreign loans, mainly in the United States. As a result, those of the belligerent countries which before the war had been creditor nations on private international account found themselves greatly weakened in this respect. On the other hand, in the United States and Japan, in Holland and the Scandinavian countries, and to a lesser extent elsewhere, the reverse occurred, and such countries emerged as substantial creditors.

Upon these shifts in private financial relations were superimposed the inter-governmental reparation and loan obligations which resulted from the war. Unlike normal international borrowing operations, the inter-governmental debts were in no way connected with economic development, while the reparation obligations were simply penalties for damages. Although the inter-Allied loans were incurred for value received, they were not used for economic expansion, and did not provide the means for their liquidation.

It was not until efforts were made to resume peacetime activities after the close of the war that the results of these economic and financial shifts manifested themselves. The European belligerents naturally and of necessity sought to rehabilitate both their agriculture and their industry. This process led to a series of conflicts of interest both among European nations and as between Europe and the outside world.

Under the influence of territorial changes, the creation of a large number of new national units, and many other factors, the post-war economic policies of European nations assumed a confused and wasteful orientation. Countries which had formerly been primarily agricultural sought to restore their agricultural production and exports, and at the same time to curtail their imports of finished products through a process of industrialization. Countries which had formerly been primarily industrial sought to re-establish production and exports of manufactured goods, and at the same time to reduce their foreign purchases of foodstuffs through an expansion of their own agriculture. These developments took place behind ever rising walls of international trade restrictions, affecting both imports and exports.

With the resurgence of productive and commercial activity in Europe, there was a distinct lessening of European demand for agricultural and industrial products from overseas, which rendered redundant some of the productive capacity that had been created during the war in the non-European countries. This, in turn, demanded swift readjustments and curtailments in non-European countries. The agricultural depression in the United States, which has continued throughout the postwar era and has brought in its wake a veritable holocaust of financial institutions, offers a striking illustration. And since these countries sought to retain as far as possible the commercial advantages acquired during the war, there was an unprecedented sharpening of international competition, countered by a constant growth of foreign trade restrictions.

These conflicts of interest were intensified by the need of inaugurating a flow of wealth from the debtor to the creditor countries in order that liquidation of the immense body of inter-governmental indebtedness resulting from the conflict might be accomplished. And such a flow was obstructed both by the disorganized economic and financial condition of the debtor countries and by the trade policies pursued by the creditor countries.

The conflicts of interest, in turn, intensified the fiscal and currency difficulties under which the war-affected areas of Europe were laboring, and lent added emphasis to maladjustments in agriculture, in industry, and in finance. The inevitable and profound changes in the currents of trade which resulted from these dislocations threw the economic world out of balance. The adjustment of international trade and financial relations which had existed before the war was disrupted at the outbreak of hostilities, and it was not regained after the restoration of peace. The economic losses resulting from the shattering of the international economic organization, by means of which men and women must earn their daily bread, extended literally to the ends of the earth.

The significance of these fundamental economic maladjustments, now generally apparent, was almost wholly unrecognized at the end of the war. The devastated areas were restored in a few short years, but the ill consequences of the disjointed economic and financial system are obviously still with us. In this connection we are tempted to recall a conversation which one of the authors had with an elderly and much traveled lady while crossing the Atlantic in the summer of 1921. They had been discussing economic conditions in Europe and he had been contending that the destructive effects of the war were not confined to Northeastern France and the other devastated areas—that indeed the losses of these countries were not at all to be measured by human casualties or destroyed houses and lands. Finally she turned upon him and said: "Young man, have you seen the devastated areas? Until you have, you will never have the slightest conception of what this war has meant." "Yes, madam," he replied, "I have seen the devastated areas. Now, may I ask, have you seen the meaning of the depreciated and oscillating exchanges, the disorganized banking and currency systems, and the disrupted trade and commercial relations of the world? Have you visualized the significance of the maladjustments in world economic organization which the war produced?" Without answering, she turned abruptly away.

II. DEBT POLICIES IN RELATION TO RECONSTRUCTION

The great problem of world economic reconstruction emerged to command the attention of statesmen as soon as hostilities ceased. Indeed, ideas for the solution of post-war problems were being formulated on both sides of the battle-front long before the end of the struggle was in sight. It will be helpful in gauging the prevailing conceptions of the post-war era to recall some of these views.

In the camp of the Central Powers, attention was being focussed on the creation of a more or less closed economic empire comprising Germany and Austria-Hungary. On the side of the Allies, a somewhat looser conception of economic collaboration was being urged, the principal features of which were embodied in the resolutions of the Inter-Allied Economic Conference, which took place at Paris in 1916. Since victory favored the Allies, only their policies need be summarized here.

In accordance with the resolutions of the conference of 1916, the Allied Powers agreed upon the following plan of post-war action: (1) to insure the re-establishment of countries which had suffered "from acts of destruction, spoilation, and unjust requisitions;" (2) to refuse enemy powers most-favored-nation treatment for a number of years after the war; (3) to conserve for themselves all their resources; (4) to protect themselves against dumping by the establishment of a system of special treatment for goods originating in enemy countries. It will be seen that the purpose of the first resolution was to obtain reparation from the defeated countries, and that the second, third, and fourth were intended to impede, if not to prevent, the economic recovery of the enemy countries.

The economic clauses of the Versailles Treaty bear a striking resemblance to the resolutions of the Paris conference of 1916. We find the same philosophy expressed in the reparation provisions, in the imposition on Germany of a "one-sided" most-favored-nation arrangement, and in the provisions with reference to the protection of industries against German competition. There was obviously no recognition, either in the conference of 1916 or in the peace treaties, of the fact that if the defeated countries were to pay reparations they must be permitted to recover economically, nor apparently was there any realization that the prosperity of the Allied countries themselves would be dependent upon the economic recovery of Central Europe. The treaties evidenced no conception of the economic interdependence of Europe or of the unity of the problem of world economic recovery.

Those provisions of the treaty which dismembered Germany and Austria and set up new states—however desirable they may have appeared from a political or racial viewpoint—were detrimental to European economic recovery. The economic and financial development of Germany before the war was transforming the larger part of Central and Eastern Europe into an integrated economic area. Much of the economic growth throughout this region was stimulated by and radiated from the financial and commercial centers of Germany and Austria. Since this great area was one of the principal markets of French, Italian, Belgian, Dutch, Scandinavian, and British exports, it should have been—but was not—clear that economic retrogression there would have serious repercussions upon the trade and industry of the Allied countries.

However, peace had not been long concluded before the economic and financial confusion in Europe, resulting from the heritage of the war and the policies that were being pursued, rendered imperative international consultation and action. At financial and economic conferences in Brussels in 1920 and in Genoa in 1922, the statesmen of Europe adopted a series of resolutions designed to guide efforts for the promotion of international economic rehabilitation. These resolutions were primarily directed toward the restoration of general financial stability. They urged balancing of government budgets and curtailment of paper money issues; return to the gold standard and stabilization of the international exchanges on a gold basis; re-establishment of the bases of international credit; and abandonment of controls and impediments to international trade.

But again there was little evidence of any real appreciation of the unified character of the problem. For example, no consideration was given to the fact that it was impossible for any of the countries concerned to return to the gold standard and maintain stable exchanges as long as the countries of Central Europe were incapable of a similar achievement, because of the reparation policies that were being pursued. It was not until Austria, Hungary, and Germany collapsed financially from the strain to which they were subjected, and were rehabilitated through the aid of extensive foreign credits, that a return to the gold standard in Europe generally became possible. And it may be added here that when the financial structure of these countries again broke down in the spring of 1931 the financial repercussions were felt around the world, Great Britain being forced off the gold standard, and even the United States narrowly escaping the same fate.

The attitude of the creditor governments toward the inter-Allied debts was substantially the same as toward the reparation payments, although it was not until 1922 that the problem of these debts was given real consideration. The policies then laid down indicated that there was no adequate appreciation of the nature of the maladjustments that needed correction if the world was to prosper, and that there was no recognition of the economic inter-dependence of Europe and the United States. The United States was to collect as much as possible from each and every country irrespective of the relation of such payments to the promotion of general economic recovery. Reparations and inter-Allied debts were to be regarded as separate and distinct problems, with American policy in no way dependent upon the outcome of the efforts to collect reparations. Finally, as we shall show in the next two chapters, no consideration was given to the relationship of reparation and inter-Allied debt payments to American prosperity.

III. PRIVATE LOANS AND RECONSTRUCTION POLICY

Following the collapse of Austria, Hungary, and Germany in 1922-23, there came a new orientation with reference to the general problem of economic rehabilitation. Central Europe could not be allowed to disintegrate in consequence of the debt policies that were being pursued. On the contrary, it was now admitted that there could be no general recovery from the war, even for the victors, unless the economic system of the heart of the European Continent could be restored. Such restoration, it was seen, required not only a breathing spell in connection with reparation payments, but also a large inflow of new wealth from the creditor countries themselves. Hence the provisions for "reconstruction" loans in the Dawes plan and in the League of Nations schemes for Austria and Hungary. These official loans were supplemented by a large variety of private credits, which were extended for the rehabilitation of the shattered economies of these countries.

At the same time, the American government and American financial institutions worked together in carrying out a similar policy with reference to the rehabilitation of other distressed debtors. As soon as satisfactory debt funding agreements were concluded, it was understood that new private loans would be made available. This policy had in view a twofold purpose: to restore the gold standard and to rehabilitate the debtor countries, thus enabling them to expand their subsequent paying capacity; and to contribute meanwhile to the prosperity of the lending countries themselves. In the words of the former Secretary of the Treasury, A. W. Mellon:

The countries of Europe must be restored to their place in civilization. . . . We have learned the folly of imposing indefinite and impossible terms from the experiment with Germany before the Dawes plan. . . . America, with its excess of capital seeking profitable investment must aid by making private loans to Europe for productive purposes. Only from these private loans during the past year have the countries abroad been able to pay for our wheat and cotton. It is these new loans which make our exports possible.[1]

The immediate results of this new policy of reconstruction and debt payment were all that could be desired. The loans stimulated American export trade and contributed greatly to the prosperity of the ensuing years. They also enabled European countries to return to the gold standard; to maintain stable exchanges for a period of years; and to restore, in substantial measure, industry, agriculture, and trade. At the same time, they made it possible for Germany and the other debtor countries to meet without difficulty the comparatively modest initial instalments of the various reparation and debt schedules.

So great was the success of this policy that the fundamentals of the problem were soon obscured and nearly all sense of reality was lost. It led, for example, to optimistic and reassuring statements on the part of the administrators of the Dawes plan, to the premature initiation of the Young plan, and to the abandonment of the safeguard provisions which had been established under the Dawes plan. Many students of economics were also confused. The phenomenal economic activity of Germany, under the stimulus of the inflowing credits and the abnormal purchasing power thus created, were regarded as of enduring character and amply assuring future capacity to pay. For example, James W. Angell in his study of Germany's recovery, wrote: "The burden now imposed by the Young plan is one which Germany

[1] Statement before the Ways and Means Committee of the House of Representatives, Jan. 4, 1926.

can carry, and under which she can grow and prosper at a reasonable, though not rapid, rate. . . . That Germany's expansion will continue in coming years seems assured."[2]

The success with which the new loan policy was meeting led many to believe that the so-called transfer problem had been proved a myth. It was urged that inasmuch as the foreign loans were, in the main, extended for productive purposes, they would ultimately lead to an export surplus on the part of Germany and automatically provide the means for German payments on both reparation and private debt accounts. The fact that no difficulties had been found in procuring the foreign exchange with which to meet reparation instalments was cited in evidence, and it was argued that, thanks to the productive character of the loans, Germany was rapidly achieving a permanent export surplus ample to meet both reparation and debt requirements. It is true that there were two periods in which Germany's trade balance appeared to be moving in the right direction. The first was in 1926, when exports and imports were in approximate equilibrium, and the second was after the beginning of the depression of 1930 when exports actually exceeded imports. This shift in the trade situation was on both occasions proclaimed as evidence that the situation was automatically working itself out. In both cases, however, the improvement was due not to an expansion of exports while imports remained relatively stationary, but to a sharp curtailment of imports as an incident of business depression—exports being reduced at the same time, though, temporarily, to a lesser degree.[3]

[2] *The Recovery of Germany*, 1930, pp. 342, 361.
[3] See p. 306 for the actual trade figures.

It was also believed that the loans to Europe, particularly to Germany, were strictly analogous to the pre-war commercial borrowings of the United States. We borrowed extensively abroad for many years for the development of our railroads, public utilities, and industries. For a considerable time the new loans each year exceeded the amount of the interest payments. In due course such payments, however, came to exceed the amount of the new borrowings; but as a result of the expansion of production, we then had an ample export surplus with which to meet the interest payments. So also, it was argued, would Germany automatically achieve the necessary export surplus.[4]

This reasoning ignored vital differences. The loans to America were at comparatively low rates of interest and went for the development of the resources of a virgin continent. The loans to Germany cost the German people on the average close to 9 per cent. Funds were borrowed, first and foremost, for the restoration of the country's monetary and credit system and for the replenishment of the depleted working capital, including raw materials, partly manufactured products, and the normal supplies of finished goods in the hands of dealers and of ultimate consumers. A substantial part of the loans was thus required merely to restore German economy to a functioning basis. Moreover, some of the loans which were devoted to expansion of plant and equipment, as for example those contracted by public utilities and municipalities,[5] were not of a character to promote directly an expansion of exports.

---

[4] A vigorous exponent of this point of view was George P. Auld, former accountant general of the Reparation Commission.

[5] It should be noted that most of the loans to municipalities were for genuine economic improvements. Those which were used to build ath-

Notwithstanding the character and cost of these loans it was assumed that they would not only expand Germany's exports sufficiently to permit the interest and amortization charges thereon to be met, but that they would also provide the means for liquidating the reparation payments as well. The fact that Germany had long been a densely populated country with its resources intensively developed and operating at or near the point of diminishing returns was regarded as of no moment. Nor were the post-war barriers to international trade apparently considered of any real significance.

The view that Germany offered remarkable investment opportunities, and that as a result of large foreign borrowing she could develop a paying capacity on the reparation account, came to be widely held immediately after the inauguration of the Dawes plan. As one of the present authors wrote in 1924, "There are bankers and business men and economists almost without number who have the notion that Germany, with her 63 millions of population on an intensively developed area two-thirds the size of the State of Texas, offers a fruitful field for the investment of foreign capital. The notion that Germany offers a rich investment market for foreign capital and that she can now meet her reparation obligations by credit transactions is simply an illusion."[6]

This is a convenient place to comment briefly upon the charge sometimes made that, in connection with these loans, Germany deliberately swindled the American public.[7] The truth is that the loans were a funda-

letica stadia and luxurious bachelor apartments, of which so much has been made by Garet Garrett in the *Saturday Evening Post*, comprise but a trivial fraction of the total.

[6] H. G. Moulton, *The Reparation Plan*, pp. 114-15.

[7] See, for example, Garet Garrett, "As Noble Lenders," *Saturday Evening Post*, Oct. 17, 1931.

mental element in the new international economic policy that had been developed. As we have seen, they were regarded as indispensable to the restoration of the gold standard, to the rebuilding of Europe, and to the prosperity of the United States. Neither the German government nor the government of any other country in Europe, nor private interests therein, engaged in any extensive propaganda in this country for the granting of loans. They sought funds through the regular financial channels, and it is no exaggeration to say that they were met more than half-way by American bankers. The bankers and their clients alike were under the spell of the times, and foreign loans—to Europe, to South America, and to other parts of the world—as well as vast issues in the domestic markets, were offered and subscribed on the basis of false economic assumptions as to the future. Foreign loans were but a phase of the "new era" psychology.

Amid the economic confusion of the time, the cumulative effects of the new borrowing were lost sight of. The total of international debt payments, required to meet annual charges in consequence of the continuing borrowing, was growing in snowball fashion. While new loans to Europe undoubtedly had a part to play in restoring economic stability following the disastrous disorganization of 1922-23, there was never the slightest justification for the wholesale extension of credit which took place. Whatever its immediate effects, in the long run it could not fail to produce new complications and to increase the existing maladjustments.

Even if the world depression had not begun at the end of 1929 and international lending had not suddenly decreased almost to the vanishing point, it was inconceivable that new loans could have continued to exceed the rising reparation and Allied debt instalments, plus interest charges on the vast volume of private indebtedness that had already been created. The loan policy which constituted the second phase of post-war reparation and inter-Allied debt policy thus did not solve the war debt problem nor lay the foundation for enduring world prosperity. It failed to accomplish the basic purposes for which it had been inaugurated.

At the end of 14 years the fundamental problems left by the war still remain unsolved. To be sure, substantial downward revisions in the volume of both reparation and debt obligations have been made, and the way has been opened for more drastic reduction; large debt payments have been effected; and private creditors have to a considerable extent taken the place of public creditors. But economic balance has not been restored, especially as between Europe and America. On the contrary, the maladjustments have been increased.

CHAPTER XVIII

THE CREDITORS' WILLINGNESS
TO RECEIVE

In no official pronouncement or agreement pertaining to reparation and inter-Allied debts is there to be found any intimation that under any possible circumstances or conditions would the creditor countries be unwilling to receive the aggregate payments due. It is assumed as a matter of elementary common sense that the more a creditor country receives the wealthier it will be. Just as an individual benefits in direct proportion to the debts he collects, so, it is reasoned, a creditor nation obviously benefits to the precise degree that it succeeds in collecting from debtor countries.

It is the purpose of this chapter to show that the governments of the creditor countries, while officially committed to the principle of debt collection, have not, in fact, pursued economic policies based on a belief that the receipt of unlimited reparation and Allied debt payments would promote their own economic welfare. In order to demonstrate the truth of this statement, it will be necessary to return to the analysis of basic principles presented in Chapter II; and then to review post-war commercial policies in relation thereto.

International debt payments, as we indicated, can in the last analysis be made only through the delivery of commodities or the rendering of services to the creditors. Moreover, the net debtor country must, in the long run, have an export surplus of goods and services and the creditor country must have an import surplus. Gold may be utilized in limited amounts, and to a somewhat

386

larger extent movable goods and capital assets, such as foreign investments, may be temporarily employed. It is necessary to say *temporarily* because the process of using capital assets is self-destructive. Similarly, borrowing the means of payment may be a useful temporary expedient which ends in increasing burdens. Over a period of years payment must be made out of the *current* excess of exports over imports. The case is precisely like that of a corporation, which can meet obligations temporarily by utilizing capital, or by borrowing, but which in the long run can rely only on net earnings.

With this fundamental truth in mind, let us now see whether the policies of creditor countries have been directed toward promoting an export surplus from Germany—the fountain source of payments—and toward procuring an adequate import surplus for themselves. While the policies of the several creditors have varied in degree, depending upon the particular problem of each, all have endeavored to restrict, in one way or another, the necessary flow of wealth. We shall consider first the policies of the reparation creditors, leaving those of the United States, the primary ultimate creditor, for separate discussion.

I. ALLIED POLICY AND GERMAN TRADE

We have already seen that at the Inter-Allied Conference of 1916 a policy was agreed upon for curbing the economic power of Germany by simultaneously restricting her imports of essential raw materials, imposing barriers against her exports to Allied countries, and denying to her "favored-nation" treatment in commercial treaties. By the time of the Peace Conference it had become apparent that it would be shortsighted for the

Allies to shut themselves out of German markets. Accordingly, they modified their policies with a view to selling as much as possible to Germany, while buying as little as possible from her. Hence the "unilateral" favored-nation provision—"favorable" to the Allies but not to Germany; the stipulation that German import duties on Allied products should not be increased during the early post-war period; and the provision that goods originating in Alsace, Lorraine, Posen, and Upper Silesia should be admitted into Germany free of duty for a number of years.[1]

There are four aspects of Allied policy with reference to German trade to be considered. The first relates to the expansion of German exports to world markets in general; the second, to the sale of German exports in Allied countries; the third, to Allied exports to Germany; and the fourth, to direct deliveries of specific goods to the Allies, the so-called payments in kind. The first three phases will be briefly reviewed below, while the fourth will be given more detailed consideration in the section which follows.

The attitude of the Allied governments as regards German exports in general has been much the same in all cases. Since the end of the war, they have looked upon an expansion of German exports as detrimental to the commerce and industry of their own countries, and have sought, by means of commercial agreements and in other ways, to prevent, in so far as possible, the recovery by Germany of her pre-war markets. The great fear in the early post-war years, when under the temporary stimulus of inflation Germany showed signs of

---

[1] Five years in the case of Alsace and Lorraine; three years in the case of the Polish provinces.

industrial recovery, was that reviving German competition in Eastern and Southern Europe, in the Near and the Far East, and in North and South America, would have a paralyzing effect upon the commerce of the Allies. This fear has been manifested more or less continuously throughout the post-war period, and was particularly prominent when the obliteration of the indebtedness of German corporations, resulting from the complete collapse of the mark, appeared to give German producers a decided cost advantage.

The Allies have been even more concerned about a possible flood of German exports into their own markets. Because of the fear of German competition, they have imposed high duties on many commodities of the type exported by Germany. It is true that the policies thus pursued did not bar all German goods from Allied markets, and that it would be wholly incorrect to say that the Allies have been unwilling to receive any goods from Germany. The significant result to be noted is that to the extent that Germany's exports were restricted, her possibilities of developing a *surplus* of exports over imports, which is essential if she is to make continuous payments, were lessened.

With reference to the maintenance of Allied exports to Germany, differences in point of view early manifested themselves, especially as between Great Britain and France. During the early post-war boom, Great Britain appeared to have little occasion for concern over German markets. But as she struggled against the economic difficulties which began to emerge in 1920, recovery of the rich German markets of former days began to appear as a vital necessity. In the years before the war Germany, next to India, was the most important outlet for British products. Exports to Germany in 1913, for example, accounted for 7.7 per cent of all British exports as compared with 5.6 per cent to the United States, 5.5 per cent to France, 4.5 per cent to Canada, and 13.4 per cent to India.

While British policy continued for a time to vacillate, since 1922 Great Britain has been steadfastly concerned with the restoration of economic prosperity in Central Europe. It was chiefly in the interests of her own export trade that Great Britain opposed the occupation of the Ruhr, took an active part in negotiations looking toward the rehabilitation of Germany and other Central European countries, and favored a complete change of front on reparation policy.

It was a much longer time before the French government came to recognize the economic importance to France of a prosperous Germany. Because of her larger degree of economic self-sufficiency and the boom which accompanied the reconstruction of the devastated areas, France's interest in a prosperous Germany did not appear of vital importance. But by 1924-25, following the breakdown of Germany and the expiration of the special privileges secured to some French industries by the treaty of peace, it began to be clear that French economic activity in no small degree depended upon economic, social, and political stability in Central Europe. It was not, however, until the effects of the great depression began to be felt in France that her attitude became comparable with that of Great Britain.

The complications of the trade problem thus produced a real dilemma for the Allied countries. With impediments to the expansion of her exports, Germany's capacity to buy the products of Allied industries would also be curtailed. Which was better: to have a restored and prosperous Germany, making substantial purchases in the Allied countries, but able to compete effectively in the matter of exports in Allied and world markets; or an economically prostrate Germany, unable to compete, but at the same time unable to buy the surplus output of British, French, Belgian, and Italian producers? Great Britain's answer to this dilemma has already been indicated. The answer of the other Allies was finally given at Lausanne.

II. PAYMENTS IN KIND

As a part of this consideration of Allied policy with reference to German trade, we must examine the so-called payments in kind, or direct deliveries to Allied countries of goods to be credited on reparation account. It is true that substantial payments were made by this process.[2] Thus on first thought it might appear that the foregoing statement of Allied policy has been exaggerated. We shall find, however, that such is not the case.

As was noted earlier, Germany was required by the treaty of peace to deliver to the Allies ships, railway equipment, livestock, supplies, and other movable property. During the period of acute shortage immediately after the war, she turned over substantial quantities of such property. The explanation of the failure to continue this process is well illustrated by the story of reparation ships. In addition to surrendering the greater part of her existing mercantile fleet, Germany was required under the treaty to build ships for the Allies at a certain rate per year. But as soon as the post-war shipping depression developed, the Allied governments in the interests of their own shipyards refused to receive any further tonnage.

[2] See p. 279.

The peace treaty also provided that Germany should devote her economic resources directly to the physical reconstruction of the invaded areas. Was it not eminently just that the nation which had devastated this region should provide the material for its restoration? Concretely, Germany was to furnish animals, machinery, equipment, tools, and like articles of a commercial character; also restoration materials, stone, brick, tile, wood, window glass, steel, lime, cement, furniture, and heating apparatus.

As soon as the German government offered to make payments in the goods specified, serious objections were raised by producers and labor organizations, especially in France, who wished to reserve for themselves the opportunity of furnishing the supplies required. In short, the French people desired to do most of their own building and then to receive cash reimbursement from Germany afterwards. Compromises were made, however, and Germany was permitted to supply such materials as French industries were unable to produce at all, or not equipped to furnish in adequate amounts. Moreover, since the coal mines of France and Belgium had been wrecked, and inasmuch as Italy normally is a large importer of coal, these countries were willing to receive free coal from Germany.

In general, it was not until the period of the Dawes plan that deliveries in kind assumed an important and regular place in the process of payment. By that time it had become recognized that if Germany was to make any substantial payments her exports must be facilitated. Under the Dawes plan, slightly over half of the German payments were in the form of deliveries in kind, chiefly coal. But, with the passage of time and the accumulation of experience as to the implications of this process with respect to trade competition, a strong movement developed among some of the creditors against a continuation of payments in kind. Under the Young plan, as we have seen, such payments were arranged on a sharply descending scale, ceasing altogether at the end of ten years. The explanation of this restriction is that while some payments in kind might be welcomed indefinitely by certain creditors who were short of particular materials, such a policy appeared to be detrimental to others of the Allies. This divergence of interest may best be illustrated by reference to the coal issue.

Immediately after the war, as the result of the destruction of French mines, the British coal trade was greatly stimulated. The government kept down the price of coal in Great Britain with a view to facilitating domestic industry, while allowing the coal operators to charge on their foreign sales "all that the traffic would bear." However, under the terms of the Spa agreement, signed in 1920, Germany was compelled to deliver 2 million tons of Ruhr coal per month. This supply exceeded the French domestic requirements even before the first post-war depression became severe, and before long French railways and sidings were literally congested with coal trains. Coal prices fell precipitately, and in order to receive as much as possible the French government began to sell excess coal to Holland, Scandinavia, and Italy for whatever price it would bring. Not only was England's market in France gone, but her shipments to other countries were also greatly curtailed. The coal strike in England, which for three months paralyzed all British industry, was a direct result of the necessity of British coal owners to compete with this indemnity coal. While the amounts that were to be paid were reduced by subsequent agreements, and smaller deliveries were consequently required from Germany, the receipt of reparation coal by France, Belgium, and Italy continued to be a direct detriment to this vitally important industry of Great Britain.

The problem of reparation coal was one of the factors responsible for the stipulation of the Dawes plan under which no deliveries in kind could be *re-exported* by the recipient countries. It was also one of the mainsprings of the British opposition to deliveries in kind at the meetings of the Young Committee and at The Hague conferences. An important part of the compromise between Great Britain and the other creditors at the first Hague conference was agreement on the part of Italy to reduce her receipts of reparation coal from Germany and to purchase specified quantities of British coal.

Great Britain steadfastly refused to accept any portion of her share in the German reparation payments in the form of deliveries in kind. She preferred to utilize the device of reparation "recovery levies," which enabled her to receive from Germany only such commodities as would normally enter into ordinary commercial intercourse between the two countries.[8]

While the other creditor countries were more willing than Great Britain to receive limited quantities of selected free goods from Germany, they were, in the end, won over to the British viewpoint with regard to deliveries in kind. The accompanying chart shows graphically how rapidly such deliveries were to disappear under The Hague agreements based on the Young plan, and how payments in cash were to increase.

[8] See pp. 274-76.

Apart from their acceptability to the creditor countries, payments in kind can afford at best but a partial solution of the problem of the debtor countries. They cannot be indefinitely continued regardless of the state of the debtor country's general international trade and financial balance. If, as a result of making deliveries in

DELIVERIES IN KIND UNDER THE HAGUE AGREEMENTS

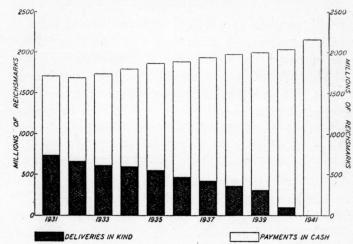

kind, a country's ordinary exports are insufficient to pay for indispensable imports, then such deliveries may require a curtailment of imports and a consequent reduction in the capacity for making subsequent payments. An excess of exports over imports—including in the exports both payments in kind and ordinary sales abroad —remains a fundamental necessity, if payments are to be continued over a period of years. Moreover, the budget problem of the debtor country is not in any way helped because foreign payments are made in the form of deliveries in kind. The debtor government still has to raise the money with which to pay the domestic producers for the goods which are to be delivered to the foreign creditors. The most that can be said for payments in kind is that they facilitate the trade problem of the debtor country by providing foreign outlets which might not otherwise be available.

III. AMERICAN POLICY AND DEBT RECEIPTS

Since the destination of the greater part of the flow of wealth required in the liquidation of the war debts is the United States, it is apparent that American policies are of paramount importance in connection with this whole problem. As the ultimate recipient, the United States, if it is to be paid, must be willing to receive from foreigners goods and services of a greater aggregate value than the value of the services which it renders and the goods which it ships to foreigners. It is not necessary that our excess of imports and services be derived directly from German and Allied sources, for the goal may be accomplished by roundabout trading operations; but it is necessary that in our international transactions with the world as a whole imports should exceed exports to the extent of the debt payments received by us.

With this fundamental necessity in mind, we may now consider those policies of the United States which have an important bearing upon the problem of debt payments. There can be no denying, in the first place, that this country is committed to a policy of protecting our markets against competitive goods. We increased our tariff schedules in 1922 nearly all along the line, with the express purpose of meeting reviving European competition. Again in 1930, the Smoot-Hawley tariff act carried still further the policy of keeping imports of competitive commodities to the very minimum.

Our protective policy affects chiefly the European countries, for the simple reason that it is only the European countries which are equipped to compete in our markets in a wide variety of lines of manufacture. Germany's chief possibilities of exports to the United States lie in such lines as textiles, metallurgical products, machinery, leather goods, chemicals, and dyestuffs, and we are doing everything in our power to restrict German sales of all these commodities in this country. Export possibilities from Great Britain and France are similar, with coal to be added for Great Britain and wines for France. British coal is not desired for one reason, and French wine is excluded for another.

But are we not willing that European countries should expand their exports to other markets, turning the proceeds over to us, and thus enabling us to purchase such necessary and non-competitive imports as nitrates, rubber, or raw silk? The answer again is in the negative. We have done everything in our power in the post-war years to overcome European competition in all the markets of the world. It has frequently been suggested by those concerned with reparation and international debt negotiations that Germany, for example, can sell vast quantities of goods in undeveloped areas and utilize the proceeds for reparation payments. But the industrialists of the Allied countries and of the United States have manifested no disposition to sit idly by and permit such potential markets to be captured by Germany.

It has also often been assumed that, as a result of triangular trade processes, the creditor can escape the necessity of receiving an import surplus. This is pure fallacy, for we cannot get payments unless we receive goods from somewhere. By virtue of triangular trade operations we have a wider variety of goods to choose from, but we do not escape the necessity of choosing and taking the goods.

American policy not only calls for a restriction of imports in all competitive lines, but also for promotion of exports in every possible direction. While seeking to meet European competition in outside markets, we are endeavoring to expand our exports to the European countries. For many years the government has sought to foster export trade by means of the promotional services of the State and Commerce Departments, by the improvement of banking and credit facilities, and by special legislation such as the Webb-Pomerene Act. Our business interests have striven to expand exports by every means in their power, including the making of great price concessions on foreign orders. Our commercial and investment banks have furthered the process by liberal, not to say over-liberal, extensions of credit.

American shipping policy also works at cross purposes with the collection of debts. In pre-war years American goods were largely carried by ships under foreign registry and the transportation charges represented a considerable income to foreigners. During and since the war, the United States has developed a substantial merchant marine, subsidized by the American taxpayers. Without entering upon any discussion as to the economic or naval desirability of developing a merchant marine, the fact is clear that we are taxing the American people in order to subsidize merchant vessels so that we can take traffic away from foreign vessels, thereby lessening the capacity of foreign countries to meet their debt payments to the United States.

American dependence upon foreign banking and insurance services has also been decreased. Before the war,

London occupied a pre-eminent place in world banking, and very substantial commissions were earned on American as well as on other trade. The business of foreign insurance companies in the United States was also very great, while that of American insurance companies abroad was relatively small. As a result of the development of the Federal Reserve system and the impairment of Great Britain's financial position resulting from the war, the United States has come to play a much more important role than heretofore in the financing of foreign trade. At the same time there has been a considerable shift in the insurance situation.

The restriction of immigration also affects the international exchange situation. While immigrants must bring some money with them, their remittances to relatives and friends greatly exceed the money brought in. In consequence, dollars are rendered available in the exchange markets which can be utilized in making debt payments. The more immigration is restricted the smaller the volume of annual remittances tends to become.

Tourist expenditures, similarly, give to foreigners income which is available for meeting international debt payments. In this important connection alone, there is no American policy which has served to restrict the earnings of foreigners.

With these general considerations in mind, we are in a position to consider the net result of the various conditions and policies just described upon America's international balance of income and outgo. Did we have an excess of imports and services from foreigners over our exports and services to foreigners during the period when large sums were received by our Treasury on the war debt account? If not, how were the payments in fact effected?

Adequate data are available for the nine years from 1922 to 1930, when, according to the calculations made by the United States Department of Commerce, the United States had a substantial excess of income from trade and services and foreign investments and war debt payments. Exclusive of loans or other capital transactions, the principal items, in millions of dollars, are as follows:

Income

Commodity exports	43,512
Foreign tourist expenditures in the United States	1,765
Interest and dividends on American private investments abroad	6,792
Instalments on war debts	1,842
Miscellaneous (net)	419
Total income	54,330

Outgo

Commodity imports	37,957
American tourist expenditures abroad	5,829
Shipping (net)	665
Immigrant remittances	1,979
Charitable and missionary contributions	494
Total	49,301
Gold imports (net)	687
Total outgo	49,988

The excess of income uncovered by gold shipments amounted to 4,342 million dollars. This net income we invested abroad. The nominal amount of new foreign loans and investments made by American citizens during this period was 7,150 million dollars, of which the foreign borrowers received 6,303 millions, discounts and commissions retained in this country aggregating 847 million dollars. At the same time, the investments of foreigners in American securities, business enterprises, etc., on long and short-term accounts, amounted to 1,961 million dollars. Thus, during the nine-year period our net creditor position was increased by 4,342 million dollars.[4]

As a result of the extension by American citizens of new foreign loans sufficient in amount to permit foreigners to cover excess purchases in the United States and to meet payments to the American Treasury on the war debts, the economic realities of the international debt problem were completely disguised. Thanks to the loans it was possible for the United States to pursue commercial policies which worked at cross purposes with a policy of debt collection.

A word may now be said as to the bearing of this analysis upon the question of the capacity of the debtors to make payments. We are not, either here or elsewhere in this volume, interested in appraising the capacity either of Germany or of the Allied debtors to make payments. We may nevertheless point out that the capacity of the debtors to pay depends in a vital way upon the capacity or willingness of the creditors to receive. Except in the Dawes report, official discussions of capacity to pay have all along been on an unreal plane because it has been assumed that this is solely a problem for the debtors. It is easy to demonstrate, theoretically, that the people of any nation could, by practicing economy, raise substantial sums with which to meet foreign debt payments. Assum-

---

[4] Since some of the items entering the balance of accounts are necessarily rough estimates, the total figures given are only approximately exact.

ing full employment for everybody and large profits from prosperous business activity, it would seem that almost any government, given a disposition to meet its obligations, could raise the necessary income. But in view of the economic interrelations of the modern world, employment and profits are directly dependent upon the state of international trade and the policies of other countries. For example, Germany, as a great commercial nation, is vitally dependent upon export markets. If these be restricted, not only may she be unable to obtain the necessary foreign exchange with which to meet external obligations, but her internal prosperity and budget situation will also be adversely affected.[5] It is, therefore, impossible to determine whether Germany—assuming complete willingness on her own part—could pay any particular stipulated sum. This is because her export problem and, as a consequence, her whole economic and fiscal position are in large degree beyond her own control.[6]

One thing is certain—that a country which is unwilling to receive payments cannot be paid.

[5] The relation of American export markets to American prosperity and the United States budget is analyzed in Chap. XIX.

[6] In H. G. Moulton and C. E. McGuire, *Germany's Capacity to Pay*, 1923, pp. 245-46, this conclusion was stated as follows: "We set no definite annual sums that Germany can pay through the development of an export surplus, for the simple reason that it is utterly impossible for anyone to know whether, in view of all the conditions that exist and that will continue to exist, Germany will be able to develop any export surplus. It depends upon wholly indeterminate factors."

CHAPTER XIX

AMERICA'S INTEREST IN THE WAR DEBTS

The virtual cancellation of reparation obligations by the Lausanne conference has focussed attention more than ever upon the future of American policy in relation to the inter-Allied debts. Should the American government follow the lead of Germany's creditors and cancel to all intents and purposes the whole mass of outstanding indebtedness? Should a new series of debt settlements be made in the light of changed conditions? Should the United States refuse to consider any further reduction of the debts? It is our purpose in this chapter to consider where the enlightened self-interest of the United States really lies.

I. WAR DEBTS AND THE AMERICAN TAXPAYER

Uppermost in the mind of the average citizen at this time is the thought that if the Treasury does not collect the war debts the American taxpayer will have to shoulder increased burdens. In view of the very difficult fiscal situation with which we are now confronted, it is not surprising that there should be the strongest objection to any remission of the debts. The attitude of the American taxpayer in this regard is, of course, identical with that of the taxpayers of Allied countries who have insisted that if reparations were not collected from Germany they would have to bear all the losses resulting from the war.

It is undeniable that from the fiscal point of view a remission of war debts would mean that the American Treasury will have to collect larger sums from the

American taxpayers than would otherwise be the case —this because the Liberty bonds are the obligation of the United States government and must be paid whether or not we collect from Europe. At first glance this fact appears to be decisive in indicating where our own economic interest lies. If we have to shoulder the increased burdens, it seems obvious that we will be made the poorer to that extent.

The problem is not as simple as it appears, however. Before accepting this popular idea as conclusive and all-embracing, attention must be directed to the fact that the fiscal problem of the United States Treasury depends upon the state of prosperity within the country as well as upon the collection of war debts. During the period of prosperity prior to 1930, our fiscal situation presented no difficulties. Tax rates were in fact being periodically reduced, and yet our revenues were more than sufficient to meet all the requirements of the national government and to enable the Treasury to effect each year a substantial reduction in the public debt. It was only with the coming of the great depression that the American budget was unbalanced and that the tax burden upon the American people became truly onerous. What prosperity means from the standpoint of Treasury receipts may be indicated by the difference between revenues of 4,033 million dollars in the fiscal year ending June 30, 1929, and 3,317 millions in the fiscal year ending June 30, 1931.

These figures furnish convincing evidence—if evidence is needed—that the paramount interest of the United States is in the recovery of economic prosperity. If war debt policies have contributed to the depression or now serve as a deterrent to business recovery, they obviously contribute to the fiscal difficulties of the United States government. Before concluding that it is to the real interest of the American taxpayer to have the debts collected, it is therefore necessary to consider the relationship of debt payments to American foreign trade and American prosperity in general.

II. WAR DEBTS AND AMERICAN TRADE

It will be remembered that if European countries are to make, and the United States is to receive, the war debt payments, those countries must have an export surplus (including services), and the United States must have a corresponding import surplus. The process of payment thus inevitably affects the currents of international trade. In the preceding chapter it was shown that our government has not desired any such alteration of trade and has pursued policies intended to prevent either an expansion of imports or a curtailment of exports. It is clear, therefore, that our fiscal policies and our trade policies have been in fundamental conflict.

In this connection it is useful to recall that between 1925 and 1930 there was a widespread belief in governmental and business circles that a way out of this dilemma had been found. Thanks to the new private loans to foreigners we were able to maintain an excess of exports and yet receive payments on account of the war debts. It was believed that if new loans continued to be made in amounts which exceeded the war debt instalments, plus the accumulating interest on the new indebtedness, the necessity for an import surplus on the part of the United States could be indefinitely avoided. It was admitted that ultimately such a surplus would be necessary; but that ultimate day was regarded as a very long way off. Such trade readjustments as might be necessary could be gradually worked out in connection with trade expansion and without perceptible effects upon the existing industrial organization. For reasons already indicated, this comfortable doctrine has disappeared along with other pleasing vagaries of the new era. Accordingly, the relationship of the debt problem to American trade must now be squarely faced.

We must consider first the general significance of American export trade. How important to the economic well-being of the United States is the maintenance of our export trade, particularly in European markets?

Throughout the nineteenth century trade between the United States and Europe was vital to the development of both Continents. The increase in population and the economic development of Europe and the United States proceeded hand in hand, and each was dependent upon the other. The opening up of sources of raw material and foodstuffs in the United States made possible the maintenance in Europe of vast industrial populations, and in turn the markets afforded by these urban populations of Europe alone made possible the prosperous and rapid expansion of American agriculture. The price of both cotton and wheat, which gave support to the larger part of our agricultural population, was vitally dependent upon European demands. During the last quarter of the nineteenth century, when our principal exports were still foodstuffs and raw materials, European markets absorbed from three-fourths to four-fifths of our total shipments abroad; in turn, Europe found in the United States much the largest single foreign market for the manifold products of her industry.

With the growth of American manufacturing and the entrance of our industries into the field of international competition, which began shortly after the turn of the century, trade relations showed significant shifts. Since American manufactured exports went chiefly to non-European markets, Europe's relative share in our trade began to decline. During the last five years preceding the war Europe took 62 per cent of our exports, while since the war she has been taking only a little more than half. Nevertheless, the aggregate European purchases of American products continued to expand; it was only in relative terms that there was any decline. Moreover, as late as 1929 Europe took as much as four-fifths of our exports of cotton and copper, and approximately two-thirds of our foreign shipments of such important products as tobacco, wheat, lard, and petroleum products.

It should also be borne in mind that European trade is important to the United States in indirect ways. In 1929, for example, Europe as a whole purchased 35 per cent of Canada's exports, 67 per cent of Australia's, 80 per cent of Argentina's, 45 per cent of Brazil's, 50 per cent of India's, 20 per cent of China's, and 31 per cent of Chile's. Japan is, in fact, the only important country which does not depend directly upon European markets. Inasmuch as 18 per cent of American exports in 1929 went to Canada, 12 per cent to the Far East, and 10 per cent to South America, it is apparent that the ability of those countries to sell in Europe has an important bearing upon their total trade capacity and thus affects their power to buy in the United States.

Notwithstanding the continuing importance of Europe in American foreign trade, it is sometimes argued that the total export trade is now unimportant in comparison with our vast domestic trade and thus has no real relation to American prosperity. While an export figure of over 5 billion dollars in 1929 sounds impressive, this is after all less than 10 per cent of our total domestic production. Could we not readily lop off this 10 per cent, or at least the 5 per cent which goes to Europe, and make it up by an expansion of our domestic markets?

The argument that our export trade is unimportant and has no real bearing upon our prosperity sounds plausible, but it is fundamentally erroneous. The assumption that domestic trade could be expanded simultaneously with the curtailment of foreign trade is without foundation. On the contrary, as we shall see, a decline in foreign trade inevitably carries with it also a decline in domestic trade. So widespread has become the notion that our foreign trade is relatively unimportant that we must give careful consideration to the economics of this problem.

American farms, mines, and factories turn out each year an immense variety of commodities which, taken together, comprise our aggregate trade. Many of these commodities do not enter the export trade at all, or appear in negligible amounts, while in other cases the sales abroad comprise a substantial part of the total. The 10 per cent figure for our export trade is merely a general average relating to our total production and trade, and does not in any way indicate the vital significance of the export trade to certain important lines of production or manufacture. Cotton, tobacco, wheat, lard, copper, petroleum products, automobiles and machinery together account for about three-fifths of our total exports, and in nearly every one of these cases the percentage of the product which is sold abroad is very much higher than the general export average of 10 per cent.

The truth is that foreign trade is of vital importance for many basic American industries. The following figures show the percentage of the annual production of each of the designated commodities shipped abroad in the year 1929:[1]

Commodity	Per Cent	Commodity	Per Cent
Cotton	54.8	Gasolene	13.8
Tobacco	41.2	Typewriters	40.1
Lard	33.3	Printing machinery	29.2
Wheat	17.9	Sewing machines	28.0
Copper	36.0	Agricultural machinery	23.3
Kerosene	34.7	Locomotives	20.8
Lubricating oils	31.0	Passenger automobiles	14.0

In such lines of production as these a loss of exports is obviously a matter of paramount significance. Even in the case of wheat, where our exports amounted to less than 18 per cent, the price is profoundly affected by fluctuations in the foreign demand; in such cases as cotton and tobacco the price is fundamentally dependent upon foreign demand. While the price is also affected by changes in the domestic demand, the decline in the foreign demand alone could readily make the difference between 16 and 6 cent cotton, and perhaps 70 and 50 cent wheat.

The domestic demand for these commodities cannot be increased to offset a loss of foreign demand. It would be idle to suggest the possibility that the domestic de-

---

[1] Figures are based on physical volume, except in the case of machinery, where values constitute the base.

mand for American cotton, tobacco, kerosene, lubricating oils, agricultural machinery, or locomotives would be expanded proportionately to a decline of foreign demand. These industries have been developed to take care of a large foreign demand in addition to supplying domestic requirements. The American people cannot purchase greatly increased quantities of these commodities if foreign demand for them should disappear. The consequent fall in price and the cheapening of the product might result in some increase in demand; but this would be offset by the general impoverishment of the American people.

The loss of foreign markets would, in fact, lead to a shrinkage in the domestic market. If the cotton, tobacco, or wheat producing areas are seriously depressed as a result of the loss of foreign markets, the purchasing power among vast sections of our population is curtailed, and, in consequence, their ability to purchase goods in the domestic market is lessened. Within the last few years we have been witnessing in a most convincing way the effects of agricultural depression not only upon the demand for manufactured commodities but upon our whole economic and financial organization. The agricultural depression has brought with it the failure of thousands of banks, the impairment of the investments of insurance companies, and widespread default on municipal and other local securities. In a similar way, the depression in areas producing raw materials and in industries which sell products abroad has had its repercussions throughout the entire economic system.

It may be suggested, however, that we could shift the capital and the population that is now engaged in the production of goods for export into other lines whose output could be sold in the domestic market. In the long run, it would seem that in a country of such vast resources as the United States we might gradually reorganize so as to become completely independent of the outside world. Such a reorganization is theoretically possible, but as a practical matter it is beset with virtually insuperable obstacles. The primary difficulty is that we are now equipped to produce in nearly all lines, goods in excess of the absorptive capacity of our own markets, and it is difficult indeed to find lines of production which are capable of being expanded so as to absorb capital and labor released from other lines. For some years we have been endeavoring to effect agricultural readjustments, and even during the period of expansion we met with little success. It is doubtful indeed whether our economic system could survive amid the difficulties that would be involved in effecting the wholesale shifts that would be required to make this country independent of foreign trade.

The conclusion, therefore, is that as a practical proposition it is impossible for us to maintain, much less expand, our domestic markets unless we maintain at the same time our export markets and the prosperous conditions which such markets mean for many important basic lines of American agriculture and industry. There never was a more complete economic fallacy than the one now prevalent—that this country can turn its back on Europe and prosper by so doing.

What, now, is the bearing of the war debts upon American export trade? The answer is clear as to the tendency, though it is impossible to measure the effects mathematically. To the extent that European countries must use the proceeds of their exports to pay the war debts, their ability to purchase American exports is curtailed. Indeed, as things work out, the reduction in the demand for American exports is likely to be much greater than the actual amount of the debts because of the inevitable widespread effects of the restrictive trade policies which it would be necessary for the European governments to invoke. The most serious effects would, of course, occur if pressure for payments led to financial instability and consequent social and political unrest. In such an event, the experience with Germany has amply shown that the trade of the creditor countries may be profoundly affected.[2]

It is clear from this analysis that the interests of the farmers of the cotton, tobacco, grain, and livestock producing areas of this country would be promoted by anything which tended to increase the purchasing power of the markets of Europe. It is also clear that it is to the interest of workmen in industries which produce for the export trade, or for sale to the cotton, tobacco, grain and livestock producing areas of this country, that European markets should expand. Similarly, it is to the interests of financial and trading groups whose solvency is dependent upon a return of prosperity in these great

[2] The contention may be advanced that if the payment of war debts adversely affects the creditor country, it should also be true that no foreign loan could ever be paid without damaging the creditor country. Such conclusion would, however, be untenable, for the reparations and war debts are not analogous to normal business loans. Under ordinary circumstances, foreign loans are extended for the development of economic enterprises. The lending country, instead of expanding its own industries, is furnishing the funds and the materials with which the borrowing country may expand its productive equipment. Industrial and trade changes, both in the creditor and the debtor countries, thus accompany the very process of international credit extension. In due course the creditor country can receive an import surplus without any disorganizing effects upon its economic life. This is amply illustrated by the experience of England as a creditor country.

producing areas that European recovery be promoted.

The serious shortcoming of public discussions of the debt question has been the failure to focus upon the trade aspects of the problem, thereby obscuring the larger interests of the American Treasury itself. What has not been seen in contemplating the fiscal problem is that the losses to the Treasury from a remission of the debts would undoubtedly be greatly outweighed by the gains which would accrue to the Treasury with the recovery of business activity. Given prosperous cotton, tobacco, and wheat areas and thriving industries, the American tax problem will take care of itself as it did during the period from 1925 to 1929. The extent to which American prosperity may be said to be dependent upon European and world prosperity will be further considered in the final chapter.

III. SIGNIFICANCE OF OUR CREDITOR POSITION

The financial exigencies of the war, as we have already seen, involved the liquidation by European investors of large blocks of American securities and also led to extensive borrowing in American markets on private account.[3] Thus, quite apart from inter-governmental borrowing, the international investment position of the United States shifted from that of a debtor to that of a substantial creditor. This change has been greatly magnified by the extensive foreign loans of the post-war period. The sweeping nature of the transformation which has taken place in our international financial position is indicated by the following data.

The foreign investments of the American people amounted in 1912 to 1.9 billion dollars; by 1922, exclusive of the war debts to the United States Treasury,

[3] See pp. 32-34.

they had risen to 8 billions, and by the end of 1930 to 15.5 billions. On the eve of the war we were a *net debtor* to the extent of about 3 billion dollars, while to-day we are a *net creditor*, apart from the war debt, in the amount of approximately 11 billion dollars.[4]

Aside from the war debts, if the interest on the private indebtedness is to be paid, without recourse to new loans, the United States must have a substantial excess of imports. On the basis of the situation in 1930, it would have been necessary for us, if the annual charges on American private investments abroad were to be met out of current earnings by foreigners, to increase our imports or decrease our exports by approximately 400 million dollars. A much greater trade adjustment would have been required if the war debt payments were also taken into account.

Thus it will be seen that even if the war debt problem were removed as a complicating factor, our position as a creditor nation on private account must inevitably involve trade readjustments of considerable magnitude. We must increase our imports relatively to our exports until we have the import surplus by means of which alone international debts of any kind can be paid.

The growth of private indebtedness abroad has thus created a new interest on the part of American people in the prosperity of other countries. At the same time it has given rise to new problems in international trade relations. Even with the war debts out of the picture it will be necessary for the United States to modify its

---

[4] These figures are based on a study of American investments abroad made by Paul D. Dickens of the Finance and Investment Division of the United States Department of Commerce. See *Trade Information Bulletin No. 767.*

tariff and other international commercial policies in order to permit an adequate increase of imports, if interest on private investments abroad is to be collected. It is impossible for any nation to play the role of a creditor successfully, and at the same time impose ever increasing restrictions upon imports. Such an effort is as foredoomed to failure as the proverbial attempts to make water run up hill of its own accord.

It is our belief that the necessary readjustments of commercial policies required by the changed position of the United States in the world can be carried out with fewer transitional dislocations if the complications presented by the war debts are eliminated. There will in any event be difficulties enough in effecting the industrial and agricultural readjustments which are inevitably in store for this country.

CHAPTER XX

WAR DEBTS AND WORLD PROSPERITY

In the opening paragraph of this book we referred to the fact that the coming of the world-wide economic depression has caused the war debt problem to emerge more than ever as a dominating factor in the whole international scene. Whatever one's theories as to the depression as a whole, there is an indubitable relation between its causes and the war debt problem, and an even closer relationship between the process of recovery from its disastrous effects and the continued existence of a vast body of inter-governmental obligations. It is with appraising these relationships that we are here mainly concerned.

The immediate cause of the world economic reaction cannot be assigned directly to the war debt situation. When the recession began, the foreign loan program was still in operation and no difficulties were being experienced in meeting either reparation or Allied debt instalments. But although the first haltings of world prosperity did not occur primarily in Europe, the underlying maladjustments of the international situation played a contributing part in bringing on the reaction which began in the autumn of 1929.

The second stage of the depression, ushered in by the financial breakdown of Central Europe which occurred in the first half of 1931, was directly connected with the war debt problem, and especially with its reparation aspect. German finances and the German economic system could not stand the strain of meeting the reparation obligations in a period of economic depression, especially when the stream of inflowing credits was no longer forthcoming. Moreover, the existence of a great volume of short-term foreign credits, resulting in part from the preceding attempts at reparation fulfillment, rendered Germany particularly vulnerable the moment a loss of confidence manifested itself.

The financial crisis which began in Austria and Germany quickly spread to other countries, and the effects extended to the most remote corners of the earth. The economic inter-dependence of the modern world was never more strikingly manifested than in the international ramifications of the German debacle. The shock to public confidence as well as the direct effects upon international trade immediately increased the difficulties of maintaining financial stability in other countries.

The repercussions of the German crisis upon British credit resources, together with the resort to heroic fiscal measures by the British government, produced an exchange panic in Great Britain. The Bank of England was forced to suspend specie payments and the export of gold in order to prevent a complete dissipation of the nation's gold supply. A number of other countries were immediately forced to follow suit, while still others found it necessary to impose stringent foreign exchange restrictions. Thus the results of years of post-war endeavor to restore the gold standard as the basis of sound international commercial and financial development were practically undone.

In the United States the effects were quickly manifested in the extraordinary decline in the value of both foreign and domestic stocks and bonds. The loss of confidence in American financial stability led to the withdrawal of bank deposits and to the liquidation of American securities held by foreigners. The persistent drain upon our gold supply induced a widespread feeling of panic within the country and led to an enormous volume of hoarding, which in turn contributed to the difficulties of the banks and the further demoralization of the security markets.

The direct effects upon agriculture and industry were as pronounced as the effects upon the financial markets. The shrinkage of exports resulted in a further collapse of commodity prices, particularly of such great export staples as cotton and wheat. This calamity in its turn produced its chain of adverse consequences throughout the entire economic and financial structure. Resort to extraordinary financial methods and utilization of all the credit resources of the government were required to prevent a general financial collapse that would have paralyzed the economic life of the country.

In the light of this extraordinary manifestation of the economic inter-dependence of the modern world, a new understanding of the significance of the war debt problem was inevitable. Increasing numbers of people have come to realize that the industry and trade of Western Europe are linked with that of Central Europe, that the prosperity of the United States is dependent upon that of Europe as a whole, and that all nations are bound together by ties of mutual interest. After years of illusion, the unity of the problem of world economic recovery is at last coming to be appreciated.

This analysis of the economic history of the postwar era may be briefly summed up in the following terms. The basically significant economic result of the World War was the destruction of the economic equilibrium between nations which exists under conditions of normal trade and financial development. The relations between Europe and America, in particular, were thrown completely out of balance. A primary requirement for the restoration of world prosperity after the war, was the re-establishment of equilibrium, for only thus could the stability upon which production and trade depend be achieved.

The policies laid down at the end of the war were not based upon a recognition of this fundamental requirement. As a result they brought about increasing international economic maladjustments. In effect, it may be said that we sought to promote world economic recovery from the destruction and disorganization wrought by the war by means of reparation and debt policies requiring a flow of wealth from the relatively poorer to the relatively richer nations.

The war-time nations which suffered most heavily from the conflict, both directly in the form of wealth destruction, and indirectly through the disorganization of the general financial and economic mechanism, were the nations of Continental Europe. The nation least affected by the war was the United States, with Great Britain occupying an intermediate position. Leaving Russia out of the picture, the Continental nations which suffered most heavily were the Central Powers, followed by France and Belgium. While the Central Powers sustained comparatively little land devastation, their indirect or "invisible" losses were vastly greater than those of any of the Allies, because of the terrific strain of waging war almost entirely out of their own resources, the loss of territory, and the destruction of their pre-war international commercial organization and markets.

The liquidation of reparations and of inter-Allied debts requires, in its final effect, a great flow of wealth from Central Europe to the United States of America. As the frontispiece map indicates, a relatively small portion of this would remain with the Allies, but the bulk would eventually accrue to the United States. It can, therefore, fairly be stated that reparation and debt policies called for payments by the relatively poor to the relatively rich.

This policy became effective so far as reparations were concerned immediately after the war. Its results were first manifested two years after the reparation "settlement" of 1921, when the German financial and economic system broke down completely, resulting in chaotic conditions in Central Europe and producing serious dislocations in the economic life not only of all Europe, but of the outside world as well. With this collapse the German nation went—so to speak—into the hands of foreign receivers for purposes of reorganization. It had become apparent that a condition of prosperity in Germany was essential not only to a program of reparation payment but also to the general economic welfare of the world as a whole.

With the advent of the Dawes plan the direction of the flow of wealth was reversed. Nominally the policy of debt collections remained unchanged, but it was supplemented by a policy of new loans to the debtor countries. As a result, there began a net flow of wealth from the United States to the impoverished nations of Europe and particularly to Germany. The Dawes plan provided for a large loan to Germany and encouraged extensive private loans. The inter-Allied debt settlements required, in most cases, small payments in the first five years; and the agreements were usually followed by American loans very greatly in excess of the current debt instalments. Thus, on balance—whatever may have been true of particular countries—instead of America's being paid, Europe was going even more heavily into debt.

During the years from 1924 to 1929, when wealth was moving from the United States to Europe, it appeared that real progress was being made by the impoverished nations of Europe toward financial and economic stability. It may be recalled that the gold standard was restored, that the exchanges were stabilized, that fiscal conditions were improved, that industrial production was re-established, and that international trade was greatly extended. In fact, the goals set up in the early post-war conferences at Brussels and Genoa seemed to be in prospect of realization.

But the structure of this apparent prosperity was built on insecure foundations. As the mounting payments prescribed in the reparation and debt settlements were met out of new foreign borrowing, there came into existence a rapidly growing volume of new indebtedness. The process of liquidating international obligations by means of new borrowings, which increased the indebtedness in snowball fashion and which was not accompanied by corresponding changes in basic industrial and trade conditions and relations, could not continue indefinitely. A collapse was sooner or later inevitable.

In 1930 the direction of the flow of wealth was in fact once more reversed. The diminishing loans did not cover the reparation and debt instalments, plus interest on private debts. Germany, the fountain-head, was again obliged to pay from her own resources. The result, as we have seen, was an early financial breakdown, followed by a world-wide financial and economic disaster, the cost of which in terms of material losses and human suffering has already become comparable to that of the war itself.

Our answer to the two fundamental questions with which this analysis has been primarily concerned is unequivocal:

1. A complete obliteration of all reparation and war debt obligations would promote, rather than retard, world economic prosperity.

2. The collection of these inter-governmental debts would be economically detrimental, rather than beneficial, to the creditor countries.

The basic economic implications of the war debt problem are clear. The attempts to collect obligations, resulting not from productive economic developments but from the destructive processes of the war, have only served to impede the restoration of international economic equilibrium and world prosperity. While the obliteration of the war debts would not solve all the manifold difficulties under which the world is laboring, economic analysis leads unmistakably to the conclusion that the restoration and maintenance of world prosperity will be rendered much easier if the disorganizing effects of the war debt payments are eliminated once and for all.

STATISTICAL APPENDIXES

APPENDIX A

DETAILS OF WAR BORROWING
AND LENDING

I. ALLIED INTER-GOVERNMENTAL LOANS PRIOR TO APRIL 1, 1917[a]
(In millions of dollars)

Borrowing Country	From Great Britain	From France	Total
Russia[b]	1,657.5	426.5	2,084.0
Italy[c]	673.5	—	673.5
France[d]	555.0	—	555.0
Belgium	242.8	48.3	291.1
Serbia (Yugoslavia)[e]	59.0	35.8	94.8
Rumania	60.8	—	60.8
Portugal	9.7	—	9.7
Greece	7.1	3.9	11.0
Belgian Congo	4.5	—	4.5
British dominions and colonies[f]	544.5	—	544.5
Total	3,814.4	514.5	4,328.9

[a] Based on H. E. Fisk, *The Inter-Ally Debts*, 1924, p. 121. All conversions at par of exchange.

[b] Adjusted for gold shipments amounting to $291,960,000 and book credit of $973,000,000.

[c] Adjusted for gold shipments amounting to $80,674,000.

[d] Adjusted for gold shipments amounting to $375,900,000.

[e] Including a small loan to Montenegro.

[f] Canada's debt is adjusted by subtracting the amount lent by her to Great Britain.

II. ALLIED INTER-GOVERNMENTAL INDEBTEDNESS AT THE TIME OF THE ARMISTICE[a]
(In millions of dollars)

Borrowing Country	From United States	From Great Britain	From France	Total	Change since April 1917
Great Britain.....	3,696.0	—	—	3,789.4[b]	+3,789.4
British dominions.	—	249.4[c]	—	249.4	− 295.1
Russia...........	187.7	2,471.8[d]	955.2	3,614.7	+1,530.7
Italy.............	1,031.0	1,855.0[e]	75.0[f]	2,961.0	+2,287.5
France...........	1,970.0[g]	1,682.8[h]	—	3,652.8	+3,097.8
Belgium..........	171.8	422.3	534.6	1,128.7	+ 837.6
Serbia (Yugoslavia)	10.6	91.6[i]	297.4	399.6	+ 304.8
Rumania.........	—	78.1	220.4	298.5	+ 237.7
Greece...........	—	90.3	155.0	245.3	+ 234.3
Portugal.........	—	61.3	—	61.3	+ 51.6
Cuba............	10.0	—	—	10.0	+ 10.0
Belgian Congo....	—	11.9	—	11.9	+ 7.4
Total.........	7,077.1	7,014.5	2,237.6	16,422.6[b]	+12,093.7
Increase in total since April 1917	7,077.1	3,200.1	1,723.1	12,093.7[b]	

[a] Based on Fisk, *Inter-Ally Debt*, p. 345. All conversions at par of exchange.

[b] Including loan from Great Britain to the government of Argentina amounting to $93,427,000.

[c] This figure consists of loans made by Great Britain to various dominions and colonies, aggregating 693.3 millions less loans made to Great Britain by Canada, amounting to 443.9 millions.

[d] Adjusted for gold shipments amounting to $291,960,000 and book credit of $973,000.000.

[e] Adjusted for gold shipments and credits to Great Britain, amounting to $152,314,000.

[f] Adjusted for credits to France, amounting to $96,625,000.

[g] A debt of $382,719,000 was owing to France at the time of the Armistice; it was adjusted later.

[h] Adjusted for gold shipments and credits to Great Britain, amounting to $431,796,000.

[i] Including a small loan to Montenegro.

III. Credits Established by the United States Treasury in Favor of Foreign Governments, Advances Made to Them, and Expenditures Reported by Them, April 6, 1917 to November 1, 1920
(In millions of dollars)
A. War Period: April 6, 1917 to November 30, 1918

Particulars	Great Britain	France	Italy	Belgium	Russia	Others	Total
Established credits..........	3,945.0	2,445.0	1,210.0	210.1	450.0	61.5	8,321.6
Less credits withdrawn....	—	—	—	—	125.0	—	125.0
Net credits..............	3,945.0	2,445.0	1,210.0	210.1	325.0	61.5	8,196.6
Cash advanced.............	3,796.0	2,010.0	1,091.0	185.5	192.7	25.8	7,301.0
Less refunds and repayments	—	—	—	—	5.0	—	5.0
Net advances.............	3,796.0	2,010.0	1,091.0	185.5	187.7	25.8	7,296.0
Expenditures for:							
Munitions including remounts	1,179.5	668.1	229.7	7.5	58.7	3.9	2,147.4
Munitions for other governments.................	204.0	—	—	—	—	—	204.0
Exchange and cotton.......	1,570.7	505.4	37.9	—	53.2	—	2,167.2
Cereals..................	1,214.6	—	.7	2.3	—	—	1,217.6
Other foods..............	878.4	77.8	58.8	13.4	1.7	—	1,030.1
Tobacco.................	63.6	18.4	—	2.4	—	—	84.4
Other supplies...........	165.6	86.7	34.9	4.1	49.3	—	340.6
Transportation..........	—	24.6	57.1	.7	2.2	—	84.6
Shipping.................	48.9	62.0	.8	—	1.3	—	113.0
Reimbursements..........	—	876.0	577.8	10.6	—	—	1,464.4
Interest.................	270.0	125.9	29.2	5.5	4.1	.3	435.0
Maturities..............	307.0	159.8	—	—	5.0	—	471.8
Relief..................	—	89.0	—	139.5	—	11.6	240.1
Silver..................	132.8	3.8	—	—	—	—	136.6
Food for northern Russia..	7.0	—	—	—	—	—	7.0
Purchases from neutrals...	—	—	5.9	—	—	—	5.9
Special credit against credits to be established for United States government war purchases in Italy.......	—	—	25.0	—	—	—	25.0
Miscellaneous...........	29.3	14.0	34.0	1.2	3.1	10.0	91.6
Total reported expenditures..	6,071.4	2,711.5	1,091.8	187.2	178.6	25.8	10,266.3
Less:							
Reimbursements from United States credits to other governments...........	1,464.4	—	—	—	—	—	1,464.4
Dollar payments by United States government for foreign currencies..........	122.6	692.3	10.2	—	—	—	825.1
Proceeds of rupee credits and gold from India.....	67.8	—	—	—	—	—	67.8
Total deductions.............	1,654.8	692.3	10.2	—	—	—	2,357.3
Net expenditures...........	4,416.6	2,019.2	1,081.6	187.2	178.6	25.8	7,909.0

[a] Compiled from *Annual Report of the Secretary of the Treasury*, 1920, pp. 338–48.

III. Credits Established by the United States Treasury (*Continued*)
(In millions of dollars)
B. Post-War Period: December 1, 1918 to November 1, 1920

Particulars	Great Britain	France	Italy	Belgium	Russia	Others	Total
Established credits..........	450.0	630.5	460.1	143.3	—	133.0	1,816.9
Less credits withdrawn....	118.0	27.5	3.8	4.2	137.3	12.2	303.0
Net credits.................	332.0	603.0	456.3	139.1	—137.3	120.8	1,513.9
Cash advanced	481.0	987.5	540.3	163.7	—	112.3	2,284.8
Less refunds and repayments	80.2	31.5	—	—	—	2.9	114.6
Net advances...............	400.8	956.0	540.3	163.7	—	109.4	2,170.2
Expenditures for:							
Munitions including remounts	151.1	159.1	29.5	6.6	—	—	346.3
Munitions for other governments.................	1.5	—	—	—	—	—	1.5
Exchange and cotton......	111.7	301.2	49.6	—	—	15.0	477.5
Cereals..................	160.8	—	41.1	3.0	—	—	204.9
Other foods..............	290.7	217.4	82.6	8.8	—	—	599.5
Tobacco.................	35.6	22.4	—	2.8	—	—	60.8
Other supplies...........	49.8	189.9	28.6	4.3	—	—	272.6
Transportation..........	—	7.9	42.9	.7	—	—	51.5
Shipping................	—	60.4	—	—	—	—	60.4
Reimbursements..........	19.3	169.8	206.1	12.7	.6	—	408.5
Interest.................	117.8	142.9	28.4	5.5	—	.9	295.5
Maturities...............	46.5	129.9	—	—	—	—	176.4
Relief...................	16.0	54.1	16.0	125.0	—	86.9	298.0
Silver...................	128.8	2.5	—	—	—	—	131.3
Food for northern Russia..	—	—	—	—	—	—	—
Purchases from neutrals...	—	—	12.9	—	—	—	12.9
Special credit against credits to be established for United States government war purchases in Italy.......	—	—	22.3	—	—	—	76.8
Miscellaneous...........	18.4	27.3	22.3	1.9	—	6.9	76.8
Total reported expenditures...	1,148.0	1,484.8	560.0	171.3	.6	109.7	3,474.4
Less:							
Reimbursements from United States credits to other governments..........	389.2	19.3	—	—	—	—	408.5
Dollar payments by United States government for foreign currencies	326.7	333.2	4.2	1.2	—	—	665.3
Proceeds of rupee credits and gold from India.....	13.6	—	—	—	—	—	13.6
Total deductions...........	729.5	352.5	4.2	1.2	—		1,087.4
Net expenditures...........	418.5	1,132.3	555.8	170.1	.6	109.7	2,387.0

III. Credits Established by the United States Treasury (*Continued*)
(In millions of dollars)
C. Whole Period

Particulars	Great Britain	France	Italy	Belgium	Russia	Others	Total
Established credits..........	4,395.0	3,075.5	1,670.1	353.4	450.0	194.5	10,138.5
Less credits withdrawn....	118.0	27.5	3.8	4.2	262.3	12.2	428.0
Net credits.................	4,277.0	3,048.0	1,666.3	349.2	187.7	182.3	9,710.5
Cash advanced.............	4,277.0	2,997.5	1,631.3	349.2	192.7	138.1	9,585.8
Less refunds and repayments	80.2	31.5	—	—	5.0	2.9	119.6
Net advances...............	4,196.8	2,966.0	1,631.3	349.2	187.7	135.2	9,466.2
Expenditures for:							
Munitions including remounts	1,330.6	827.2	259.2	14.1	58.7	3.9	2,493.7
Munitions for other governments.................	205.5	—	—	—	—	—	205.5
Exchange and cotton......	1,682.4	806.6	87.5	—	53.2	15.0	2,644.7
Cereals..................	1,375.4	—	41.8	5.3	—	—	1,422.5
Other foods..............	1,169.1	295.2	141.4	22.2	1.7	—	1,629.6
Tobacco.................	99.2	40.8	—	5.2	—	—	145.2
Other supplies...........	215.4	276.6	63.5	8.4	49.3	—	613.2
Transportation...........	—	32.5	100.0	1.4	2.2	—	136.1
Shipping.................	48.9	122.4	.8	—	1.3	—	173.4
Reimbursements..........	19.3	1,045.8	783.9	23.3	.6	—	1,872.9
Interest.................	387.8	268.8	57.6	11.0	4.1	1.2	730.5
Maturities...............	353.5	289.7	—	—	5.0	—	648.2
Relief...................	16.0	143.1	16.0	264.5	—	98.5	538.1
Silver...................	261.6	6.3	—	—	—	—	267.9
Food for northern Russia..	7.0	—	—	—	—	—	7.0
Purchases from neutrals...	—	—	18.8	—	—	—	18.8
Special credit against credits to be established for United States government war purchases in Italy.......	—	—	25.0	—	—	—	25.0
Miscellaneous............	47.7	41.3	56.3	3.1	3.1	16.9	168.4
Total reported expenditures..	7,219.4	4,196.3	1,651.8	358.5	179.2	135.5	13,740.7
Less:							
Reimbursements form United States credits to other governments...........	1,853.6	19.3	—	—	—	—	1,872.9
Dollar payments by United States government for foreign currencies........	449.3	1,025.5	14.4	1.2	—	—	1,490.4
Proceeds of rupee credits and gold from India.....	81.4	—	—	—	—	—	81.4
Total deductions............	2,384.3	1,044.8	14.4	1.2	—	—	3,444.7
Net expenditures...........	4,835.1	3,151.5	1,637.4	357.3	179.2	135.5	10,296.0

IV. FOREIGN GOVERNMENT OBLIGATIONS HELD BY THE UNITED
THEREON, AS OF THE LAST INTEREST PERIOD
(In thousands

Country	Acquired under Liberty Loan Acts		Acquired from Sales of Surplus War Material (Act of July 9, 1918)		Acquired by American Relief Administration on Account of Relief (Act of Feb. 25, 1919)	
	Principal	Interest	Principal	Interest	Principal	Interest
Armenia.......	—	—	—	—	8,028.4	1,204.3
Austria........	—	—	—	—	—	—
Belgium.......	347,251.0	60,073.4	29,872.7	—^{bc}	—	—
Cuba..........	7,740.5	—^{c}	—	—	—	—
Czechoslovakia.	61,974.0	10,136.2	20,612.3	2,959.4	6,428.1	964.2
Esthonia.......	—	—	12,213.4	1,832.0	1,785.8	257.6
Finland........	—	—	—	—	8,281.9	1,012.4
France........	2,933,405.1	503,386.0	407,341.1	—^{c}	—	—
Great Britain...	4,135,818.4^d	611,044.2^e	—	—	—	—
Greece.........	15,000.0	750.0	—	—	—	—
Hungary.......	—	—	—	—	—	—
Italy..........	1,648,034.0	284,681.5	—	—	—	—
Latvia.........	—	—	2,521.9	252.0	2,610.4	391.6
Liberia........	26.0	3.5	—	—	—	—
Lithuania......	—	—	4,159.5	623.9	822.1	123.3
Nicaragua.....	—	—	170.6	—^{b}	—	—
Poland........	—	—	59,678.6	7,042.8	51,671.8	7,750.8
Rumania......	23,205.8	3,925.7	12,922.7	1,938.4	—	—
Russia.........	187,729.8	39,214.3	406.1	10.2	4,465.5	488.2
Yugoslavia.....	26,126.6	4,611.7	24,978.0	3,382.4	—	—
Total.......	9,386,311.2	1,517,826.5	574,876.9	18,041.1	84,094.0	12,192.4

^{a} From *Combined Annual Reports of the World War Foreign Debt Commission*, 1927, p. 10.
^{b} No interest was due on Nicaraguan notes until maturity, as was also the case of certain
^{c} Interest was paid as it became due.
^{d} Includes $61,000,000 of British obligations which were given for Pittman silver ad-
^{e} Great Britain paid $50,000,000 on Oct. 16, 1922 and $50,000,000 on Nov. 15, 1922, on

STATES, TOGETHER WITH ACCRUED AND UNPAID INTEREST
PRIOR TO OR ENDING WITH NOVEMBER 15, 1922[a]
of dollars)

Held by United States Grain Corporation on Account of Sales of Flour (Act of Mar. 30, 1920)		Total		Total Indebtedness
Principal	Interest	Principal	Interest	
3,931.5	473.0	11,959.9	1,677.3	13,637.2
24,055.7	2,886.7	24,055.7	2,886.7	26,942.4
—	—	377,123.7	60,073.4[b]	437,197.1
—	—	7,740.5	—[c]	7,740.5
2,873.3	344.8	91,887.7	14,404.6	106,292.3
—	—	13,999.2	2,089.6	16,088.8
—	—	8,281.9	1,012.4	9,294.3
—	—	3,340,746.2	503,386.0	3,844,132.2
—	—	4,135,818.4[d]	611,044.2[e]	4,746,862.6
—	—	15,000.0	750.0	15,750.0
1,685.8	202.3	1,685.8	202.3	1,888.1
—	—	1,648,034.0	284,681.5	1,932,715.5
—	—	5,132.3	643.6	5,775.9
—	—	26.0	3.5	29.5
—	—	4,981.6	747.2	5,728.8
—	—	170.6	—[b]	170.6
24,312.5	2,825.2	135,662.9	17,618.8	153,281.7
—	—	36,128.5	5,864.1	41,992.6
—	—	192,601.4	39,712.7	232,314.1
—	—	51,104.6	7,994.1	59,098.7
56,858.8	6,732.0	10,102,140.9	1,554,792.0	11,656,932.9

Belgian obligations aggregating $2,284,151.40.

vances and for which a special agreement for payment was made.
account of interest on other than Pittman silver obligations.

APPENDIX B

INTER-GOVERNMENTAL DEBT
PAYMENT SCHEDULES

The schedules given here comprise all inter-governmental debt payments still outstanding as of July 1, 1931, with the exception of those indicated in the notes prefacing each group. The grouping of schedules is somewhat arbitrary, but it is designed (1) to provide a ready method of finding separate schedules and (2) to show the payments to be received and made by the principal creditors and debtors. All instalments are shown in the original currencies stipulated in the debt agreements, and a conversion table for these currencies is given below. The sources from which the schedules have been taken and such details as those relating to dates of payment, postponement provisions, and other stipulations contained in the agreements are given in the text of the book, to which cross reference is made.

Currency Equivalents
(At par of exchange)

1 pound sterling = $4.8666	1 Danish krone ⎫
1 French franc (pre-war) = $0.1929	1 Norwegian krone ⎬ = $0.26798
1 French franc (post-war) = $0.0392	1 Swedish krone ⎭
1 Italian lira (post-war) = $0.0526	1 Canadian dollar = $1.00
1 Swiss franc = $0.1929	1 reichsmark = $0.2382
1 Dutch florin = $0.402	1 gold crown = $0.2026
	1 gold franc = $0.1929

I. DEBTS TO THE UNITED STATES

The amounts shown here represent the original payment schedules, as embodied in the debt funding agreements, for all countries, with the exception of Esthonia, Hungary, Latvia, Lithuania, and Poland. These five countries had exercised certain postponement options, explained in Chapter V, and the schedules given for them embody the adjustments rendered necessary by the funding of the deferred instalments. Payments due to the United States from Germany are shown on page 470. For the details of the debt agreements see Chapter V.

A. SCHEDULE OF PAYMENTS BY AUSTRIA

1929–33	5 annuities, each of............................$	287,556
1934–43	10 annuities, each of..........................	460,093
1944–68	25 annuities, each of..........................	743,047
	Total...................................	$24,614,885

B. SCHEDULE OF PAYMENTS BY BELGIUM

1. Pre-Armistice Debt

Calendar Year	Principal Payment
1926–27	$ 1,000,000
1928	1,250,000
1929	1,750,000
1930	2,250,000
1931	2,750,000
1932–86	2,900,000
1987	2,280,000
Total	$171,780,000

2. Post-Armistice Debt

Fiscal Year	Annual Interest Payments	Annual Principal Payments	Total Annual Payments	Fiscal Year	Annual Interest Payments	Annual Principal Payments	Total Annual Payments
1926...	1,740,000	1,100,000	2,840,000	1958...	6,331,500	3,500,000	9,831,500
1927...	2,000,000	1,100,000	3,100,000	1959...	6,209,000	3,600,000	9,809,000
1928...	2,250,000	1,200,000	3,450,000	1960...	6,083,000	3,700,000	9,783,000
1929...	2,500,000	1,200,000	3,700,000				
1930...	2,750,000	1,200,000	3,950,000	1961...	5,953,500	3,800,000	9,753,500
				1962...	5,820,500	4,000,000	9,820,500
1931...	3,250,000	1,300,000	4,550,000	1963...	5,680,500	4,100,000	9,780,500
1932...	3,750,000	1,300,000	5,050,000	1964...	5,537,000	4,300,000	9,837,000
1933...	4,250,000	1,300,000	5,550,000	1965...	5,386,500	4,400,000	9,786,500
1934...	4,750,000	1,400,000	6,150,000	1966...	5,232,500	4,600,000	9,832,500
1935...	5,250,000	1,400,000	6,650,000	1967...	5,071,500	4,700,000	9,771,500
1936...	8,172,500	1,600,000	9,772,500	1968...	4,907,000	4,900,000	9,807,000
1937...	8,116,500	1,700,000	9,816,500	1969...	4,735,500	5,100,000	9,835,500
1938...	8,057,000	1,800,000	9,857,000	1970...	4,557,000	5,300,000	9,857,000
1939...	7,994,000	1,800,000	9,794,000				
1940...	7,931,000	1,900,000	9,831,000	1971...	4,371,500	5,400,000	9,771,500
				1972...	4,182,500	5,600,000	9,782,500
1941...	7,864,500	1,900,000	9,764,500	1973...	3,986,500	5,800,000	9,786,500
1942...	7,798,000	2,000,000	9,798,000	1974...	3,783,500	6,000,000	9,783,500
1943...	7,728,000	2,100,000	9,828,000	1975...	3,573,500	6,300,000	9,873,500
1944...	7,654,500	2,100,000	9,754,500	1976...	3,353,000	6,600,000	9,953,000
1945...	7,581,000	2,200,000	9,781,000	1977...	3,122,000	6,800,000	9,922,000
1946...	7,504,000	2,300,000	9,804,000	1978...	2,884,000	7,000,000	9,884,000
1947...	7,423,500	2,400,000	9,823,500	1979...	2,639,000	7,200,000	9,839,000
1948...	7,339,500	2,500,000	9,839,500	1980...	2,387,000	7,500,000	9,887,000
1949...	7,252,000	2,500,000	9,752,000				
1950...	7,164,500	2,600,000	9,764,500	1981...	2,124,500	7,800,000	9,924,500
				1982...	1,851,500	8,100,000	9,951,500
1951...	7,073,500	2,700,000	9,773,500	1983...	1,568,000	8,400,000	9,968,000
1952...	6,979,000	2,800,000	9,779,000	1984...	1,274,000	8,600,000	9,874,000
1953...	6,881,000	2,900,000	9,781,000	1985...	973,000	8,900,000	9,873,000
1954...	6,779,500	3,000,000	9,779,500	1986...	661,500	9,300,000	9,961,500
1955...	6,674,500	3,100,000	9,774,500	1987...	336,000	9,600,000	9,936,000
1956...	6,566,000	3,300,000	9,866,000				
1957...	6,450,500	3,400,000	9,850,500	Total.	310,050,500	246,000,000	556,050,500

C. SCHEDULE OF PAYMENTS BY CZECHOSLOVAKIA
1. First 18 Years

Fiscal Year	Interest Due	Principal Due	Total Amount Due	Total Amount to Be Paid	Amount Deferred Each Year	Value of Each Deferred Amount on 19th Year
1926	$ 3,450,000	$ 575,000	$ 4,025,000	$ 3,000,000	$ 1,025,000	$ 1,761,086.23
1927	3,432,750	595,000	4,027,750	3,000,000	1,027,750	1,714,379.79
1928	3,414,900	610,000	4,024,900	3,000,000	1,024,900	1,659,831.06
1929	3,396,600	630,000	4,026,600	3,000,000	1,026,600	1,614,158.82
1930	3,377,700	645,000	4,022,700	3,000,000	1,022,700	1,561,192.58
1931	3,358,350	665,000	4,023,350	3,000,000	1,023,350	1,516,684.65
1932	3,338,400	690,000	4,028,400	3,000,000	1,028,400	1,479,775.62
1933	3,317,700	710,000	4,027,700	3,000,000	1,027,700	1,435,697.46
1934	3,296,400	730,000	4,026,400	3,000,000	1,026,400	1,392,117.83
1935	3,274,500	750,000	4,024,500	3,000,000	1,024,500	1,349,068.77
1936	3,794,000	770,000	4,564,000	3,000,000	1,564,000	1,989,842.79
1937	3,767,050	795,000	4,562,050	3,000,000	1,562,050	1,920,156.21
1938	3,739,225	825,000	4,564,225	3,000,000	1,564,225	1,857,806.57
1939	3,710,350	855,000	4,565,350	3,000,000	1,565,350	1,796,273.56
1940	3,680,425	885,000	4,565,425	3,000,000	1,565,425	1,735,613.31
1941	3,649,450	915,000	4,564,450	3,000,000	1,564,450	1,675,877.95
1942	3,617,425	945,000	4,562,425	3,000,000	1,562,425	1,617,109.87
1943	3,584,350	980,000	4,564,350	3,000,000	1,564,350	1,564,350.00
Total	$63,199,575	$13,570,000	$76,769,575	$54,000,000	$22,769,575	$29,641,023.07

2. Remaining 44 Years

Fiscal Year	Interest	Principal	Total	Fiscal Year	Interest	Principal	Total
1944	$ 4,587,485.81	$ 1,296,023.07	$ 5,883,508.88	1968	$ 2,925,825.00	$ 2,955,000.00	$ 5,880,825.00
1945	4,542,125.00	1,340,000.00	5,882,125.00	1969	2,822,400.00	3,060,000.00	5,882,400.00
1946	4,495,225.00	1,385,000.00	5,880,225.00	1970	2,715,300.00	3,165,000.00	5,880,300.00
1947	4,446,750.00	1,435,000.00	5,881,750.00				
1948	4,396,525.00	1,485,000.00	5,881,525.00	1971	2,604,525.00	3,280,000.00	5,884,525.00
1949	4,344,550.00	1,540,000.00	5,884,550.00	1972	2,489,725.00	3,395,000.00	5,884,725.00
1950	4,290,650.00	1,590,000.00	5,880,650.00	1973	2,370,900.00	3,510,000.00	5,880,900.00
				1974	2,248,050.00	3,635,000.00	5,883,050.00
1951	4,235,000.00	1,645,000.00	5,880,000.00	1975	2,120,825.00	3,760,000.00	5,880,825.00
1952	4,177,425.00	1,705,000.00	5,882,425.00	1976	1,989,225.00	3,890,000.00	5,879,225.00
1953	4,117,750.00	1,765,000.00	5,882,750.00	1977	1,853,075.00	4,030,000.00	5,883,075.00
1954	4,055,975.00	1,825,000.00	5,880,975.00	1978	1,712,025.00	4,170,000.00	5,882,025.00
1955	3,992,100.00	1,890,000.00	5,882,100.00	1979	1,566,075.00	4,315,000.00	5,881,075.00
1956	3,925,950.00	1,960,000.00	5,885,950.00	1980	1,415,050.00	4,465,000.00	5,880,050.00
1957	3,857,350.00	2,025,000.00	5,882,350.00				
1958	3,786,475.00	2,100,000.00	5,886,475.00	1981	1,258,775.00	4,625,000.00	5,883,775.00
1959	3,712,975.00	2,170,000.00	5,882,975.00	1982	1,096,900.00	4,785,000.00	5,881,900.00
1960	3,637,025.00	2,245,000.00	5,882,025.00	1983	929,425.00	4,950,000.00	5,879,425.00
				1984	756,175.00	5,125,000.00	5,881,175.00
1961	3,558,450.00	2,325,000.00	5,883,450.00	1985	576,800.00	5,305,000.00	5,881,800.00
1962	3,477,075.00	2,405,000.00	5,882,075.00	1986	391,125.00	5,490,000.00	5,881,125.00
1963	3,392,900.00	2,490,000.00	5,882,900.00	1987	198,975.00	5,685,000.00	5,883,975.00
1964	3,305,750.00	2,575,000.00	5,880,750.00				
1965	3,215,625.00	2,665,000.00	5,880,625.00	Total..	$127,740,410.81	$131,071,023.07	$258,811,433.88
1966	3,122,350.00	2,760,000.00	5,882,350.00	Add total amount received first 18 years.....			54,000,000.00
1967	3,025,750.00	2,855,000.00	5,880,750.00	Grand total...			$312,811,433.88

D. SCHEDULE OF PAYMENTS BY ESTHONIA

1. First 8 Years

Calendar Year	Interest Due	Interest Paid (Under options)	Amount to be Funded	Calendar Year	Interest Due	Interest Paid (Under options)	Amount to be Funded
1923	$ 418,011.75	—	$ 418,011.75	1928	470,525.40	200,000.00	270,525.40
1924	430,443.23	—	430,443.23	1929	476,239.75	250,000.00	226,239.75
1925	442,812.15	—	442,812.15	1930	480,402.15	300,000.00	180,402.15
1926	454,366.73	100,000.00	354,366.73	Total	$3,636,012.87	$1,000,000.00	$2,636,012.87
1927	463,211.71	150,000.00	313,211.71				

2. Remaining 54 Years

Calendar Year	Interest	Principal	Total	Calendar Year	Interest	Principal	Total
1931	$ 493,980.39	$ 108,012.87	$ 601,993.26	1959	$ 403,655.00	$ 279,000.00	$ 682,655.00
1932	490,740.00	111,000.00	601,740.00	1960	393,890.00	289,000.00	682,890.00
1933	568,645.00	114,500.00	683,145.00				
1934	564,637.50	118,500.00	683,137.50	1961	383,775.00	299,000.00	682,775.00
1935	560,490.00	122,000.00	682,490.00	1962	373,310.00	310,000.00	683,310.00
1936	556,220.00	126,000.00	682,220.00	1963	362,460.00	320,000.00	682,460.00
1937	551,810.00	131,000.00	682,810.00	1964	351,260.00	331,000.00	682,260.00
1938	547,225.00	136,000.00	683,225.00	1965	339,675.00	343,000.00	682,675.00
1939	542,465.00	141,000.00	683,465.00	1966	327,670.00	355,000.00	682,670.00

Year				Year			
1940	537,530.00	146,000.00	683,530.00	1967	315,245.00	368,000.00	683,245.00
				1968	302,365.00	380,000.00	682,365.00
				1969	289,065.00	394,000.00	683,065.00
				1970	275,275.00	407,000.00	682,275.00
1941	532,420.00	151,000.00	683,420.00	1971	261,030.00	422,000.00	683,030.00
1942	527,135.00	156,000.00	683,135.00	1972	246,260.00	436,000.00	682,260.00
1943	521,675.00	161,000.00	682,675.00	1973	231,000.00	452,000.00	683,000.00
1944	516,040.00	167,000.00	683,040.00	1974	215,180.00	468,000.00	683,180.00
1945	510,195.00	172,000.00	682,195.00	1975	198,800.00	484,000.00	682,800.00
1946	504,175.00	178,000.00	682,175.00	1976	181,860.00	501,000.00	682,860.00
1947	497,945.00	184,000.00	681,945.00	1977	164,325.00	519,000.00	683,325.00
1948	491,505.00	190,000.00	681,505.00	1978	146,160.00	537,000.00	683,160.00
1949	484,855.00	198,000.00	682,855.00	1979	127,365.00	556,000.00	683,365.00
1950	477,925.00	205,000.00	682,925.00	1980	107,905.00	575,000.00	682,905.00
1951	470,750.00	212,000.00	682,750.00	1981	87,780.00	595,000.00	682,780.00
1952	463,330.00	219,000.00	682,330.00	1982	66,955.00	616,000.00	682,955.00
1953	455,665.00	227,000.00	682,665.00	1983	45,395.00	637,000.00	682,395.00
1954	447,720.00	235,000.00	682,720.00	1984	23,100.00	660,000.00	683,100.00
1955	439,495.00	243,000.00	682,495.00	Total	$20,241,632.89	$16,466,012.87	$36,707,645.76
1956	430,990.00	251,000.00	681,990.00	Add total amount paid under options	1,000,000.00	—	1,000,000.00
1957	422,205.00	260,000.00	682,205.00	Grand total	$21,241,632.89	$16,466,012.87	$37,707,645.76
1958	413,105.00	270,000.00	683,105.00				

E. Schedule of Payments by Finland

Calendar Year	Interest	Principal	Total
1923	$270,000	$45,000	$315,000
1924	268,650	45,000	313,650
1925	267,300	47,000	314,300
1926	265,890	49,000	314,890
1927	264,420	50,000	314,420
1928	262,920	52,000	314,920
1929	261,360	53,000	314,360
1930	259,770	55,000	314,770
1931	258,120	55,000	313,120
1932	256,470	58,000	314,470
1933	297,185	62,000	359,185
1934	295,015	62,000	357,015
1935	292,845	65,000	357,845
1936	290,570	67,000	357,570
1937	288,225	69,000	357,225
1938	285,810	71,000	356,810
1939	283,325	74,000	357,325
1940	280,735	76,000	356,735
1941	278,075	79,000	357,075
1942	275,310	82,000	357,310
1943	272,440	84,000	356,440
1944	269,500	87,000	356,500
1945	266,455	90,000	356,455
1946	263,305	93,000	356,305
1947	260,050	96,000	356,050
1948	256,690	100,000	356,690
1949	253,190	103,000	356,190
1950	249,585	107,000	356,585
1951	245,840	110,000	355,840
1952	241,990	114,000	355,990
1953	238,000	118,000	356,000
1954	233,870	122,000	355,870

Calendar Year	Interest	Principal	Total
1955	$229,600	$126,000	$355,600
1956	225,190	131,000	356,190
1957	220,605	136,000	356,605
1958	215,845	141,000	356,845
1959	210,910	146,000	356,910
1960	205,800	151,000	356,800
1961	200,515	156,000	356,515
1962	195,055	162,000	357,055
1963	189,385	167,000	356,385
1964	183,540	173,000	356,540
1965	177,485	179,000	356,485
1966	171,220	185,000	356,220
1967	164,745	192,000	356,745
1968	158,025	199,000	357,025
1969	151,060	206,000	357,060
1970	143,850	213,000	356,850
1971	136,395	220,000	356,395
1972	128,695	228,000	356,695
1973	120,715	236,000	356,715
1974	112,455	244,000	356,455
1975	103,915	253,000	356,915
1976	95,060	262,000	357,060
1977	85,890	271,000	356,890
1978	76,405	280,000	356,405
1979	66,605	290,000	356,605
1980	56,455	301,000	357,455
1981	45,920	312,000	357,920
1982	35,000	322,000	357,000
1983	23,730	333,000	356,730
1984	12,075	345,000	357,075
Total	$12,695,055	$9,000,000	$21,695,055

F. Schedule of Payments by France

Fiscal Year	Interest	Principal	Total	Fiscal Year	Interest	Principal	Total
1926	—	$30,000,000.00	$30,000,000.00	1958	59,573,740.79	65,426,259.21	125,000,000.00
1927	—	30,000,000.00	30,000,000.00				
1928	—	32,500,000.00	32,500,000.00	1959	69,525,701.18	55,474,298.82	125,000,000.00
1929	—	32,500,000.00	32,500,000.00	1960	67,861,472.21	57,138,527.79	125,000,000.00
1930	—	35,000,000.00	35,000,000.00	1961	66,147,316.38	58,852,683.62	125,000,000.00
				1962	64,381,735.87	60,618,264.13	125,000,000.00
1931	38,650,000.00	1,350,000.00	40,000,000.00	1963	62,563,187.95	62,436,812.05	125,000,000.00
1932	38,636,500.00	11,363,500.00	50,000,000.00	1964	60,690,083.58	64,309,916.42	125,000,000.00
1933	38,522,865.00	21,477,135.00	60,000,000.00	1965	58,760,786.09	66,239,213.91	125,000,000.00
1934	38,308,093.65	36,691,906.35	75,000,000.00				
1935	37,941,174.59	42,058,825.41	80,000,000.00	1966	66,235,877.95	58,764,122.05	125,000,000.00
1936	37,520,586.33	52,479,413.67	90,000,000.00	1967	64,179,133.68	60,820,866.32	125,000,000.00
1937	36,995,792.20	63,004,207.80	100,000,000.00	1968	62,050,403.36	62,949,596.64	125,000,000.00
1938	36,365,750.12	68,634,249.88	105,000,000.00	1969	59,847,167.48	65,152,832.52	125,000,000.00
1939	35,679,407.62	74,320,592.38	110,000,000.00	1970	57,566,818.34	67,433,181.66	125,000,000.00
1940	34,936,201.70	80,063,798.30	115,000,000.00				
				1971	55,206,656.98	69,793,343.02	125,000,000.00
1941	68,271,127.42	51,728,872.58	120,000,000.00	1972	52,763,889.98	72,236,110.02	125,000,000.00
1942	67,236,549.98	57,763,450.02	125,000,000.00	1973	50,235,626.12	74,764,373.88	125,000,000.00
1943	66,081,280.97	58,918,719.03	125,000,000.00	1974	47,618,873.04	77,381,126.96	125,000,000.00
1944	64,902,906.59	60,097,093.41	125,000,000.00	1975	44,910,533.60	80,089,466.40	125,000,000.00
1945	63,700,964.72	61,299,035.28	125,000,000.00	1976	42,107,402.27	82,892,597.73	125,000,000.00
1946	62,474,984.02	62,525,015.98	125,000,000.00	1977	39,206,161.35	85,793,838.65	125,000,000.00
1947	61,224,483.70	63,775,516.30	125,000,000.00	1978	36,203,377.00	88,796,623.00	125,000,000.00
1948	59,948,973.37	65,051,026.63	125,000,000.00	1979	33,095,495.19	91,904,504.81	125,000,000.00
1949	58,647,952.84	66,352,047.16	125,000,000.00	1980	29,878,837.52	95,121,162.48	125,000,000.00
1950	57,320,911.90	67,679,088.10	125,000,000.00				
				1981	26,549,596.84	98,450,403.16	125,000,000.00
1951	69,959,162.67	55,040,837.33	125,000,000.00	1982	23,103,832.73	101,896,167.27	125,000,000.00
1952	68,583,141.73	56,416,858.27	125,000,000.00	1983	19,537,466.87	105,462,533.13	125,000,000.00
1953	67,172,720.29	57,827,279.71	125,000,000.00	1984	15,846,278.21	109,153,721.79	125,000,000.00
1954	65,727,038.29	59,272,961.71	125,000,000.00	1985	12,025,897.95	112,974,102.05	125,000,000.00
1955	64,245,214.24	60,754,785.76	125,000,000.00	1986	8,071,804.38	116,928,195.62	125,000,000.00
1956	62,726,344.60	62,273,655.40	125,000,000.00	1987	3,979,317.53	113,694,786.64	117,674,104.17
1957	61,169,503.21	63,830,496.79	125,000,000.00				
				Total	$2,822,674,104.17	$4,025,000,000.00	$6,847,674,104.17

G. Schedule of Payments by Great Britain

Calendar Year	Interest	Principal	Total
1923	$138,000,000	$23,000,000	$161,000,000
1924	137,310,000	23,000,000	160,310,000
1925	136,620,000	24,000,000	160,620,000
1926	135,900,000	25,000,000	160,900,000
1927	135,150,000	25,000,000	160,150,000
1928	134,400,000	27,000,000	161,400,000
1929	133,590,000	27,000,000	160,590,000
1930	132,780,000	28,000,000	160,780,000
1931	131,940,000	28,000,000	159,940,000
1932	131,100,000	30,000,000	161,100,000
1933	151,900,000	32,000,000	183,900,000
1934	150,780,000	32,000,000	182,780,000
1935	149,660,000	32,000,000	181,660,000
1936	148,540,000	32,000,000	180,540,000
1937	147,420,000	37,000,000	184,420,000
1938	146,125,000	37,000,000	183,125,000
1939	144,830,000	37,000,000	181,830,000
1940	143,535,000	42,000,000	185,535,000
1941	142,065,000	42,000,000	184,065,000
1942	140,595,000	42,000,000	182,595,000
1943	139,125,000	42,000,000	181,125,000
1944	137,655,000	46,000,000	183,655,000
1945	136,045,000	46,000,000	182,045,000
1946	134,435,000	46,000,000	180,435,000
1947	132,825,000	51,000,000	183,825,000
1948	131,040,000	51,000,000	182,040,000
1949	129,255,000	51,000,000	180,255,000
1950	127,470,000	53,000,000	180,470,000
1951	125,615,000	55,000,000	180,615,000
1952	123,690,000	57,000,000	180,690,000
1953	121,695,000	60,000,000	181,695,000
1954	119,595,000	64,000,000	183,595,000
1955	$117,355,000	$64,000,000	$181,355,000
1956	115,115,000	64,000,000	179,115,000
1957	112,875,000	67,000,000	179,875,000
1958	110,530,000	70,000,000	180,530,000
1959	108,080,000	72,000,000	180,080,000
1960	105,560,000	74,000,000	179,560,000
1961	102,970,000	78,000,000	180,970,000
1962	100,240,000	78,000,000	178,240,000
1963	97,510,000	83,000,000	180,510,000
1964	94,605,000	85,000,000	179,605,000
1965	91,630,000	89,000,000	180,630,000
1966	88,515,000	94,000,000	182,515,000
1967	85,225,000	96,000,000	181,225,000
1968	81,865,000	100,000,000	181,865,000
1969	78,365,000	105,000,000	183,365,000
1970	74,690,000	110,000,000	184,690,000
1971	70,840,000	114,000,000	184,840,000
1972	66,850,000	119,000,000	185,850,000
1973	62,685,000	123,000,000	185,685,000
1974	58,380,000	127,000,000	185,380,000
1975	53,935,000	132,000,000	185,935,000
1976	49,315,000	136,000,000	185,315,000
1977	44,555,000	141,000,000	185,555,000
1978	39,620,000	146,000,000	185,620,000
1979	34,510,000	151,000,000	185,510,000
1980	29,225,000	156,000,000	185,225,000
1981	23,765,000	162,000,000	185,765,000
1982	18,095,000	167,000,000	185,095,000
1983	12,250,000	175,000,000	187,250,000
1984	6,125,000	175,000,000	181,125,000
Total	$6,505,965,000	$4,600,000,000	$11,105,965,000

H. SCHEDULE OF PAYMENTS BY GREECE

1. War Debt

July 1, 1928................	$20,000	
Jan. 1, 1929................	20,000	
July 1, 1929................	25,000	
Jan. 1, 1930................	25,000	
July 1, 1930................	30,000	
Jan. 1, 1931................	30,000	
July 1, 1931................	110,000	
Jan. 1, 1932................	$110,000	
July 1, 1932................	130,000	
Jan. 1, 1933................	130,000	
July 1, 1933, and semi-annually thereafter to Jan. 1, 1938, 10 payments each of....	150,000	
July 1, 1938, and semi-annually thereafter to Jan. 1, 1990, 104 payments each of....	175,000	

2. Loan of 1928

Due Date	Interest	Principal	Total
Nov. 10, 1929...	$243,340	$201,000	$444,340
May 10, 1930...	239,320	206,000	445,320
Nov. 10, 1930...	235,200	210,000	445,200
May 10, 1931...	231,000	214,000	445,000
Nov. 10, 1931...	226,720	218,000	444,720
May 10, 1932...	222,360	222,000	444,360
Nov. 10, 1932...	217,920	227,000	444,920
May 10, 1933...	213,380	231,000	444,380
Nov. 10, 1933...	208,760	236,000	444,760
May 10, 1934...	204,040	240,000	444,040
Nov. 10, 1934...	199,240	245,000	444,240
May 10, 1935...	194,340	251,000	445,340
Nov. 10, 1935...	189,320	256,000	445,320
May 10, 1936...	184,200	261,000	445,200
Nov. 10, 1936...	178,980	266,000	444,980
May 10, 1937...	173,660	271,000	444,660
Nov. 10, 1937...	168,240	276,000	444,240
May 10, 1938...	162,720	282,000	444,720
Nov. 10, 1938...	157,080	288,000	445,080
May 10, 1939...	151,320	293,000	444,320
Nov. 10, 1939...	145,460	300,000	445,460
May 10, 1940...	139,460	305,000	444,460
Nov. 10, 1940...	133,360	312,000	445,360
May 10, 1941...	$127,120	$318,000	$445,120
Nov. 10, 1941...	120,760	324,000	444,760
May 10, 1942...	114,280	330,000	444,280
Nov. 10, 1942...	107,680	337,000	444,680
May 10, 1943...	100,940	344,000	444,940
Nov. 10, 1943...	94,060	350,000	444,060
May 10, 1944...	87,060	358,000	445,060
Nov. 10, 1944...	79,900	365,000	444,900
May 10, 1945...	72,600	372,000	444,600
Nov. 10, 1945...	65,160	380,000	445,160
May 10, 1946...	57,560	387,000	444,560
Nov. 10, 1946...	49,820	395,000	444,820
May 10, 1947...	41,920	403,000	444,920
Nov. 10, 1947...	33,860	411,000	444,860
May 10, 1948...	25,640	419,000	444,640
Nov. 10, 1948...	17,260	427,000	444,260
May 10, 1949...	8,720	436,000	444,720
Total........	$5,623,760	$12,167,000	$17,790,760

I. Schedule of Payments by Hungary
1. First 2 Years

Fiscal Year	Interest Due	Interest Paid	Interest Funded (Under options)	Principal Payment
1924	$ 43,845.64	$29,303.14	$14,542.50	$ 9,672.50
1925	73,511.94	44,498.94	29,013.00	10,018.00
Total	$117,357.58	$73,802.08	$43,555.50	$19,690.50

2. Remaining 60 Years

Fiscal Year	Interest	Principal	Total	Fiscal Year	Interest	Principal	Total
1926	$ 58,885.96	$ 10,230.00	$ 69,115.96	1961	$ 46,001.55	$ 32,715.00	$ 78,716.55
1927	58,579.06	10,435.00	69,014.06	1962	44,856.53	33,750.00	78,606.53
1928	58,266.02	10,640.00	68,906.02	1963	43,675.28	35,780.00	79,455.28
1929	57,946.80	11,245.00	69,191.80	1964	42,422.98	36,815.00	79,237.98
1930	57,609.45	11,755.00	69,364.45	1965	41,134.45	38,845.00	79,979.45
				1966	39,774.88	40,880.00	80,654.88
1931	57,256.80	12,270.00	69,526.80	1967	38,344.08	41,910.00	80,254.08
1932	56,888.70	12,285.00	69,173.70	1968	36,877.23	42,945.00	79,822.23
1933	56,520.15	12,785.00	69,305.15	1969	35,374.15	44,975.00	80,349.15
1934	65,492.70	12,800.00	78,292.70	1970	33,800.03	46,010.00	79,810.03

Year				Year			
1935	65,044.70	13,310.00	78,354.70	1971	32,189.68	48,040.00	80,229.68
1936	64,578.85	13,820.00	78,398.85	1972	30,508.28	49,075.00	79,583.28
1937	64,095.15	13,830.00	77,925.15	1973	28,790.65	51,105.00	79,895.65
1938	63,611.10	14,345.00	77,956.10	1974	27,001.98	52,130.00	79,131.98
1939	63,109.03	14,850.00	77,959.03	1975	25,177.43	54,180.00	79,357.43
1940	62,589.28	15,360.00	77,949.28	1976	23,281.13	56,235.00	79,516.13
1941	62,051.68	15,865.00	77,916.68	1977	21,312.90	58,280.00	79,592.90
1942	61,496.40	16,365.00	77,861.40	1978	19,273.10	60,320.00	79,593.10
1943	60,923.63	17,370.00	78,293.63	1979	17,161.90	63,365.00	80,526.90
1944	60,315.68	17,885.00	78,200.68	1980	14,944.13	65,415.00	80,359.13
1945	59,689.70	18,390.00	78,079.70	1981	12,654.60	67,480.00	80,134.60
1946	59,046.05	19,390.00	78,436.05	1982	10,292.80	69,570.00	79,862.80
1947	58,367.40	19,905.00	78,272.40	1983	7,857.85	72,675.00	80,532.85
1948	57,670.73	20,915.00	78,585.73	1984	5,314.23	74,785.00	80,099.23
1949	56,938.70	21,430.00	78,368.70	1985	2,696.75	77,050.00	79,746.75
1950	56,188.65	22,450.00	78,638.65	Total	$2,698,073.84	$1,962,865.00	$4,660,938.84
1951	55,402.90	22,965.00	78,367.90	Add total amount paid prior to 1930	73,802.08	19,690.50	93,492.58
1952	54,599.13	23,980.00	78,579.13	Grand total	$2,771,875.92	$1,982,555.50	$4,754,431.42
1953	53,759.83	24,495.00	78,254.83				
1954	52,902.50	25,510.00	78,412.50				
1955	52,009.65	26,535.00	78,544.65				
1956	51,080.93	27,565.00	78,645.93				
1957	50,116.15	28,095.00	78,211.15				
1958	49,132.83	29,125.00	78,257.83				
1959	48,113.45	29,655.00	77,768.45				
1960	47,075.53	30,685.00	77,760.53				

J. Schedule of Payments by Italy

Fiscal Year	Interest	Principal	Total	Fiscal Year	Interest	Principal	Total
1926	—	$ 5,000,000	$ 5,000,000	1958	$ 7,552,500	$ 29,600,000	$ 37,152,500
1927	—	5,000,000	5,000,000	1959	7,404,500	30,500,000	37,904,500
1928	—	5,000,000	5,000,000	1960	7,252,000	31,500,000	38,752,000
1929	—	5,000,000	5,000,000				
1930	—	5,000,000	5,000,000	1961	10,641,750	32,500,000	43,141,750
				1962	10,398,000	33,500,000	43,898,000
1931	2,521,250	12,100,000	14,621,250	1963	10,146,750	34,500,000	44,646,750
1932	2,506,125	12,200,000	14,706,125	1964	9,888,000	35,500,000	45,388,000
1933	2,490,875	12,300,000	14,790,875	1965	9,621,750	36,500,000	46,121,750
1934	2,475,500	12,600,000	15,075,500	1966	9,348,000	38,000,000	47,348,000
1935	2,459,750	13,000,000	15,459,750	1967	9,063,000	39,500,000	48,563,000
1936	2,443,500	13,500,000	15,943,500	1968	8,766,750	41,500,000	50,266,750
1937	2,426,625	14,200,000	16,626,625	1969	8,455,500	43,500,000	51,955,500
1938	2,408,875	14,600,000	17,008,875	1970	8,129,250	44,500,000	52,629,250
1939	2,390,625	15,200,000	17,590,625				
1940	2,371,625	15,800,000	18,171,625	1971	10,394,000	46,000,000	56,394,000
				1972	9,934,000	47,500,000	57,434,000

Fiscal Year	Interest	Principal	Total
1941	4,703,750	16,400,000	21,103,750
1942	4,662,750	17,000,000	21,662,750
1943	4,620,250	17,600,000	22,220,250
1944	4,576,250	18,300,000	22,876,250
1945	4,530,500	19,000,000	23,530,500
1946	4,483,000	19,600,000	24,083,000
1947	4,434,000	20,000,000	24,434,000
1948	4,384,000	20,600,000	24,984,000
1949	4,332,500	21,200,000	25,532,500
1950	4,279,500	22,000,000	26,279,500
1951	8,449,000	23,000,000	31,449,000
1952	8,334,000	23,800,000	32,134,000
1953	8,215,000	24,600,000	32,815,000
1954	8,092,000	25,400,000	33,492,000
1955	7,965,000	26,500,000	34,465,000
1956	7,832,500	27,500,000	35,332,500
1957	7,695,000	28,500,000	36,195,000

Fiscal Year	Interest	Principal	Total
1973	9,459,000	49,000,000	58,459,000
1974	8,969,000	50,500,000	59,469,000
1975	8,464,000	52,000,000	60,464,000
1976	7,944,000	54,000,000	61,944,000
1977	7,404,000	56,000,000	63,404,000
1978	6,844,000	59,000,000	65,844,000
1979	6,254,000	61,000,000	67,254,000
1980	5,644,000	62,000,000	67,644,000
1981	10,048,000	64,000,000	74,048,000
1982	8,768,000	67,000,000	75,768,000
1983	7,428,000	69,000,000	76,428,000
1984	6,048,000	72,000,000	78,048,000
1985	4,608,000	74,000,000	78,608,000
1986	3,128,000	77,000,000	80,128,000
1987	1,588,000	79,400,000	80,988,000
Total	$365,677,500	$2,042,000,000	$2,407,677,500

K. SCHEDULE OF PAYMENTS BY LATVIA

1. First 8 Years

Calendar Year	Interest Due	Interest Paid (Options)	Amount to be Funded	Calendar Year	Interest Due	Interest Paid (Options)	Amount to be Funded
1923	$ 174,549.38	—	$ 174,549.38	1928	$ 195,732.29	80,000.00	115,732.29
1924	179,740.58	—	179,740.58	1929	198,322.20	90,000.00	108,322.20
1925	184,877.83	$ 87,000.00	97,877.83	1930	200,572.35	100,000.00	100,572.35
1926	187,435.80	—	187,435.80	Total	$1,513,664.20	$ 400,000.00	$ 1,113,664.20
1927	192,433.77	43,000.00	149,433.77				

2. Remaining 54 Years

Calendar Year	Interest	Principal	Total	Calendar Year	Interest	Principal	Total
1931	$ 206,659.93	$ 44,664.20	$ 251,324.13	1961	$ 161,539.00	$ 123,800.00	$ 285,339.00
1932	205,320.00	46,200.00	251,520.00	1962	157,206.00	127,700.00	284,906.00
1933	237,923.00	47,500.00	285,423.00	1963	152,736.50	133,600.00	286,336.50
1934	236,260.50	48,800.00	285,060.50	1964	148,060.50	138,500.00	286,560.50
1935	234,552.50	50,200.00	284,752.50	1965	143,213.00	142,500.00	285,713.00
1936	232,795.50	52,500.00	285,295.50	1966	138,225.50	147,500.00	285,725.50
1937	230,958.00	53,900.00	284,858.00	1967	133,063.00	153,500.00	286,563.00
1938	229,071.50	56,200.00	285,271.50	1968	127,690.50	159,500.00	287,190.50
1939	227,104.50	57,600.00	284,704.50	1969	122,108.00	164,600.00	286,708.00
1940	225,088.50	60,000.00	285,088.50	1970	116,347.00	171,800.00	288,147.00

Year			
1941	222,988.50	62,500.00	285,488.50
1942	220,801.00	63,900.00	284,701.00
1943	218,564.50	66,400.00	284,964.50
1944	216,240.50	68,800.00	285,040.50
1945	213,832.50	71,300.00	285,132.50
1946	211,337.00	73,800.00	285,137.00
1947	208,754.00	76,300.00	285,054.00
1948	206,083.50	78,900.00	284,983.50
1949	203,322.00	81,400.00	284,722.00
1950	200,473.00	85,000.00	285,473.00
1951	197,498.00	87,600.00	285,098.00
1952	194,432.00	91,200.00	285,632.00
1953	191,240.00	93,800.00	285,040.00
1954	187,957.00	97,500.00	285,457.00
1955	184,544.50	100,200.00	284,744.50
1956	181,037.50	103,900.00	284,937.50
1957	177,401.00	107,600.00	285,001.00
1958	173,635.00	111,400.00	285,035.00
1959	169,736.00	115,200.00	284,936.00
1960	165,704.00	119,000.00	284,704.00

Year			
1971	110,334.00	178,000.00	288,334.00
1972	104,104.00	184,200.00	288,304.00
1973	97,657.00	190,500.00	288,157.00
1974	90,989.50	196,800.00	287,789.50
1975	84,101.50	204,100.00	288,201.50
1976	76,958.00	211,500.00	288,458.00
1977	69,555.50	219,000.00	288,555.50
1978	61,890.50	226,500.00	288,390.50
1979	53,963.00	234,000.00	287,963.00
1980	45,773.00	242,700.00	288,473.00
1981	37,278.50	251,400.00	288,678.50
1982	28,479.50	260,100.00	288,579.50
1983	19,376.00	270,900.00	290,276.00
1984	9,894.50	282,700.00	292,594.50
Total..	$8,501,858.93	$6,888,664.20	$15,390,523.13
Add total amount paid under options............	400,000.00	—	400,000.00
Grand total............	$8,901,858.93	$6,888,664.20	$15,790,523.13

L. Schedule of Payments by Lithuania

1. First 5 Years

Fiscal Year	Interest Due	Interest Paid	Interest Funded (Under options)	Principal Payment
1925	$180,900.00	$135,675.00	$ 45,225.00	$ 30,000.00
1926	182,031.76	92,031.76	90,000.00	30,225.00
1927	183,821.63	94,271.63	89,550.00	31,960.00
1928	185,545.85	96,460.85	89,085.00	33,507.50
1929	187,209.56	98,604.56	88,605.00	35,098.00
Total	$919,508.80	$517,043.80	$402,465.00	$160,790.50

2. Remaining 57 Years

Fiscal Year	Interest	Principal	Total	Fiscal Year	Interest	Principal	Total
1930	$ 188,150.24	$ 36,467.50	$ 224,617.74	1961	$ 150,548.19	$ 104,755.00	$ 255,303.19
1931	187,056.21	37,525.00	224,581.21	1962	146,881.77	108,980.00	255,861.77
1932	185,930.46	38,615.00	224,545.46	1963	143,067.47	112,205.00	255,272.47
1933	184,772.01	39,705.00	224,477.01	1964	139,140.30	116,430.00	255,570.30
1934	183,580.86	41,795.00	225,375.86	1965	135,065.25	119,655.00	254,720.25
1935	212,714.84	42,885.00	255,599.84	1966	130,877.32	123,880.00	254,757.32
1936	211,213.87	44,975.00	256,188.87	1967	126,541.52	128,105.00	254,646.52
1937	209,639.75	46,065.00	255,704.75	1968	122,057.85	132,330.00	254,387.85

Year			
1938	256,182.47	48,155.00	208,027.47
1939	255,587.05	49,245.00	206,342.05
1940	255,953.47	51,335.00	204,618.47
1941	255,246.75	52,425.00	202,821.75
1942	255,501.87	54,515.00	200,986.87
1943	255,683.85	56,605.00	199,078.85
1944	255,837.67	58,740.00	197,097.67
1945	255,916.77	60,875.00	195,041.77
1946	255,966.15	63,055.00	192,911.15
1947	255,889.22	65,185.00	190,704.22
1948	255,742.75	67,320.00	188,422.75
1949	255,571.55	69,505.00	186,066.55
1950	255,273.87	71,640.00	183,633.87
1951	254,901.47	73,775.00	181,126.47
1952	255,499.35	76,955.00	178,544.35
1953	255,935.93	80,085.00	175,850.93
1954	255,272.95	82,225.00	173,047.95
1955	255,575.08	85,405.00	170,170.08
1956	255,765.90	88,585.00	167,180.90
1957	255,845.42	91,765.00	164,080.42
1958	255,903.65	95,035.00	160,868.65
1959	255,847.42	98,305.00	157,542.42
1960	255,631.75	101,530.00	154,101.75
1969	253,981.30	136,555.00	117,426.30
1970	254,426.87	141,780.00	112,646.87
1971	254,689.57	147,005.00	107,684.57
1972	254,769.40	152,230.00	102,539.40
1973	254,666.35	157,455.00	97,211.35
1974	254,380.42	162,680.00	91,700.42
1975	253,913.62	167,907.00	86,006.62
1976	253,264.88	173,135.00	80,129.88
1977	253,430.15	179,360.00	74,070.15
1978	253,377.55	185,585.00	67,792.55
1979	253,102.08	191,805.00	61,297.08
1980	254,283.90	199,700.00	54,583.90
1981	254,194.40	206,600.00	47,594.40
1982	254,863.40	214,500.00	40,363.40
1983	255,730.90	222,875.00	32,855.90
1984	255,705.28	230,650.00	25,055.28
1985	256,857.53	239,875.00	16,982.53
1986	253,926.90	245,340.00	8,586.90
Total	$14,391,707.27	$6,271,674.50	$8,120,032.77
Add amount paid prior to 1930	677,834.30	160,790.50	517,043.80
Grand total	$15,069,541.57	$6,432,465.00	$8,637,076.57

M. SCHEDULE OF PAYMENTS BY POLAND
1. First 7 Years

Calendar Year	Interest Due	Interest Paid (Under options)	Amount to be Funded
1923	$ 5,396,976.00	$ —	$ 5,396,976.00
1924	5,557,554.00	—	5,557,554.00
1925	5,708,124.58	1,000,000.00	4,708,124.59
1926	5,835,388.15	1,500,000.00	4,335,388.15
1927	5,944,828.36	2,000,000.00	3,944,828.36
1928	6,038,447.83	2,500,000.00	3,538,447.83
1929	4,302,978.44a	3,000,000.00	1,302,978.44
Total	$ 38,784,297.37	$ 10,000,000.00	$ 28,784,297.37

2. Remaining 55 Years

Calendar Year	Interest	Principal	Total	Calendar Year	Interest	Principal	Total
1930	$6,220,328.92	$1,287,297.37	$7,507,626.29	1961	$ 4,898,355.00	$ 3,737,000.00	$ 8,635,355.00
1931	6,181,710.00	1,325,000.00	7,506,710.00	1962	4,767,560.00	3,859,000.00	8,626,560.00
1932	6,141,960.00	1,357,000.00	7,498,960.00	1963	4,632,495.00	3,982,000.00	8,614,495.00
1933	7,118,125.00	1,393,000.00	8,511,125.00	1964	4,493,125.00	4,106,000.00	8,599,125.00
1934	7,069,370.00	1,452,000.00	8,521,370.00	1965	4,349,415.00	4,231,000.00	8,580,415.00
1935	7,018,550.00	1,485,000.00	8,503,550.00	1966	4,201,330.00	4,356,000.00	8,557,330.00
1936	6,966,575.00	1,520,000.00	8,486,575.00	1967	4,048,870.00	4,483,000.00	8,531,870.00
1937	6,913,375.00	1,554,000.00	8,467,375.00	1968	3,891,965.00	4,610,000.00	8,501,965.00
1938	6,858,985.00	1,589,000.00	8,447,985.00	1969	3,730,615.00	4,739,000.00	8,469,615.00

Year			
1939	6,803,370.00	1,623,000.00	8,426,370.00
1940	6,746,565.00	1,659,000.00	8,405,565.00
1941	6,688,500.00	1,720,000.00	8,408,500.00
1942	6,628,300.00	1,781,000.00	8,409,300.00
1943	6,565,965.00	1,842,000.00	8,407,965.00
1944	6,501,495.00	1,905,000.00	8,406,495.00
1945	6,434,820.00	1,967,000.00	8,401,820.00
1946	6,365,975.00	2,055,000.00	8,420,975.00
1947	6,294,050.00	2,143,000.00	8,437,050.00
1948	6,219,045.00	2,232,000.00	8,451,045.00
1949	6,140,925.00	2,321,000.00	8,461,925.00
1950	6,059,690.00	2,411,000.00	8,470,690.00
1951	5,975,305.00	2,527,000.00	8,502,305.00
1952	5,886,860.00	2,667,000.00	8,553,860.00
1953	5,793,515.00	2,784,000.00	8,577,515.00
1954	5,696,075.00	2,900,000.00	8,596,075.00
1955	5,594,575.00	3,018,000.00	8,612,575.00
1956	5,488,945.00	3,136,000.00	8,624,945.00
1957	5,379,185.00	3,255,000.00	8,634,185.00
1958	5,265,260.00	3,374,000.00	8,639,260.00
1959	5,147,170.00	3,494,000.00	8,641,170.00
1960	5,024,880.00	3,615,000.00	8,639,880.00

Year			
1970	3,564,750.00	4,868,000.00	8,432,750.00
1971	3,394,370.00	4,998,000.00	8,392,370.00
1972	3,219,440.00	5,130,000.00	8,349,440.00
1973	3,039,890.00	5,362,000.00	8,401,890.00
1974	2,852,220.00	5,596,000.00	8,448,220.00
1975	2,656,360.00	5,831,000.00	8,487,360.00
1976	2,452,275.00	6,067,000.00	8,519,275.00
1977	2,239,930.00	6,304,000.00	8,543,930.00
1978	2,019,290.00	6,543,000.00	8,562,290.00
1979	1,790,285.00	6,983,000.00	8,773,285.00
1980	1,545,880.00	7,425,000.00	8,970,880.00
1981	1,286,005.00	8,067,000.00	9,353,005.00
1982	1,003,660.00	8,712,000.00	9,715,660.00
1983	698,740.00	9,558,000.00	10,256,740.00
1984	364,210.00	10,406,000.00	10,770,210.00
Total	264,330,483.92	207,344,297.37	471,674,781.29
Plus total amount paid under options	10,000,000.00	—	10,000,000.00
Grand total	$274,330,483.92	$207,344,297.37	$481,674,781.29

a Less a credit of $1,813,428.69.

N. Schedule of Payments by Rumania

1. First 14 Years

Fiscal Year	Interest Due	Principal Due	Total Amount Due	Total Amount to be Paid	Amount Deferred	Value of Each Deferred Amount on 15th Year
1926	$1,337,700.00	$ 222,000.00	$ 1,559,700.00	$ 200,000.00	$1,359,700.00	$ 2,035,817.04
1927	1,331,040.00	229,000.00	1,560,040.00	300,000.00	1,260,300.00	1,831,651.22
1928	1,324,170.00	236,000.00	1,560,170.00	400,000.00	1,160,170.00	1,637,355.26
1929	1,317,090.00	243,000.00	1,560,090.00	500,000.00	1,060,090.00	1,452,535.10
1930	1,309,800.00	250,000.00	1,559,800.00	600,000.00	959,800.00	1,276,814.6
1931	1,302,300.00	258,000.00	1,560,300.00	700,000.00	860,300.00	1,111,117.32
1932	1,294,560.00	265,000.00	1,559,560.00	800,000.00	759,560.00	952,433.76
1933	1,286,610.00	273,000.00	1,559,610.00	1,000,000.00	559,610.00	681,272.62
1934	1,278,420.00	282,000.00	1,560,420.00	1,200,000.00	360,420.00	425,997.58
1935	1,269,960.00	290,000.00	1,559,960.00	1,400,000.00	159,960.00	183,567.62
1936	1,471,470.00	296,000.00	1,767,470.00	1,600,000.00	167,470.00	185,676.84
1937	1,461,110.00	338,890.00	1,800,000.00	1,800,000.00	—	—
1938	1,449,248.85	550,751.15	2,000,000.00	2,000,000.00	—	—
1939	1,429,972.56	770,027.44	2,200,000.00	2,200,000.00	—	—
Total	$18,863,451.41	$4,503,668.59	$23,367,120.00	$14,700,000.00	$8,667,120.00	$11,774,239.02

2. Remaining 48 Years

Fiscal Year	Interest	Principal	Total
1940	$1,815,119.62	$ 430,560.43	$2,245,680.05
1941	1,800,050.00	445,000.00	2,245,050.00
1942	1,784,475.00	462,000.00	2,246,475.00

Fiscal Year	Interest	Principal	Total
1966	$1,192,310.00	$1,053,000.00	$2,245,310.00
1967	1,155,455.00	1,090,000.00	2,245,455.00
1968	1,117,305.00	1,129,000.00	2,246,305.00

Year				Year			
1943	1,768,305.00	478,000.00	2,246,305.00	1969	1,077,790.00	1,168,000.00	2,245,790.00
1944	1,751,575.00	494,000.00	2,245,575.00	1970	1,036,910.00	1,209,000.00	2,245,910.00
1945	1,734,285.00	512,000.00	2,246,285.00				
1946	1,716,365.00	529,000.00	2,245,365.00	1971	994,595.00	1,252,000.00	2,246,595.00
1947	1,697,850.00	548,000.00	2,245,850.00	1972	950,775.00	1,295,000.00	2,245,775.00
1948	1,678,670.00	567,000.00	2,245,670.00	1973	905,450.00	1,341,000.00	2,246,450.00
1949	1,658,825.00	587,000.00	2,245,825.00	1974	858,515.00	1,387,000.00	2,245,515.00
1950	1,638,280.00	608,000.00	2,246,280.00	1975	809,970.00	1,436,000.00	2,245,970.00
				1976	759,710.00	1,486,000.00	2,245,710.00
1951	1,617,000.00	629,000.00	2,246,000.00	1977	707,700.00	1,539,000.00	2,246,700.00
1952	1,594,985.00	651,000.00	2,245,985.00	1978	653,835.00	1,592,000.00	2,245,835.00
1953	1,572,200.00	673,000.00	2,245,200.00	1979	598,115.00	1,648,000.00	2,246,115.00
1954	1,548,645.00	697,000.00	2,245,645.00	1980	540,435.00	1,706,000.00	2,246,435.00
1955	1,524,250.00	722,000.00	2,246,250.00				
1956	1,498,980.00	747,000.00	2,245,980.00	1981	480,725.00	1,765,000.00	2,245,725.00
1957	1,472,835.00	773,000.00	2,245,835.00	1982	418,950.00	1,827,000.00	2,245,950.00
1958	1,445,780.00	800,000.00	2,245,780.00	1983	355,005.00	1,891,000.00	2,246,005.00
1959	1,417,780.00	828,000.00	2,245,780.00	1984	288,820.00	1,957,000.00	2,245,820.00
1960	1,388,800.00	857,000.00	2,245,800.00	1985	220,325.00	2,026,000.00	2,246,325.00
				1986	149,415.00	2,097,000.00	2,246,415.00
1961	1,353,805.00	887,000.00	2,245,805.00	1987	76,020.00	2,172,000.00	2,248,020.00
1962	1,327,760.00	918,000.00	2,245,760.00				
1963	1,295,630.00	950,000.00	2,245,630.00	Total	$55,945,699.62	$51,860,560.43	$107,806,260.05
1964	1,262,380.00	984,000.00	2,246,380.00				
1965	1,227,940.00	1,018,000.00	2,245,940.00				

Plus total amount received first 14 years..... 14,700,000.00

Grand total.......... $122,506,260.05

O. Schedule of Payments by Yugoslavia

Fiscal Year	Interest	Principal	Total
1926	—	$200,000.00	$ 200,000.00
1927	—	200,000.00	200,000.00
1928	—	200,000.00	200,000.00
1929	—	200,000.00	200,000.00
1930	—	200,000.00	200,000.00
1931	—	225,000.00	225,000.00
1932	—	250,000.00	250,000.00
1933	—	275,000.00	275,000.00
1934	—	300,000.00	300,000.00
1935	—	325,000.00	325,000.00
1936	—	350,000.00	350,000.00
1937	—	375,000.00	375,000.00
1938	$ 74,687.50	400,000.00	474,687.50
1939	74,187.50	450,000.00	524,187.50
1940	73,625.00	488,000.00	561,625.00
1941	292,060.00	524,000.00	816,060.00
1942	289,440.00	562,000.00	851,440.00
1943	286,630.00	604,000.00	890,630.00
1944	283,610.00	648,000.00	931,610.00
1945	280,370.00	697,000.00	977,370.00
1946	276,885.00	707,000.00	983,885.00
1947	273,350.00	718,000.00	991,350.00
1948	269,760.00	729,000.00	998,760.00
1949	266,115.00	746,000.00	1,012,115.00
1950	262,385.00	764,000.00	1,026,385.00
1951	258,565.00	782,000.00	1,040,565.00
1952	254,655.00	801,000.00	1,055,655.00
1953	250,650.00	820,000.00	1,070,650.00
1954	246,550.00	838,000.00	1,084,550.00
1955	484,720.00	855,000.00	1,339,720.00
1956	476,170.00	873,000.00	1,349,170.00
1957	467,440.00	892,000.00	1,359,440.00
1958	917,040.00	912,000.00	1,829,040.00
1959	898,800.00	938,000.00	1,836,800.00
1960	880,040.00	961,000.00	1,841,040.00

Fiscal Year	Interest	Principal	Total
1961	$1,506,435.00	$ 984,000.00	$2,490,435.00
1962	1,471,995.00	1,018,000.00	2,489,995.00
1963	1,436,365.00	1,054,000.00	2,490,365.00
1964	1,399,475.00	1,090,000.00	2,489,475.00
1965	1,361,325.00	1,129,000.00	2,490,325.00
1966	1,321,810.00	1,168,000.00	2,489,810.00
1967	1,280,930.00	1,209,000.00	2,489,930.00
1968	1,238,615.00	1,251,000.00	2,489,615.00
1969	1,194,830.00	1,295,000.00	2,489,830.00
1970	1,149,505.00	1,340,000.00	2,489,505.00
1971	1,102,605.00	1,388,000.00	2,490,605.00
1972	1,054,025.00	1,436,000.00	2,490,025.00
1973	1,003,765.00	1,486,000.00	2,489,765.00
1974	951,755.00	1,538,000.00	2,489,755.00
1975	897,925.00	1,592,000.00	2,489,925.00
1976	842,205.00	1,648,000.00	2,490,205.00
1977	784,525.00	1,706,000.00	2,490,525.00
1978	724,815.00	1,765,000.00	2,489,815.00
1979	663,040.00	1,827,000.00	2,490,040.00
1980	599,095.00	1,891,000.00	2,490,095.00
1981	532,910.00	1,957,000.00	2,489,910.00
1982	464,415.00	2,026,000.00	2,490,415.00
1983	393,505.00	2,097,000.00	2,490,505.00
1984	320,110.00	2,170,000.00	2,490,110.00
1985	244,160.00	2,246,000.00	2,490,160.00
1986	165,550.00	2,324,000.00	2,489,550.00
1987	84,210.00	2,406,000.00	2,490,210.00
Total...	$32,327,635.00	$62,850,000.00	$95,177,635.00

II. DEBTS TO GREAT BRITAIN

In addition to the payments shown in these schedules, Great Britain also receives debt instalments from the following countries:

Germany (reparation debt), as shown on pages 472-73;

Hungary (reparation debt), as shown on page 477;

Bulgaria (reparation debt), as shown on page 476;

Czechoslovakia (liberation debt), as shown on page 256;

France, Belgium, and Italy (The Hague arrangement), as shown on page 205;

Austria, Poland, Rumania, Esthonia, and Yugoslavia (relief debts), as shown on pages 461-66;

Poland (Upper Silesia agreement), as shown on page 467;

Lithuania (Memel agreement), as shown on page 467.

These instalments are not included in the schedules that follow either because they are in the form of uniform annuities and are given in the text of the book, or else because they are, for convenience, grouped under the paying countries. For the details of Great Britain's funding agreements with her debtors and the sources from which the payment schedules are derived see pages 115-22. It should be noted that the schedules for the post-war debt payments by Belgian Congo, Rumania, Poland, Czechoslovakia, Greece, and Lithuania, as given in Table B, are taken from German Statistical Office, *Die interalliierten Schulden,* 1930, pages 40-41.

A. SCHEDULES OF WAR DEBT PAYMENTS
(Annual payments by the countries indicated, in
thousands of pounds sterling)

Financial Year Ending March 31	France	Italy[a]	Portugal	Yugo-slavia	Rumania	Greece
1926........	—	2,000	—	—	—	—
1927........	4,000	4,000	125	—	50	50
1928........	6,000	4,000	250	150	100	200
1929........	8,000	4,000	300	200	150	200
1930........	10,000	4,000	350	250	200	250
1931........	12,500	4,000	350	300	250	300
1932........	12,500	4,000	350	300	250	350
1933–35......	12,500	4,118	350	300	250	350
1936........	12,500	4,118	350	300	275	350
1937–39......	12,500	4,118	350	350	275	400
1940........	12,500	4,118	400	350	275	400
1941–42......	12,500	4,118	400	400	275	400
1943–45......	12,500	4,118	400	600	275	400
1946–57......	12,500	4,118	400	600	500	400
1958–67......	14,000	4,118	400	600	500	400
1968–87......	14,000	4,118	400	600	750	400
1988........	14,000	2,060	400	600	750	400
1989........	—	—	200	600	—	—
Total......	799,500	254,550	23,975	32,800	31,250	23,550

[a] Net payments after deduction for the return of gold deposits. See p. 120.

B. Schedules of Post-War Debt Payments
(Annual payments by the countries indicated, in thousands
of pounds sterling)

Financial Year Ending March 31	Belgium	Belgian Congo	Rumania	Poland	Czechoslovakia	Greece	Latvia	Esthonia	Lithuania
1924	—	—	—	—	—	—	—	—	—
1925	—	—	—	11.1	—	—	—	—	—
1926	—	—	—	22.3	—	—	—	—	—
1927	378.7	177.7	5.0	22.3	106.0	10.8	74.9	40.0	—
1928	450.0	180.0	5.0	22.3	106.0	10.8	74.9	40.0	30.0
1929	450.0	180.0	5.0	22.3	106.0	10.8	74.9	40.0	36.0
1930	450.0	180.0	5.0	22.3	106.0	10.8	74.9	40.0	34.5
1931	450.0	180.0	5.0	22.3	106.0	10.8	74.9	40.0	33.0
1932	640.0	225.0	5.0	22.3	106.0	10.8	74.9	40.0	31.5
1933	635.5	256.2	5.0	22.3	106.0	10.8	74.9	40.0	—
1934	640.7	257.2	5.0	22.3	106.0	10.8	74.9	40.0	—
1935	640.2	258.0	5.0	11.1	106.0	10.8	74.9	40.0	—
1936	639.2	253.5	—	—	106.0	10.8	74.9	40.0	—
1937	637.7	254.0	—	—	—	—	77.5	40.0	—
1938	635.7	254.2	—	—	—	—	77.5	40.0	—
1939	638.2	254.2	—	—	—	—	77.5	40.0	—
1940	640.0	254.0	—	—	—	—	77.5	40.0	—
1941	636.0	258.5	—	—	—	—	77.5	40.0	—
1942	636.5	257.5	—	—	—	—	77.5	80.0	—
1943	641.2	256.2	—	—	—	—	77.5	80.0	—
1944	640.0	254.7	—	—	—	—	77.5	80.0	—
1945	638.0	253.0	—	—	—	—	77.5	80.0	—
1946	640.2	256.0	—	—	—	—	77.5	80.0	—
1947	640.5	253.5	—	—	—	—	77.5	80.0	—
1948	637.0	255.7	—	—	—	—	77.5	80.0	—
1949	641.5	257.5	—	—	—	—	77.5	80.0	—
1950	639.7	253.7	—	—	—	—	77.5	80.0	—
1951	637.0	254.7	—	—	—	—	77.5	80.0	—
1952	638.2	255.2	—	—	—	—	77.5	80.0	—
1953	638.2	255.2	—	—	—	—	77.5	80.0	—
1954	637.0	254.7	—	—	—	—	77.5	80.0	—
1955	639.5	253.7	—	—	—	—	77.5	80.0	—
1956	640.5	257.2	—	—	—	—	77.5	80.0	—
Total	18,146.9	7,251.0	45.0	222.9	1,060.0	108.0	2,229.0	1,800.0	165.0

III. DEBTS TO FRANCE

In addition to the payments shown in these schedules, France also receives debt instalments from the following countries:

Germany (reparation debt), as shown on page 472;

Hungary (reparation debt), as shown on page 477;

Bulgaria (reparation debt), as shown on page 476;

Czechoslovakia (liberation debt), as shown on page 256;

Austria, Poland, and Rumania (relief debts), as shown on pages 461-66.

Poland (Upper Silesia agreement), as shown on page 467;

Lithuania (Memel agreement), as shown on page 467;

Latvia (post-war debt), as shown on page 128;

Yugoslavia (The Hague agreement), as shown on page 469.

These instalments are not included in the schedules that follow for the same reasons as those stated in connection with Great Britain on page 455. For the details of France's funding agreements with her debtors and the sources from which the payment schedules are derived see pages 124-28.

A. Schedules of War Debt Payments
(Annual payments by the countries indicated, in thousands of French francs,[a]
except those from Rumania, which are in thousands
of pre-war francs[a])

Year	Rumania	Yugoslavia	Greece		Poland		Czecho-slovakia
			Tranche A	Tranche B	Tranche A	Tranche B	
1928......	1,261	—	—	—	—	—	—
1929......	1,831	3,153	252	145	—	—	—
1930......	1,709	9,459	757	539	—	—	10,000
1931......	2,278	12,613	1,009	737	3,385	15,314	10,000
1932......	2,848	15,766	1,262	934	6,179	15,314	10,000
1933......	2,848	15,766	1,262	934	9,268	15,314	10,000
1934......	2,848	15,766	1,262	934	12,358	15,314	10,000
1935......	2,848	15,766	1,262	934	15,447	15,314	10,000
1936......	2,848	15,766	1,262	934	15,447	20,419	10,000
1937–40....	3,132	17,342	1,388	1,023	15,447	20,419	10,000
1941–42....	3,132	17,342	1,388	1,023	16,992	25,524	10,000
1943–45....	3,739	20,700	1,657	1,243	16,992	25,524	10,000
1946.......	3,739	20,700	1,657	1,243	20,282	38,286	10,000
1947–49....	6,798	37,636	3,012	2,302	20,282	38,286	10,000
1950......	6,798	37,636	3,012	2,302	36,876	38,286	10,000
1951–55 ...	6,798	37,636	3,012	2,302	36,876	51,048	10,000
1956–65....	6,798	37,636	3,012	2,302	36,876	52,351	10,000
1966.......	10,925	18,818	1,506	1,125	36,876	52,351	10,000
1967–70....	22,577	—	—	—	36,876	52,351	10,000
1971.......	22,577	—	—	—	36,876	—	10,000
1972–79....	22,577	—	—	—	55,314	—	10,000
1980–87....	22,577	—	—	—	55,314	—	—
1988......	11,288	—	—	—	55,314	—	—
1989–92....	—	—	—	—	55,314	—	—
Total....	680,559	1,024,809	82,018	62,064	2,262,826	1,538,220	500,000

[a] See table of currency equivalents on p. 432.

IV. DEBTS TO ITALY

In addition to the payments shown below, Italy also receives debt instalments from the following countries:

Germany (reparation debt), as shown on page 472;
Hungary (reparation debt), as shown on page 477;
Bulgaria (reparation debt), as shown on page 476;
Czechoslovakia (liberation debt), as shown on page 256;
Austria (relief debt), as shown on page 461;
Poland (Upper Silesia agreement), as shown on page 467;
Czechoslovakia (war debt), as shown on page 467;
Bulgaria (repatriation debt), as shown on page 130;
France (The Hague arrangement), as shown on page 223.

These instalments are not shown here for the same reasons as those stated in connection with Great Britain on page 455. For the details of Italy's funding agreements with her debtors and the sources from which the payment schedules are derived see pages 128-30.

A. War Debt Payments by Rumania

Period		Italian Lire
1927–36	10 annuities, each of	2,250,000
1937–46	10 annuities, each of	4,000,000
1947–56	10 annuities, each of	5,500,000
1957–66	10 annuities, each of	6,500,000
1967–76[a]	10 annuities, each of	6,500,000

[a] These annuities were cancelled by the agreement of Jan. 20, 1930. See p. 129.

V. RELIEF DEBTS

The schedules given here represent all payments on account of relief debts, with the exception of those to the United States, which are shown under "Debts to the United States." For the details of the relief debt agreements see pages 130-35. For the dollar equivalents of the currencies indicated see page 432.

A. AUSTRIAN RELIEF DEBT SCHEDULE
(Annual payments to countries and in currencies indicated)

Creditor Country	Currency	1929–33	1934–43	1944–68	Total
Great Britain..	Pounds sterling	68,523	109,637	177,064	5,865,585
	Dollars	186,486	298,378	481,881	15,963,235
France........	French francs	244,023	390,437	630,556	20,888,385
	Lire	148,884	238,214	384,716	12,744,460
	Dollars	187,685	300,296	484,977	16,065,810
	Pounds sterling	731	1,169	1,888	62,545
Switzerland....	Swiss francs	286,250	458,000	739,670	24,503,000
Holland.......	Florins	192,229	307,567	496,720	16,454,815
Italy.........	Dollars	223,482	357,572	577,479	19,130,105
	Pounds sterling	2,546	4,074	6,579	217,945
	Lire	229,252	366,805	592,389	19,624,035
Denmark.....	Kroner	14,261	22,818	36,851	1,220,760
Sweden.......	Kroner	864	1,383	2,233	73,975
Norway.......	Kroner	19,722	29,955	48,377	1,607,585
	Pounds sterling	24	38	62	2,050

B. Polish Relief
(Payments to countries

Date	Great Britain (Pounds sterling)	France (French francs)	Switzerland (Swiss francs)	Holland (Florins)
July 1, 1925...	119,250. –.–	7,000	2,250	13,000
Jan. 1, 1926 ...	119,250. –.–	7,000	2,250	13,000
July 1, 1926...	155,025. –.–	9,100	2,925	16,900
Jan. 1, 1927 ...	154,130.12.6	9,048	2,908	16,803
July 1, 1927 ...	165,161. 5.–	9,695	3,116	18,005
Jan. 1, 1928 ...	163,968.15.–	9,625	3,094	17,875
July 1, 1928 ...	174,701. 5.–	10,255	3,296	19,045
Jan. 1, 1929 ...	173,210.12.6	10,167	3,268	18,882
July 1, 1929...	183,645. –.–	10,780	3,465	20,020
Jan. 1, 1930 ...	181,856. 5.–	10,675	3,431	19,825
July 1, 1930 ...	275,467.10.–	16,170	5,198	30,030
Jan. 1, 1931 ...	271,293.15.–	15,925	5,119	29,575
July 1, 1931...	279,045. –.–	16,380	5,265	30,420
Jan. 1, 1932 ...	274,573. 2.6	16,118	5,181	29,933
July 1, 1932 ...	282,026. 5.–	16,555	5,321	30,745
Jan. 1, 1933 ...	277,256. 5.–	16,275	5,231	30,225
July 1, 1933 ...	284,411. 5.–	16,695	5,366	31,005
Jan. 1, 1934 ...	279,343. 2.6	16,397	5,271	30,452
July 1, 1934 ...	286,200. –.–	16,800	5,400	31,200
Jan. 1, 1935 ...	280,833.15.–	16,485	5,299	30,615
July 1, 1935 ...	275,467.10.–	16,170	5,198	30,030
Jan. 1, 1936 ...	270,101. 5.–	15,855	5,096	29,445
July 1, 1936...	276,660. –.–	16,240	5,220	30,160
Jan. 1, 1937 ...	270,995.12.6	15,908	5,113	29,543
July 1, 1937...	289,181. 5.–	16,975	5,456	31,525
Jan. 1, 1938 ...	282,920.12.6	16,607	5,338	30,842
July 1, 1938...	288,585. –.–	16,940	5,445	31,460
Jan. 1, 1939 ...	282,026. 5.–	16,555	5,321	30,745
July 1, 1939 ...	275,467.10.–	16,170	5,198	30,030
Jan. 1, 1940 ...	268,908.15.–	15,785	5,074	29,315
Total........	7,160,962.10.–	420,350	135,113	780,650

[a] In addition to these payments, Poland is also obligated to pay Sweden, ments of approximately 379,000 kroner each, during the last ten years of

DEBT SCHEDULE
and in currencies indicated)

Denmark (Kroner)	Sweden[a] (Kroner)	Norway		Date
		(Kroner)	(Pounds sterling)	
10,500	12,000	508,000	37.10. –	...July 1, 1925
10,500	12,000	508,000	37.10. –	...Jan. 1, 1926
13,650	15,600	660,400	48.15. –	...July 1, 1926
13,571	15,510	656,590	48. 9. 5	...Jan. 1, 1927
14,543	16,620	703,580	51.18. 9	...July 1, 1927
14,438	16,500	698,500	51.11. 3	...Jan. 1, 1928
15,383	17,580	744,220	54.18. 9	...July 1, 1928
15,251	17,430	737,870	54. 9. 4	...Jan. 1, 1929
16,170	18,480	782,320	57.15. –	...July 1, 1929
16,013	18,300	774,700	57. 3. 9	...Jan. 1, 1930
24,255	27,720	1,173,480	86.12. 6	...July 1, 1930
23,888	27,300	1,155,700	85. 6. 3	...Jan. 1, 1931
24,570	28,080	1,188,720	87.15. –	...July 1, 1931
24,176	27,630	1,169,670	86. 6.11	...Jan. 1, 1932
24,833	28,380	1,201,420	88.13. 9	...July 1, 1932
24,413	27,900	1,181,100	87. 3. 9	...Jan. 1, 1933
25,043	28,620	1,211,580	89. 8. 9	...July 1, 1933
24,596	28,110	1,189,990	87.16.10	...Jan. 1, 1934
25,200	28,800	1,219,200	90. –. –	...July 1, 1934
24,728	28,260	1,196,340	88. 6. 3	...Jan. 1, 1935
24,255	27,720	1,173,480	86.12. 6	...July 1, 1935
23,783	27,180	1,150,620	84.18. 9	...Jan. 1, 1936
24,360	27,840	1,178,560	87. –. –	...July 1, 1936
23,861	27,270	1,154,430	85. 4. 4	...Jan. 1, 1937
25,463	29,100	1,231,900	90.18. 9	...July 1, 1937
24,911	28,470	1,205,230	88.19. 5	...Jan. 1, 1938
25,410	29,040	1,229,360	90.15. –	...July 1, 1938
24,833	28,380	1,201,420	88.13. 9	...Jan. 1, 1939
24,255	27,720	1,173,480	86.12. 6	...July 1, 1939
23,678	27,060	1,145,540	84.11. 3	...Jan. 1, 1940
630,530	720,600	30,505,400	2,251.17. 6	......Total

under the second relief debt agreement, signed in 1929, semi-annual instal-
the period.

C. Rumanian Relief
(Payments to countries and

Date	Great Britain (Pounds sterling)	France (French francs)	Switzerland (Swiss francs)	Australia (Pounds sterling)
July 1, 1925.....	55,000. –.–	12,250	4,000	3,000. –.–
Jan. 1, 1926.....	55,000. –.–	12,250	4,000	3,000. –.–
July 1, 1926.....	55,000. –.–	12,250	4,000	3,000. –.–
Jan. 1, 1927.....	55,000. –.–	12,250	4,000	3,000. –.–
July 1, 1927.....	55,000. –.–	12,250	4,000	3,000. –.–
Jan. 1, 1928.....	55,000. –.–	12,250	4,000	3,000. –.–
July 1, 1928.....	55,000. –.–	12,250	4,000	3,000. –.–
Jan. 1, 1929.....	55,000. –.–	12,250	4,000	3,000. –.–
July 1, 1929.....	55,000. –.–	12,250	4,000	3,000. –.–
Jan. 1, 1930.....	55,000. –.–	12,250	4,000	3,000. –.–
July 1, 1930.....	104,500. –.–	23,275	7,600	5,700. –.–
Jan. 1, 1931.....	103,262.10.–	22,999	7,510	5,632.10.–
July 1, 1931.....	107,525. –.–	23,949	7,820	5,865. –.–
Jan. 1, 1932.....	106,150. –.–	23,643	7,720	5,790. –.–
July 1, 1932.....	104,775. –.–	23,336	7,620	5,715. –.–
Jan. 1, 1933.....	103,400. –.–	23,030	7,520	5,640. –.–
July 1, 1933.....	107,525. –.–	23,949	7,820	5,865. –.–
Jan. 1, 1934.....	106,012.10.–	23,612	7,710	5,782.10.–
July 1, 1934.....	104,500. –.–	23,275	7,600	5,700. –.–
Jan. 1, 1935.....	102,987.10.–	22,938	7,490	5,617.10.–
July 1, 1935.....	106,975. –.–	23,826	7,780	5,835. –.–
Jan. 1, 1936.....	105,325. –.–	23,459	7,660	5,745. –.–
July 1, 1936.....	103,675. –.–	23,901	7,540	5,655. –.–
Jan. 1, 1937.....	107,525. –.–	23,949	7,820	5,865. –.–
July 1, 1937.....	105,737.10.–	23,551	7,690	5,767.10.–
Jan. 1, 1938.....	103,950. –.–	23,153	7,560	5,670. –.–
July 1, 1938.....	102,162.10.–	22,754	7,430	5,572.10.–
Jan. 1, 1939.....	105,875. –.–	23,581	7,700	5,775. –.–
July 1, 1939.....	103,950. –.–	23,153	7,560	5,670. –.–
Jan. 1, 1940.....	107,525. –.–	23,949	7,820	5,865. –.–
July 1, 1940.....	105,462.10.–	23,489	7,670	5,752.10.–
Jan. 1, 1941.....	103,400. –.–	23,030	7,520	5,640. –.–
July 1, 1941.....	106,837.10.–	23,796	7,770	5,827.10.–
Jan. 1, 1942.....	104,637.10.–	23,306	7,610	5,707.10.–
July 1, 1942.....	102,437.10.–	22,816	7,450	5,587.10.–
Jan. 1, 1943.....	105,737.10.–	23,551	7,690	5,767.10.–
July 1, 1943.....	103,400. –.–	23,030	7,520	5,640. –.–
Jan. 1, 1944.....	106,562.10.–	23,734	7,750	5,812.10.–
July 1, 1944.....	104,087.10.–	23,183	7,570	5,677.10.–
Jan. 1, 1945.....	107,112.10.–	23,857	7,790	5,842.10.–
Total........	3,703,012.10.–	825,574	269,310	201,982.10.–

DEBT SCHEDULE
in currencies indicated)

Denmark (Kroner)	Sweden (Kroner)	Norway		Date
		(Kroner)	(Pounds sterling)	
3,000	2,250	1,250	50. –.–	...July 1, 1925
3,000	2,250	1,250	50. –.–	...Jan. 1, 1926
3,000	2,250	1,250	50. –.–	...July 1, 1926
3,000	2,250	1,250	50. –.–	...Jan. 1, 1927
3,000	2,250	1,250	50. –.–	...July 1, 1927
3,000	2,250	1,250	50. –.–	...Jan. 1, 1928
3,000	2,250	1,250	50. –.–	...July 1, 1928
3,000	2,250	1,250	50. –.–	...Jan. 1, 1929
3,000	2,250	1,250	50. –.–	...July 1, 1929
3,000	2,250	1,250	50. –.–	...Jan. 1, 1930
5,700	4,275	2,375	95. –.–	...July 1, 1930
5,633	4,224	2,347	93.17.6	...Jan. 1, 1931
5,865	4,399	2,444	97.15.–	...July 1, 1931
5,790	4,343	2,413	96.10.–	...Jan. 1, 1932
5,715	4,286	2,381	95. 5.–	...July 1, 1932
5,640	4,230	2,350	94. –.–	...Jan. 1, 1933
5,865	4,399	2,444	97.15.–	...July 1, 1933
5,783	4,337	2,409	96. 7.6	...Jan. 1, 1934
5,700	4,275	2,375	95. –.–	...July 1, 1934
5,618	4,213	2,341	93.12.6	...Jan. 1, 1935
5,835	4,376	2,431	97. 5.–	...July 1, 1935
5,745	4,309	2,394	95.15.–	...Jan. 1, 1936
5,655	4,241	2,356	94. 5.–	...July 1, 1936
5,865	4,399	2,444	97.15.–	...Jan. 1, 1937
5,768	4,326	2,403	96. 2.6	...July 1, 1937
5,670	4,253	2,363	94.10.–	...Jan. 1, 1938
5,573	4,179	2,322	92.17.6	...July 1, 1938
5,775	4,331	2,406	96. 5.–	...Jan. 1, 1939
5,670	4,253	2,363	94.10.–	...July 1, 1939
5,865	4,399	2,444	97.15.–	...Jan. 1, 1940
5,753	4,314	2,397	95.17.6	...July 1, 1940
5,640	4,230	2,350	94. –.–	...Jan. 1, 1941
5,828	4,371	2,428	97. 2.6	...July 1, 1941
5,708	4,281	2,378	95. 2.6	...Jan. 1, 1942
5,588	4,191	2,328	93. 2.6	...July 1, 1942
5,768	4,326	2,403	96. 2.6	...Jan. 1, 1943
5,640	4,230	2,350	94. –.–	...July 1, 1943
5,813	4,359	2,422	96.17.6	...Jan. 1, 1944
5,678	4,258	2,366	94.12.6	...July 1, 1944
5,843	4,382	2,434	97. 7.6	...Jan. 1, 1945
201,989	151,489	84,161	3,366. 7.6	......Total

D. Relief Debt Payments by Yugoslavia and Esthonia
to Great Britain
(In pounds sterling)

Date	By Yugoslavia	By Esthonia
July 1, 1925..........	—	7,530
Jan. 1, 1926..........	—	7,530
July 1, 1926..........	—	7,530
Jan. 1, 1927..........	—	7,530
July 1, 1927..........	51,721	7,530
Jan. 1, 1928..........	51,721	7,530
July 1, 1928..........	67,237	7,530
Jan. 1, 1929..........	66,849	7,530
July 1, 1929..........	71,633	7,530
Jan. 1, 1930..........	71,116	7,530
July 1, 1930..........	75,772	15,199
Jan. 1, 1931..........	75,125	15,199
July 1, 1931..........	79,650	15,199
Jan. 1, 1932..........	78,875	15,199
July 1, 1932..........	119,476	15,199
Jan. 1, 1933..........	117,666	15,199
July 1, 1933..........	121,028	15,199
Jan. 1, 1934..........	119,088	15,199
July 1, 1934..........	122,320	15,199
Jan. 1, 1935..........	120,252	15,199
July 1, 1935..........	123,355	15,199
Jan. 1, 1936..........	121,157	15,199
July 1, 1936..........	124,130	15,199
Jan. 1, 1937..........	121,803	15,199
July 1, 1937..........	119,475	15,199
Jan. 1, 1938..........	117,148	15,199
July 1, 1938..........	119,993	15,199
Jan. 1, 1939..........	117,536	15,199
July 1, 1939..........	125,423	15,199
Jan. 1, 1940..........	122,708	15,199
July 1, 1940..........	125,165	—
Jan. 1, 1941..........	122,320	—
July 1, 1941..........	119,475	—
Jan. 1, 1942..........	116,631	—
Total............	3,105,848	379,280

VI. MISCELLANEOUS DEBTS

The schedules given here represent payments on various inter-governmental accounts, not shown elsewhere. In addition to the instalments indicated here, payments are also made by Belgium to Holland, as shown on page 135. For dollar equivalents of the currencies indicated see page 432.

A. Payments by Poland under the Upper-Silesia Agreement[a]
(Annual payments to countries and in currencies indicated)

Year	France (In French francs)	Great Britain (In pounds sterling)	Italy (In lire)
1931–35.........	7,112,918	24,077	1,531,062
1936–40.........	8,891,143	30,096	1,913,829
1941–50.........	10,669,374	36,115	2,296,590
1951–65.........	11,543,870	39,075	2,484,828
Total.........	359,872,095	1,218,140	77,462,775

[a] See p. 122 for the details of the agreement.

B. Payments by Lithuania under the Memel Agreement[a]
(Payments to countries and in currencies indicated)

Year	France (In French francs)	Great Britain (In pounds sterling)	Italy (In lire)
Within 15 days of signature......	4,725,998	908. 8. 2	—
Dec. 15, 1930.....	5,886,373	1,131. 8. 0	16,273
Dec. 15, 1931.....	5,907,505	1,135. 9. 0	—
Dec. 15, 1932.....	5,907,505	1,135. 9. 0	—
Total.........	22,427,381	4,310.14. 2	16,273

[a] See p. 122 for the details of the agreement.

C. Payments by Greece to Canada[a]
(In Canadian dollars)

Date	Principal	Interest	Total	Date	Principal	Interest	Total
June 30, 1924....	80,000	400,000	480,000	June 30, 1937....	155,000	252,000	407,000
Dec. 31, 1924....	85,000	396,000	481,000	Dec. 31, 1937....	160,000	244,250	404,250
June 30, 1925....	85,000	391,750	476,750	June 30, 1938....	165,000	236,250	401,250
Dec. 31, 1925....	90,000	387,500	477,500	Dec. 31, 1938....	170,000	228,000	398,000
June 30, 1926....	90,000	383,000	473,000				
Dec. 31, 1926....	95,000	378,500	473,500	June 30, 1939....	170,000	219,500	389,500
June 30, 1927....	95,000	373,750	468,750	Dec. 31, 1939....	175,000	211,000	386,000
Dec. 31, 1927....	100,000	369,000	469,000	June 30, 1940....	180,000	202,250	382,250
June 30, 1928....	100,000	364,000	464,000	Dec. 31, 1940....	185,000	193,250	378,250
Dec. 31, 1928....	100,000	359,000	459,000	June 30, 1941....	190,000	184,000	374,000
				Dec. 31, 1941....	195,000	174,500	369,500
June 30, 1929....	105,000	354,000	459,000	June 30, 1942....	200,000	164,750	364,750
Dec. 31, 1929....	110,000	348,750	458,750	Dec. 30, 1942....	205,000	154,750	359,750
June 30, 1930....	110,000	343,250	453,250	June 30, 1943....	210,000	144,500	354,500
Dec. 31, 1930....	115,000	337,750	452,750	Dec. 31, 1943....	215,000	134,000	349,000
June 30, 1931....	115,000	332,000	447,000				
Dec. 31, 1931....	120,000	326,250	446,250	June 30, 1944....	220,000	123,250	343,250
June 30, 1932....	120,000	320,250	440,250	Dec. 31, 1944....	225,000	112,250	337,250
Dec. 31, 1932....	125,000	314,250	439,250	June 30, 1945....	230,000	101,000	331,000
June 30, 1933....	130,000	308,000	438,000	Dec. 31, 1945....	235,000	89,500	324,500
Dec. 31, 1933....	130,000	301,500	431,500	June 30, 1946....	245,000	77,750	322,750
				Dec. 31, 1946....	250,000	65,500	315,500
June 30, 1934....	135,000	295,000	430,000	June 30, 1947....	255,000	53,000	308,000
Dec. 31, 1934....	140,000	288,250	428,250	Dec. 31, 1947....	260,000	40,250	300,250
June 30, 1935....	140,000	281,250	421,250	June 30, 1948....	270,000	27,250	297,250
Dec. 31, 1935....	145,000	274,250	419,250	Dec. 31, 1948....	275,000	13,750	288,750
June 30, 1936....	150,000	267,000	417,000				
Dec. 31, 1936....	150,000	259,500	409,500	Total........	8,000,000	12,200,250	20,200,250

[a] See pp. 135–36 for the details of the agreement.

D. Payments by Yugoslavia to France under Special Agreement
Based on the Young Plan[a]
(Annual payments in thousands of reichsmarks)

1929	251.8
1930	394.2
1931	225.6
1932	186.7
1933–1935	207.0
1936	292.2
1937	487.6
1938	597.8
1939	647.8
1940	747.8
1941	897.8
1942	1,284.7
1943	1,833.6
1944	2,595.6
1945	3,095.6
1946	3,049.2
1947	3,031.5
1948	3,060.1
1949	4,060.1
1950–1953	5,060.1
1954	5,310.1
1955–1958	7,560.1
1959	8,810.1
1960–1965	10,060.1
1966	5,030.0
Total	157,352.3

[a] See pp. 222–23 for the details of the agreement.

VII. PAYMENTS BY GERMANY

The details of the arrangements under which the payments shown here are to be made are given in Chapter X. It should be noted that Germany is entitled to small receipts from Italy, as indicated on page 223. For the dollar equivalents of the currencies indicated see page 432.

A. PAYMENT SCHEDULE IN THE AMERICAN-GERMAN AGREEMENT
(Annual payments in thousands of reichsmarks)

Year	Costs of the Army of Occupation	Mixed Claims	Total
1929............	—	20,400	20,400
1930............	37,850	40,800	78,650
1931............	25,400	40,800	66,200
1932............	25,300	40,800	66,100
1933............	21,950	40,800	62,750
1934–36........	18,600	40,800	59,400
1937............	17,500	40,800	58,300
1938............	16,400	40,800	57,200
1939............	17,500	40,800	58,300
1940............	18,600	40,800	59,400
1941............	21,950	40,800	62,750
1942–48........	25,300	40,800	66,100
1949............	30,300	40,800	71,100
1950–65........	35,300	40,800	76,100
1966............	17,650	40,800	58,450
1967–80	—	40,800	40,800
1981............	—	20,400	20,400
Total........	1,048,100	2,121,600	3,169,700

B. GERMAN REPARATION ANNUITIES AND ALLIED WAR DEBT PAYMENTS
(In millions of reichsmarks)

German Fiscal Year Ending March 31	Reparation Annuity			Aggregate Allied Payments on the War Debts
	Total[a]	Unconditional	Conditional	
First Period				
1931	1,641.6	612.0	1,029.6	965.1
1932	1,618.9	612.0	1,006.9	942.3
1933	1,672.1	612.0	1,060.1	995.4
1934	1,744.9	612.0	1,132.9	1,136.4
1935	1,807.5	612.0	1,195.5	1,199.0
1936	1,833.5	612.0	1,221.5	1,224.9
1937	1,880.3	612.0	1,268.3	1,271.8
1938	1,919.8	612.0	1,307.8	1,334.0
1939	1,938.1	612.0	1,326.1	1,352.5
1940	1,983.4	612.0	1,371.4	1,375.0
1941	2,096.1	612.0	1,484.1	1,487.6
1942	2,114.6	612.0	1,502.6	1,437.9
1943	2,131.9	612.0	1,519.9	1,455.1
1944	2,128.2	612.0	1,516.2	1,451.5
1945	2,141.4	612.0	1,529.4	1,464.7
1946	2,137.7	612.0	1,525.7	1,460.9
1947	2,133.4	612.0	1,521.4	1,456.5
1948	2,149.1	612.0	1,537.1	1,472.3
1949	2,143.9	612.0	1,531.9	1,467.1
1950	2,240.7	612.0	1,628.7	1,461.6
1951	2,283.1	612.0	1,671.1	1,503.9
1952	2,267.1	612.0	1,655.1	1,487.9
1953	2,270.1	612.0	1,658.1	1,491.0
1954	2,277.2	612.0	1,665.2	1,498.1
1955	2,288.5	612.0	1,676.5	1,509.4
1956	2,283.7	612.0	1,671.7	1,504.5
1957	2,278.1	612.0	1,666.1	1,499.1
1958	2,285.7	612.0	1,673.7	1,506.7
1959	2,317.7	612.0	1,705.7	1,538.6
1960	2,294.5	612.0	1,682.5	1,515.4
1961	2,304.4	612.0	1,692.4	1,525.4
1962	2,322.2	612.0	1,710.2	1,543.2
1963	2,314.1	612.0	1,702.1	1,535.0
1964	2,326.5	612.0	1,714.5	1,547.4
1965	2,326.0	612.0	1,714.0	1,546.8
1966	2,352.7	612.0	1,740.7	1,573.7
Second Period				
1967	1,566.9	—	—	1,566.9
1968	1,566.1	—	—	1,566.1
1969	1,575.9	—	—	1,575.9
1970	1,589.2	—	—	1,589.2
1971	1,602.9	—	—	1,602.9
1972	1,613.1	—	—	1,613.1
1973	1,621.5	—	—	1,621.5
1974	1,624.9	—	—	1,624.9
1975	1,627.6	—	—	1,627.6
1976	1,634.2	—	—	1,634.2
1977	1,637.9	—	—	1,637.9
1978	1,644.6	—	—	1,644.6
1979	1,654.7	—	—	1,654.7
1980	1,659.6	—	—	1,659.6
1981	1,670.5	—	—	1,670.5
1982	1,687.6	—	—	1,687.6
1983	1,691.8	—	—	1,691.8
1984	1,703.3	—	—	1,703.3
1985	1,683.5	—	—	1,683.5
1986	925.1	—	—	925.1
1987	931.4	—	—	931.4
1988	897.8	—	—	897.8

[a] The instalments due the United States from the Young plan annuities, as shown in the following table, have been subtracted from these totals.

C. German Reparation Annuities under the Young Plan[a]

(In millions of reichsmarks)

German Fiscal Year Ending March 31	France	British Empire	Italy	Belgium	Yugo-slavia	Rumania	Japan	Portugal	Greece	Poland	United States	Total
First Period												
1930[b]	418.8	53.1	42.5	70.7	72.1	—	13.2	6.0	—	0.5	65.9	742.8
1931	900.7	366.8	156.0	98.2	79.4	10.0	13.2	13.2	3.6	0.5	66.3	1,707.9
1932	838.4	362.0	190.8	102.6	79.3	12.0	13.2	13.2	6.7	0.5	66.1	1,685.0
1933	879.8	364.5	196.3	105.3	79.4	13.0	13.2	13.2	6.9	0.5	66.1	1,738.2
1934	879.1	454.8	192.4	100.3	72.4	13.9	11.9	12.6	7.2	0.4	59.4	1,804.3
1935	941.8	450.1	193.6	102.8	72.5	14.7	11.9	12.6	7.2	0.4	59.4	1,866.9
1936	962.8	444.9	195.2	110.0	72.6	16.1	11.9	12.6	7.2	0.4	59.4	1,892.9
1937	1,004.1	438.1	197.2	116.9	73.8	17.2	11.9	12.6	8.3	0.4	59.4	1,939.7
1938	1,031.8	452.6	198.6	114.7	71.5	18.3	11.4	12.4	8.3	0.4	57.2	1,977.0
1939	1,052.4	447.1	200.2	114.8	71.8	19.1	11.4	12.4	8.5	0.4	57.2	1,995.3
1940	1,087.3	442.5	204.1	117.0	74.5	23.7	11.9	13.6	8.4	0.4	59.4	2,042.8
1941	1,179.9	457.1	211.5	117.1	76.1	20.1	11.9	13.6	8.4	0.4	59.4	2,155.5
1942	1,171.2	456.3	223.1	123.9	83.9	20.0	13.2	14.2	8.3	0.5	66.1	2,180.7
1943	1,191.4	446.0	225.5	124.1	88.2	20.6	13.2	14.2	8.3	0.5	66.1	2,198.0
1944	1,190.8	439.8	227.8	124.2	88.3	21.1	13.2	14.2	8.3	0.5	66.1	2,194.3
1945	1,190.7	430.5	230.5	123.9	88.5	21.1	13.2	14.2	8.3	0.5	66.1	2,207.5
1946	1,190.8	439.1	233.3	124.0	88.7	25.7	13.2	14.2	8.3	0.5	66.1	2,203.8
1947	1,188.1	432.4	235.6	124.1	88.7	28.4	13.2	14.2	8.3	0.5	66.1	2,199.5
1948	1,185.2	446.6	237.1	124.1	88.8	31.2	13.2	14.2	8.3	0.5	66.1	2,215.2
1949	1,185.1	439.1	239.4	124.2	88.8	31.2	13.2	14.2	8.3	0.5	66.1	2,210.0
1950	1,248.6	439.6	248.1	134.6	99.8	31.1	15.2	15.1	8.1	0.6	76.1	2,316.8
1951	1,277.9	440.5	260.1	134.7	99.9	31.1	15.2	15.1	8.1	0.6	76.1	2,359.2
1952	1,248.5	441.1	272.8	134.7	100.0	31.1	15.2	15.1	8.1	0.6	76.1	2,343.2
1953	1,248.3	441.4	275.6	134.7	100.0	31.1	15.2	15.1	8.1	0.6	76.1	2,346.2
1954	1,248.2	445.6	278.5	134.7	100.1	31.1	15.2	15.1	8.1	0.6	76.1	2,353.3
1955	1,248.1	453.6	281.3	134.7	100.7	31.1	15.2	15.1	8.1	0.6	76.1	2,364.6
1956	1,248.2	444.2	285.4	134.7	101.2	31.1	15.2	15.1	8.1	0.6	76.1	2,359.8

1957	1,248.1	434.7	289.0	134.9	101.2	31.1	15.2	15.1	8.1	0.6	76.1	2,354.2
1958	1,278.6	407.3	292.6	134.9	102.2	31.1	15.2	15.1	8.1	0.6	76.1	2,361.8
1959	1,302.8	410.2	292.7	134.8	103.1	31.1	15.2	15.1	8.1	0.6	76.1	2,393.8
1960	1,278.4	408.3	299.8	134.8	103.2	31.1	15.2	15.1	8.1	0.6	76.1	2,370.6
1961	1,278.2	406.1	310.8	134.7	104.5	31.1	15.2	15.1	8.1	0.6	76.1	2,380.5
1962	1,278.2	412.0	321.5	134.5	105.9	31.1	15.2	15.1	8.1	0.6	76.1	2,398.3
1963	1,278.1	400.5	324.8	134.8	105.9	31.1	15.2	15.1	8.1	0.6	76.1	2,390.2
1964	1,278.0	410.1	327.8	134.6	106.0	31.1	15.2	15.1	8.1	0.6	76.1	2,402.6
1965	1,277.9	406.3	331.0	134.9	106.0	31.1	15.2	15.1	8.1	0.6	76.1	2,402.1
1966	1,297.5	410.6	334.0	134.5	106.0	31.1	15.2	15.1	8.1	0.6	76.1	2,428.8
Second Period												
1967	794.2	357.2	290.1	53.1	22.7	31.7	—	8.2	9.7	—	40.8	1,607.7
1968	794.1	346.7	295.1	52.8	22.7	36.8	—	8.2	9.7	—	40.8	1,606.9
1969	790.9	349.4	302.3	53.0	22.7	39.8	—	8.2	9.7	—	40.8	1,616.7
1970	787.7	355.7	309.3	53.1	22.7	42.9	—	8.2	9.7	—	40.8	1,630.0
1971	787.5	361.2	317.6	53.2	22.7	42.9	—	8.2	9.7	—	40.8	1,643.7
1972	787.3	361.8	327.7	52.8	22.7	42.9	—	8.2	9.7	—	40.8	1,653.9
1973	787.1	366.1	332.0	52.8	22.6	42.9	—	8.2	9.7	—	40.8	1,662.3
1974	786.9	365.4	336.3	52.8	22.6	42.9	—	8.2	9.7	—	40.8	1,665.7
1975	786.8	364.1	340.5	52.8	22.6	42.9	—	8.2	9.7	—	40.8	1,668.4
1976	786.6	366.4	344.6	53.5	22.6	42.9	—	8.2	9.7	—	40.8	1,675.0
1977	786.3	363.8	350.8	53.3	22.6	42.9	—	8.2	9.7	—	40.8	1,678.7
1978	786.1	364.8	356.9	53.3	22.6	42.9	—	8.2	9.7	—	40.8	1,685.4
1979	785.9	365.1	367.1	53.2	22.6	42.9	—	8.2	9.7	—	40.8	1,695.5
1980	785.7	364.7	372.9	52.9	22.6	42.9	—	8.2	9.7	—	40.8	1,700.4
1981	785.5	363.5	385.1	53.1	22.6	42.9	—	8.2	9.7	—	40.8	1,711.3
1982	785.2	365.7	400.1	53.3	22.6	42.9	—	8.2	9.7	—	—	1,687.6
1983	785.0	362.9	407.2	53.4	22.6	42.9	—	8.2	9.7	—	—	1,691.8
1984	784.7	372.0	409.8	53.4	22.6	42.9	—	8.2	9.7	—	—	1,703.3
1985	784.4	346.2	416.5	53.0	22.6	42.9	—	8.2	9.7	—	—	1,683.5
1986	784.1	−414.1[c]	418.8	53.3	22.6	42.9	—	8.2	9.7	—	—	925.1
1987	783.9	−414.1[c]	425.0	53.3	22.6	42.9	—	8.2	9.7	—	—	931.4
1988	753.3	−372.1[c]	382.6	50.6	22.6	42.9	—	8.2	9.7	—	—	897.8

[a] There are slight discrepancies in the totals, due to rounding off.
[b] The year 1929–30 comprises only the 7 months September 1929 to March 1930.
[c] These sums correspond to the excess war debt receipts of Great Britain over war debt payments during these three years.

German Fiscal Year Ending March 31	France	Great Britain	Italy	Belgium
1931..........	408,400	172,900	75,000	33,700
1932..........	381,200	161,400	70,000	31,500
1933..........	353,900	149,800	65,000	29,200
1934..........	326,700	138,300	60,000	27,000
1935..........	299,500	126,800	55,000	24,700
1936..........	272,300	115,300	50,000	22,500
1937..........	245,000	103,700	45,000	20,200
1938..........	217,800	92,200	40,000	18,000
1939..........	190,600	80,700	35,000	15,700
1940..........	163,300	69,100	30,000	13,500
Total.......	2,858,700	1,210,200	525,000	236,000

II. As Established by

German Fiscal Year Ending March 31	France			Great Britain Reparation Recovery Act Levies[a]	Italy
	Deliveries	Reparation Recovery Act Levies[b]	Total		
1930[c].......	272,293.0	21,507.0	293,800	46,036.00	37,000
1931........	364,090.4	36,609.6	400,700	190,964.00	52,500
1932........	305,540.0	32,860.0	338,400	186,638.70	52,500
1933........	306,180.6	30,219.4	336,400	140,718.85	52,500
1934........	304,506.3	29,693.7	334,200	138,270.60	52,500
1935........	274,773.4	27,226.6	302,000	126,782.50	52,500
1936........	225,977.9	23,182.1	249,160	107,948.70	52,500
1937........	196,314.9	20,545.1	216,860	95,669.70	52,500
1938........	166,674.6	17,985.4	184,660	83,750.10	52,500
1939........	137,124.4	15,335.6	152,460	71,411.25	52,500
1940[d].......	45,274.5	4,710.5	49,985	21,934.60	15,500
Total.....	2,598,750.0	259,875.0	2,858,625	1,210,125.00	525,000

[a] For the details of the reparation recovery act levies see pp. 274–75.

[b] The Hague agreement provides that "if the Rumanian government and the shall be exceeded, a corresponding reduction shall be applied by agreement between respect of the other powers shall, however, not be changed."

[c] Period covering seven months, from Sept. 1, 1929, to Mar. 31, 1930.

[d] Period covering five months, from April 1, 1939 to Aug. 31, 1939.

DELIVERIES IN KIND
of Reichsmarks)
the Young Committee

Yugoslavia	Rumania	Japan	Portugal	Greece	Total
37,500	8,300	5,600	5,600	3,000	750,000
35,000	7,700	5,200	5,200	2,800	700,000
32,500	7,200	4,900	4,900	2,600	650,000
30,000	6,600	4,500	4,500	2,400	600,000
27,500	6,100	4,100	4,100	2,200	550,000
25,000	5,500	3,700	3,700	2,000	500,000
22,500	5,000	3,400	3,400	1,800	450,000
20,000	4,400	3,000	3,000	1,600	400,000
17,500	3,900	2,600	2,600	1,400	350,000
15,000	3,300	2,300	2,300	1,200	300,000
262,500	58,000	39,300	39,300	21,000	5,250,000

The Hague Agreement

Belgium	Yugo-slavia	Rumania[b]	Japan	Portugal	Greece	Total
24,500.00	26,000	—	2,550	4,600	—	434,486.00
33,750.00	7,500	9,000	5,625	6,548	3,000	739,587.00
31,500.00	35,000	6,950	5,250	4,800	2,800	663,838.70
29,250.00	32,500	7,150	4,875	4,500	2,600	610,493.85
27,000.00	30,000	6,600	4,500	4,402	2,400	599,872.60
24,750.00	27,500	6,050	4,125	4,125	2,200	550,032.50
20,837.50	23,300	5,500	3,750	3,328	2,000	468,324.20
17,756.25	19,400	4,950	3,375	2,742	1,800	415,052.95
14,675.00	16,600	4,400	3,000	2,156	1,600	363,341.10
11,593.75	13,200	3,850	1,825	1,570	1,400	309,810.00
637.50	1,500	3,300	500	604	1,200	95,161.10
236,250.00	262,500	57,750	39,375	39,375	21,000	5,250,000.00

German firms subsequently agree that the quota fixed in respect of a given period
the German and Rumanian governments to the other annuities; the distribution in

E. Payments to Belgium under the German Marks Agreement[a]
(In thousands of reichsmarks)

1929–30	1 annuity of	16,200
1930–33	3 annuities each of	21,500
1933–41	8 annuities each of	26,000
1941–49	8 annuities each of	20,100
1949–66	17 annuities each of	9,300

Total...607,600

[a] By a special arrangement, Belgium agreed to turn over to Luxemburg 3.063912 per cent of each annuity. See p. 135.

VIII. OTHER REPARATION DEBTS

A. Bulgarian Reparation Payments and Their Distribution[a]
(Annual amounts in gold francs)

Creditor	1930	1930–40	1940–50	1950–66
Greece	5,000,000	7,673,000	8,823,950	9,602,942
Rumania	—	1,300,000	1,495,000	1,626,981
Yugoslavia	—	500,000	575,000	625,762
France	—	166,300	191,245	208,128
Italy	—	159,900	183,885	200,119
Czechoslovakia	—	100,000	115,000	125,152
Great Britain	—	70,400	80,960	88,107
Belgium	—	25,600	29,440	32,039
Japan	—	2,400	2,760	3,004
Portugal	—	2,400	2,760	3,004
Total	5,000,000	10,000,000	11,500,000	12,515,238

[a] See pp. 249–53 for the details of the agreement.

B. Hungarian Reparation Payments and their Distribution[a]
(Annual amounts in gold crowns)

Creditor	1930	1931	1932	1933	1934	1935	1936-41	1942-43	1944-46
Greece	5,371,100	6,138,400	6,905,700	7,673,000	8,440,300	9,207,600	9,974,900	10,742,200	—
Rumania	910,000	1,040,000	1,170,000	1,300,000	1,430,000	1,560,000	1,690,000	1,820,000	—
Yugoslavia	140,000	160,000	180,000	200,000	220,000	240,000	260,000	280,000	—
Czechoslovakia	70,000	80,000	90,000	100,000	110,000	120,000	130,000	140,000	—
France	198,100	226,400	254,700	283,000	311,300	339,600	367,900	396,200	6,100,000
Italy	190,400	217,600	244,800	272,200	299,200	326,400	353,600	380,800	
Great Britain [b]	84,000	96,000	108,000	120,000	132,000	144,000	156,000	168,000	
Belgium	30,800	35,200	39,600	44,000	48,400	52,800	57,200	61,600	
Japan	2,800	3,200	3,600	4,000	4,400	4,800	5,200	5,600	
Portugal	2,800	3,200	3,600	4,000	4,400	4,800	5,200	5,600	
Fund B	—	—	—	—	—	—	—	—	7,400,000
Total	7,000,000	8,000,000	9,000,000	10,000,000	11,000,000	12,000,000	13,000,000	14,000,000	13,500,000

[a] See pp. 238-46 for the details of the agreement.
[b] Assigned to Fund A.

APPENDIX C

DETAILS OF INTER-GOVERNMENTAL DEBT PAYMENTS PRIOR TO JULY 1, 1931

I. Estimates by the German Government and by the Reparation Commission of Payments Made by Germany[a]

(In millions of gold marks)

Items	German Government	Reparation Commission
I. PRIOR TO SEPTEMBER 1, 1924........................	56,577	10,027
Cash..	2,356	2,345
Reparation recovery levies	373	373
Coal, coke, and by-products....................	2,374	927
Dyestuffs and pharmaceutical products.........	250	107
Livestock....................................	204	147
Railway materials............................	1,803	1,103[b]
Motor trucks................................	59	32
Agricultural machinery.......................	21	21
Ocean shipping..............................	4,486	711
Inland water craft...........................	56	50
Cables......................................	78	53
Harbor material.............................	80	—
Abandoned non-military materials..............	5,041	140
Naval vessels................................	1,338	—
Other deliveries in kind and miscellaneous........	401	399
Ruhr payments in kind........................	820	504
Clearing payments...........................	617	—
Labor of German prisoners of war..............	1,200	—
Ceded properties of the Reich, the federal states, and private interests........................	19,845	2,312
Share of the public debt not taken over by ceded territories..................................	657	24
Armies of occupation.........................	2,012	779
Costs of Inter-Allied Commission..............	106	—
Military disarmament (including scuttled warships)	8,500	—
Industrial disarmament.......................	3,500	—
Adjustment of frontiers, referendums, etc........	400	—
II. AFTER SEPTEMBER 1, 1924[c]......................	11,096	
Payments under the Dawes plan................	7,993	
Payments under the Young plan, the American-German agreement, and the Marks agreement	3,103	
GRAND TOTAL	67,673	

[a] See pp. 261–63. The German figures are from a statement issued by the German government through the Wolff Telegraphic Bureau on Jan. 29, 1932; the Reparation Commission's figures are from its report entitled *Payements-Livraisons-Cessions effectués par l'Allemagne en dehors du Plan des Experts du 9 Avril 1924.*

[b] Including a provisional credit of 270 million marks.

[c] The Reparation Commission's figures for this period do not extend beyond May 17, 1930 and are left out of this account. For a discussion pertaining to this period see pp. 264–66 of the text.

II. Amounts Received by the Creditor Powers under the Administration of the Agent General for Reparation Payments, September 1, 1924 to May 17, 1930[a]

(In millions of reichsmarks)

Items, by Countries	Dawes Plan September 1, 1924– May 17, 1930	Young Plan September 1, 1929– May 17, 1930	Total
FRANCE..................................	3,939.2	443.0	4,382.2
Army of Occupation costs.................	319.5	—	319.5
Reparation Recovery Act..................	259.2	25.6	284.8
Cash transfers (in foreign currencies)........	961.0	208.3	1,169.3
Services rendered by Germany prior to September 1, 1924.........................	5.6	—	5.6
Deliveries in kind, including transportation...	2,389.2	208.5	2,597.7
Miscellaneous payments..................	4.7	.6	5.3
GREAT BRITAIN...........................	1,654.4	103.6	1,758.0
Army of Occupation costs.................	96.5	1.4	97.9
Reparation recovery levies................	1,250.9	67.2	1,318.1
Cash transfers (in foreign currencies)........	291.0	35.0	326.0
Services rendered by Germany prior to September 1, 1924.........................	11.5	—	11.5
Deliveries in kind, including transportation...	4.5	—	4.5
Miscellaneous payments..................	—	—	—
ITALY..................................	555.1	66.9	622.0
Cash transfers (in foreign currencies)........	134.7	25.5	160.2
Deliveries in kind, including transportation...	420.4	41.4	461.8
Miscellaneous payments..................	—	—	—
BELGIUM................................	527.4	82.8	610.2
Army of Occupation costs.................	36.1	.2	36.3
Cash transfers (in foreign currencies)........	85.2	57.3	142.5
Services rendered by Germany prior to September 1, 1924.........................	.1	—	.1
Deliveries in kind, including transportation...	406.0	25.3	431.3
Miscellaneous payments..................	—	—	—
YUGOSLAVIA..............................	275.2	75.1	350.3
Cash transfers (in foreign currencies)........	37.6	51.2	88.8
Deliveries in kind, including transportation...	236.5	23.6	260.1
Miscellaneous payments..................	1.1	.3	1.4
RUMANIA................................	67.2	0.6	67.8
Cash transfers (in foreign currencies)........	1.3	—	1.3
Deliveries in kind, including transportation...	65.9	0.6	66.5
Miscellaneous payments..................	—		

[a] Compiled from *Reports of the Agent General for Reparation Payments*, 1925–30.

II. Amounts Received by the Creditor Powers (*Continued*)

Items, by Countries	Dawes Plan September 1, 1924– May 17, 1930	Young Plan September 1, 1929– May 17, 1930	Total
PORTUGAL..............................	44.9	7.3	52.2
Cash transfers (in foreign currencies)........	5.8	1.6	7.4
Deliveries in kind, including transportation...	39.1	5.7	44.8
JAPAN..................................	45.1	5.0	50.1
Cash transfers (in foreign currencies)........	14.7	2.7	17.4
Deliveries in kind, including transportation...	30.4	2.3	32.7
GREECE.................................	23.7	0.7	24.4
Cash transfers (in foreign currencies)........	4.1	0.7	4.8
Deliveries in kind, including transportation...	19.6	—	19.6
POLAND.................................	1.4	0.6	2.0
Cash transfers (in foreign currencies)........	0.1	0.2	0.3
Deliveries in kind, including transportation...	1.3	0.4	1.7
UNITED STATES OF AMERICA.................	300.4	77.0	377.4
Cash transfers (in foreign currencies)........	183.4	52.2	235.6
Deliveries under special agreement..........	117.0	24.8	141.8
ALL COUNTRIES...........................	7,434.2	862.9	8,297.1
Army of Occupation costs..................	452.1	1.6	453.7
Reparation recovery levies.................	1,510.1	92.8	1,602.9
Cash transfers (in foreign currencies)........	1,718.9	434.8	2,153.7
Services rendered by Germany prior to September 1, 1924.......................	17.3	—	17.3
Deliveries in kind, including transportation...	3,612.8	308.0	3,920.8
Deliveries under special agreement..........	117.0	24.8	141.8
Miscellaneous payments..................	6.0	.9	6.9
COSTS OF COMMISSIONS, AND OTHER PRIOR CHARGES..............................	75.0	6.1	81.1
GRAND TOTAL............................	7,509.2	869.0	8,378.2[b]

[b] In addition to these amounts, the Agent General also received and disbursed the following sums required for the service of the German External Loan of 1924: under the Dawes plan, 439.8 million reichsmarks; under the Young plan, 67.7 millions; a total of 507.5 millions.

III. Payments Made to the United States Treasury
(In dollars, by fiscal

Country	1918			1919	
	Principal	Interest	Total	Principal	Interest
Austria	—	—	—	—	—
Belgium	—	2,070,868.42	2,070,868.42	—	8,836,413.13
Czechoslovakia	—	—	—	—	304,178.09
Esthonia	—	—	—	—	—
Finland	—	—	—	—	—
France	—	33,270,096.54	33,270,096.54	7,570,000.00	91,830,097.54
Great Britain	—	59,320,616.66	59,320,616.66	—	171,791,790.25
Greece	—	—	—	—	—
Hungary	—	—	—	—	—
Italy	—	11,375,216.05	11,375,216.05	—	46,223,636.57
Latvia	—	—	—	—	—
Lithuania	—	—	—	—	—
Poland	—	—	—	—	—
Rumania	—	—	—	—	108,904.11
Yugoslavia	—	95,895.88	95,895.88	—	540,163.26
Total	—	106,132,693.55	106,132,693.55	7,570,000.00	319,635,182.95

Country	1921			1922	
	Principal	Interest	Total	Principal	Interest
Austria	—	—	—	—	—
Belgium	—	1,379,429.06	1,379,429.06	440,552.83	1,379,429.06
Czechoslovakia	—	—	—	—	—
Esthonia	—	—	—	—	—
Finland	—	—	—	—	—
France	34,567,861.81	12,679,100.12	47,246,961.93	—	20,695,395.37
Great Britain	46,517,633.57	13,244,444.73	59,762,078.30	30,500,000.00	4,575,000.00
Greece	—	784,153.34	784,153.34	—	375,000.00
Hungary	—	—	—	—	—
Italy	—	—	—	—	—
Latvia	—	126,266.19	126,266.19	—	—
Lithuania	—	—	—	—	—
Poland	—	1,811,948.20	1,811,948.20	—	231,250.09
Rumania	—	—	—	—	—
Yugoslavia	653,890.97	—	653,890.97	—	—
Total	81,739,386.35	30,025,341.64	111,764,727.99	30,940,552.83	27,256,074.52

Country	1924			1925	
	Principal	Interest	Total	Principal	Interest
Austria	—	—	—	—	—
Belgium	172.01	1,376,734.47	1,376,906.48	—	1,376,730.50
Czechoslovakia	—	—	—	—	—
Esthonia	—	—	—	—	—
Finland	45,000.00	269,325.00	314,325.00	45,000.00	267,975.00
France	85,672.74	20,367,057.25	20,452,729.99	4,660.51	20,367,057.25
Great Britain	53,500,000.00	138,241,385.87	191,741,385.87	23,000,000.00	136,965,000.00
Greece	—	—	—	—	—
Hungary	—	15,295.54	15,295.54	9,672.50	29,666.33
Italy	146,772.94	—	146,772.94	—	—
Latvia	—	—	—	—	—
Lithuania	—	—	—	30,000.00	137,221.97
Poland	—	—	—	—	505,025.99
Rumania	—	—	—	—	—
Yugoslavia	65,601.65	—	65,601.65	—	—
Total	53,843,219.34	160,269,798.13	214,113,017.47	23,089,333.01	159,648,677.04

ON THE WAR DEBT ACCOUNT TO JULY 1, 1931[a]
years ending June 30)

1919	1920			Country
Total	Principal	Interest	Total	
—	—	—	—	Austria
8,836,413.13	1,522,901.66	728,207.81	2,251,109.47	Belgium
304,178.09	—	—	—	Czechoslovakia
—	—	—	—	Esthonia
—	—	—	—	Finland
99,400,097.54	21,823,490.00	1,810,441.50	23,633,931.50	France
171,791,790.25	64,164,007.99	1,200,333.86	65,364,341.85	Great Britain
—	—	—	—	Greece
—	—	—	—	Hungary
46,223,636.57	—	—	—	Italy
—	—	—	—	Latvia
—	—	—	—	Lithuania
—	—	—	—	Poland
108,904.11	1,794,180.48	154,409.63	1,948,590.11	Rumania
540,163.26	—	—	—	Yugoslavia
327,205,182.95	89,304,580.13	3,893,392.80	93,197,972.93	Total

1922	1923			Country
Total	Principal	Interest	Total	
—	—	—	—	Austria
1,819,981.89	94,003.87	1,378,595.76	1,472,599.63	Belgium
—	—	—	—	Czechoslovakia
—	—	—	—	Esthonia
20,695,395.37	—	444,315.27	444,315.27	Finland
35,075,000.00	251,216.23	20,367,057.25	20,618,273.48	France
375,000.00	30,500,000.00	176,178,085.74	206,678,085.74	Great Britain
—	—	—	—	Greece
—	—	—	—	Hungary
—	18,080.00	—	18,080.00	Italy
—	—	—	—	Latvia
—	—	—	—	Lithuania
231,250.09	—	—	—	Poland
—	—	—	—	Rumania
—	1,107.54	—	1,107.54	Yugoslavia
58,196,627.35	30,864,407.64	198,368,054.02	229,232,461.66	Total

1925	1926			Country
Total	Principal	Interest	Total	
—	—	—	—	Austria
1,376,730.50	2,100,000.00	1,757,234.66	3,857,234.66	Belgium
—	3,000,000.00	—	3,000,000.00	Czechoslovakia
—	—	51,441.88	51,441.88	Esthonia
312,975.00	47,000.00	266,595.00	313,595.00	Finland
20,371,717.76	20,203,888.19	—	20,203,888.19	France
159,965,000.00	24,000,000.00	136,260,000.00	160,260,000.00	Great Britain
—	—	—	—	Greece
39,338.83	10,018.00	59,036.23	69,054.23	Hungary
—	5,199,466.34	—	5,199,466.34	Italy
—	—	91,562.76	91,562.76	Latvia
167,221.97	30,225.00	92,031.76	122,256.76	Lithuania
505,025.99	—	1,250,000.00	1,250,000.00	Poland
—	204,451.54	—	204,451.54	Rumania
—	207,112.39	—	207,112.39	Yugoslavia
182,738,010.05	55,002,161.46	139,827,902.29	194,830,063.75	Total

III. PAYMENTS MADE TO THE UNITED STATES TREASURY
(In dollars, by fiscal

Country	1927			1928	
	Principal	Interest	Total	Principal	Interest
Austria........	—	—	—	—	—
Belgium.......	2,100,000.00	2,000,000.00	4,100,000.00	2,450,000.00	2,250,000.00
Czechoslovakia.	3,000,000.00	—	3,000,000.00	3,000,000.00	—
Esthonia......	—	125,000.00	125,000.00	—	175,000.00
Finland........	49,000.00	265,155.00	314,155.00	50,000.00	263,670.00
France........	30,533,109.12	—	30,533,109.12	32,031,169.06	—
Great Britain...	25,000,000.00	135,525,000.00	160,525,000.00	25,000,000.00	134,775,000.00
Greece........	—	—	—	—	—
Hungary.......	10,230.00	58,732.51	68,962.51	10,435.00	58,422.54
Italy..........	5,000,000.00	—	5,000,000.00	5,000,000.00	—
Latvia.........	—	8,000.00	8,000.00	—	75,000.00
Lithuania......	31,960.00	94,271.63	126,231.63	33,507.50	96,460.85
Poland........	—	1,750,000.00	1,750,000.00	—	2,250,000.00
Rumania......	300,000.00	—	300,000.00	400,000.00	—
Yugoslavia.....	200,000.00	—	200,000.00	200,000.00	—
Total......	66,224,299.12	139,826,159.14	206,050,458.26	68,175,111.56	139,943,553.39

Country	1930			1931	
	Principal	Interest	Total	Principal	Interest
Austria........	575,112.00	—	575,112.00	287,556.00	—
Belgium.......	3,450,000.00	2,750,000.00	6,200,000.00	4,050,000.00	3,250,000.00
Czechoslovakia.	3,000,000.00	—	3,000,000.00	3,000,000.00	—
Esthonia......	—	275,000.00	275,000.00	—	396,990.19
Finland.......	53,000.00	260,565.00	313,565.00	55,000.00	258,945.00
France........	57,251,463.26	—	57,251,463.26	1,350,000.00	38,650,000.00
Great Britain...	27,000,000.00	133,185,000.00	160,185,000.00	28,000,000.00	132,360,000.00
Greece........	457,000.00	482,660.00	939,660.00	484,000.00	466,200.00
Hungary.......	11,245.00	57,778.13	69,023.13	11,755.00	57,433.13
Italy..........	5,000,000.00	—	5,000,000.00	12,100,000.00	2,521,250.00
Latvia.........	—	95,000.00	95,000.00	—	153,337.84
Lithuania......	36,467.50	188,150.24	224,617.74	37,525.00	187,056.21
Poland........	—	4,637,365.89	4,637,365.89	1,287,297.37	6,173,410.01
Rumania......	600,000.00	—	600,000.00	700,000.00	—
Yugoslavia.....	200,000.00	—	200,000.00	225,000.00	—
Total......	97,634,287.76	141,931,519.26	239,565,807.02	51,588,133.37	184,474,622.38

a Data furnished by the United States Treasury. Only payments by the 15 war debtors
following payments on the war debt account: Cuba, $12,286,751.58; Liberia, $36,471.56; Nica-

ON THE WAR DEBT ACCOUNT TO JULY 1, 1931[a] (*continued*)
years ending June 30)

1928	1929				Country
Total	Principal	Interest	Total		
4,700,000.00	2,950,000.00	2,500,000.00	5,450,000.00		...........Austria
3,000,000.00	3,000,000.00	—	3,000,000.00		..........Belgium
175,000.00	—	225,000.00	225,000.00		.....Czechoslovakia
313,670.00	52,000.00	262,140.00	314,140.00		..........Esthonia
32,031,169.06	20,367,057.26	—	20,367,057.26		...........Finland
159,775,000.00	27,000,000.00	133,995,000.00	160,995,000.00		...........France
—	42,922.67	—	42,922.67		......Great Britain
68,857.54	10,640.00	58,106.41	68,746.41		...........Greece
5,000,000.00	5,000,000.00	—	5,000,000.00		..........Hungary
75,000.00	—	85,000.00	85,000.00		..............Italy
129,968.35	35,098.00	98,604.56	133,702.56		...........Latvia
2,250,000.00	—	2,750,000.00	2,750,000.00		.........Lithuania
400,000.00	500,000.00	—	500,000.00		...........Poland
200,000.00	200,000.00	—	200,000.00		..........Rumania
					.........Yugoslavia
208,118,664.95	59,157,717.93	139,973,850.97	199,131,568.90		.........Total

1931	1918–31				Country
Total	Principal	Interest	Total		
287,556.00	862,668.00	—	862,668.00		...........Austria
7,300,000.00	19,157,630.37	33,033,642.87	52,191,273.24		..........Belgium
3,000,000.00	18,000,000.00	304,178.09	18,304,178.09		.....Czechoslovakia
396,990.19	—	1,248,432.07	1,248,432.07		..........Esthonia
313,945.00	396,000.00	2,558,685.27	2,954,685.27		...........Finland
40,000,000.00	226,039,588.18	260,036,302.82	486,075,891.00		...........France
160,360,000.00	404,181,641.56	1,507,616,657.11	1,911,798,298.67		......Great Britain
950,200.00	983,922.67	2,108,013.34	3,091,936.01		...........Greece
69,188.13	73,995.50	394,470.82	468,466.32		..........Hungary
14,621,250.00	37,464,319.28	60,120,102.62	97,584,421.90		..............Italy
153,337.84	—	634,166.79	634,166.79		...........Latvia
224,581.21	234,783.00	893,797.22	1,128,580.22		.........Lithuania
7,460,707.38	1,287,297.37	21,359,000.18	22,646,297.55		...........Poland
700,000.00	4,498,632.02	263,313.74	4,761,945.76		..........Rumania
225,000.00	1,952,712.55	636,059.14	2,588,771.69		.........Yugoslavia
236,062,755.75	715,133,190.50	1,891,206,822.08	2,606,340,012.58		.........Total

who have negotiated funding agreements are shown here. In addition, the Treasury received the
ragua, $168,783.13; Russia, $8,748,878.87; a total of $21,240,885.14.

APPENDIX D

BALANCE SHEET OF THE WAR DEBTS

In the two tables which follow an attempt is made to give a balance sheet of all inter-governmental obligations resulting from the war. These tables require a number of explanatory remarks.

The data contained in the tables are derived from the payment schedules given in Appendix B and in various portions of the text. For the sake of comparability, all payments have been converted into dollars at the par of exchange. This method of conversion is open to criticism in view of the fact that some of the currencies involved, notably the British pound sterling and the Scandinavian kroner, are, at the present time, at a discount with respect to their nominal gold values. It has been thought, however, that, since the payments presented here cover a long future period, conversion at par of exchange would give a more useful set of data than if the conversion were made on the basis of the rates of exchange prevailing at the time when the tables were prepared.

Table I represents for each country the aggregate amounts of interest and amortization payments which it was, as of July 1, 1931, obligated to make to all other countries, or entitled to receive from all other countries, in accordance with the schedules of payments in force on that date. In cases in which a country makes payments to another country on several accounts, all such payments have been consolidated. For example, while Poland is indebted to Great Britain on three different accounts, the payments required are not shown separately, but are added together to indicate the total payments due to Great Britain from Poland. The last three columns show both the gross and the net creditor or debtor position of each of the countries concerned.

Table II indicates the movement of inter-governmental debt payments which were scheduled for the fiscal year 1931-32, that is, the period covered by the Hoover moratorium. Here, again, all payments by one country to another have been consolidated, and in the last three columns the creditor or debtor position of every country is given for the year in question.

486

Debts owed by governments to governments are dealt with in these tables,[1] but not debts owed by governments to private parties. Accordingly, payments by Germany on account of the Dawes loan of 1924 and of the "mobilization" loan of 1930, as well as the instalments due to the United States in liquidation of the mixed claims awards, are not included. Similarly, such payments as those which Greece is obligated to make to Bulgaria under the Molloff-Caphandaris agreement and the contributions of various countries to the Hungarian Funds are also excluded.

Finally, no account is taken in Table I of current interest on the amounts postponed during the year 1931-32, as prescribed in the London protocol of August 11, 1931, and in the similar agreements among the various debtors and creditors.

---

[1] All such debts are included here, except the obligations between the government of Great Britain and those of the British dominions. See footnote 1 on p. 5.

ments by

t n	Greece	Hungary	Italy	Latvia	Lithuania	Poland
	—	—	—	—	—	—
	—	7.6	—	—	—	—
	70.5	—	—	—	—	—
	886.5	—	—	—	—	—
	—	17.2	—	—	—	—
	—	—	—	—	—	13.
	—	—	—	—	—	—
	—	—	—	—	—	—
	77.3	48.7	—	—	231.6	1,067.
	—	—	52.6	—	—	—
	1,755.8	20.7	21,753.4	364.5	158.8	2,919.
	—	1,321.4	—	—	—	—
	—	—	—	—	—	—
	—	46.8	—	—	—	80.
	—	.7	—	—	—	—
	—	—	—	—	—	—
	—	—	—	—	—	—
	—	—	—	—	—	24.
	—	—	—	—	—	632.
	—	—	—	—	—	—
	—	.7	—	—	—	—
	—	223.9	—	—	—	—
	—	—	—	—	—	218.
	—	—	—	—	—	2.
0.0	1,109.1	69.2	14,706.1	250.7	224.5	7,486.
	—	34.4	—	—	—	—
0.0	3,899.2	1,791.3	36,512.1	615.2	614.9	12,445.

Portugal	Rumania	Yugo-slavia	Total Receipts	Total Payments	Net Receipts (+) Net Pay-ments (−)
—	56.7	—	56.7	—	+56.7
—	—	—	—	1,406.0	−1,406.0
—	—	—	29,833.6	14,923.8	+14,909.8
—	—	482.4	552.9	2,269.6	−1,716.7
—	—	—	886.5	—	+886.5
—	—	—	36.5	6,885.3	−6,848.8
—	3.1	—	20.0	—	+20.0
—	—	—	—	943.0	−943.0
—	—	—	—	312.3	−312.3
—	496.2	605.3	193,675.1	115,631.0	+78,044.1
—	—	—	52.6	384,716.9	−384,664.3
1,703.3	2,280.8	2,231.4	189,743.4	159,520.0	+30,223.4
—	—	—	4,828.1	3,899.2	+928.9
—	—	—	—	1,791.3	−1,791.3
—	118.4	—	47,448.5	36,512.1	+10,936.4
—	—	—	2,993.8	—	+2,993.8
—	—	—	—	615.2	−615.2
—	—	—	—	614.9	−614.9
—	—	—	153.6	—	+153.6
—	—	—	1,897.0	—	+1,897.0
—	2.2	—	640.5	—	+640.5
—	—	—	119.1	12,445.5	−12,326.4
—	—	—	3,098.7	1,703.3	+1,395.4
—	—	—	3,721.6	3,762.7	−41.1
—	2.3	—	220.6	—	+220.6
—	3.0	—	60.2	—	+60.2
—	800.0	250.0	252,605.1	—	+252,605.1
—	—	—	18,877.1	3,569.1	+15,308.0
1,703.3	3,762.7	3,569.1	751,521.2	751,521.2	—

ᵃ Conversion is all cases at par of exchange.   Includes payments ag

INDEX

489

PUBLICATIONS OF THE BROOKINGS INSTITUTION*

INSTITUTE OF ECONOMICS SERIES

(1.) GERMANY'S CAPACITY TO PAY.
   By Harold G. Moulton and Constantine E. McGuire. 384 pp. 1923. $2.50.

(2.) RUSSIAN DEBTS AND RUSSIAN RECONSTRUCTION.
   By Leo Pasvolsky and Harold G. Moulton. 247 pp. 1924. $2.50.

(3.) MAKING THE TARIFF IN THE UNITED STATES.
   By Thomas Walker Page. 281 pp. 1924. $3.

(4.) AMERICAN AGRICULTURE AND THE EUROPEAN MARKET.
   By Edwin G. Nourse. 333 pp. 1924. $2.50.

(5.) SUGAR IN RELATION TO THE TARIFF.
   By Philip G. Wright, 312 pp. 1924. $2.50.

(6.) MINERS' WAGES AND THE COST OF COAL.
   By Isador Lubin. 316 pp. 1924. Out of print.

(7.) THE REPARATION PLAN.
   By Harold G. Moulton. 325 pp. 1924. $2.50.

(8.) THE FRENCH DEBT PROBLEM.
   By Harold G. Moulton and Cleona Lewis. 459 pp. 1925. $2.

(9.) THE RUHR-LORRAINE INDUSTRIAL PROBLEM.
   By Guy Greer. 328 pp. 1925. $2.50.

(10.) THE CASE OF BITUMINOUS COAL.
   By Walton H. Hamilton and Helen R. Wright. 310 pp. 1925. $2.50.

(11.) INTEREST RATES AND STOCK SPECULATION.
   By Richard N. Owens and Charles O. Hardy. 221 pp. rev. ed. 1930. $2.50.

(12.) THE FEDERAL INTERMEDIATE CREDIT SYSTEM.
   By Claude L. Benner. 375 pp. 1926. Out of print.

(13.) THE TARIFF ON WOOL.
   By Mark A. Smith. 350 pp. 1926. $2.50.

* The parentheses indicate that the volume itself does not carry the number since it was given subsequent to publication.

LIST OF PUBLICATIONS

44. JAPAN: AN ECONOMIC AND FINANCIAL APPRAISAL.
    By Harold G. Moulton with the collaboration of
    Junichi Ko. 645 pp. 1931. $4.
45. CREDIT POLICIES OF THE FEDERAL RESERVE SYSTEM.
    By Charles O. Hardy. 374 pp. 1932. $2.50.
46. WAR DEBTS AND WORLD PROSPERITY.
    By Harold G. Moulton and Leo Pasvolsky. 498 pp.
    1932. $3.

INSTITUTE FOR GOVERNMENT RESEARCH SERIES

Studies in Administration

(1.) THE SYSTEM OF FINANCIAL ADMINISTRATION OF
     GREAT BRITAIN.
     By W. F. Willoughby, W. W. Willoughby, and S.
     M. Lindsay. 362 pp. 1917. $3.
(2.) THE BUDGET: A TRANSLATION.
     By René Stourm. 619 pp. 1917. $4.
(3.) THE PROBLEM OF A NATIONAL BUDGET.
     By W. F. Willoughby. 220 pp. 1918. Out of print.
(4.) THE MOVEMENT FOR BUDGETARY REFORM IN THE
     STATES.
     By W. F. Willoughby. 254 pp. 1918. $3.
(5.) THE CANADIAN BUDGETARY SYSTEM.
     By H. C. Villard and W. W. Willoughby. 379 pp.
     1918. $3.
(6.) ORGANIZED EFFORTS FOR THE IMPROVEMENT OF
     METHODS OF ADMINISTRATION IN THE UNITED
     STATES.
     By Gustavus A. Weber. 391 pp. 1919. $3.
(7.) TEACHERS' PENSION SYSTEMS IN THE UNITED STATES.
     By Paul Studensky. 460 pp. 1920. $3.
(8.) THE FEDERAL SERVICE: A STUDY OF THE SYSTEM OF
     PERSONNEL ADMINISTRATION OF THE UNITED
     STATES GOVERNMENT.
     By Lewis Mayers. 607 pp. 1922. $5.
(9.) THE REORGANIZATION OF THE ADMINISTRATIVE
     BRANCH OF THE NATIONAL GOVERNMENT.
     By W. F. Willoughby. 298 pp. 1923. Out of print.

(10.) THE DEVELOPMENT OF NATIONAL ADMINISTRATIVE ORGANIZATION IN THE UNITED STATES.

By Lloyd M. Short. 514 pp. 1923. $5.

(11.) THE STATISTICAL WORK OF THE NATIONAL GOVERNMENT.

By Laurence F. Schmeckebier. 574 pp. 1925. $5.

(12.) MANUAL OF ACCOUNTING AND REPORTING FOR THE OPERATING SERVICES OF THE NATIONAL GOVERNMENT.

By Henry P. Seidemann. 399 pp. 1926. $5.

(13.) THE NATIONAL GOVERNMENT AND PUBLIC HEALTH.

By James A. Tobey. 423 pp. 1926. $3.

(14.) THE NATIONAL BUDGET SYSTEM, WITH SUGGESTIONS FOR ITS IMPROVEMENT.

By W. F. Willoughby. 343 pp. 1927. $3.

(15.) THE DEPARTMENT OF JUSTICE OF THE UNITED STATES.

By Albert Langeluttig. 318 pp. 1927. $3.

(16.) THE LEGAL STATUS AND FUNCTIONS OF THE GENERAL ACCOUNTING OFFICE.

By W. F. Willoughby. 193 pp. 1927. $3.

(17.) THE PROBLEM OF INDIAN ADMINISTRATION.

By Lewis Meriam and Associates. 872 pp. 1928. $5.

(18.) THE DISTRICT OF COLUMBIA: ITS GOVERNMENT AND ADMINISTRATION.

By Laurence F. Schmeckebier. 943 pp. 1928. $5.

(19.) THE DEVELOPMENT OF GOVERNMENTAL FOREST CONTROL IN THE UNITED STATES.

By Jenks Cameron. 471 pp. 1928. $3.

(20.) MANUAL OF ACCOUNTING, REPORTING, AND BUSINESS PROCEDURE FOR THE TERRITORIAL GOVERNMENT OF HAWAII.

By Henry P. Seidemann. 570 pp. 1928. $5.

(21.) THE GOVERNMENT AND ADMINISTRATION OF GERMANY.

By Frederick F. Blachly and Miriam E. Oatman. 770 pp. 1928. $5.

(22.) GROUP REPRESENTATION BEFORE CONGRESS.

By E. Pendleton Herring. 309 pp. 1929. $3.

Principles of Administration

SERVICE MONOGRAPHS OF THE UNITED STATES GOVERNMENT

8. Steamboat-Inspection Service. 130 pp. 1922. $1.
9. Weather Bureau. 87 pp. 1922. $1.
10. Public Health Service. 298 pp. 1923. $2.
11. National Park Service. 172 pp. 1922. $1.
12. Employees' Compensation Commission. 86 pp. 1922. $1.
13. General Land Office. 224 pp. 1923. $1.50.
14. Bureau of Education. 157 pp. 1923. $1.
15. Bureau of Navigation. 124 pp. 1923. $1.
16. Coast and Geodetic Survey. 107 pp. 1923. $1.
17. Federal Power Commission. 126 pp. 1923. $1.
18. Interstate Commerce Commission. 169 pp. 1923. Out of print.
19. Railroad Labor Board. 83 pp. 1923. $1.
20. Division of Conciliation. 37 pp. 1923. $1.
21. Children's Bureau. 83 pp. 1925. $1.
22. Women's Bureau. 31 pp. 1923. $1.
23. Office of the Supervising Architect. 138 pp. 1923. $1.
24. Bureau of Pensions. 111 pp. 1923. $1.
25. Bureau of Internal Revenue. 270 pp. 1923. $1.50.
26. Bureau of Public Roads. 123 pp. 1923. $1.
27. Office of the Chief of Engineers. 166 pp. 1923. $1.
28. United States Employment Service. 130 pp. 1923. $1.
29. Bureau of Foreign and Domestic Commerce. 180 pp. 1924. $1.
30. Bureau of Immigration. 247 pp. 1924. $1.50.
31. Patent Office. 127 pp. 1924. Out of print.
32. Office of Experiment Stations. 178 pp. 1924. $1.
33. Customs Service. 191 pp. 1924. Out of print.
34. Federal Farm Loan Bureau. 160 pp. 1924. $1.
35. Bureau of Standards. 299 pp. 1925. $2.
36. Government Printing Office. 143 pp. 1925. $1.
37. Bureau of the Mint. 90 pp. 1926. $1.
38. Office of the Comptroller of the Currency. 84 pp. 1926. $1.
39. Naval Observatory. 101 pp. 1926. $1.
40. Lighthouse Service. 158 pp. 1926. $1.
41. Bureau of Animal Industry. 190 pp. 1927. $1.50.
42. Hydrographic Office. 112 pp. 1926. $1.
43. Bureau of Naturalization. 108 pp. 1926. $1.

44. Panama Canal. 413 pp. 1927. $2.50.
45. Medical Department of the Army. 161 pp. 1927. $1.50.
46. General Accounting Office. 215 pp. 1927. $1.50.
47. Bureau of Plant Industry. 121 pp. 1927. $1.
48. Office of Indian Affairs. 591 pp. 1927. $3.
49. United States Civil Service Commission. 153 pp. 1928. $1.50.
50. Food, Drug and Insecticide Administration. 134 pp. 1928. $1.50.
51. Coast Guard. 265 pp. 1929. $1.50.
52. Bureau of Chemistry and Soils. 218 pp. 1928. $1.50.
53. Bureau of the Census. 224 pp. 1929. $1.50.
54. Bureau of Biological Survey. 339 pp. 1929. $2.
55. Bureau of Dairy Industry. 74 pp. 1929. $1.50.
56. Bureau of Engraving and Printing. 111 pp. 1929. $1.50.
57. Bureau of Prohibition. 333 pp. 1929. $2.
58. Forest Service. 268 pp. 1930. $2.
59. Plant Quarantine and Control Administration. 198 pp. 1930. $1.50.
60. Bureau of Entomology. 177 pp. 1930. $1.50.
61. Aeronautics Branch: Department of Commerce. 147 pp. 1930. $1.50.
62. Bureau of Home Economics. 95 pp. 1930. $1.50.
63. United States Shipping Board. 338 pp. 1931. $2.50.
64. The Personnel Classification Board. 160 pp. 1931. $1.50.
65. The Federal Radio Commission. 159 pp. 1932. $1.50.

MISCELLANEOUS SERIES

PORTO RICO AND ITS PROBLEMS.
  By Victor S. Clark and Associates. 707 pp. 1930. $5.
STEPHEN J. FIELD: CRAFTSMAN OF THE LAW.
  By Carl Brent Swisher. 473 pp. 1930. $4.
THE SPIRIT OF '76 AND OTHER ESSAYS.
  By Carl Becker, J. M. Clark, and William E. Dodd. 135 pp. 1927. $1.50.
ESSAYS ON RESEARCH IN THE SOCIAL SCIENCES.
  By W. F. G. Swann and others. 194 pp. 1931. $2.

LIST OF PUBLICATIONS

THE SOCIETY OF NATIONS: ITS ORGANIZATION AND CONSTITUTIONAL DEVELOPMENT.
By Felix Morley. 678 pp. 1932. $3.50.

PAMPHLETS

No. 1. RECENT GROWTH OF THE ELECTRIC LIGHT AND POWER INDUSTRY.
By Charles O. Hardy. 53 pp. 1929. 50 cents.

No. 2. FIRST MORTGAGES IN URBAN REAL ESTATE FINANCE.
By John H. Gray and George W. Terborgh. 69 pp. 1929. 50 cents.

No. 3. THE ABSORPTION OF THE UNEMPLOYED BY AMERICAN INDUSTRY.
By Isador Lubin. 36 pp. 1929. 50 cents.

No. 4. SOME TRENDS IN THE MARKETING OF CANNED FOODS.
By Leverett S. Lyon. 57 pp. 1929. 50 cents.

No. 5. THE FECUNDITY OF NATIVE AND FOREIGN-BORN WOMEN IN NEW ENGLAND.
By Joseph J. Spengler. 63 pp. 1930. 50 cents.

No. 6. SOURCES OF COAL AND TYPES OF STOKERS AND BURNERS USED BY ELECTRIC PUBLIC UTILITY POWER PLANTS.
By William H. Young. 83 pp. 1930. 50 cents.

No. 7. FEDERAL SERVICES TO MUNICIPAL GOVERNMENTS.
By Paul V. Betters. 100 pp. 1931. 50 cents.

No. 8. REORGANIZATION OF THE FINANCIAL ADMINISTRATION OF THE DOMINICAN REPUBLIC.
By Taylor G. Addison. 105 pp. 1931. 50 cents.

No. 9. ADVISORY ECONOMIC COUNCILS.
By Lewis L. Lorwin, 84 pp. 1931. 50 cents.

No. 10. UNEMPLOYMENT INSURANCE IN AUSTRIA.
By Mollie Ray Carroll. 52 pp. 1932. 50 cents.